Breaking Into Sports:
The Real Guide to Landing Your Dream Job

From *I Love Sports* to *I Work in Sports*. What Actually Gets You Hired

Stuart Sokoloff

Edited by Kirsten Mancosky
Cover design by Sam Leventhal

First Edition
ISBN: 979-8-9944586-0-0

Printed in the United States of America

www.StuartSokoloff.com

For my dad,

You showed me what it means to work hard, dream big, and never settle for ordinary. You're the reason I chose sales, the reason I kept pushing when things got hard, and the reason I believe I can achieve anything I set my mind to. Though you left us too early, I know you're watching down on me, probably keeping a closer eye on my sales numbers than anyone else. This book, this career, is all because you believed in me first.

I miss you every day. I hope I'm making you proud.

"All of us who have been lucky enough to have a career in professional sports have an obligation to give back. One way to do that is to assist young people with ability and desire in finding that first job in the business" **Rob Manfred, Commissioner, MLB**

"Breaking into sports has never been about shortcuts or luck; it's about preparation meeting opportunities. Passion will get you started, but preparation, resilience, and leadership will sustain your career. I've always believed real success comes from rolling up your sleeves, learning the business from the ground up, and being willing to fail forward. Young people who are coachable, committed to excellence, and focused on serving others give themselves the best chance to break in and make a meaningful impact. Those of us fortunate enough to have had long careers in this industry owe it to the next generation to share what we know and help clear the path for them." **Jerry Colangelo, Chairman, Naismith Memorial Basketball Hall of Fame, Basketball Hall of Famer, Former Owner & Chairman, Arizona Diamondbacks & Phoenix Suns and Mercury, Former Managing Director, USA Basketball**

"Throughout our lives, there will be people and experiences that help to shape who we are and who we might become. Sport, at all levels, is one of those experiences, and your coaches, your teammates, those that come to watch you compete, your coworkers, can often be those people. Sport, and the challenges and triumphs therein, mimic life. If you look at sport as more than just a game, you will recognize the opportunities to grow and become the best version of yourself on the field, or pitch, or court, or rink, and beyond it, as a person, and potentially as an athlete. Whether it is the former or the latter, seize the opportunity and embrace the relationships you build along the way. In doing so, you will not only give yourself a chance to do something you love as a career but you will also be in a position to breathe into and support the next young person who aspires to have a career in sports, just like Stuart did!" **Tony Clark, Executive Director, MLB Players Association**

"As someone who founded a sports media company while still in college, this book matters because it's so informative. It gives students a real, practical roadmap for navigating the grind of breaking in and building a sustainable career. Resources like this are how we better prepare the next generation and strengthen the sports industry as a whole." **Adam White, Founder & CEO, Front Office Sports**

"Stuart's insight into the ever-changing world of sports gives young people the perspective and confidence they need to move forward. The sports industry can be challenging, but with the right guidance, it becomes a place full of opportunity. Stuart understands not just the business of sports, but the people in it, and that's what helps students navigate their own path with purpose." **Annie Meyers Drysdale, Olympian, Basketball Hall of Famer, Only Woman to try out with an NBA Team**

"Stuart's journey from intern to industry professional embodies everything this book teaches. I've watched him navigate the challenges of breaking into sports with persistence, authenticity, and genuine relationship-building. What sets this book apart is that Stuart isn't theorizing, he's done it, through internships and a decade of real experience. He understands what it actually takes to go from loving sports to working in sports, and he knows how to explain it in a way that gives students actionable guidance they can use immediately." **Alan Nero, Managing Director, Baseball, Octagon**

"I've known Stuart since he was trying to break into the sports industry, and what he writes in this book is what he's actually lived. Think of it as a diary about how to get in, how to progress, and how to succeed in this business. This isn't theory, it's the real path he took. Stuart didn't just observe the industry from the outside; he worked his way through it, made the mistakes, learned the lessons, and figured out what actually works. That experience shows on every page." **Pat O'Conner, Former MiLB President**

"This is still an in-person, live entertainment business, and that's how a career in sports starts. Being present matters. Showing up, building relationships, and learning by doing are still the foundation of this industry. Some of the most important lessons come from being in the room, and taking pride in the work, whether it's glamorous or not. If you're reliable, curious, and invested in the people around you, others will invest in you. That's how trust is built, and trust is what ultimately opens doors." **Sam Kennedy, President & CEO, Boston Red Sox**

"There are many different avenues to gaining a career in sports. Some people land the job because they played the sport, others from internships, and others from connections within. However you get in, there is no substitute for being slow to speak and quick to listen and remembering to always be humble with a teachable spirit. If you can do that, you have a better chance of a career with longevity." **Dana Brown, General Manager, Houston Astros**

"After more than 40 years in this business and working with over 30,000 students from 163 countries, I can tell you one thing with certainty: passion alone doesn't get you in anymore. Everyone who applies for that entry-level job loves sports. What separates the ones who actually build careers is preparation, strategy, and a willingness to do the unglamorous work before anyone's watching. Stuart is someone who got that early. He completed 16 internships and professional experiences while still in college, built his network with intention, and proved his value before he ever applied for his first full-time job. That's the walk-on mentality I preach every day, and it's exactly what this book teaches. If you're serious about breaking into sports, this is the honest, practical guidance you actually need." **Dr. Lynn Lashbrook, President & Founder, Sports Management Worldwide**

Table of Contents

Acknowledgements

Rob, you spoke to my class freshman year and within an hour provided me with an opportunity to interview with my hometown minor league baseball team. You gave me my first real chance and showed me that professionals in this industry genuinely want to help.

Bridget, you gave me my first internship and showed me what the best can do. The first lesson I learned from you became my career mantra: "It's better to ask for forgiveness than permission."

Taneka, you taught me real sales, sprinting up three flights of stairs because the elevator takes too long and we could be making cold calls. You showed me that hustle isn't just a buzzword; it's how you work, think, and win.

Jentry and Cara, who truly taught me how to sell. Jentry, thank you for pushing me when I needed it. Cara, thank you for always caring and being there through the ups and downs, and of course, for teaching me that groups are life.

To my Suns family, Adam, Bobby, Courtney, Eric, Hillary, Josh, Kyle, Matt, Nick, and so many more, thank you for guiding me through inside sales and my early career. From answering my endless questions to celebrating every milestone, you made Phoenix home.

To my mentors, Alan, Anthony, Barry, Jeff, Keith, Marc, Mike, Ray, and Taylor, I wouldn't be here without you. As a wide-eyed college student, getting on calls with executives from teams I'd only dreamed of working for changed everything. Thank you for seeing potential in me and investing your time to guide my career.

To the friends I've made throughout my career, Alex, Johanna, Kayla, Marnae, Morgan, Morria, Rachael, Scott, Seth, Zoe, and many more, thank you for making the late nights manageable and celebrating every win together. It's been incredible growing in this industry with you.

Adam, Ali, and Nate, thank you for believing in me and providing opportunities beyond my wildest dreams. You showed me how to carry myself with professionalism and poise when the spotlight is brightest and the pressure is greatest, and you reminded me to have fun along the way.

Last but certainly not least, my family. Amber, my wife, thank you for sticking by my side through thick and thin, from courtside to client dinners, even when it means me being gone for two weeks on a road trip. I love you and you're my best friend. Mom and Harrison, thank you for believing in me and allowing me to pursue my dreams without limits.

Prologue

If you're reading this, you probably love sports. That passion is important; it's what draws us to this industry. But passion alone won't get you hired, won't help you survive the 70-hour weeks, and won't build the career you're imagining.

When I started at Springfield College as a sport management student, I thought loving sports and working hard would be enough. However, it wasn't. Breaking into this industry requires strategy, relentless hustle, genuine relationships, and a willingness to do things most people won't do. Over four years, I completed 16 professional experiences across internships, part-time roles, and volunteer opportunities, said yes to every opportunity, built relationships with anyone who'd give me fifteen minutes, and moved across the country chasing opportunities. I learned by doing, failing, adjusting, and doing it again until I figured out what actually worked.

That journey, from a student who had no direction, to building a decade-long career with numerous professional sports teams, including the Phoenix Suns & Mercury, Baltimore Orioles, Cleveland Guardians & Cincinnati Reds Spring Training facility, San Francisco Giants, Athletes Unlimited, Baseball and Basketball Halls of Fames, and more, taught me everything in this book. These aren't theories from a classroom. These are strategies, tactics, and mindset shifts I used to break in and build a career I genuinely love. This is what I teach my students. This is what I wish someone had told me before I started.

This book takes you from "I love sports" to "I work in sports" by walking through every stage of building a sports career. We start with the most important question, "Why do you want to work in sports?", and explore passion versus purpose, lifestyle design, and how the industry actually works. Then we tackle choosing the right school, gaining experience through internships and creative alternatives, embracing geographic flexibility, and building genuine relationships through strategic networking, informational interviews, mentors, and social media. Finally, we prepare you for your first job and how to build a sustainable career that lasts.

I'm not going to sugarcoat this - breaking into sports is hard. Opportunities are limited, competition is intense, pay is often low early on, and hours are brutal. Many people start down this path and don't make it, not because they lack talent or passion, but because they don't know what it actually takes. This book won't make the journey easy, but it will make it clearer. It shows you what actually works versus what sounds good but doesn't translate to results.

If you're willing to do the work, really do it, not just read about it, this book gives you the best possible chance to turn your sports passion into your career. I'll give you the roadmap. You have to walk the path.

Time to step onto the field.

Introduction

I didn't plan on jumping over the dugout fence in front of tens of thousands of fans at loanDepot Park during the World Baseball Classic, but when Garrett Stubbs' two-run double cleared the left fielder's glove on March 12, 2023, my instincts took over. We weren't just celebrating a go-ahead hit; we were punching our ticket to the 2026 World Baseball Classic. For Team Israel, that moment represented years of improbable dreams crystallizing into reality.

The truth is, I had no business being there. My path to that dugout wasn't solely paved by connections or careful planning. Leaving high school, I didn't have any connections, nor a plan (not to mention failing a class).

What I did possess was an unshakable hunger and relentless drive to get a job in professional sports. Sixteen internships and professional experiences, hundreds of cold emails, dozens of handwritten thank-you notes, and a stubborn refusal to quit led me to working with four MLB teams, an NBA & WNBA team, the Israel National Baseball team, the Baseball and Basketball Hall of Fame Induction and Enshrinement ceremonies, a few minor league teams, a college professor, started two companies, and the list goes on.

This is the story of how I found a career in sports business and what I've learned from nearly a decade in the game. What you'll learn are tools and advice I've seen the best do, or done myself. This isn't a how-to-get-rich-or-famous-in-sports book. Instead, I'm offering something more valuable: a battle-tested strategy for doing meaningful work, cultivating authentic relationships, and building a career with genuine purpose.

So here's the deal I'll make with you. Take what I've learned and experienced, put it into practice, and I guarantee you'll have the best opportunity to pursue your dream career. Together, we'll transform "I love sports" into "I work in sports."

Part I: Getting in the Game

(Laying the Foundation)

Breaking into sports business through three essential foundations: discovering your authentic "why" and designing the lifestyle you actually want (Chapter 1), understanding how the sports industry really works with detailed career paths across almost every department from operations to analytics (Chapter 2), finding where you actually fit within the industry based on your personality, strengths, and long-term career goals (Chapter 3), and choosing the right educational program based on hands-on opportunities, alumni networks, and access to internships rather than rankings (Chapter 4).

"As an athlete or entrepreneur, we question ourselves about whether we made the right decision or not. Make a decision, find a path and commit to it. Make the necessary adjustments along the way." **Barry Larkin, Baseball Hall of Famer**

"As an athlete who meets a lot of people, you're always cautious as to who you let into your circle. Easily upon meeting Stuart I knew that genuineness was something I picked up immediately. When you have good people around you, I believe you try and keep them around as they want to protect you and try their hardest to make sure a good time is had. That's all I've had with our interactions. I'm sure I'm not the only one and that's the best part of the story. Good people are simply good people." **Adam Jones, Baltimore Orioles Hall of Famer**

"Breaking into the sports industry requires a strategic approach that combines passion with practicality. When I first met Stuart while playing for the Israel National baseball team, this was the impression he quickly radiated. Being great at listening and paying attention to detail will build relationships fast and lead to trust. Those attributes allow you to climb the sports industry ladder with ease. Stuart 100% knows this, and has lived all of that." **Ian Kinsler, Texas Rangers Hall of Famer**

"As an athlete one thing you find out quickly is when you find success, there are always people who want something from you or are willing to give you a hand. At first it is overwhelming on what things come your way as well as what doors open. Shortly after you find that, a lot of those come with strings attached. It's not everyday you meet someone in the industry as genuine as Stuart who wants the best for you. I was lucky enough to have met him and we continue to have a friendship long after my playing career is over." **Kevin Pillar, MLB Veteran (10+ Seasons)**

"Individuals beginning a career in sports management need a solid roadmap to begin or advance their journey. Stuart provides great perspective and action oriented recommendations to give a leg up on the competition and set a solid foundation for growth and success." **John Doleva, President and CEO, Naismith Memorial Basketball Hall of Fame**

"Grit, character, and a team-first mindset shape a career. In sports, the greatest elevate the team before themselves, because the team, not individual applause, defines true success. Sports management follows the same rule. Servant leadership isn't just a style, it's the spark that elevates others and lights the path to lasting impact." **Jamie Dinsmore, President and CEO, Hockey Hall of Fame**

"We are all grateful for having a career in sports and for someone initially believing in us to get our start. Stuart's ability to share his knowledge with those looking to get into this space, as well as his passion to help others, is unmatched. We all could have used this advice and perspective when looking for that break, and we never forget those who responded to our requests for advice and interviews in the beginning. It should be our responsibility to do the same for others." **Derrick Hall, President & CEO of the Arizona Diamondbacks**

"For any college students hoping to join the professional ranks, I really have one piece of good advice. Throw away your watches. Pro sports and specifically baseball is not a 9-5 job. I have made many sacrifices through the years – no Friday night movies, no Sundays at the beach, no summer vacations. I never worried about the hours because I loved what I did. So if you want to make the jump to the pros, understand what lies ahead. I have been with the Mets now for 46 years and wouldn't change a thing." **Jay Horwitz, New York Mets Hall of Fame Achievement Award Winner, 55+ Year Sports Executive**

Chapter 1: The Opening Quarter

Before polishing your resume, or submitting that first internship application, pause. Ask yourself one fundamental question:

Why do I want to work in sports?

This may seem like a simple question. But trust me, it's not. As a matter of fact, it's one of the most important questions you'll answer on this journey. As you search for your answer, understand this: you must become a fan of the business before you can be a fan of the sport. Somewhere beneath our professional aspirations, we're all still kids at heart, and that's precisely why sports careers captivate so many of us. Whether we competed on the field, or cheered from the bleachers, sports shaped our formative memories. Athletics ignited our passion and showed us that play could become something more, maybe even a career.

Finding Your Why

Let's start with the fundamentals. What part of sports genuinely excites you the most? Is it the electric atmosphere of game day? The meticulous behind-the-scenes planning? The art of storytelling? The depth of statistics? The chess match of strategy? Ask yourself: What do you find yourself gravitating toward, even when nobody is watching? Reading, watching, or doing? What's the thing that genuinely lights you up? Your answer doesn't need to be perfectly polished right now, but it does need to be honest. Because working in sports isn't highlight reels and celebrity access. It's early mornings, long nights, tight budgets, pressure-packed moments, and yes, it can even be getting hung up on 76 times a day. (Trust me, I've counted.)

David Scrivines, 25+ year Professional Baseball Scout says "When I ask students why they should get hired, the most common responses are, 'I'm hard working, have a passion for the game, and am very enthusiastic, and I've played since I was four.' Passion alone won't get you hired. You need to look for separators that make you valuable and different from the competition in ways that will actually help the team. If someone spoke five languages, that would be a separator. In my case, my separator is that I have hundreds of contacts in the independent leagues who provide highly valid information. But these are sources I've built relationships with and maintained over time. How many people connect on LinkedIn and then that's the end of it? Starting relationships, building them, and then maintaining them is what matters".

So Why Keep Showing Up?

But even with a clear "why," there will be days when showing up feels pointless. You'll work a game where everything goes wrong, nobody notices the things you fixed, and you drive home exhausted, wondering if any of it matters. Those days are not the exception in this industry. They're practically part of the job description.

So why keep showing up? Because the sports industry rewards people who stay. Not blindly, not without direction, but consistently. The relationships that open doors don't happen after one networking event or working a few games. The reputation that gets you recommended for a job doesn't come from one great game. It's built drip by drip, shift by shift, season by season. The person who hired me for one of my biggest opportunities didn't remember a single conversation we had. They remembered that every time they looked up, I was there, doing the work.

There's also something that nobody tells you early on: the industry is smaller than it looks. People move between teams, leagues, and markets constantly. The intern you worked alongside at a minor league stadium might be a director somewhere in three years. The vendor you treated well during a chaotic event might recommend you for a role you didn't even know existed. How you show up, every single time, is the long game.

And sometimes, showing up is how you figure out what you actually want. You think you want to be in marketing until you spend a season watching the operations team work and realize that's where you come alive. You can't discover that from the outside. You find it by being in the building, saying yes to the unglamorous stuff, and paying attention to what energizes you versus what drains you.

Showing up is the answer. It's not a phase you push through to get to the real work. It is the real work.

For me, it started with a simple idea: I wanted to create memories that would last a lifetime for fans. At the time, this didn't feel particularly revolutionary. But that perspective shifted dramatically after I survived two major terrorist attacks. When you come face-to-face with mortality like that, something clicks. Life isn't just short, it's precious and fragile. And if I'm going to pour my energy into something, why not dedicate it to giving people the best day of their lives? Why not create those unforgettable memories where a family walks out of a stadium still buzzing about what they just witnessed together? That realization kept me anchored when I found myself deep in the trenches, grinding through fourteen-hour gamedays, sweating through my dress shirt, all while coordinating an on-court performance and simultaneously troubleshooting a ticketing issue. When the details threatened to overwhelm me, I'd remember: someone out there is experiencing something they'll tell their grandkids about. That's why I do this.

Here's what I've learned: your "why" will evolve over time. It should. You'll grow, your goals will shift, and your understanding of the industry will deepen. But establishing a strong starting point through your personal mission statement gives you direction.

Passion vs. Purpose

Let's chat about two words that casually get tossed around the "follow your dreams" conversation: passion and purpose. They sound similar, but they're not.

Passion is what excites you.
Purpose is what sustains you.

Millions of people are passionate about sports. They live for game day. They memorize stats, debate trades, and never miss a broadcast. That doesn't mean they're meant to work in the sports industry. There's a vast difference between being a devoted fan and being an effective professional. Think about it this way: passion gets you through the highlight moments - the championship celebrations, the sold-out crowds, the behind the scenes access, etc. Purpose gets you through everything else. And trust me, there's a lot of "everything else." If you're thinking about breaking into sports, make sure your purpose runs deeper than just loving the game. The people who thrive in this industry, the ones who build sustainable, fulfilling careers, all share one characteristic: their purpose outlasts their passion. This industry will test you. The hours will drain you. The pay might disappoint you. But if your purpose is solid, you'll keep showing up.

The truth is if your answers feel uncertain right now, that's okay. Self-awareness is the first step. But if you can't articulate a purpose beyond "I love sports," you're not ready yet, and that's valuable information too. Because at the end of the day, passion might get you in the door. Purpose keeps you in the building. Before you go further, ask yourself these questions:

Am I prepared to do meaningful work that isn't always glamorous? Most days won't involve championship rings or viral moments. They'll involve spreadsheets, vendor negotiations, and solving problems nobody will ever thank you for. Can you find purpose in that?

Can I stay focused when it gets repetitive, chaotic, or underappreciated? You'll send the same email seventeen times. You'll coordinate events that attendees take for granted. You'll work weekends while your friends are celebrating holidays. Will your purpose carry you through those moments, or will your passion fizzle out?

Do I want to contribute to the game, not just consume it? There's profound satisfaction in being part of the machinery that creates the experiences fans cherish. But it requires shifting your identity from consumer to creator, from spectator to contributor. Are you ready for that transformation?

Designing Your Lifestyle

Here's the question nobody asks you in college, but everyone should: What kind of lifestyle do you actually want? Not what sounds impressive. Not what you think you're supposed to want. What do *you* want your daily life to look like five years from now? This might seem tangential to a book about sports management, but it's actually foundational. Because the lifestyle demands of this industry, especially early in your career, are significant and non-negotiable. Sports will consume your nights, weekends, and holidays. It will demand flexibility when you crave routine. It often means modest paychecks, high-pressure situations, and relentless hustle.

The question isn't whether these demands exist. They do. The question is: Does that align with your goals? Your personality? Your other priorities? Let me paint you a picture of what the lifestyle of entry careers in sports often looks like. You'll work when everyone else is off. Game days are weekends. Playoffs are holidays. Your friends are planning beach trips in July, and you're coordinating fan experiences for upcoming games. You'll earn less than your college roommate who took the corporate job, sometimes significantly less. The "working in sports" premium works in reverse: people will pay *you* less because there is a line out the door of people willing to take your job. You'll hustle constantly, not just physically (though yes, you'll be on your feet) but mentally. You'll juggle multiple roles, solve problems in real-time, and operate with minimal margin for error, all while maintaining a smile for fans, partners, and colleagues.

Does this scare you off? Maybe it does. It should be realistic. But here's the other side: some people genuinely thrive in this environment. They love the adrenaline of live events. They get energized by the unpredictability. They'd rather work a hundred Saturday nights in an arena than spend Monday through Friday in a cubicle, regardless of the pay difference. Some people crave the rush of live events and game-day chaos. Others thrive in analytical, strategic, or behind-the-scenes roles that offer more structure and predictability. There's no one universally right path, but there is absolutely a right path *for you*.

Before you commit to this industry, get brutally honest with yourself. What energizes you? Do you come alive in high-pressure, real-time environments? Or do you do your best work with time to think, analyze, and strategize? What drains you? Is it repetitive tasks? Constant social interaction? Lack of structure? Knowing your energy drains helps you avoid roles that will burn you out. What are your non-negotiables? Maybe it's being home for dinner most nights. Maybe it's earning a certain income by 30. Maybe it's having weekends free for the family. There's no judgment here, but you need to know your boundaries before the industry tests them.

Here's what people won't tell you: designing your lifestyle intentionally doesn't mean you lack ambition. It means you're strategic enough to pursue a path you can actually sustain. Burnout doesn't make you noble, it makes you ineffective. The people who build long, successful careers in sports aren't the ones who ignore lifestyle fit. They're the ones who find roles that align with how they're wired, then pour everything into those roles because the fit is right. So before you start applying to every sports job posting you can find, pause. Get clear on what kind of life you want to build. A dream job that creates a nightmare lifestyle isn't a dream, but a countdown to your exit. Find the intersection of what you love, what the industry needs, and what your life requires. That's where sustainable careers are built.

Dream Without Limits

Once you've explored your "why" and considered what kind of lifestyle you want, let's try something you were always told as a kid: dream without limits. Take money completely out of the equation and ignore what's "realistic." Forget what your parents expect, what your professors suggest, or what sounds impressive on LinkedIn. Strip away every practical consideration and honestly answer, "What's your dream job?" Not the job you think you can get, not the role that makes financial sense, not the position that checks all the responsible boxes, but just a dream. The thing that makes your chest tighten with excitement when you imagine it. The role you'd pursue even if nobody understood why. For me, the dream was always simple: I wanted a job I'd genuinely look forward to every single day and didn't want to dread on Sunday nights, or count down to Friday afternoons. I wanted to feel like I had a paid hobby rather than a job, something I'd probably do even if the paycheck disappeared. That became my north star. When work feels like something I *get* to do instead of something I *have* to do, I know I'm in the right place.

This exercise isn't frivolous. It's essential. Because you can't steer a ship to harbor if you never decide which harbor you're sailing toward. You'll optimize for safety, prestige, or salary and wake up one day wondering why success feels so hollow. Your dream might look completely different, and that's exactly the point. Maybe your dream is building a championship-caliber analytics department from scratch, maybe it's becoming the voice fans associate with their favorite team, maybe it's creating youth sports programs that change kids' lives, maybe it's negotiating billion-dollar broadcast deals, or designing stadiums that become architectural landmarks. Or maybe it's something that doesn't even exist yet, a role you'll have to create because nobody's imagined it before.

The specifics don't matter right now. What truly matters is allowing yourself to want what you genuinely desire, rather than settling for what feels realistic or acceptable. Because what I've learned is that the gap between where you are and where you dream of being isn't nearly as insurmountable as it appears. However, you can't chase a dream you're too afraid to acknowledge.

I'm not suggesting you ignore reality entirely. Bills need paying and experience needs building. We'll get to the practical steps, the internships, the networking, the right opportunities. But all of that tactical work becomes exponentially more effective when it's guided by a genuine vision of where you're headed.

Think of your dream job as the journey and the destination. You might not drive straight there. You'll probably take detours, make strategic stops, and adjust your route as you learn more about the terrain. But knowing your destination determines which roads you take, which opportunities you pursue, and which compromises you're willing to make along the way. As you journey through your career, you'll make lifelong friends, unforgettable memories, and maybe even earn a championship ring. When you achieve your dream job, you'll look back and be grateful for the journey that got you there.

So right now, before we dive into resumes and applications, interviews and emails, give yourself the gift of dreaming without limits. Write it down. Say it out loud. Let yourself want it fully, even if it feels audacious or improbable. Because the people who end up in extraordinary places all started by admitting they wanted something extraordinary. Your dream job exists. Maybe not in its exact form today, but in some version, somewhere, it's waiting. The question is whether you're brave enough to name it and bold enough to chase it.

John Michos, Premium Sales Manager for the New York Mets looks back and thinks, "If you told 8-year-old John who grew up a Mets fan that he would work for other NL East rivals Washington Nationals, Miami Marlins and then eventually come full circle to work for his hometown New York Mets, he would not believe this dream he gets to call life."

Dream Big, But Plan Smart

We just spent the last part talking about dreaming without limits and identifying what you truly want without letting practical concerns constrain your vision. That advice stands, you need to know your destination to chart your course. Now I'm going to give you advice that seems contradictory, but equally as important, to have a backup plan. Not because you're going to fail at your dream, but because succeeding in sports requires being strategic, not just passionate. The biggest thing is having a plan, knowing what you want, where you're headed, and how you're going to get there. That clarity gives you direction and purpose when the path gets difficult. But the reality nobody talks about in career workshops is sometimes organizations fold, positions get eliminated, ownership changes, or the opportunity you were counting on disappears overnight. I've seen talented, hardworking people lose jobs through no-fault-of-their-own budget cuts, front office turnover, or a new regime that brings their own people. Having a backup plan doesn't mean you lack commitment or confidence. It means you're strategic enough to protect yourself while pursuing your dream. Maybe your backup is developing transferable skills that work outside of sports, or maybe it's building a network in adjacent industries. Maybe it's keeping your certifications current, or maintaining relationships in other fields. Whatever it is, don't put all your eggs in one basket with an industry this volatile. Chase your sports career with everything you have, but be smart enough to have options if circumstances beyond your control force you to pivot. The people who last longest in sports aren't just the most passionate, they're the most adaptable.

The Foundation Before the Hustle

I know you're itching to jump into the actionable stuff, the job search strategy, and the networking guidance. If you rush past this, you'll wonder why nothing feels right. You need three things locked in before moving forward: know your "why," know your dream, and know what kind of life you want to build.

These answers matter most when you're grinding through your seventh consecutive day of late nights, exhausted and questioning everything, and someone casually mentions that your job "must be fun because you work in sports." In that moment, you'll smile, not because it's glamorous, but because you know exactly why you're doing it. You'll remember your purpose when passion alone would've sent you packing. You'll feel grounded in your dream when the daily grind threatens to break you.

That clarity doesn't come from skipping ahead to the tactical chapters. It comes from doing this uncomfortable, introspective work right now. So take the time and answer the hard questions. Write it down. Get honest with yourself. Because the tactics only work when you know where you're going.

Pat O'Conner, the former MiLB President, reminds students and young professionals, "If you love baseball, go buy a ticket and enjoy the game. Working in sports isn't about being a fan. You have to be honest with yourself about why you're doing this. Are you chasing autographs, fame, fortune? Because you don't get famous working in sports, and if you want to make a lot of money, you need your name on the back of the jersey, not on your front (your name tag). You have to be committed to the work."

Your Foundation Blueprint

Before moving forward, complete this essential self-assessment. In a journal or document, write detailed answers to these questions:

1. Why do I want to work in sports? Go beyond "I love sports" and identify the specific impact you want to have.

2. What does my ideal day look like five years from now? Describe it hour by hour, including work responsibilities, lifestyle elements, and personal priorities.

3. What is my dream job in sports, with no limitations on feasibility? Be specific about the role, organization type, and what you'd be doing daily.

4. What are three non-negotiables for my career and life? These might include location flexibility, work-life balance, earning potential, or specific types of work.

5. What skills and experiences do I currently have that are valuable to sports organizations? Be honest about your starting point. Save this document and review it every six months as your answers evolve. This clarity will guide every decision you make from here forward.

"The key is to just start and get your hands dirty, try, test, experiment, and learn. When I began as an intern, I had no idea I would end up loving what I do every single day, but once you start, people sometimes take a chance on you, and what matters is what you do with that chance. I became obsessed with learning and growing, studying everything I could about storytelling, entertainment, and creativity, because that obsession to never settle, to never be satisfied with past work, and to keep pushing to get better is what makes the difference. From Walt Disney and the entertainment industry, P.T. Barnum, WWE, SNL, Pixar, Cirque du Soleil, you name it, I studied it. Too many people show up with just a resume, but if you want a real break, do what others won't – create something, show value, ask questions, and give without expecting anything in return. Early on, I didn't get paid, I had to prove it and build it first, and that's the mindset that creates opportunity. So just start, get your hands dirty, become obsessed with learning, and don't be afraid to stand out. We weren't born to fit in, we were born to stand out." **Jesse Cole, Owner of Savannah Bananas, Creator of Banana Ball, Author of *Fans First* & *Find Your Yellow Tux***

"You need to gain experience in a solid business. Learn and identify the type of business you're best suited for, such as accounting, sales, PR, marketing, sponsorships, TV, or advertising. Sports is one of the top three industries in the country. Read trade magazines and newsletters to stay informed as much as you can. Learn what's happening in the industry and who the key players are. Be someone others turn to for ideas!" **Brandon Steiner, CEO of CollectibleXchange and Founder of Steiner Sports**

"Learn your craft. Know your industry and your field inside and out. Number two, study leadership. Study successful leaders and unsuccessful leaders. Both. You'll learn the common threads of what makes someone succeed and what makes them fail. You'll have patterns to aspire to and patterns to avoid." **Dave Gettleman, Former NFL League General Manager**

"Sports is more than a business. It's a passion. Learn from the experiences of Stuart who has been there. These positions require creativity, teamwork, and dedication to an intense schedule. The best in the business bring experiences from other places, so the fact that you have not worked in sports can be a plus. Here you will find a guide to navigating your way into a role where you can be noticed. Don't be afraid to stick your neck out and prove before you are hired why you are the candidate they need – even if there is no job posting!" **Janet Marie Smith, Executive Vice President Planning & Development, Los Angeles Dodgers and Chairman & Co-Founder, Canopy Team**

"Sports are built on preparation, relationships, and trust. My advice to students is to focus on the fundamentals, stay patient, and be willing to learn from anyone. None of us get here alone, and supporting the next generation is one of the most important responsibilities we have as professionals." **Ryan Norys, Chief Revenue Officer, Tottenham Hotspur Football Club**

Chapter 2: How the Sports Industry Works and Where It Can Go

If you asked a random person on the street what a sports career looks like, they'd probably say a player, coach, agent, or maybe marketing. That's about it. The average fan can't imagine how many individuals it takes to put on an event. There's an entire ecosystem of professionals making it happen, people in roles that have nothing to do with athletic performance, but everything to do with whether the franchise succeeds. Here's the reality: for every player on the field, there are dozens, sometimes hundreds, of people working behind the scenes. The sports industry isn't just about the game. It's about the business of the game. And that business is massive, complex, and full of opportunities most people never consider.

The Non-Linear Reality of Sports Careers

If you're waiting for someone to hand you a career roadmap with clear milestones and guaranteed timelines, you'll be waiting forever. Sports careers don't work that way. The person who's now a VP of Marketing might have started in ticket sales, spent three years in minor league baseball, moved to sponsorship at a different organization, took what seemed like a lateral move to get into a bigger market, and finally landed in marketing leadership fifteen years later. That's not a failure to follow a plan, that's a successful sports career.

This chapter breaks down typical career progressions across different departments in sports, but you need to understand that these paths are frameworks, not formulas. You'll see the general trajectory from entry-level to leadership, competencies at each stage, and typical timelines. But your path will zigzag. You'll take lateral moves that turn out to be the best decisions of your career. You'll pivot between departments, you'll move between organizations, leagues, and sometimes leave sports entirely before coming back.

The goal isn't to follow these paths exactly, but to understand the landscape well enough to make informed decisions about where you're going and what you're building toward.

"It's okay if what you originally thought you wanted to do turns out to be completely different than what you thought it would be. Be willing to pivot, try new things, and find what you are passionate about," says Chrissy Cuda, the Director of Stadium Production at the Nashville Soccer Club.

Understanding Progression Fundamentals

Before diving into specific departments, let's establish how progression typically works across the industry. Most sports organizations follow similar hierarchical structures, though titles vary. The general ladder looks like this:

Coordinator/Assistant → Manager/Account Executive (AE) → Senior Manager/Senior AE → Director → Senior Director → Vice President (VP) → Senior VP → Executive VP/Chief Officer

It's important to understand this because it'll save you time in the application process. If you're a senior in college, do not start applying for Vice President-level roles. You need real experience first. When I was a senior I was applying to any and all jobs, with little direction. Time-frames vary dramatically based on performance, organizational growth, and opportunities, but rough averages are 1-3 years from Coordinator to Manager, 2-4 years from Manager to Senior Manager/Director, 3-5 years from Director to VP, and 5+ years from VP to SVP/EVP. These aren't guarantees, as some people move faster, many move slower, and plenty of successful careers plateau at Director or VP levels without ever reaching the C-suite.

What drives progression? It could be a combination of factors: Performance and results that are measurable and consistent. Expanding scope by taking on more responsibility, bigger accounts, or additional teams. Organizational growth, because growing companies create more senior positions. Strategic moves between organizations to access opportunities that don't exist in your current structure. And perhaps most importantly, building political capital by developing relationships with decision-makers who advocate for your advancement.

The biggest mistake young professionals make is expecting linear progression within one organization. The reality is that strategic moves between organizations often accelerate your career more than waiting for the next opening at your current employer. Don't view changing organizations as disloyalty; rather, view it as agency over your career trajectory.

The Sports Ecosystem

The sports industry isn't one thing. It's an interconnected web of organizations, each playing a specific role in bringing sports to fans. Understanding this ecosystem is critical because your dream job might not be where you think it is – not the sanitized version you see on ESPN, but the real structure, who does what, how money flows, and where you might actually fit into all of it.

Professional teams and franchises are what most people picture when they think of a "sports job." These are your MLB, NBA, NFL, NHL, MLS teams, plus countless minor league and independent organizations. But the landscape is expanding rapidly beyond traditional major leagues. Women's professional sports are experiencing unprecedented growth with leagues like the WNBA gaining tremendous momentum, the Professional Women's Hockey League (PWHL) launching with massive fan support, and innovative formats like Athletes Unlimited (the AUSL) revolutionizing how leagues operate with its player-focused model and rotating team structure. Unrivaled, a new 3-on-3 basketball league, is attracting top WNBA talent with competitive salaries and a compact season.

Both the massive franchises and the budding organizations generate revenue through ticket sales, sponsorships, merchandise, broadcasting rights, concessions, etc. They employ everyone from the general manager to the person scanning tickets at the gate. The core functions remain consistent across leagues, sales, marketing, operations, and community engagement, but the scale, resources, growth trajectories, and lifestyle demands vary dramatically.

These emerging leagues present unique opportunities for aspiring professionals. They're building infrastructure from scratch, which means fewer entrenched hierarchies and more chances to wear multiple hats and gain diverse experience quickly. Early employees in these organizations often have tremendous impact and faster career progression than they would in established leagues, where structures are rigid and competition for advancement is higher. Additionally, many of these newer leagues are intentionally designed with better work-life balance in mind. Shorter seasons, more concentrated schedules, and leaner operations often mean more sustainable workloads compared to the grinding 162-game MLB season or 82-game NBA schedule. If you're willing to embrace some uncertainty and help build something new, these leagues offer ground-floor opportunities that simply don't exist in mature organizations, often with more reasonable schedules.

Jason Klein, the founder of Force3 Pro Gear, reiterates, "Sports functions as one ecosystem. Every part depends on the others. Team staff, brands, vendors, and equipment companies all keep the game running. When you understand that, you build stronger relationships and you move farther than the people who chase titles instead of people. Students focus on team jobs, but the strongest opportunities come from understanding how the full system works. This circle is small. You deal with the same people for years. Your behavior and your relationships decide how far you go.

The job you start with is not the job you end with. The right attitude and steady performance open the path forward."

Before we get into the traditional team-side roles, let's talk about the team-adjacent opportunities first. These positions orbit around teams without being directly employed by them, and they're often overlooked by people trying to break into the industry.

Before diving in, grab a highlighter or pen. As you read through the roles in this chapter, mark the ones that spark your interest, even if you don't fully understand them yet. When I first explored the range of departments and positions in sports, I was surprised by just how many paths existed beyond the obvious ones. My hope is that you experience that same sense of discovery and start to see possibilities you may not have considered before.

Leagues and Governing Bodies operate above individual teams, functioning as the strategic center of the sport itself. Organizations like the MLB, MLS, NBA, NFL, and NCAA set rules, negotiate massive broadcast deals worth billions, manage schedules, enforce policies, and protect the brand integrity of the entire league. These entities employ lawyers who handle complex labor negotiations and legal compliance, marketing professionals who promote the sport globally, operations specialists who coordinate logistics across dozens of teams, policy experts who shape the future of the game, and business development executives who expand into new markets.

The scope of what league offices handle can be staggering. At the American Hockey League (AHL) level, for example, the league office doesn't just manage the schedule, they actually build the entire 1,152 game schedule by hand. Beyond scheduling, the league maintains a central registry that tracks every transaction across all teams, from trades and recalls to signings and professional tryout agreements. The Team Marketing & Business Operations (TMBO) and/or Team Business Services (TBS), depending on what league, plays a particularly crucial role in keeping member clubs healthy and growing. They work directly with teams on ticket sales, corporate partnerships, marketing (social media, paid marketing, email marketing, websites, and beyond), and sharing best practices across the league. They're constantly looking at financial reports to understand the overall health of the league and identify any teams that might be struggling compared to others. One of the most valuable things that TMBO and TBS does is provide professional development for team staff. They run sales training sessions and help people navigate the challenges that come up in professional sports organizations, everything from managing up, to dealing with staff turnover, to working with the C-suite and navigating personalities. "This group is key to the league because they have a pulse and strong relationships with all member clubs," Emily Vance, the Senior Marketing Manager for the Hartford Wolf Pack and former Manager of Business Analytics at the AHL, notes, "They're able to connect individuals from member teams to one another, especially when teams are interested in certain promotions or ticket packages that other teams are running, or if teams are having issues with things unique to one another." The All-Star Game represents another major event that the league office coordinates each season, bringing together planning, marketing, and operations expertise from across the organization.

Chris Olsen, the Senior Director of Football Administration at the Atlanta Falcons, mentions, "Starting at the NFL league office taught me the importance of the integrity of compliance to ensure all Clubs compete on a level playing-field. I spent years reviewing contracts, coordinating draft eligibility, serving as a liaison between the Clubs-and the players' union, but equally as important, I served as a labor relations resource for the Clubs in an ever-evolving salary cap system. That experience gave me a bird's-eye view of how 32 organizations operate differently within the same framework. When you work at a league office, you're building relationships across the entire sport, and that network becomes incredibly valuable throughout your career, no matter where you end up."

Beyond day-to-day problem solving, league offices orchestrate the sharing of institutional knowledge that elevates every team's business operations. Annual league meetings bring together staff from across clubs to discuss league-wide trends in ticketing, marketing, and social media performance. Many leagues organize club performance groups where teams can benchmark their results against peers and learn what's actually working in the market right now. "We're constantly looking at how we can help teams improve their business operations," says Jonathan White, a sports business executive. "That means bringing clubs together to share what's working, whether that's through performance groups where teams can compare their metrics or connecting individual teams who are facing similar challenges."

When teams are evaluating new venues or planning renovation projects, the league office becomes an invaluable resource. White explains, "Teams are always looking at new venues or renovation spaces, and this is where the league can be extremely valuable as a resource to help guide these decisions. We connect them with other clubs who've recently gone through similar processes, and we help them think through the business implications of those decisions." This collective intelligence helps smaller markets avoid costly mistakes and allows successful strategies to spread quickly across the entire league. "This is really how we help elevate team business," White notes. "It's about making sure every club has access to the best thinking across the entire league."

The TBS department at the American League level is viewed as one of the most respected, trusted, and valued departments by member clubs. This department is unique in the sense that members in this department typically build their career on the team side first. "The staff in TMBO typically built their careers on the team side first, so when they enter this department, they have real-life experience," Vance explains. "They understand the struggles that staff on the team side face on a firsthand basis and can provide insight into how to handle certain situations." This experience is what makes them so effective. They're talking with teams almost daily, building strong relationships that allow them to connect clubs facing similar challenges. When Hartford wanted to run an Emo Night promotion, TBS connected them with San Diego who had run a successful Emo Night the prior season. When Hartford was curious about glow-in-the-dark jerseys, they got introduced to Cleveland. And when Hartford switched from Ticketmaster to AXS for their ticketing system, the league office connected them with Bakersfield, Ontario, and San Diego, teams that had already made that transition and could share what they learned. Vance has seen both sides of this relationship and understands how critical these central operations are to keeping the entire league running smoothly.

League offices tend to be more corporate in culture and function than team-level positions – think traditional business hours, structured hierarchies, and strategic long-term planning rather than the daily chaos of game operations. From a work-life balance perspective, league positions often offer more predictable schedules since they're not tied to the rhythm of individual games and seasons in the same way team employees are. You'll still work intensely during major events like drafts, playoffs, and championship series, but the day-to-day tends to be more sustainable. These roles also typically offer competitive corporate salaries and benefits that rival or exceed what teams pay for similar positions.

Sports Agencies represent athletes, coaches, and brands, but they're far more than just contract negotiators. Major agencies like Wasserman, Octagon, CAA Sports, Excel Sports Management, and Klutch Sports Group have evolved into full-service operations offering marketing, branding, media production, event management, and strategic consulting. Wasserman works with everyone from individual athletes to Fortune 500 companies on talent representation and brand consulting, while Octagon specializes in athlete representation but also manages major events and global sponsorship activation. Beyond the headline-grabbing contract negotiations that happen during free agency, agencies employ lawyers who draft and review complex contracts, marketing coordinators who secure endorsement deals and manage brand partnerships, financial advisors who help athletes manage wealth and plan for life after sports, PR specialists who handle media relations and crisis management, and business development professionals who identify new revenue opportunities for clients. If you work for an agency, you might represent talent directly, service corporate clients looking to enter the sports space, or manage the business operations that keep everything running behind the scenes. Smaller boutique agencies offer more personalized service, closer relationships with clients, and potentially faster career growth if you're looking for a tighter-knit environment where you can make an immediate impact. The work-life balance at agencies varies dramatically depending on your role and clients. Agent life can be grueling; you're always on call for your athletes, traveling constantly, and working around their schedules. But roles in marketing, operations, or finance within agencies often offer more structure and predictability, especially at larger firms with established systems and support staff.

Brands and Sponsors invest billions in sports annually, making them one of the most lucrative sectors of the industry. Companies like Nike, Gatorade, State Farm, Coca-Cola, and countless others aren't just buying logo placement; they're buying access to passionate, engaged audiences who will associate their emotional connection to sports with the brand itself. "Brands leverage sports partnerships to connect with their target audiences where they are most passionate," explains Caitlyn Ranson, the Director of Brand Partnerships & Events Activation at Bridgestone Americas. "Brands that do it correctly identify the intersectionality of engaging with fans in shared spaces so that their brand can show up in an authentic and meaningful way." These companies employ entire teams dedicated to sports marketing strategy, partnership activation, experiential marketing, content creation, and measuring return on investment. If you work on the brand side, you're figuring out how to leverage sports to sell products, build brand loyalty, and create memorable consumer experiences. You might develop activations like Nike's athlete-driven campaigns, Gatorade's integration into training and performance, or State Farm's community-focused sponsorships that connect with fans beyond just logo visibility.

When evaluating potential partnerships, Ranson looks for specific indicators of success. "I prioritize alignment on shared values and long-term vision. Partners who embrace innovation and community impact signal opportunities for meaningful collaboration beyond short-term logo placements." She emphasizes that audience overlap is equally critical, noting that authentic partnerships thrive when both brands genuinely serve similar communities. She also seeks partners with a flexible, collaborative mindset, where co-creation and openness to experimentation replace rigid deliverables. That said, the brand side comes with its own set of challenges. Ranson points out slower pace and more bureaucracy, limited autonomy, measurement challenges in proving value and securing necessary investment as obstacles that professionals should consider. The corporate structure that provides stability can also mean more layers of approval, longer timelines for decisions, and constant pressure to justify ROI in ways that teams don't always face. If you want to work in sports but value structure, compensation, and balance, the brand side might be your best path. Just know that you'll be trading the fast-paced intensity of team environments for the methodical approach of corporate marketing.

Brand-side roles typically offer significantly better work-life balance than team-side positions. You're operating on corporate schedules rather than game schedules, which means more predictable hours, weekends off (unless you're activating at an event), and traditional vacation time. The pay is also generally higher, as corporate marketing budgets dwarf team budgets, and brands compete for talent with the broader business world, not just sports.

Venues and Facilities are the physical backbone of live sports, yet they're often completely overlooked by people trying to break into the industry. Stadiums, arenas, training facilities, multi-use complexes, and sports entertainment districts all require sophisticated management operations. Venue operations encompass everything from event coordination and scheduling to food and beverage service, to security and crowd management, to capital improvement projects and infrastructure upgrades. Teams need professionals who understand building systems, vendor management, safety protocols, hospitality operations, and how to create exceptional guest experiences across thousands of interactions per event. Some venues are owned and operated by teams themselves, while others are independent entities managed by companies like Oak View Group, ASM Global, AEG Worldwide, or Legends that host multiple sports franchises, concerts, conventions, and community events. Working for a venue management company can actually offer more diverse experience and better career trajectory than working for a single team because you're exposed to different sports, events, and operational challenges.

"Many roles on the venue side are closer to fans than any other department within a sports organization. They are the ushers, the ticket takers, the concessionaires, etc. that are interacting directly with fans on a daily basis. They are both the backbone and the front lines of the team. I think being so close to the fan experience is a very valuable experience to get while breaking into the industry," shares Hannah Butler, the Director of Operations at the Charlotte Sports Foundation. She also mentions, "Being on the venue side is a great place to start when you don't know where to start because it touches nearly every single department within an organization. It's a fantastic opportunity to learn how an organization operates and get access to all of the different functions of the business." From a lifestyle perspective, venue roles often mean evening and weekend work during events, but many positions, such as facility management, capital projects, and business operations, operate on more traditional schedules during the week. These roles also tend to offer more stability than team positions because venues host events year-round and don't experience the same seasonal intensity or playoff volatility that defines team employment.

Technology and Analytics have fundamentally revolutionized how teams, leagues, and brands operate. Front offices now employ data scientists building predictive models, software engineers creating custom platforms, analysts transforming raw data into actionable insights, and product managers bridging technical teams with business stakeholders. These professionals use advanced metrics and machine learning to evaluate player performance, optimize ticket pricing in real-time, personalize fan experiences, and make strategic decisions grounded in evidence rather than intuition. Companies like StatCast, Whoop, and Sportlogiq build the sophisticated tools that teams and leagues now consider essential infrastructure. Working for a sports tech company offers the best of both worlds: you're in the sports industry but operating with the compensation, equity opportunities, and work culture typical of the tech sector. Analytics and strategy departments are increasingly common, especially in major markets. Forward-thinking teams leverage data scientists & engineers, business analysts, visualization specialists, and strategy professionals to help uncover insights to give their organization a winning edge. Team sizes vary greatly depending on the organization.

Getting in right out of college is competitive. Strong candidates have quantitative degrees, demonstrate analytical skills, possess programming abilities, and display a genuine passion for sports. Advanced degrees are becoming a prerequisite to these jobs at an increasing rate. Alex Forbes, the Senior Manager of Business Intelligence with the Phoenix Suns & Mercury, says, "What makes sports analytics unique is that there's less red tape than most industries. Analysts aren't stuck in the back office; they have a seat at the table, helping shape decisions and driving real results in real time. The strongest candidates bring quantitative degrees in fields like statistics, math, computer science, or economics, along with programming skills in Python, R, and SQL. But here's what really matters: you need to translate data into clear, actionable insights that people can actually use, and you've got to have genuine passion for sports. That combination is what opens doors."

Work-life balance in these departments is seen as more commonplace in relation to operations roles. You're working on projects with defined timelines, not reacting to game-day chaos. However, this can also vary greatly depending on the team and organization. Seth Greenberg, the Manager of Revenue and Insights at Learfield, remembers his time with the Kansas City Chiefs, when he had to send parking reports to higher-ups every 15 minutes to help diagnose traffic flow and keep track of gate openings through the beginning of the games. Remote work is often available, and typical weeks run 45-50 hours with flexibility. Compensation is competitive: entry-level analysts earn \$55,000-\$75,000, senior roles \$85,000-\$120,000+, and directors can command \$150,000+.

Vendors and Service Providers support the entire sports ecosystem from behind the scenes, and they employ thousands of professionals whose work makes everything else possible. Hospitality and food service companies like Aramark and Delaware North, ticketing platforms like Ticketmaster and SeatGeek, transportation services that move teams and equipment, marketing agencies that create campaigns and activations, legal firms specializing in sports law, construction companies that build and renovate facilities, and technology vendors providing everything from Wi-Fi infrastructure to CRM systems – all of these make their living serving sports organizations.

But the vendor ecosystem goes even deeper than that. Behind major platforms like Ticketmaster, there's a vast network of third-party companies plugging in to help support live events. Ticketmaster's Nexus program, for example, connects partners with an entire marketplace of vendors, from companies like Fevo that help drive group sales, to Vozzi, a texting platform making waves in fan engagement. Check out Ticketmaster's Nexus partner site to see just how expansive this network really is. New companies are constantly entering the space, disrupting traditional models and finding innovative ways to solve problems for teams and fans alike. The doors are wide open for entrepreneurs to launch their own companies and break into the sports business with fresh ideas. Teams seem more receptive than ever to trying new approaches to grow revenues, even if it means investing significant resources in emerging technology. "On the vendor and service provider side, you need to understand the full scope of what we do. Vendors work with teams, brands, leagues, venues, players, and cities. That gives us a wider view of the industry than many team roles offer. The work moves fast and your reputation follows you everywhere. Trust matters more than anything. Teams stay with vendors who deliver and communicate well. Students should know that vendor roles build long-term relationships across the entire industry, not just one organization. On the brand side, the stability and structure are accurate, but students need to understand these roles are relationship driven. You deal with teams, leagues, vendors, and agencies every day. Brands expect people who execute with consistency and communicate clearly. These positions are competitive. Every decision affects the business. Students should approach brand roles as business jobs, not fan jobs," says Klein.

That said, starting team-side and then transitioning to vendors can be a strategic path. That early experience working inside a sports organization helps you understand the clientele you'll be serving from the vendor side, making you far more effective at anticipating their needs and speaking their language. Moving into the vendor space also helps broaden your skill set and prevents you from feeling pigeonholed in the sports world. You still get a taste of sports, but it opens up your next career moves, making it easier to break directly into adjacent industries like tech, marketing, or hospitality. In fact, because of factors like compensation and work-life balance, vendors and tech companies have become a natural next step for professionals leaving team-side roles. These companies actively seek out people with vast networks and deep understanding of how sports organizations operate. That team-side experience becomes your competitive advantage when landing your next role in tech or the broader vendor ecosystem.

These roles often offer significantly better work-life balance than working directly for teams because you're operating on traditional business timelines and corporate structures, rather than being at the mercy of game schedules and playoff intensity. Vendors also tend to pay better because they're competing for talent across multiple industries, not just sports. You still get to work in sports, attending games, collaborating with teams, and solving interesting problems, but with more reasonable hours, better benefits, and often the opportunity to work with multiple clients rather than being tied to one organization's fate.

Inside a Sports Organization: How Teams Actually Work

Let's now zoom in on a professional sports team, because that's where most people want to start. Here's what the organizational structure typically looks like and what each department actually does, how many people work in each area, and what your realistic chances are of breaking in right out of college. Traditionally, most teams and organizations do their hiring during the offseason, or shortly after their major annual event, whether that's a championship game, a tournament, or another flagship competition. Understanding this hiring cycle helps you time your outreach strategically.

Sport Operations (baseball ops, football ops, basketball ops, etc.) are what fans think of as "the front office," or the decision makers who build championship rosters. This is where the real roster magic happens: the general manager (GM) and assistant GMs set organizational philosophy and make final personnel decisions; directors of player development oversee minor league systems and prospect progression; scouts evaluate amateur and professional talent across the country and internationally; video coordinators break down game film and prepare scouting reports; and analysts use advanced metrics to inform everything from draft strategy to in-game tactics. Many MLB teams employ 100+ people in baseball operations (including scouts and minor league staff), NBA teams typically have 15-25 in basketball operations, and NFL teams range from 25-40, making these departments relatively small, but incredibly influential. "At our baseball operations organizational meetings three years ago, we had approximately 300 people in that group. This includes scouts, front office, coaches, player development, sport psychologists, video coordinators, analysts, strength and development, research and development, baseball data systems, and more. As a point of reference, this group consisted of about 100 people 20 years ago," Scrivines remembers. "How I think about baseball operations is that it covers a lot of different areas, one of which is the front office. But I do think they're different. I don't think our Triple-A manager is working in the front office, for example."

Simon Rosenbaum, the Director of Player Programs & Integration at Tampa Bay Rays, points out how many aspiring professionals don't realize the breadth of opportunities within baseball ops. "People asked me what areas of baseball operations I was interested in and I genuinely did not have an answer. Now that I'm on this side, I do think it's helpful for candidates to have thought about more specific areas within baseball ops that they're most interested in." His advice for standing out? "Do and share your own work. That's the thing that will separate you from other candidates. It's much harder to separate based on resumes and cover letters."

Teams seldom hire for these positions, and rarely at the entry-level. However, depending on the team, interns can get hired more frequently. "We hire a number of interns every year and have hired many of our full-time staff, including me, from that internship pipeline. It's the best interview the teams and candidates can get," says Rosenbaum. Getting in right out of college is extremely difficult. These are among the most highly competitive, hardest-to-access roles in the entire industry that require deep sport-specific knowledge, often advanced degrees (especially for analytics roles), and typically years of grinding in lower levels. Think unpaid internships, minor league gigs, or assistant positions where you're proving yourself through 80-hour weeks and complete devotion to the craft. Most successful candidates have either played the sport at high levels, worked in minor leagues for years, or have advanced degrees (MBA, analytics, sports management) combined with multiple relevant internships. Scrivenes mentions, "Job descriptions change. The job as a scout has changed and includes more video and data now. So we have to have a growth mindset and be able to adapt and learn. And we can't underestimate the value of being a team player. There are many skilled people that are all qualified for positions, but team players and those that go above and beyond have a better chance of getting into the industry and staying in the industry."

The work-life balance here is virtually nonexistent during the season; baseball operations professionals work year-round: scouting during the season, evaluating in the playoffs, making moves in free agency, preparing for the draft, and managing player development in the offseason. If you're married to the idea of roster construction and player personnel, understand that it requires sacrificing nearly everything else, at least until you've established yourself at higher levels where you have more control over your schedule. The pay at entry levels is shockingly low for the hours demanded: $35,000-$50,000 for analysts/coordinators, though compensation improves significantly as you climb the ladder. Directors can earn $150,000+, and GMs earn millions. This path is for people who genuinely can't imagine doing anything else.

Olsen says, "Football operations roles are about mastering complexity under pressure. Whether you're negotiating a multimillion-dollar contract extension or managing roster moves on cut-down day, you need to know the nuances of the CBA and the Constitution & By-Laws, understand cap implications years out, and build trust with agents, coaches, and front office executives simultaneously. The hours are long, the decisions are consequential, and there's not much margin for error when you're dealing with someone's livelihood and your team's competitive future. But if you love the strategic chess match of roster construction and you're willing to put in years learning the craft, there's nothing quite like striving to win a championship."

Ticket Sales is where most sports careers begin, and it offers some of the clearest progression paths because success is quantifiable. However, even in sales, advancement isn't automatic. You need to consistently hit numbers, develop new skills, and position yourself for the next level. Ticket sales is your most realistic entry point into professional sports because teams need to sell tickets to survive, which means they're always hiring. Sales roles have high turnover because the job is demanding, the hours are long, and not everyone can handle the constant rejection. That creates openings. More importantly, sales teaches you the fundamentals of the business. You learn how to communicate, how to handle pressure, how to work with different departments, and how to deliver results when it matters. Ticket sales teams are typically divided into specialized verticals, such as new business (prospecting new season ticket holders), experience or retention (keeping current customers engaged and renewing), premium products (suites and club seats), and group sales (groups starting from 10+ tickets). All of these verticals focus on generating the revenue that keeps teams operational.

Something critical that students often miss is you should actually want to be in sales, not just use it as a stepping stone to business intelligence, player development, or some other department you think is more glamorous. If you're only in sales to get your foot in the door, it shows. You won't perform at the level needed to advance, and you'll burn out before you get anywhere. The people who succeed in sales and eventually move into other roles are the ones who genuinely embrace the work, hit their numbers, and build relationships across the organization. Teams promote from within when they see someone who delivers, not someone who's just waiting for something better to open up.

With the high turnover rate, teams are constantly hiring. The upside? Once you're in and prove yourself, you can transition to other departments. Many successful executives in marketing, partnerships, and operations started in ticket sales because it teaches you the fundamentals faster than any other path. You learn how to communicate under pressure, how to manage relationships, how to work cross-functionally with marketing and operations, and how to deliver results when it matters. Those skills transfer everywhere.

The work is demanding, from making calls during business hours, attending games at night, working weekends, and hitting monthly quotas. Picture this: on a standard office day, you're arriving by 8 or 9 A.M. and immediately diving into calls. You're working through a list of prospects, hearing "no" far more often than "yes," tracking every interaction in the CRM, and trying to hit your daily call quota before the afternoon slows down. You're coordinating with marketing on promotions, following up on leads from digital campaigns, and prepping for evening outreach when people are more likely to pick up the phone. Then there's the administrative work: updating accounts, sending proposals, processing renewals, and sitting in team meetings to review numbers and strategy.

Now flip to game day. You're still in the office making calls during the day, but as game time approaches, your role shifts entirely. You're greeting clients at will call, walking premium suite holders to their seats, handling last-minute issues with tickets that didn't get delivered, and networking with prospects you invited to the game. You're not watching the game like a fan. You're working the concourse, shaking hands, answering questions, and positioning yourself for the follow-up call you'll make the next morning. By the time you leave, it's 11 P.M. or midnight, and you're back at your desk the next day doing it all over again.

Anthony Parilla, the Vice President of Property Sales at Elevate, explains that game days can be the best way to separate yourself. "Whether you're working a 40- or 70-hour week, what really matters is what you accomplish during those hours. Most salespeople don't fully realize the opportunity that a game night presents. The average salesperson will see the event as 'check-in and check-out.' The top performers will see the event as their competitive edge: an opportunity to make a great first impression on people who are already buying the product and experiencing the game in real time." He continues, "Give out 30 business cards. Grab ten new phone numbers. Help five people sitting courtside understand how the inclusive amenities work. Do this consistently over the course of a season, and you'll generate incremental sales while separating yourself from the 90% of salespeople who stick to the status quo."

The work typically means 60-70 hour weeks during peak seasons. Turnover is high for a few reasons. First, the job is performance-based. If you're not hitting your numbers, you won't last. Second, the grind wears people down. The rejection is constant. The hours are relentless. You're working while your friends are enjoying their weekends. You miss holidays, birthdays, and family events because games don't stop for your personal life. Third, many people come into sales thinking it's a stepping stone to something "better," and when they realize how hard the work actually is, they check out mentally and either leave or get let go.

So what can you do to avoid burnout? First, you have to genuinely want to be in sales, not just tolerate it until something else opens up. The people who thrive are the ones who find satisfaction in closing deals, building relationships, and competing with themselves to hit bigger numbers. Second, you need to build routines that protect your mental and physical health. That means setting boundaries where you can, finding time to exercise, and not letting the job consume every waking hour even when it feels like it should. Third, lean on your team. Sales can feel isolating when you're grinding through rejection, but the best sales cultures are built on support, shared wins, and people who genuinely want to see each other succeed.

Base salaries range from $35,000-$50,000, but strong performers can earn $70,000-$100,000+ through commissions. A typical career progression within sales follows a well-defined path:

Inside Sales Representative → Account Executive (AE) → Senior AE → Sales Manager → Director of Ticket Sales → VP of Ticket Sales

Inside Sales Representative (1-2 years of experience at this role): You're making high-volume calls, learning the fundamentals, and proving you can handle rejection while hitting activity and revenue targets. Success means consistently hitting monthly quotas, developing strong product knowledge, and demonstrating coachability. A typical base salary across professional sports can range from $20,000-$35,000. The key milestone is proving you can sell consistently, not just having one good month followed by three low ones. Pay attention to the size and structure of the team you're joining. Are you going to be one of twenty reps fighting for a promotion, or part of a smaller crew of five where you'll get more attention and opportunity? Also, look at how often they promote from within versus hiring managers from outside. It tells you whether there's actually a path up or if you'll hit a ceiling.

Account Executive (2-4 years of experience at this role): You've graduated to managing bigger accounts, groups, season tickets, or premium seating. You're spending less time on the phone and more time building face-to-face relationships. Success means growing your book of business, maintaining high retention rates, and upselling existing clients. The transition from inside to outside sales usually requires 12-24 months of consistent performance, though some organizations hire directly into outside roles.

Senior Account Executive (2-3 years of experience at this role): You're managing the largest, most complex accounts or breaking into sponsorship sales. You might be mentoring newer AEs informally. Success means significant revenue generation (often $500K+ annually), long-term client retention, and demonstrating leadership qualities.

Sales Manager (3-5 years of experience at this role): You've transitioned from individual contributor to managing a team of 4-12 sales-people. Success now relies on your team's numbers, not just your own. You're coaching, recruiting, conducting performance reviews, and thinking strategically about process improvements. The jump to management is significant; many great salespeople struggle because managing sellers requires entirely different skills than selling.

Director of Ticket Sales (3-5 years of experience at this role): You're overseeing multiple sales teams (inside sales, season tickets, groups, or maybe premium), managing managers, and thinking about departmental strategy, pricing, and process. You're working closely with marketing, operations, and finance. This role requires balancing team leadership with strategic thinking about revenue optimization.

VP of Ticket Sales/Chief Revenue Officer (5+ years of experience at this role): You're in senior leadership, setting organizational revenue strategy, managing directors, interfacing with ownership, and making major decisions about pricing, inventory, and go-to-market strategies. Getting here usually requires 10-15+ years in the industry with a track record of consistent revenue growth and team leadership.

Parilla mentions about getting into leadership, "There are plenty of prerequisites to stepping into sales leadership: being a top sales performer, a positive cultural asset, and a great time manager, to name a few. That said, as you work your way into middle management and senior leadership, it's important to think intentionally about your core leadership values so you can truly lean into them and regularly audit yourself. My core leadership values are simple: (1) Care About People, (2) Do the Right Thing, (3) Challenge, and (4) Support. What are yours? Take your time developing what your true leadership values are. Once they're established, you'll have a much sharper vision for how to effectively lead your team."

Partnership Teams secure and manage the corporate sponsors who provide massive revenue streams beyond ticket sales, everything from stadium naming rights worth millions to promotional theme nights, digital advertising, and everything in between. These roles blend sales, account management, and market strategy. Broadly speaking, the partnership team works to identify prospects, craft customized proposals, negotiate contracts, and manage activations to ensure sponsors achieve their business objectives and ex-tend the partnership for years to come.

One critical structural nuance that Rob Crain, the Senior Director of Corporate Partnerships for the Boston Celtics, emphasizes is that partnerships departments are typically split into two distinct teams: activation and sales. "The VP is typically the head of partnership sales," Crain explains, highlighting how the leadership structure reflects this division. Understanding this split is essential because the career paths differ significantly. "It's not as typical to see partnership sales people come from the activation side," Crain notes. Instead, successful partnership sales professionals usually come from media and broadcast sales backgrounds, where they've developed experience selling media inventory. "They usually always have a number attached to their name," meaning they've proven themselves in quota-driven, results-oriented environments where their revenue generation is directly tracked and measured. The activation side requires a fundamentally different skill set, even though both teams work toward partnership success. Activation professionals, as Crain emphasizes, "need to be very detail oriented" because they're responsible for flawlessly executing the complex deliverables that make partnerships work. While sales people are hunting new deals and managing the revenue relationship, activation people are ensuring every promised benefit, from signage placement to social media posts to hospitality events, gets delivered correctly and on time. This operational excellence is what makes sponsors feel valued and drives renewals, but the path from activation coordinator to partnership sales is less common than moving into sales from other revenue-generating roles where you've already proven you can close deals and hit numbers.

The term "activation" is critical in the partnerships world. It's what separates a logo on a sign from a meaningful partnership that drives business results. Activation is how sponsors bring their partnerships to life and extract value from their investment. Simply put, when a company pays $500,000 to sponsor your team, they're not just buying their logo on the outfield wall. They're buying the right to leverage that partnership to reach customers, build brand awareness, and drive sales. Your job in partnerships isn't just to sell the deal. It's to help sponsors activate their investment effectively so they renew year after year. Sherrick Bader, the Senior Manager of Partnership Strategy & Service with the Phoenix Suns & Mercury, puts it this way: "The activation vertical holds the keys to all upsell revenue, and in some cases has a number tied to their name as well. The sales mentality is growing in the activation space because those team members are closest to their partners and act as another arm of their business. I start every onboarding call with a very similar

statement: 'I am effectively a new employee at your company.'"
That's the mindset you need to succeed in this role.

Activation takes countless forms, such as on-site experiences like branded fan zones or halftime contests that put the sponsor's product in fans' hands, digital campaigns leveraging the team's social media reach to amplify sponsor messaging, hospitality events where sponsors entertain clients in premium spaces, community programs where sponsors participate in team charity initiatives to build goodwill, content integration where sponsors appear in team-produced videos or podcasts, and data-driven targeting where sponsors access fan databases for email marketing or exclusive offers. The best partnership professionals think like marketers and are an extension of the brand. They understand their sponsors' business objectives, target demographics, and success metrics, then work closely with partners to develop and execute activations that deliver measurable ROI. The best partnerships happen when teams and sponsors collaborate throughout the process, with partners often taking an active role in shaping how their brand comes to life at games and events. A beverage company is not solely interested in signage because of the logo inclusion; instead, they may look at the signage asset as an opportunity to communicate sampling events which can lead to increased brand affinity, social media presence to emphasize brand awareness and drive social engagement on their channels, or in-stadium sales lift helping to maintain their market advantage. A bank may look at entitling a community event as a way of highlighting brand association with cause-driven initiatives or engaging with the local community that they serve. Partnership activation is where you deliver on what was sold. Once deals are signed, activation teams ensure every promised benefit gets executed flawlessly, sponsors feel valued, and relationships strengthen toward renewal.

Partnership sales is where you hunt for new revenue and bring sponsors into the organization. Your job is finding companies that want visibility, designing packages that deliver value, and closing deals that can range from $25,000 to multimillion-dollar naming rights agreements. These departments are much smaller than ticket sales (typically 5-15 people, depending on market size and individual team member scope), so opportunities are limited. Breaking in right out of college tends to be more difficult than your standard ticket sales development role, but it is not completely uncommon. The most successful candidates have previous experience through internships or work history, or have worked in the industry for a handful of years but in other capacities. Partnership sales requires a fundamentally different skill set than ticket sales. You're selling complex, customized solutions rather than standardized inventory. You're navigating corporate bureaucracies with multiple decision-makers rather than individual consumers. The sales cycle also tends to be much longer than traditional ticket sales transactions, with many iterations of the partnership terms along the way. You're thinking of multi-year agreements worth six or seven figures rather than transactional purchases. And critically, you're often judged not just on closing deals, but on retention and renewals, though this varies by organization. Some teams have their partnership sales staff handle the entire relationship from initial sale through renewals and upselling, while others transition accounts to an activation or account management team after the deal closes. Either way, if your sponsors don't achieve their objectives and renew, the partnership hasn't actually succeeded. The most successful partnership professionals become strategic advisors to their clients, deeply understanding their business challenges and positioning the team partnership as a solution that drives real business outcomes.

Success requires relentless prospecting, creativity in packaging assets, persistence through rejection, and the ability to understand what drives value for corporate partners. You need strong negotiation skills and the ability to craft deals that offer value on both sides. You're constantly networking, attending industry events, researching potential sponsors, building presentations, and sitting through countless meetings trying to convince companies to invest. It's high-pressure, quota-driven work, but if you're motivated by competition and closing deals, partnership sales offers unlimited earning potential and rapid advancement for top performers. Responsibilities include driving contractual deliverables, coordinating with internal departments to customize marketing opportunities for partners, and building strong client relationships. You're the primary relationship owner, coordinating signage installation, managing gameday activations, tracking deliverable completion, creating recap reports with ROI data, identifying upsell opportunities, and ensuring partners feel their investment is paying off. Success requires exceptional organizational skills, project management abilities, attention to detail, and genuine relationship-building talent. Effective communication is key, keeping sponsors informed about results and being responsive to their needs. Brand Activation Specialists focus on seamlessly integrating sponsors' branding into sports events through digital campaigns, in-stadium signage, or fan engagement activities.

As with any job in sports, the role is demanding when it comes to work-life balance. You can expect 40-50 hour weeks during the season with regular game attendance, occasional travel, and partnership events/activations. Work-life balance is better than sales roles, typical 45-50 hour weeks with occasional evening and weekend events, and the satisfaction comes from seeing partnerships succeed and sponsors renewing year after year.

Base salaries range from $50,000-$75,000 with bonuses at the end of each year that can push total compensation to $90,000-$150,000+ for senior roles. Entry-level partnership sales roles typically pay between $55,000-$75,000 base salary, with the real money coming from commissions on closed deals. Sales managers can earn total compensation around $125,000 annually when including bonuses and commissions. The career path moves from Partnership Sales Coordinator handling smaller prospects and supporting senior sellers, to Account Executive managing your own deals ($50,000-$100,000 deal size), to Senior Account Executive or

Sales Manager closing major partnerships ($150,000-$500,000+ deal size), to Director of Partnership Sales leading the sales team and strategy, and finally to VP of Corporate Partnerships overseeing the entire revenue operation and closing transformational deals.

The career path typically moves from Partnership Services Coordinator supporting fulfillment and logistics ($40,000-$55,000 salary), to Account Manager owning existing partnerships and managing renewals ($55,000-$75,000 salary), to Senior Account Manager managing the organization's largest accounts ($75,000-$100,000ha salary), to Director or Senior Director of Partner-ship Activation leading the activation team and strategy ($100K-$150K+ salary), and eventually to VP-level roles overseeing the entire partnership experience.

Business Intelligence and Analytics departments in a sports organization make decisions constantly. How do we price these seats? Which season ticket holders are most likely not to renew? Did that sponsorship activation actually move the needle? For most of sports history, those questions got answered by gut instinct and experience. Business Intelligence (BI) changed that. Now there's a small team of people whose entire job is to make sure the organization stops guessing and starts knowing.

BI teams in pro sports sit at the intersection of almost every revenue-generating function. They're pulling data from ticketing systems, customer relationship management (CRM) platforms, sponsorship activation reports, marketing campaigns, and fan surveys, then building dashboards, models, and reports that help sales reps, partnership managers, and executives make smarter decisions. On the ticketing side, that means dynamic pricing analysis, forecasting attendance, identifying which fans are flight risks before they lapse, and figuring out the right promotional offer to get a lapsed buyer back in the building. On the partnerships side, BI analysts measure whether a sponsor's activation is actually performing, calculate the return on a deal, and help the sales team build a data-backed story when they're pitching a renewal. For marketing, they're segmenting fan databases, tracking campaign performance, and helping the team understand who their customers actually are.

The work is deeply cross-functional. A good BI analyst isn't just running queries in a back office somewhere. They're sitting in meetings with the ticket sales director explaining what the churn model is showing, walking the partnerships team through a deck on sponsor ROI, and translating genuinely complex data into something a VP can act on. The technical skills matter a lot, things like SQL, Python or R, Tableau or Power BI, and familiarity with CRM systems like Salesforce or Hubspot. But the ability to communicate what the data means, in plain language, to people who didn't go to school for statistics, is honestly what separates the people who thrive in these roles from the ones who struggle.

These departments tend to be small, typically 3-8 people, depending on the size of the organization and how seriously leadership has committed to data-driven decisionmaking. Some teams have a dedicated BI director overseeing analysts who specialize by function (one focused on ticketing, one on partnerships, and one on marketing). Smaller organizations might have one or two analysts doing all of it. That means you're often wearing a lot of hats, and the work is varied enough to keep things interesting.

Getting in right out of college is genuinely possible here, more so than in departments like finance or legal. Teams actively post entry-level analyst roles, and a degree in business analytics, statistics, economics, or information systems translates directly. What will help you stand out: actual technical proficiency (not just "familiar with Excel"), some experience with SQL or a BI platform, and a portfolio or coursework that shows you can tell a story with data rather than just produce it. Internships with sports teams, leagues, or even sports tech vendors like SeatGeek or Ticketmaster can open doors quickly. If you don't have sports experience yet, analytical roles in retail, hospitality, or any high-volume transactional environment are genuinely valued because the data problems are similar.

The lifestyle is more stable than most sports departments. You're generally working standard business hours, though game days can pull you in when something needs to be tracked in real time or a dashboard needs to be ready for a post-game debrief. There's no grinding through 70-hour weeks the way you might in ticket sales, and the work doesn't stop and start with the season the way community relations does. It's a role where you can build deep expertise and grow methodically over time.

Pay for entry-level analysts typically runs $45,000-$65,000, with managers earning $70,000-$100,000 and directors in larger markets pushing higher than that. The technical skills you build here are also genuinely portable. If you ever want to leave sports, organizations across every industry are hungry for people who can work with data, build dashboards, and connect analysis to business decisions. It's one of the more sustainable paths into the industry if you have the analytical inclination, because the skills compound over time and the demand for good data people in sports is only going one direction.

Marketing builds the property's brand, builds fan engagement, and ultimately helps fill seats and drive revenue across all channels. Marketing teams are multifaceted operations that run integrated advertising campaigns across traditional and digital media, manage social media presence and community engagement, coordinate game-day promotions and special events, create compelling content (video, graphics, written) that keeps fans emotionally connected to the team year-round, analyze fan data to personalize messaging and improve targeting, and collaborate closely with sales to drive ticket revenue and with partnerships to activate sponsor relationships. "Here's how I'd explain 'integrated' in that context to a college student wanting to break into sports: 'Integrated' here means all your marketing efforts work together as one cohesive strategy instead of being separate, disconnected pieces. Think of it this way, instead of your social media team doing their own thing, your email team doing something completely different, and your billboard ads saying something else entirely, an integrated campaign means they're all telling the same story and reinforcing each other." Kevin Feinberg, the Director of Partnership Marketing for Little League International, says this cross-collaboration with other departments is one of the reasons he was drawn to sports marketing in the first place. Marketing doesn't exist in a vacuum; it only works when you have strong relationships with communications, operations, partnerships, and other departments across the organization.

For example, let's say your team is promoting a big weekend series. An integrated campaign might launch a teaser video on social media, follow it up with targeted emails to season ticket holders, run digital ads that match the same creative and messaging, put up billboards with the same visual theme, and have your in-arena promotions tie into the whole thing. Each piece amplifies the others because they're all working toward the same goal with a consistent look, feel, and message. It's like a band playing together versus a bunch of musicians playing different songs at the same time. When it's integrated, everything hits harder because it's all in sync. That's what makes modern sports marketing effective, nothing exists in isolation.

Marketing in sports has evolved dramatically. It's no longer just billboards and bobblehead nights. Modern sports marketing teams include content creators, graphic designers, video producers, social media managers, email marketing specialists, brand strategists, and data analysts. Teams typically employ 10-20 people in marketing, depending on whether content creation and social media are housed within marketing or separated into their own departments, or even outsourced altogether to third-party agencies.

Getting in right out of college is moderately difficult, but it can be more accessible than partnerships or operations. Strong candidates have portfolios including marketing internships and demonstrating creation skills (video editing, graphic design, writing), social media management experience, and increasingly valuable digital-native skills (SEO, analytics platforms, social media algorithms). It's also worth noting that everyone's path into sports marketing looks different. You might start as a social media intern, move into a content creation role, then shift to broader marketing strategy before eventually landing in a director-level position overseeing campaigns. Or you could come from a sales background and transition into marketing because you understand the revenue side. Someone else might start in minor league baseball, build their skills there, and eventually move up to a major league team or a different sport entirely. There's no single roadmap. The key is gaining experience, understanding how different departments work together, and being ready to adapt as the industry evolves.

The COVID-19 pandemic forced sports properties to completely reimagine how they stayed relevant when fans couldn't fill stadiums. Teams had to find new ways to keep their communities engaged, which meant a massive pivot to digital content and creative storytelling. Whether it was virtual watch parties, behind-the-scenes content with players at home, or interactive social media campaigns, organizations learned they could build deeper connections with fans even without live events. Many of those strategies stuck around because they worked. Teams realized they could reach fans year-round, not just on game days, and that digital engagement could be just as powerful as the in-person experience.

The work is creative, fast-paced, and increasingly digital-first. From a lifestyle perspective, marketing roles typically offer better balance than sales or game operations. You'll attend games regularly and work some evenings and weekends during activations or content shoots, but much of the work happens during normal business hours, with remote work increasingly common for content creation roles. Expect 45-50 hour weeks during the season and lighter workloads in the offseason.

The pay is moderate at entry levels ($40,000-$55,000 for coordinators) but improves as you specialize and advance, with Senior Marketing Managers earning $80,000-$120,000+, plus there's significant creative satisfaction in seeing your campaigns resonate with thousands of fans. Marketing progression is less linear than sales because the discipline is broader and more specialized. You might start in social media, move to brand marketing, pivot to content creation, then end up leading an integrated marketing team. In most marketing organizations, career advancement tends to follow a predictable progression:

Marketing Coordinator/Content Creator → Marketing Manager → Senior Marketing Manager → Director of Marketing → VP of Marketing/CMO

Marketing Coordinator/Content Creator (1-3 years of experience at this role): You're executing campaigns, managing social media accounts, creating content, coordinating with vendors, and supporting senior marketers. Success means quality execution, meeting deadlines, growing engagement metrics, and showing creative thinking. The key is building a portfolio of work that demonstrates both creativity and business impact.

Marketing Manager (2-4 years of experience at this role): You're managing specific marketing functions, maybe digital marketing, brand partnerships, game presentation, or creative services. You might have 1-2 direct reports. Success means campaign results that drive measurable business outcomes (ticket sales, sponsorship activation, brand awareness). The transition requires moving from execution to strategy and from individual contributor to managing others or complex projects.

Senior Marketing Manager (3-5 years of experience at this role): You're managing bigger budgets, more complex campaigns, and leading cross-functional initiatives. Success means demonstrating ROI on marketing spend, building strong agency and vendor relationships, and contributing to organizational strategy. This is often where careers plateau for people who are excellent executors but struggle with strategic thinking or managing complex relationships.

Director of Marketing (4-6 years of experience at this role): You're leading an entire marketing function with multiple managers reporting to you. You're setting department strategy, managing six-figure budgets, partnering with sales and corporate partnerships on integrated campaigns. Getting here requires proving you can think strategically about the business, not just create great campaigns.

VP of Marketing/CMO (7+ years of experience at this role): You're setting organizational brand strategy, overseeing all marketing functions, managing a substantial budget, and sitting at the executive leadership table. This typically requires 12-15+ years of overall experience with a track record of building brands and driving business results.

The Creative Team captures the moments that define sports. These roles have evolved dramatically with digital transformation and the social media explosion. What started as a "capture the moment" initiative has transformed into a "capitalize on the moment" movement. Teams now need constant content for websites, social platforms, broadcasts, and marketing campaigns.

Team photographers and videographers document games, practices, community events, and behind-the-scenes moments. They capture content for immediate social media use, marketing campaigns, and historical archives. Beyond game coverage, these roles include producing feature videos, creating sponsor content, developing original programming, and creating in-venue entertainment collateral like print materials and video board displays. What's crucial to understand is how interconnected these creative roles have become. Photography, videography, graphic design, and social media teams work heavily together across the industry, so much so that each person needs to know how to do, or at least understand at a base level, a piece of something else, since the work affects everyone's job. How a photographer shoots affects how a graphic is made. What a designer is thinking about affects what shot the photographer might need to get. What the design says or feels like can affect what a social media manager can caption that post. How a videographer shoots affects how someone else can edit it. With this creative boom across the sports industry, more positions are being added or even contracted out as teams create additional platforms and cover more events. At the same time, people in current positions are being asked to do more and learn skill sets that transcend multiple roles.

Breaking into sports photography and creative roles requires an exceptional portfolio demonstrating your abilities. Portfolios don't always need to be a fancy or super put-together website, although that route is favorable and looks more professional; even a well-curated Instagram account that showcases your work may suffice. But the key is that your portfolio should be a "best of" showcase, not a dump of everything you've ever created. Show what you consider your best stuff and demonstrate variety. From a photography standpoint, that means different photographic styles, such as action, portrait, studio, panning, detail, behind-the-scenes. For designers, show a range of social media graphics, in-venue displays, ticketing imagery (in the sometimes 10-20 sizes that are requested), print material, and logo design. For videographers, include social media clips, long-form content, stingers, and commercials.

Start building your portfolio immediately. Shoot local high school games, college sports, or amateur leagues. Quality matters more than where you shot it. Create an online portfolio website and share work on social media. When posting your work, don't forget to comment on posts of other photographers and repost content that's inspired you. In the creative industry, there's this phenomenon of referring to people you've never met but followed and interacted with online, your "Instagram friends." Those small pieces of online interaction may seem insignificant, but they're quickly expanding your network. Your network is your net worth in this industry, who you know and the people you interact with matter enormously.

When you're just getting started, the best thing you can get are repetitions. Steph Curry wouldn't be a better shooter if he shot less, right? You won't be a better designer if you never design, a better social media manager if you never post, a better photographer or videographer if you never shoot or edit. Get those reps from anyone willing to give them to you. Local high school games are a great place to start, and if you can't start there, try your little brother's Little League game. Shoot for anyone willing to give you a credential in the beginning. You're not going to operate that way forever, but to get your foot in the door, it's a great way to begin. Internships and freelance opportunities are common entry points. Offer to shoot content for minor league teams or college programs initially. Many team photographers started as freelancers. Doing this work consistently may help generate some movement in creating relationships with freelance clients and kickstart your career a little faster. Networking matters enormously.

One under looked part of this industry is the time spent completing the administrative work. For photographers and videographers, that could be labeling photos and footage or adding metadata to clips and images. For designers, it's creating libraries of logos or naming layers in a template for someone else to use. For social media managers, it could be learning scheduling software or setting up broadcast streams that they'll clip at the game later that day. People always look at the glamorous part of the industry without realizing these other parts are just as important to learn, even if they're not the most fun. Early in your career, expect to work every game and event. Your schedule will be dictated by the team's calendar, nights, weekends, holidays. You'll haul equipment and work in challenging conditions. But if you're passionate about capturing the moments that make sports special, it's worth every minute.

Entry-level positions include assistant photographers, production assistants, junior graphic designers, and social media coordinators starting between $35,000-$55,000. Staff photographers, videographers, graphic designers, and social media managers earn $50,000-$80,000. Senior photographers, editors, senior designers, and senior social media managers can make $70,000-$100,000. Art directors typically fall in the $80,000-$120,000 range, depending on the team and market. Directors at major teams can earn $100,000-$150,000+. Many professionals supplement salaries with freelance work.

Game Presentation and Event Production make game day actually happen. They're the orchestrators ensuring that everything fans experience is seamless, entertaining, and memorable. This department serves as the gatekeeper of almost all visual and auditory content fans consume in the venue, filtering every request and obligation to maximize entertainment value, production quality, and brand compatibility while making room for sponsored content and brand campaigns. The ultimate goal is creating an experience so seamless that fans never notice the machine working behind the curtain. This team coordinates every detail from the moment gates open until the last fan leaves, the national anthem performers, between-inning entertainment, halftime shows, in-game promotions, mascot appearances, fan contests, video board content, music and sound cues, lighting and pyrotechnics, ceremony coordination, and emergency protocols. They work closely with external vendors, manage minute-by-minute rundowns, troubleshoot inevitable problems in real-time (because something always goes wrong), and ensure fans have an exceptional experience regardless of what's happening on the court or field. Teams typically employ 2-6 full-time game operations staff, plus dozens of part-time game-day employees, with larger venues that host multiple events having 15+ full-time operations staff. This role can go from staffing one-off events to a full season. Depending on what the production is, game presentations can staff upwards of 100 people.

Getting full-time roles right out of college is moderately difficult, but part-time and seasonal game-day positions are highly accessible and can lead to full-time opportunities. Strong candidates have event management experience, internships in game presentation, volunteer experience managing logistics for large events, and demonstrated ability to stay calm under pressure. Game presentation professionals need to thrive under pressure, think on their feet, communicate clearly with dozens of stakeholders simultaneously, and maintain composure when chaos erupts, with technical skills in audio/visual production, event management software, and emergency protocols becoming increasingly important.

This is not a desk job; you're on your feet for 12-15 hours on game days, running around the venue, solving problems, and managing controlled chaos. The work-life balance is challenging. Your busiest days are when everyone else is off (nights, weekends, holidays), the season is intense and relentless, and you're exhausted by the end of it, though the offseason offers recovery time while also requiring planning and preparation for the next season. But for people energized by live events and variety who get bored sitting still, this role offers unmatched excitement and visible impact. You see fans enjoying experiences you created, which provides immediate satisfaction that desk-based roles can't match.

Entry-level coordinators earn $35,000-$50,000, managers earn $55,000-$80,000, and directors of game operations at major league level can earn $90,000-$130,000+. Career trajectory within the department typically follows the following:

Game Presentation Coordinator → Presentation Manager → Senior Presentation Manager → Director of Game Presentation → VP of Presentation

Presentation Coordinator (1-3 years of experience at this role): You're supporting game day execution, managing part-time staff, coordinating logistics, and solving problems in real time. Success means reliability, calm under pressure, and attention to detail. This role is about proving you can handle the chaos of live events without melting down.

Presentation Manager (2-4 years of experience at this role): You're managing specific operational areas, such as venue operation, event production, or facilities coordination. You have direct reports and broader responsibility. Success means smooth event execution, strong vendor relationships, and staff development.

Senior Presentation Manager (4-6 years of experience at this role): You're managing multiple operational functions or serving as assistant director, and often serve as the primary script writer and show caller for game day. You're involved in strategic planning and potentially managing other managers. The jump requires systems thinking, seeing how all operational pieces interconnect. The producing skills you develop here translate well to freelance opportunities in live event production outside sports.

Director of Game Presentation (5-8 years of experience at this role): You're leading the entire operations department, managing managers, setting operational strategy, and overseeing budgets. As the primary script writer and show caller, you're orchestrating every moment of the fan experience while ensuring all stakeholders get their moments without disrupting the flow. You're the person ultimately responsible when things go wrong on game day. This requires both operational excellence and leadership capability, with your production skills often opening doors to high-level freelance work across entertainment and live events.

VP of Presentation (10+ years of experience at this role): You're at the executive level, overseeing all venue operations, facilities, and potentially other business operations functions. Getting here typically requires 12-15+ years and a reputation for operational excellence across multiple organizations.

Fan Experience and Guest Services focus on making sure every fan who walks through the gates feels valued and has a positive experience, regardless of the final score. This department encompasses customer service operations (handling complaints, solving problems, managing feedback), premium hospitality programs for high-value ticket holders, fan feedback and survey initiatives to continuously improve, accessibility services ensuring all fans can enjoy the venue, and enhancing the overall stadium experience through training staff and implementing service standards. Teams typically employ 6-12 full-time staff who manage hundreds of part-time guest services employees (ushers, ticket takers, hospitality staff), making this a department with significant operational scope but limited full-time positions.

Getting in right out of college is accessible, especially if you start part-time and prove yourself. Hospitality experience from hotels, restaurants, or customer service translates well, and strong candidates demonstrate emotional intelligence, problem solving under pressure, and genuine service orientation. These roles require genuine patience, exceptional problem-solving skills under pressure, emotional intelligence to deescalate frustrated fans, and authentic care about people's experiences. You're often dealing with fans at their worst, when something's gone wrong, when they're upset, or when expectations weren't met, and your job is to turn those moments around. Hannah Conlisk, the Guest Services Coordinator at AT&T Stadium and the Dallas Cowboys, says, "Professionals in Guest Services and Fan Experience roles are expected to demonstrate a deep understanding of the operational logistics behind large-scale events, always with a fans-first, customer-centric mindset. These individuals remain composed under pressure, consistently embody the organization's values during high-stress moments, and genuinely care about creating memorable, positive experiences for every guest. You get a front row seat to watch sports impact those at your venue. Remember: guests attend events for a wide range of reasons, whether entertaining clients, celebrating team loyalty, supporting a favorite player/team, continuing tradition, or simply out of pure passion. Regardless of their background or motivation, the Guest Services responsibility is to ensure that every guest has an unforgettable experience while they're at your venue."

The lifestyle mirrors game operations: you work when games happen, which means nights and weekends, though daytime administrative work (training, planning, analyzing feedback) happens during business hours.

The pay is typically modest, especially at entry levels ($35,000-$48,000 for coordinators) and managers earn $50,000-$70,000, but these roles offer deep satisfaction for people genuinely motivated by service and impact. You're directly improving people's experiences and creating loyalty that keeps families coming back for generations.

Community Relations, Community Engagement, and/or Corporate Social Responsibility connects the team to its city, building goodwill and ensuring the franchise is viewed as a valued community partner rather than just a business. This department also handles the team's community involvement and social responsibility work. This department runs youth sports programs that introduce kids to the sport, coordinates charity initiatives and fundraising events, manages player appearances at schools and hospitals, oversees grassroots marketing efforts in underserved communities, partners with local nonprofits on social impact programs, and represents the organization at community events year-round. That means running voter registration drives, supporting equal rights initiatives, responding when tragedies happen, and finding ways to help local businesses.

These departments are small, typically 3-8 people per team, depending on the organization's commitment to community engagement, which means opportunities are extremely limited. Getting in right out of college is difficult for full-time roles because teams value experience working with nonprofits, running programs, managing comm-unity partnerships, and event management, though internships in community relations are available and can lead to full-time opportunities if you prove exceptional. Volunteering with youth sports organizations, nonprofit experience, and bilingual abilities strengthen applications significantly. Community relations professionals need genuine passion for social impact (not just sports), strong project management skills to juggle multiple programs simultaneously, relationship management abilities to work effectively with nonprofit partners and community leaders, and cultural competence to engage authentically with diverse populations.

The work is meaningful but demanding; you're attending evening events regularly, working weekends at community festivals and youth clinics, coordinating player schedules (which change constantly), and often doing more with limited budgets than seems possible. Work-life balance is challenging during the season but often improves in the offseason when programming scales back.

The pay is typically lower than revenue-generating departments like sales or partnerships; entry-level coordinators earn $35,000-$48,000 and managers earn $50,000-$70,000, even up to $80,000-$90,000 in bigger markets, but the mission-driven nature attracts people who measure success by impact rather than income.

Finance and Legal handle the business fundamentals that keep the organization running, compliant, and financially healthy. Finance teams manage budgets across all departments, forecast revenue and expenses, handle payroll and benefits administration, produce financial reports for ownership, evaluate potential investments or business opportunities, and ensure fiscal responsibility. Legal teams draft and review contracts (like player contracts, although sometimes this is done by player personnel, vendor agreements, partnership deals, ticket-related deals, and potentially policy creation), manage compliance with league rules and government regulations, handle litigation when it arises, protect intellectual property, and provide counsel on business decisions with legal implications.

Getting in right out of college is very difficult. Finance roles typically require accounting degrees, CPA certification, or finance experience, while legal roles require law degrees and often 3-5 years of experience in sports law, entertainment law, or corporate law, meaning entry-level opportunities are rare and most candidates transition from law firms or corporate finance roles after establishing themselves professionally. "If you want to work in sports, don't just focus on getting in, focus on becoming great at something teams actually need. Finance and legal teams value people who've already proven themselves. When you make the jump, you're not starting over, you're taking on a more complex, higher-stakes version of the work," says Varun Desai, the CFO of the Blue Crow Sports Group. Finance and legal are some of the toughest departments to break into straight out of college. Teams want people who already know what they're doing because mistakes in these areas can be really expensive. You need to build your credibility somewhere else first, whether that's at a CPA firm, a corporate finance role, or a law firm, and then make the jump to sports once you've proven yourself. Desai continues that the rationale is simple: professionals who build their careers as CPAs or in Big Law develop deep expertise in the foundational work these roles require. For finance professionals, that means a strong understanding of financial reporting, controls, and long-term implications, knowledge that directly influences how teams make decisions and manage risk over time. Finance and legal professionals enjoy better job security than many other departments and develop transferable skills valuable across industries.

Many people don't realize how small these departments are relative to their responsibility. You might have six people in finance managing a $200 million operation. Every decision you make affects the entire organization, from whether we can afford to hire another scout, to how we structure a naming rights deal. It's high-stakes work, but if you do it well, you become one of the most trusted people in the building. Teams typically employ 5-10 people in finance and 2-5 in-house attorneys plus outside counsel as needed, making these among the smallest departments with the most specialized requirements. However, this can depend on the team, the market, and if the team owns the building. These roles offer stability, competitive compensation, and critical importance to organizational health, even though they operate behind the scenes rather than in the spotlight. If you want to work in sports but value predictability and don't need to be close to the on-field action, these paths offer sustainable careers with steady progression, though you'll need to establish yourself in the profession first before sports organizations will hire you. The nice thing about finance and legal is that you're recession-proof in a way that other departments aren't. When teams need to cut costs, they're not cutting the people who manage the budget or handle contracts. And if you ever want to leave sports, your resume is actually stronger because you've worked in a complex, high-pressure environment.

Compensation is competitive with corporate equivalents; finance analysts start at $55,000-$70,000 and managers earn $80,000-$120,000, while attorneys start at $80,000-$120,000 with senior counsel earning $150,000-$250,000+. However, this varies greatly by league, team, and industry.

Human Resources and IT keep the entire organization running smoothly, but they're more than just service departments. They're strategic partners who create value and protect the business from serious risk. HR manages recruiting and hiring, onboarding and training, benefits administration, employee relations, performance management, organizational culture initiatives, and compliance with employment law. But it's not just processing paperwork. HR also sits in the room with leadership when big decisions get made, helping think through the implications of restructuring a department, navigating sensitive employee situations, and making sure compensation strategies actually retain talent instead of burning people out. They're the ones making sure the organization doesn't get sued and that workplace policies align with long-term business goals. IT maintains the technology infrastructure everyone depends on: computer systems, networks, software applications, cybersecurity, data management, and increasingly the digital platforms fans interact with. But there's another critical piece most people don't think about: IT is essential to sponsorship deals. When a company pays millions to sponsor your team, a lot of what they're buying runs through technology. Digital signage in the arena, branded content on your app, data reporting on fan engagement, and interactive activations at games. If the Wi-Fi crashes on game day and a sponsor's activation doesn't work, you're not just dealing with an IT problem, you're potentially in breach of a million-dollar contract. IT partners work closely with the commercial and marketing teams to make sure sponsor deliverables actually happen and the tech performs when it matters most.

Getting in right out of college is moderately difficult, but the good news is these roles emphasize functional expertise over sports-specific experience. If you're studying HR or IT, your skills transfer. An HR coordinator at a tech company can absolutely move into sports. Same with IT support. Candidates with HR certifications, IT degrees or certifications, or operations management experience can transition from other industries, and entry-level IT support or HR coordinator roles are accessible with relevant degrees and internships. Something important about IT in sports right now: despite all the headlines about AI, these jobs aren't disappearing. If anything, they're becoming more critical. AI tools need people who understand how to implement them responsibly, integrate them into existing systems, and make sure they deliver actual value instead of creating new headaches. Someone still needs to manage your ticketing platform, protect fan data from cyber threats, keep the WiFi working on game days when 20,000 people are trying to post on social media, ensure that new AI chatbot connects to your CRM and comply with data privacy rules, and make sure sponsor-facing technology meets contractual requirements. The technology gets more sophisticated, which means you need more sophisticated people managing it, not fewer people. Bradley Koenen, the IT User Support Specialist with the Milwaukee Bucks, says this about his role: "If I was doing IT for a stuffy accounting firm, then I don't know how long I would last. But IT in the NBA reaches so many different fascinating worlds, from broadcast tech to cyber, to basketball analytics to ticket analytics. I'll never be stuck doing one thing in the NBA. The whole nature of the league is to be competitive, and we always innovate our competitiveness, and what we can 'do' with computers."

These roles offer stability, transferable skills, reasonable work-life balance, and the satisfaction of enabling everyone else's success. While they're not uniquely "sports" roles, they're essential to sports organizations and can provide entry points for people with relevant skills who want to transition into the industry. The lifestyle is generally more sustainable. Business hours are common (40-45 hours weekly), stress levels are typically lower than revenue or game operations roles, though IT may have occasional evening or weekend work for system maintenance, live events, or making sure sponsor activations run smoothly. Team sizes vary by organization, with HR departments typically having 3-8 people and IT teams ranging from 5-12.

Compensation is competitive with non-sports industries for similar functions: entry-level positions pay $40,000-$55,000, managers earn $65,000-$95,000, and directors command $100,000-$150,000+.

Retail and Merchandise in sports is a massive business extending far beyond team stores at stadiums. Sports merchandise generates billions annually, requiring sophisticated retail operations, supply chain management, and creative product development. The industry operates through three distinct models depending on the team or venue's contract structure: team-operated stores, concessionaire partnerships, or direct vendor relationships with brands like Adidas or Nike. Major concessionaires, including Delaware North, Aramark, Legends, and Fanatics, manage retail operations across multiple venues. When working for a concessionaire, you'll handle everything from inventory management and merchandising to maintaining client relationships with the buildings and teams they serve. On the brand side, professionals work on product development, licensing agreements, and production planning.

The retail field is accessible within sports because it values retail experience from other industries. Starting in part-time or gameday positions at team stores is one common path, allowing you to build relationships and position yourself for full-time opportunities. However, there are multiple entry points into the industry depending on your background and target role. For corporate positions with concessionaires or brands, target companies directly through their career pages. Internships at major brands or concessionaires provide strong pipelines to full-time positions. Entry-level positions include store associates, inventory coordinators, and e-commerce assistants. Mid-level roles involve category management, merchandising strategy, and vendor management. Senior positions include retail directors and licensing managers who oversee entire retail operations or product portfolios.

If you start in a store role, expect to work directly with customers during evenings, weekends, and holidays when games happen. In corporate roles, early responsibilities include coordinating inventory, processing orders, creating sales reports, and supporting client relationships.

Broadcast and Media bring sports to life for millions of fans. Traditional networks like ESPN and FOX still dominate, but streaming platforms are changing everything. This evolution creates incredible opportunities for people who understand both sports and digital media. Behind every broadcast are producers, directors, technical directors, camera operators, audio engineers, graphics coordinators, and production assistants. Beyond live games, media companies need content creators for podcasts, documentaries, and digital programming. Writers develop scripts. Editors transform raw footage. Social media managers create platform-specific content.

But there's another side to sports broadcasting that most people don't think about: brand partnerships. Dylan Ruskin, the Manager of NFL Brand Partnerships at FOX Sports, explains how his role bridges broadcast and marketing. Working on FOX NFL Kickoff, FOX NFL Sunday, in-game coverage, and postgame shows, Ruskin coordinates between the production team in Los Angeles and the Ad Sales team in New York. "From my brand partnership perspective in the broadcast and media space, it's going beyond the commercial ad unit," Ruskin says. "It's about integrating a brand into a network and even including the talent, like Brady and Gronk for FOX NFL, into a brand's marketing content."

His team manages inventory for segments, features, and sponsorship positions like presenting partnerships. "It's not enough to just have ad units anymore," Ruskin explains. "While the ad units are the bread and butter, it's about elevating your brand using the network's platform and reach." FOX NFL Sunday has been the leading pregame show for 31 years, which gives his team leverage when connecting with brands and media agencies. The streaming side presents both opportunities and challenges. "The streaming perspective is part of the latest and greatest of ways brands can extend their reach to different, and in most cases, younger demographics," Ruskin notes. However, he points out barriers to entry: "The number of inflated subscriptions and price per subscription, along with these companies still learning how to navigate elevating brands within live sports and media."

Breaking into sports media is highly competitive but achievable with the right preparation. Production assistant and coordinator roles are the most accessible entry points straight out of college. Campus media experience is invaluable. Working for your college's athletic department broadcast, student newspaper, radio station, or TV station demonstrates real-world capability. Learn technical skills before you graduate. Master editing software like Adobe Premiere, graphics software like After Effects, or camera operation. Create a portfolio, even if the work is unpaid. Film highlights, produce podcasts, or create social media content that showcases your abilities. Internships at ESPN, FOX Sports, NBC Sports, and regional sports networks teach professional workflows and often convert to full-time roles. Apply early and apply often. For brand partnership roles, Ruskin's path shows the value of starting in sponsorship or partnership roles at college athletic departments, conference networks, or multimedia rights holders like LEARFIELD before transitioning to network positions.

For digital and social media roles, build an online presence that demonstrates your ability to create engaging sports content. Networks want to see that you understand platform-specific content and can grow an audience. Expect long and irregular hours, especially early in your career. Production assistants and coordinators work whenever games happen, which means nights, weekends, and holidays. A typical NFL Sunday might mean arriving at 6 A.M. for a noon kickoff and not leaving until 8 P.M. or later. Production roles often involve 50-60+ hour weeks during the season, with some relief in the offseason depending on the sport. Brand partnership roles like Ruskin's tend to be more traditional business hours during the week, but ramp up significantly around major events and sales cycles.

Technical positions like camera operators and audio engineers work on a per-event basis, which can mean feast-or-famine scheduling. Editors might work more consistent hours in post-production facilities, but crunch around deadlines. As you advance, you gain more control over your schedule, but the nature of live sports means flexibility is always required. Senior producers and directors still work games, but they're compensated accordingly and often have teams supporting them. Entry-level positions including production assistants, coordinators, and brand partnership coordinators start between $35,000-$60,000. These roles require hustle and often involve unglamorous work like handling logistics and equipment, but they're your foot in the door. Mid-level positions like producers, editors, and social media managers earn $60,000-$100,000. At this level, you're trusted with more creative freedom and managing aspects of production or content strategy. Senior producers, directors, and brand partnership managers make $100,000-$250,000+. These positions require years of experience and a proven track record of success. Social media directors and managers at major networks can reach $80,000-$120,000. On-air talent and top executives earn significantly more, but those positions typically require extensive experience or specialized expertise. The path to higher earnings comes through proving yourself reliable, developing specialized skills, and building relationships within the industry.

Multimedia Journalism and Sports Reporting cover the stories, analysis, and breaking news that inform fans and hold sports organizations accountable. This field spans traditional beat reporting, long-form feature writing, investigative journalism, opinion and commentary, podcasting, and digital content creation. The industry has transformed dramatically. Newspapers have shrunk while digital-first outlets and independent content creators have proliferated.

Sports journalists report on games, athletes, teams, and the business of sports. Beat reporters cover specific teams daily, attending practices and games, interviewing players and coaches, breaking news, and providing analysis. Columnists provide commentary rather than straight reporting. Investigative journalists dig into deeper stories requiring months of reporting. Digital journalists create podcasts, video content, and interactive graphics.

Editors assign stories and manage workflows. Social media editors curate content for platforms like Twitter/X, YouTube, and TikTok.

The work itself has evolved beyond just game recaps. Modern sports journalism digs into the how and why, particularly at outlets like Sports Business Journal where deeper explainer pieces and trend-based analysis matter as much as breaking news. You're not just reporting that a team signed a player, you're explaining the salary cap implications, the analytics that drove the decision, and what it means for the competitive landscape. Your audience includes fans, but also executives, scouts, and agents who rely on quality reporting to stay informed.

Justina Quagliata, the Director of Digital and Social Strategy for the Nashville Predators, has this to say: "Look for inspiration! Save work that speaks to you and refer back to it. Try and keep a good understanding of what other teams and clubs are creating and how they're performing. Who is doing well hyping up their players? Who has a good community presence? Who is pushing trends forward? Have fun with it! (Bonus: this topic often comes up in job interviews!)"

Breaking into sports journalism requires building a portfolio of published work demonstrating writing ability and sports knowledge. Start immediately. Write for your college newspaper, start a blog, or freelance for small outlets. Create podcasts or YouTube videos. Post video breakdowns and analysis on TikTok or Twitter/X. Build an audience wherever you can. The traditional path used to run from school newspaper to newspaper intern to website job, but that route looks different now. Digital platforms have opened new doors.

Internships at newspapers or digital outlets provide invaluable experience and often lead to full-time positions. Apply widely. Competition is intense. Networking and self-promotion matter more than ever. Build relationships with editors, engage with journalists on social media, and share your work online consistently.

Relationship building and source development are massively important. The best journalists cultivate sources over years, not days.

Many journalists have degrees in journalism or communications, but what matters is demonstrable writing ability and proven reporting chops. Early journalism careers involve covering less glamorous beats and working demanding schedules. You'll work nights and weekends when games happen. That's the job.

Quagliata continues with, "Take breaks. Seriously. Creatives often get stuck into a pattern of creating, scrolling, brainstorming, and scrolling some more, before diving back into the creative process. Make sure you're taking time to log off, go for a walk, and be a human being. Go get dinner. Head out for a walk. Hang out with your friends and talk about things that don't solely live on the internet. Observe the world around you. We're all more well-rounded creatives when we come from a place of observation and inspiration, instead of endless pressure and doomscrolling."

Entry-level reporters at small outlets start at $30,000-$45,000. Mid-level beat reporters earn $45,000-$70,000. Senior writers and editors can make $70,000-$150,000+. National journalists at top outlets can earn $100,000-$300,000+, but these positions are rare and competitive. Freelance rates vary widely.

Medical and Performance Professionals keep athletes healthy, recover injured players, and optimize physical and mental performance. These roles include Strength and Conditioning coaches, Athletic Trainers, Physical Therapists, Mental Skills, and Sport Dietitians, requiring specialized education, certifications, and clinical expertise.

Strength and Conditioning coaches design training programs to improve athletic performance, building strength, power, speed, and endurance while reducing injury risk through proper movement patterns and load management. They play a crucial role in injury resiliency and return-to-play protocols, working alongside athletic trainers and physical therapists to track assessments, monitor workload, and ensure athletes are physically prepared for the demands of their sport. Strength and Conditioning requires a degree in exercise science or kinesiology, with extra credentials from the National Strength and Conditioning Association (NSCA) becoming essential. Starting January 1, 2030, a degree from an accredited program will be required for the Certified Strength and Conditioning Specialist (CSCS) exam. For U.S. candidates, this means a bachelor's degree from a program accredited by the NSCA-approved Commission on Accreditation of Strength and Conditioning Education (CASCE) will be necessary to take the exam. Breaking in involves starting with internships and building relationships. Assistant strength coaches start around $46,500-$90,000. You can then further pursue residencies in sports physical therapy or work at sports medicine clinics. Breaking in involves starting with internships at college programs. Head Strength Coaches can earn $110,000-$130,000.

Athletic Trainers are healthcare professionals who prevent, diagnose, and treat injuries. They're present at every practice and game, conducting assessments, providing immediate care, and managing rehabilitation protocols. Athletic Training requires a bachelor's or master's from a The Commission on Accreditation of Athletic Training Education (CAATE)-accredited program, passing the Board of Certification (BOC) exam, and state licensure. Brad Epstein, the Head Athletic Trainer for the Milwaukee Brewers, mentions that currently Athletic Training requires a masters or doctorate. Epstein says, "If you're serious about working in sports, look into internships or associate positions in athletic training or fellowships and residencies in physical therapy. Several major league organizations offer upper extremity fellowships for physical therapists that serve as direct pipelines into the sport." "Networking is key," says Kyle Belski, the former Physical Therapist, San Francisco Giants. "Whether it's through an internship, clinical rotation, continuing education course, or simply a DM on LinkedIn.

If you don't know people in the field, or at least someone with connections who can vouch for you, your resume will never make it to the top of the pile." The internships and fellowships with baseball connections are limited and extremely competitive, which means aspiring sports PTs need to get creative. "You might have to find other ways to get there," Belski explains. "That means reaching out to those in the field to inquire about clinical rotations with their organization, or even an opportunity to shadow them for a few days." Belski recommends looking beyond traditional pathways to build connections. "Find out what continuing education courses are hot in baseball right now. There are a ton in Arizona and Florida during the off season, and they are crawling with baseball PTs and ATCs."

He also encourages students not to underestimate the power of direct outreach. "Shoot your shot on LinkedIn. Students send me stuff all the time, and I am happy to give them advice. I have even had some of them shadow me. Others in the field will likely do the same." Entry-level Athletic Training positions start between $42,500-$60,000. Head Athletic Trainers can earn $80,000-$150,000+.

Physical Therapists (PT) focus on rehabilitation from injuries or surgeries. They develop detailed rehabilitation programs, use manual therapy techniques, and guide athletes through return-to-sport protocols. Physical Therapists are not just doing post-injury rehab (though that's a big part of it). They're constantly assessing players, catching small issues before they become big ones, and designing programs to prevent injuries in the first place. Think of them as part detective, part mechanic. They're watching how a pitcher's shoulder moves during bullpen sessions, noticing when a running back's gait looks off, or figuring out why a player's hamstring keeps tightening up. They work closely with the strength coaches, trainers, and team doctors to create individualized plans for each athlete.

Mornings might involve manual therapy or treatment sessions with injured players, then they're on the practice field observing movement patterns and biomechanics. During games, they're on the sidelines ready to evaluate injuries as they happen and make quick calls about whether someone can safely return to play. After games, they're often the last ones in the facility, treating players and setting up recovery protocols. The relationship between a team PT and the athletes is built on trust because players need to be honest about pain and limitations, even when there's pressure to play through everything. These therapists have to balance what's best for the player's long-term health with the immediate demands of winning games, which can be a really tough position to be in. Physical therapy requires a doctorate degree in physical therapy, passing the national exam, and state licensure. Physical Therapists earn $60,000-$90,000, with senior PTs making $90,000-$130,000+.

Mental Skills coaches work with athletes on performance psychology, helping them develop focus, manage pressure, build confidence, and maintain mental resilience during competition and recovery. While they're not psychologists, they teach practical techniques like visualization, goal-setting, and mindfulness to help athletes perform at their best when it matters most. Most Mental Skills coaches have the Certified Mental Performance Consultant (CMPC) certification. This is the credential that mental performance professionals across major sports leagues are pursuing and being encouraged to obtain. You'll also notice the field has moved toward using "mental performance" rather than "mental skills" as the preferred terminology.

Sport Dietitians' path to becoming a Certified Specialist in Sports Dietetics (CSSD) requires significant educational commitment. It starts with an undergraduate Didactic Program in Dietetics, followed by a demanding one-year dietetic internship where candidates complete between 1,000-1,200 hours of supervised work. Once the internship is complete, you're eligible to sit for the board exam to become a Registered Dietitian (RD). Certain states also require licensure and continuing education credits. Many aspiring sports dietitians pursue a master's degree, ideally in sports nutrition or a related field like anatomy, though the degree can be in any discipline. Some programs combine the dietetic internship with a master's degree to streamline the process. Sports Dietitians design nutrition plans tailored to each athlete's position, training schedule, and body composition goals, ensuring they have the right fuel for performance and recovery. They work closely with strength coaches and medical staff to optimize everything from pre-game meals to post-workout nutrition and supplement protocols.

To earn the CSSD credential, you need to work as an RD for two years and accumulate 1,500-2,000 hours of supervised experience under a sports dietitian before sitting for another board exam. The certification must be renewed every five years. Emily Kaley, MS, RDN, LDN, CSSD, ISAK 2, former MLB Sports Nutrition Coordinator, also points out the evolving landscape of the profession: "In many organizations, dietitians work alongside or even oversee strength and conditioning staff because of their advanced education requirements. Some dietitians even earn their CSCS certification to broaden their expertise. While strength and conditioning has been established in sports for much longer, sports dietetics is rapidly catching up in recognition and importance. You'll now find chef RDs managing entire kitchen and nutrition spaces for professional teams." Sport Dietitians salaries can range from $55,000 to over $100,000.

Sports science professionals use data and technology to analyze player performance, injury risk, and game strategy, turning numbers into actionable insights that help coaches make better decisions. They work with wearable technology, biomechanics, and statistical analysis to give teams a competitive edge in player development, roster construction, and in-game tactics.

Organizations to get involved in:

- Athletic Training: Professional Baseball Athletic Trainers Society (PBATS)
- Strength and Conditioning: The Professional Baseball Strength and Conditioning Coaches Society (PBSCCS)
- Physical Therapy: Professional Baseball Physical Therapy Society (PBPTS)
- Mental Skills: Association for Applied Sport Psychology (AASP) and the Professional Baseball Mental Performance Society (PBMPS)
- Registered Dietitian: American Sports and Performance Dietitians Association (ASPDA)

The Professional Baseball Athletic Trainers Society is a fantastic organization to join if you're an athletic trainer. Morgan Leichtenberger, a Minor League Athletic Trainer with the Minnesota Twins, recommends checking out each society's website for resources about how to break into the game of baseball.

Education, Certification, and Licensure Requirements:

Athletic Trainer

- Master's degree from a CAATE-accredited program (as of 2022, a bachelor's is no longer sufficient)
- Board of Certification (BOC) certification
- State licensure (varies by state)
- CPR/AED & Emergency Cardiac Care

Strength and Conditioning *Not legally licensed, but credentialing matters a lot*

- CPR/AED

Physical Therapists

- Doctor of Physical Therapy (DPT)
- National board exam (NPTE)
- State licensure (varies by state)
- Sports residency *not required*
- Board-Certified Sports Clinical Specialist (SCS) *not required*

Mental Skills

If not practicing psychology

- Certified Mental Performance Consultant (CMPC) *industry standard*

If practicing psychology or therapy

- State licensure as a psychologist or counselor (PhD/PsyD/LPC/etc.) *legally required*

Sport Dietitian

- Registered Dietitian (RD/RDN)
- State licensure (LD, LDN, etc)
- Board Certified Specialist in Sports Dietetics (CSSD) *optional*
- International Society for the Advancement of Kinanthropometry (ISAK) *optional*
- Certified Strength & Conditioning Specialist (CSCS) *optional*

Equipment Management and Clubhouse Operations are behind-the-scenes roles ensuring athletes have everything they need to perform. Equipment managers handle uniforms, gear, and playing equipment. Clubhouse managers direct locker rooms, coordinate travel logistics, and create the daily environment where athletes prepare.

Breaking into these roles requires starting at the bottom and proving yourself indispensable. Most enter through internships, part-time positions, or seasonal work with minor league teams or college programs. The key is demonstrating work ethic, reliability, and attention to detail. Networking and persistence matter enormously. Reach out to equipment managers expressing genuine interest and ask about opportunities. Be willing to relocate to smaller markets offering more accessible entry points. The Athletic Equipment Managers Association (AEMA) offers professional development but no formal certification. What matters most is hands-on experience and technical knowledge. The AEMA offers a certification that isn't mandatory yet, but the organization and equipment managers across the industry are pushing hard to make it a requirement. To qualify, you must be a member in good standing and provide employment verification showing two years of full-time, paid, non-student work through an official letter from your Athletic Director or Personnel office that verifies your start and end dates plus duties. (Student manager hours need to be on AEMA Student Manager Time Logs signed by your supervisor.) You'll also need proof of age and education like transcripts or your diploma, and you have to score at least 70 on the certification exam. The fact that this certification is gaining momentum tells you something important about the professionalization of the field. Even if it's not required for your next job, having it shows you're serious about the craft and committed to industry standards, and that distinction matters when you're competing against other candidates.

Equipment managers oversee all playing equipment and uniforms, such as ordering inventory, fitting players, repairing damaged items, managing relationships with manufacturers, and coordinating travel logistics. Every sport has specialized equipment requirements that managers must master. Clubhouse managers run locker room operations, preparing food and beverages, maintaining cleanliness, coordinating player requests, and managing travel details. These professionals become trusted team members, developing close relationships with players. Adam Braun, former Director of Football Equipment Operations at numerous colleges and universities, mentions, "In football, the fitting of protective equipment is everything. Helmets, shoulder pads, footwear, getting those right were always my first priority as an equipment manager. Player safety comes before anything else. Whether it's properly fitted gear or making sure everything is sanitized correctly, we're the first line of defense protecting these athletes. Without equipment managers, the game doesn't happen. You can play hungry, you can play hurt, but you can't play naked." Braun says this about equipment operations: "The athletics industry can be as rewarding as it can be disheartening.

There are only a finite number of positions for such a large prospective pool of employees. Being an equipment manager means being a part of something bigger than yourself. It's not the most glamorous job, and you most likely won't make life changing money doing the job. However, you will gain experiences, knowledge, and relationships unlike any other field. If you want to be an equipment manager, you need to be service oriented and selfless. You are constantly putting the needs and wants of others before your own." He continues, "Treat everyone as you would like to be treated. You never know when that Graduate Assistant (GA), Creative Director, Athletic Trainer, or Dietitian that you helped or proved yourself to accept a position as a Head Coach, Administrator, or General Manager." Braun continues with, "Don't be afraid of adopting new technologies. The game of football and football equipment has changed dramatically over the last five, ten, and fifteen years. To be successful means to continue learning and growing within your role."

When you start, expect long hours and physically demanding work. You'll arrive hours before practices to prepare equipment and stay late cleaning up. When you start, expect long hours and physically demanding work.

Entry-level positions start between $30,000-$45,000, often as seasonal roles. Assistant positions earn $40,000-$60,000. Head equipment managers can make $60,000-$100,000+. Head clubhouse managers can earn $60,000-$100,000+.

Coaching is the most visible and romanticized role in sports, involving teaching athletes, developing strategy, and leading teams to victory. It's also one of the most competitive, unstable, and demanding career paths. Coaches develop athletes' skills, design game strategies, manage in-game tactics, and create team culture. Head coaches make final decisions on personnel and strategy. Assistant coaches specialize in specific areas and handle detailed game planning and film breakdown.

Breaking into coaching usually requires playing experience, a deep knowledge of your sport, and willingness to start from the bottom. Most begin volunteering or taking low-paid positions at high schools or small colleges. Graduate assistant positions at college programs are common entry points; you'll work 60-80+ hour weeks while pursuing a master's degree. Networking is absolutely critical. Expect to move frequently, chasing opportunities wherever they exist. High school coaching often requires teaching certification. Some sports have governing bodies offering coaching certifications. At college levels, no universal certifications exist. Coaching requires deep sport-specific knowledge, teaching ability, and leadership skills. The pathway to professional or high-level college coaching often involves decades of grinding through lower levels. Early coaching positions involve relentless work with minimal recognition. You'll watch endless films and create practice plans.

Entry-level positions often pay up to $30,000 for graduate assistants and volunteers, however, the pay can be far less depending on each role, level, and sport. Low-level assistants earn $30,000-$60,000 in full-time positions, but can be less depending on factors listed previously. Full-time assistants at major programs can make $100,000-$500,000+, although this is extremely sport dependent. Head coaches at major programs earn wildly varying salaries. College football and professional head coaches can earn millions. However, most coaches at high school or small college levels earn modest salaries and face constant job uncertainty.

"You cannot make emotional decisions. Your decision-making process has to be information-oriented. It can be as simple as pros and cons. If you're getting ready to spend big money on a player, take a sheet of paper and write down what the team looks like with him and then without him. Making good decisions requires you to be as educated as possible. You have to gather all the information you need and make decisions with the information you have at that time," says Dave Gettleman, the former General Manager of the Carolina Panthers and New York Giants.

College Athletic Departments operate as massive organizations managing dozens of sports, hundreds of athletes, and multi-million dollar budgets. These departments need diverse professionals across operations, communications, development, compliance, academic support, facilities, events, marketing, and administration. College athletics offer unique opportunities because programs exist at every level: Division I, II, III, NAIA, and junior colleges. Operations professionals manage schedules and coordinate travel. Communications professionals manage media relations and write press releases. Development officers solicit donations and manage fundraising campaigns. Compliance officers navigate complex NCAA rules and monitor recruiting. Academic support advisors help student-athletes balance athletic and academic commitments. Marketing professionals promote teams and sell tickets. Facilities managers oversee stadiums and practice facilities. Event coordinators plan gameday operations. Video coordinators film practices and games.

Breaking into college athletics often begins with internships or graduate assistant positions. Graduate assistantships provide hands-on experience while earning a master's degree, though they're typically capped at 20 hours per week. Because of this limit, departments often bring on post-graduate interns to handle additional work. But what most students should know is that the best time to get involved is during undergrad. Reach out directly to athletic departments and ask about opportunities, whether that's gameday staff, tutoring, team management, or something else entirely. Take a football team, for example : they have 15 managers with responsibilities ranging from operations to analytics. Those roles are goldmines for building experience and connections before you even think about graduate school. Many professionals start at Division II, III, or NAIA programs where competition is less intense. Networking through professional organizations is critical. National Association of Collegiate Directors of Athletics (NACDA) serves as the umbrella organization for groups like National Association of Collegiate Marketing Administrators (NACMA), College Sports Information Directors of America (CoSIDA), and National Association of Academic and Student-Athlete Development Professionals (N4A). However, the structure seems to shift, so some groups are part of NACDA and some aren't depending on when you check. Master's degrees are increasingly expected for full-time professional roles. Early career roles involve supporting senior staff and learning departmental operations. You'll coordinate logistics, manage schedules, and handle administrative tasks.

Entry-level positions at smaller programs pay $30,000-$45,000, while similar roles at Power Five schools start at $40,000-$60,000. Mid-level directors earn $50,000-$90,000. Senior associate ADs can make $90,000-$200,000+. Athletic Directors at Division I schools earn widely varying salaries; smaller D-I programs pay $150,000-$300,000, while Power Five ADs earn $500,000 up to the millions. Graduate assistant positions offer stipends of $10,000-$25,000 plus tuition waivers.

Career Paths You May Have Not Considered

Most people enter this industry with a narrow vision of what they want to do, then discover something completely different that fits them better. The paths below don't get enough attention in career conversations, but they offer genuine opportunities, often with less competition than the obvious roles everyone chases.

Player Relations and Services sits at the fascinating intersection of baseball, basketball, football operations and high-end hospitality (on the team side). These professionals handle everything players and their families need off the field so athletes can focus entirely on performance. This includes coordinating complex travel arrangements for players and families (including international travel and visa issues), managing housing and relocation logistics when players are traded or called up, providing translation services for international players, organizing family support during road trips and extended travel, handling personal emergencies and sensitive situations with complete discretion, connecting players with local resources (schools, doctors, legal services), and serving as a liaison between players and the front office.

These departments are extremely small, typically just 1-3 people per team, sometimes part of a larger operations department rather than standalone, which makes opportunities incredibly rare. Getting in right out of college is extremely difficult. These roles demand maturity, exceptional relationship management and customer service skills, cultural competency, often multilingual abilities, and proven discretion. Most successful candidates have either worked in team operations for several years, served in similar roles at the minor league level, or bring backgrounds in high-end hospitality, international relations, work around professional athletes, or concierge services, combined with deep sports knowledge. These roles require exceptional organizational skills, cultural competency and language abilities (especially Spanish in baseball), absolute discretion and confidentiality, genuine empathy and care for player welfare, and the ability to solve problems creatively under pressure.

The work-life balance is unpredictable; you're essentially on call whenever players need you, which can mean late nights, emergency situations, and working around players' schedules rather than traditional business hours. However, many find the work deeply rewarding because you're directly improving lives and building genuine relationships with players who remember and appreciate your support throughout their careers.

The pay varies but is generally moderate at $50,000-$80,000 for coordinators/managers, and opportunities for advancement into front office or operations roles are real if you prove yourself reliable and trustworthy.

Ticket Operations and Box Office Management are where customer service meets revenue strategy, and it's become one of the most operationally critical and guest-facing functions in modern sports organizations. These teams manage the entire ticketing ecosystem, such as processing ticket purchases and exchanges through multiple channels (online, phone, walk-up windows), coordinating will-call operations on game days, handling customer service inquiries and resolving ticketing issues in real-time, managing ticket inventory allocation across different sales channels, overseeing box office staff and training protocols, coordinating with account executives on group and season ticket fulfillment, troubleshooting technical issues with ticketing systems during high-traffic periods, and ensuring seamless guest experiences from purchase through entry. Beyond daily operations, these teams use data analytics to optimize processes, identify bottlenecks in the purchase flow, track customer service metrics, and support revenue management strategies by providing insights into buying patterns and inventory movement. Teams typically employ 4-10 people in box office operations, depending on venue size and event frequency, plus dozens of part-time staff who work game days.

Getting in right out of college is very accessible, especially for coordinator or assistant roles. Strong candidates have customer service experience, comfort with technology and ticketing platforms, ability to stay calm under pressure during high-volume periods, and genuine service orientation. Previous experience in retail, hospitality, call centers, or other customer-facing roles translates well. The work requires exceptional customer service skills and patience with frustrated guests, technical proficiency with ticketing systems (Archtics, Provenue, Paciolan), strong organizational skills to manage complex inventory and fulfillment processes, problem-solving abilities when systems fail or issues arise on game days, attention to detail in financial reconciliation and reporting, and communication skills to coordinate across sales, operations, and guest services departments. Work-life balance is challenging during the season; you're working every game day (which means nights and weekends), handling high-stress situations when systems crash or lines back up, and managing the chaos of thousands of transactions happening simultaneously during peak periods. However, the offseason offers recovery time, and non-game-day work typically happens during more regular business hours.

Entry-level coordinators earn $35,000-$48,000, managers earn $50,000-$70,000, and directors of ticketing operations can earn $75,000-$100,000+. This path offers clear progression from coordinator to manager to director, with opportunities to transition into revenue management, sales operations, or broader guest services leadership roles. Box office experience is invaluable because you learn the entire revenue cycle, understand customer pain points intimately, and develop crisis management skills that translate across the sports industry.

Non-Profit and Non-Government Organization (NGO) Sports Organizations serve as advocates, governing bodies, and support systems for athletes, sports, and the industry. These organizations include national governing bodies like USA Triathlon, USA Judo, and USA Fencing; international bodies like the United States Olympic & Paralympic Committee (USOPC); player associations like the NFLPA and MLBPA; and alumni organizations like the MLB Players Alumni Association. These entities protect athlete rights, develop sport programming, organize competitions, and advocate for their constituents. They create opportunities for people passionate about sports governance, athlete development, and advocacy. Roles span program management, athlete services, event operations, communications, fundraising, and advocacy. Program managers develop initiatives for youth sports, coaching education, or athlete development. Event coordinators organize competitions, from local qualifiers to national championships. Communications specialists manage public relations, social media, and member engagement. Development officers pursue grants, corporate partnerships, and individual donations. Athlete services staff provide career transition support, educational resources, and wellness programs. Policy and advocacy roles work on collective bargaining, safety standards, or legislative issues.

Breaking into NGO sports requires understanding the unique mission of each organization. Research their priorities, whether athlete advocacy, grassroots development, or elite competition. Finding an organization's strategic plan can be especially helpful. Many organizations value lived experience in their sport. Former athletes have natural credibility, but non-athletes succeed through demonstrated passion and expertise. Internships provide essential entry points. The USOPC, national governing bodies, and player associations will often offer structured internship programs. Some may not have internships posted, but accept volunteers at events, competitions, or programs to build connections and experience.

Early in your career, expect modest compensation compared to professional teams or leagues. Non-profits operate with limited budgets. However, the work offers tremendous purpose. You'll directly impact athlete welfare, grow participation in sports you love, or advocate for meaningful change. You'll wear multiple hats, especially at smaller organizations. The mission-driven culture attracts people who care deeply about making sports better, creating a collaborative environment where your work has visible impact. Building relationships across the sports ecosystem opens doors to teams, leagues, or other sports organizations later in your career.

Entry-level positions include coordinators and assistants starting between $35,000-$50,000. Program managers and event coordinators earn $50,000-$75,000. Senior managers and directors make $75,000-$120,000. Executive leadership at major organizations can earn $120,000-$300,000+. Player associations typically offer higher salaries than national governing bodies.

Broadcast and Media Relations manages the critical relationships between the team and the dozens of media outlets that cover and amplify the organization. But just as importantly, they serve as the liaison between business operations and sport operations, for example, ensuring both sides of the organization are aligned on messaging and communication. This department coordinates all press conferences and media availabilities, manages media credentials and access for hundreds of reporters across the season, produces internal content for team websites and social channels, writes press releases and media guides, serves as the primary point of contact for journalists and broadcasters, handles crisis communications when sensitive situations arise, maintains statistical databases and historical records, and sometimes manages team-owned broadcast operations and radio networks. Teams typically employ 4-8 people in media relations (coordinator, managers, director of communications/PR), making this a small department with limited openings.

Getting in right out of college is difficult for full-time roles, however, media relations internships are available and highly competitive. Strong candidates have journalism degrees, sports writing experience (student newspaper, blogs, freelance), demonstrated writing portfolios, and deep knowledge of the sport and team. These professionals need exceptional writing and communication skills, deep knowledge of the sport and team history, ability to build and maintain relationships with media members (who can be demanding and sometimes adversarial), composure under pressure during crisis situations, attention to detail in managing credentials and logistics, and understanding of both traditional and digital media landscapes. The lifestyle is demanding but in different ways than other departments - you work every game day (often arriving early and staying late to accommodate media), travel with the team for road games (especially at higher levels), and are always on call when news breaks or crises emerge, with typical weeks running 50-60 hours during season. However, there's significant satisfaction in being at the center of information flow, building relationships with influential media members, and shaping how your organization is covered and perceived.

The pay is moderate; coordinators start at $40,000-$55,000, managers earn $60,000-$85,000, and directors of communications/PR earn $90,000-$140,000+. Progression generally moves from coordinator to manager to director of communications/PR, with opportunities at the league level or in corporate communications outside sports.

Operations handles the behind-the-scenes work that keeps teams functioning – facilities management, logistics, procurement, vendor relationships, and all the critical functions that don't fit neatly into other departments. The venue and arena operations team oversees the physical venue itself. From ongoing maintenance of building systems (HVAC, electrical, plumbing), capital improvement projects and renovations, event setup and breakdown, vendor management (cleaning, security, concessions, parking), safety and accessibility compliance, emergency response protocols, and maintaining playing surfaces to professional standards, operations cover a wide variety of responsibilities. Teams typically employ 10-20+ full-time staff depending on facility size and ownership structure, plus numerous part-time event staff.

Breaking into management roles right out of college is difficult, but entry-level coordinator or assistant positions are accessible, especially with relevant degrees (facilities management, engineering, construction management) or technical certifications. Many successful operations professionals started as game-day staff and worked their way up. These roles require technical knowledge of building systems, project management skills, vendor management abilities, understanding of safety regulations, and strong problem-solving skills when systems fail. The work-life balance means being present for all events, responding to facility emergencies at any hour, and managing off-season projects, but there's deep satisfaction in maintaining a facility that hundreds of thousands enjoy and seeing tangible results from your work.

Entry-level coordinators earn $40,000-$55,000, managers earn $65,000-$90,000, and directors can command $100,000-$150,000+, with highly transferable skills to facilities management outside sports.

Minor League and Affiliated Organizations employ thousands of people in roles that mirror major league structures, but with significantly more hands-on, multi-hat responsibilities that accelerate learning. Minor League Baseball, G-League (basketball), American Hockey League, and United Soccer League offer some of the most accessible entry points into professional sports. Typical minor league teams have only 8-15 full-time staff total handling all business operations, compared to the 100+ employees at major league organizations, which means everyone wears multiple hats and gains broad exposure quickly.

This is one of your most realistic paths into professional sports right out of college. Minor league teams actively hire recent graduates willing to work hard for modest pay in exchange for comprehensive experience. Having a strong work ethic, being willing to relocate to smaller markets, and having a genuine passion matter more than connections or pedigree. Many successful major league executives started in Minor League Baseball or lower-level professional leagues where they learned by doing everything.

In the minor leagues, you'll juggle multiple responsibilities. The same person might handle ticketing, coordinate promotions, manage social media, oversee game-day operations, and help with community appearances all in one week. This breadth of exposure teaches you the business holistically rather than the specialized silo experience you get at major league levels. However, the experience you gain in two years of minor league work often exceeds what takes five years to learn in a major league organization where you're narrowly focused on one function.

The work-life balance is challenging. Smaller staff means everyone does more, budgets are tighter, and you're thinking on your feet with limited resources, with typical weeks running 55-65+ hours during the season. The trade-off is real responsibility early, faster advancement opportunities, tighter team culture where you're not just a cog in a machine, and a genuine proving ground where strong performers get noticed and recruited by bigger organizations. The pay is lower, sometimes significantly lower, than major league equivalents. Entry-level positions typically pay between $28,000-$38,000 per year.

Agents and Player Representation requires a unique combination of hustle, relationship-building skills, business acumen, and often a law degree or strong background in contract negotiation and sports business. Agents negotiate player contracts with teams (which requires understanding collective bargaining agreements, salary cap rules, and contract structures), secure and manage endorsement deals with brands, provide career guidance and strategic planning throughout a player's career, handle media and public relations, connect players with financial advisors and wealth management, and represent players' interests in disputes or disciplinary matters. Beyond individual athlete representation, agencies also represent coaches, broadcasters, and executives, and larger agencies have divisions representing brands and corporations in sports partnerships.

Getting in right out of college is extremely difficult. Most agencies want law degrees or MBA backgrounds combined with proven relationships within the sport, and the typical path requires years of unpaid or low-paid apprenticeship working for established agents, building relationships within the industry, and proving you can deliver results before athletes trust you with their careers. "Team" size varies dramatically, from solo agents to large agencies with hundreds of employees across multiple sports and services. Agencies hire periodically, but it's relationship-dependent rather than following formal hiring cycles, though larger agencies (CAA Sports, Wasserman, Excel, Octagon, Boras Corporation, Klutch) have more structured internship and associate programs. The path typically involves building relationships within the industry and demonstrating results before athletes entrust you with their careers. During a recent conversation with a respected agent in the industry, they made a striking observation that captures the current state of professional sports representation: "There's no loyalty anymore." This sentiment reflects a fundamental shift in the agent-player relationship that has evolved over the past decade. Where agents once built careers on long-term partnerships with athletes, often representing them from their amateur days through retirement, the modern landscape has become increasingly transactional. Players now frequently switch agents based on immediate opportunities, perceived leverage in negotiations, or the influence of friends and family members who may lack industry experience but hold the athlete's trust. This erosion of loyalty cuts both ways, as agents are also more willing to drop clients who aren't generating significant commissions, focusing their energy on high-value athletes who can maximize their return on investment. The shift has transformed what was once a relationship-driven business into one dominated by short-term gains and constant competition, leaving little room for the mentorship and personal investment that once defined the agent-player bond. The lifestyle is demanding and unpredictable; you're always available to your clients, traveling constantly to watch them play and attend meetings, recruiting new clients relentlessly (especially during college showcases and combines), and operating in a high-pressure, relationship-dependent environment where your reputation and results determine everything. Work-life balance is essentially nonexistent, especially early in your career when you're grinding to build a client roster and establish credibility.

However, for those who succeed, it's potentially lucrative. Agents typically earn 3-5% of player contracts plus percentages of endorsements, meaning early career might see minimal income while building a roster, but successful agents with strong client lists can earn hundreds of thousands to millions annually. Plus, this job offers autonomy, variety, and the satisfaction of directly impacting players' lives and careers. It's incredibly competitive and relationship-dependent, requiring years of trust-building, but for people with the right combination of hustle, people skills, and business savvy, it can be extraordinarily rewarding both financially and personally.

Industry Mapping Exercise

Create a visual career map to understand where you might fit in the sports ecosystem. On a piece of paper, draw the organizational structure of a sports team including all departments we discussed: business operations, ticket sales, partnerships, marketing, game presentation, community relations, operations, analytics, and content. For each department, list 2-3 specific roles and write one sentence describing what each role actually does. Then, using a highlighter or different color, mark the departments and roles that genuinely interest you based on your self-assessment from Chapter 1. Next, identify three professionals currently working in those highlighted roles using LinkedIn. Don't reach out yet, just observe their career paths. Where did they start? What progression did they follow? What skills do their profiles emphasize? This exercise gives you a concrete understanding of the landscape and identifies potential career trajectories worth exploring. Keep this map visible and update it as you learn more about the industry.

"Success in baseball, like life, is about embracing every challenge and using setbacks as stepping stones. Passion and grit fuel the journey; it's not just about reaching the destination, but about the lessons learned and the relationships built along the way. Play hard, stay humble, and let your love for the game shine through. In the world of sports, the key to success lies not just in talent, but in resilience and the willingness to learn. As we rise, it's our responsibility to lift others with us." **Reggie Sanders, Cincinnati Reds Hall of Famer**

"My advice to young people is simple. Work on little things that will help you improve everyday, and remember there will be ups and downs and learn something from both. Finally, no matter how many people are in the stands, keep in mind someone is watching you. You never know where that can lead to." **Art Shamsky, Former Professional Baseball Player**

"As someone who has spent half his life in the sports field or dugout as a coach, this book will give you an ample amount of insights on the inner workings of what the sports industry entails. The good, the bad and the ugly. How to navigate those to help you make better choices on your own career path in the sports industry." **Doug Clark, Former Professional Baseball Player and Scout**

"I've spent over 40 years in baseball and still love what I do. For the past 13 years, I've been teaching a Sport Management Worldwide course to help people break into the industry. What I've learned is this: success comes down to persistence, perseverance, and talent. I've watched those qualities get rewarded again and again. But if you want real staying power in this business, you need to add one more thing, elite preparation." **Dan Evans, Former MLB General Manager**

"What has always stood out about Stuart is that he never waited for an opportunity to find him, he chased it down with preparation, ambition, and relentless effort. From the first time we connected, it was clear he understood that breaking into sports isn't about luck, it's about how you show up every single day. This book is an extension of that mindset: a real, hard-earned roadmap from someone who has lived every chapter, not just studied it." **Jentry Mullins, Sr. Vice President, Ticket Sales and Service, Brooklyn Sports & Entertainment**

"Breaking into pro sports is less about finding the perfect job posting and more about becoming someone other people trust. A lot of opportunities come from a respected person being willing to put their own reputation on the line to recommend you. That only happens when you consistently do good work, follow through, and look for ways to make the people and environments around you better, not just when you're asked. Early in your career, much of the work isn't glamorous, but those environments are where people figure out if you're dependable, coachable, and someone they want to work with. When people trust your work and value working with you, opportunities tend to follow." **Adam Virgile, Vice President, Integrated Performance Sciences, LA Clippers**

"Giving back to students matters because they are the future of our industry. If you want to break into sports, lead with a relentless work ethic, build real relationships, and don't be afraid to take risks. Put yourself out there, say yes to opportunities, and get experience wherever you can." **Chelsea Purcell, Vice President, Corporate Partnerships, PWHL**

Chapter 3: Finding Your Place in the Sports Industry

Understanding how the industry works is essential, but it's only the first step. The next step is figuring out where you actually fit within this complex ecosystem. Go back to the work you did in Chapter 1. What's your "why"? What kind of lifestyle do you want? What are you naturally good at? What energizes you rather than drains you? Now overlay those answers against everything you just learned about the sports industry structure. Where's the intersection between what you want, what you're good at, and what the industry needs?

If you love data, problem-solving, and intellectual challenges, explore analytics, revenue management, or strategy roles. If you're energized by relationships, persuasion, and helping people, consider sales, partnerships, or player services. If you care deeply about community impact and social good, look at community relations or youth programs. If you thrive in chaos, think on your feet, and get bored with routine, game operations or event production might be your calling. If you value stability, work-life balance, and transferable skills, consider roles in finance, legal, HR, IT, or working for vendors and service providers rather than teams directly.

There's no single path into sports, and there's no single definition of what a sports career looks like. The industry is vast, diverse, constantly evolving, and full of opportunities most people never consider because they're fixated on the obvious roles everyone else is chasing. Your competitive advantage comes from understanding the full landscape, identifying where you genuinely fit rather than where you think you should want to be, and pursuing opportunities strategically rather than desperately applying to everything with "sports" in the job title.

Once you know the landscape, understand how all the pieces fit together, and see where your skills and interests align with real opportunities, you can navigate strategically. You can make intentional decisions about which entry points make sense, which sacrifices are worth making, and which paths lead where you actually want to go.

Start with a Personality Test

I know what you're thinking. I just threw a bunch of different departments at you, and now you're probably more confused than when we started. Marketing, analytics, operations, content, player personnel, sales, legal, finance. It's a lot. So where do you even begin?

Here's something that might help: take a personality test. Not because it's going to reveal your destiny or tell you exactly which job title belongs on your business card, but because it can show you patterns you might not see on your own – how you work, what energizes you, what makes you want to close your laptop and take a nap. When you're staring at a list of departments, that kind of self-knowledge is actually pretty useful.

I'm not talking about those quizzes that tell you which Disney character you are. I mean legitimate assessments that have some actual framework behind them. The Myers-Briggs Type Indicator or its free cousin, 16Personalities, is a solid starting point. CliftonStrengths costs a bit more but does an excellent job showing you what you're naturally good at, which matters when you're trying to figure out where you'll actually succeed, not just survive. The Enneagram is another good one, especially if you want to understand the motivations and fears that drive your decisions. Career choices aren't just about skills. They're about what you need to be happy.

Once you've taken one of these, look for the threads. If you're someone who craves structure and clear processes, you might thrive in operations, finance, or legal. If you need variety and actually enjoy putting out fires, take a hard look at event management or team services. If you're the kind of person who can sit with spreadsheets for hours and genuinely enjoy finding patterns in the numbers, analytics or salary cap management might be your lane. If being around people energizes you rather than drains you, that points toward ticket sales, corporate partnerships, or community relations. If you're idea-driven and creative, you're probably looking at marketing, content creation, or brand strategy. And if you love the game itself, the X's and O's, the tape study, the strategy, then scouting, coaching, or player development is where you need to be.

Let me give you an example. I know someone named Sarah who took the Clifton-Strengths assessment during college. Her top strength came back as "Learner," which basically means she's energized by constantly encountering new information and acquiring new skills. She realized she didn't just want a job in sports. She wanted to be somewhere she'd never stop learning, where every day would present new problems to solve. That led her to explore sports analytics, where every game generates fresh data to dig into, where the questions never stop, and where being curious isn't just welcomed but required. She's been in the field for six years now and still loves it.

Here's the important part, though. These assessments show you where you might naturally fit, but they're not limits. They're not boxes you have to stay inside. Plenty of introverts build successful careers in sales because they're thoughtful listeners who make genuine connections. Plenty of deeply analytical people end up in creative roles because they bring structure to the chaos. The goal isn't to let a test tell you what you can and can't do. The goal is to use it as a starting point, a first step toward understanding yourself well enough to make a smart choice about where to begin. Because that's all this is, a beginning. You can always change direction later.

The Alternative Paths: Pivots, Lateral Moves, and Non-Linear Success

The career ladders above are helpful frameworks, but they don't capture how careers actually unfold. Let's talk about the moves that don't fit neatly into progression charts, but often define successful careers.

The Department Switch: Moving from sales to marketing, from operations to partnerships, from one functional area to another isn't a step backward. It's often strategic positioning.

The Minor League to Major League Jump: Starting in minor leagues or lower-division sports provides comprehensive experience but limited compensation. The strategic move is spending 2-3 years learning everything, then leveraging that experience for a major league opportunity.

The Organization-to-League or Agency Move: Teams aren't the only path. Moving to league offices, agencies, or vendors often accelerates career growth. League offices offer broader perspectives and typically better work-life balance. Agencies offer variety and often better compensation. These moves can position you for senior roles back on the team side later.

The Geographic Strategy: Sometimes the fastest path up is moving to a smaller market where opportunities are less competitive to build expertise and a track record, then leveraging that for a bigger market role. Other times it's staying in major markets where there are simply more organizations and more opportunities.

The Pause and Pivot: Many successful sports executives have left the industry for 2-5 years, gained experience in corporate environments or other industries, then returned to sports at higher levels with broader business acumen and fresh perspective. This isn't failure; it's strategic career development.

What Actually Matters for Advancement

Beyond time in role and basic competence, certain factors consistently predict who advances and who plateaus. Quantifiable impact – can you articulate specific results you delivered? Revenue generated, costs saved, problems solved, processes improved? Vague claims about being a "team player" don't drive promotions. Numbers do.

Expanding scope: Are you consistently taking on more responsibility, even before being promoted? The people who get promoted are already doing elements of the next level job.

Strategic thinking: Can you see beyond your immediate function to understand broader organizational priorities? Can you contribute to strategic conversations, not just execute tactics?

Political intelligence: Do you understand the power dynamics in your organization? Have you built relationships with decision-makers? Can you navigate organizational politics without being destroyed by them? This isn't about being manipulative; it's about understanding that advancement often depends on advocacy from people with influence.

Adaptability: Can you succeed as the organization changes, as strategies shift, as new leadership comes in? The people who thrive are the ones who can pivot without losing effectiveness.

Building others: As you move into leadership, your success depends on developing talent below you. Organizations promote people who make everyone around them better.

The Timeline Reality Check

Here's an uncomfortable truth: if you want to reach VP level in sports, you're probably looking at 12-18 years minimum from your entry-level position. Some people do it faster. Many never get there at all. There's no shame in building a successful career that plateaus at manager or director level, as most people do, and these roles can be deeply satisfying and well-compensated.

The people who reach senior leadership typically share certain patterns, such as starting in sales or operations where they learned business fundamentals. They made strategic moves between organizations rather than waiting for opportunities at one company; they built reputations as people who deliver results consistently; they developed broader business acumen beyond their specific function; and they were willing to make difficult decisions about geography, work-life balance, and career priorities.

Your timeline will depend on factors partly within your control (performance, strategic decisions, skill development) and partly beyond it (organizational growth, opportunities opening up, market conditions, sometimes just luck and timing). Focus on what you can control. Build skills. Deliver results. Develop relationships. Make strategic moves. And understand that building a career is a long game played over decades, not a sprint to the top.

Breaking In From Outside The Industry

Breaking into sports when you're already established in another career is one of the toughest transitions you can make, but it's not impossible. The challenge is that sports organizations often prioritize candidates with industry experience, even when someone from outside brings skills that are directly transferable and potentially more advanced. If you've spent ten years in corporate sales, you know how to close deals, manage accounts, and build relationships – all skills that translate perfectly to partnership sales. If you've been in marketing at a tech company, you understand digital strategy, brand positioning, and campaign execution as well as most people working for teams. The reality is you're going to face skepticism. Hiring managers will wonder if you understand the unique pressures of sports, if you can handle the hours, and if you're truly committed or just chasing a dream. Your job is to eliminate every doubt before you walk into the interview. That means doing your homework on the industry, networking relentlessly to get your foot in the door, being willing to take a step back in title or compensation, and making it crystal clear that you're not a tourist, but someone who's ready to commit to this career for the long haul.

Final Thoughts: Your Path Won't Look Like Anyone Else's

The paths in this chapter are frameworks, not prescriptions. Your career will zigzag. You'll take jobs that seem lateral or even backward, but position you for bigger moves later. You'll leave organizations, return to sports after time away, switch departments, relocate, and constantly recalibrate based on what you're learning about yourself and what you want.

That's not career confusion – that's career development. The most successful people in sports didn't follow a predetermined path. They made strategic decisions based on what they were learning, what opportunities presented themselves, and what mattered to them at different life stages. They built skills, delivered results, developed relationships, and positioned themselves to take advantage of opportunities when they appeared.

Your job isn't to follow someone else's path. It's to understand the landscape well enough to make informed decisions about where you're going, what you're building toward, and what trade-offs you're willing to make to get there. The career ladders in this chapter give you that landscape. What you do with it is up to you.

Find Your Strategic Fit

To recap this chapter, take time to honestly assess where you fit within the sports industry rather than where you think you *should* want to be. Reflect on your non-negotiables around lifestyle, compensation, location, and work environment, and identify the types of work that energize you versus those that drain you. Inventory the skills you've already proven through real results, and consider how those strengths align with actual needs across teams, leagues, agencies, and vendors. Based on that alignment, identify one primary career path and one or two alternative paths that would build similar skills or open different doors. Finally, define one concrete action you will take in the next 90 days, such as developing a specific skill, speaking with someone already in the role, or targeting a particular type of organization, to move from clarity to momentum. The goal isn't to commit to a perfect plan, but to make intentional, informed decisions rather than chasing every opportunity with "sports" in the title.

"Sports fandom connects people like nothing else on earth, and as a result, a lot of people dream of making it their profession. The competition will be high, so throw out the job descriptions & baseline expectations. Be prepared to do what nobody else will do to get that job or get that promotion. Generally, that little extra will be covered in dirty & mud, sitting outside an office without an invite, available without much notice, mostly accessible on nights, weekends & holidays. Embrace it!" **Michael Bucklin, Sr. Vice President, FOX Sports Digital**

"Early in your career, your job isn't to find the perfect role, it's to build skills, relationships, and credibility. A career in sports is a long, winding road, and the people who last are the ones who say yes to opportunities, stay coachable, and commit to getting better every single day. Just as important, you have to believe in what you're selling. In sports, you're not simply selling tickets or sponsorships, you're creating moments that drive very different outcomes for different people. Sometimes it's core memories with family and friends, sometimes it's client relationships, brand building, employee engagement, or community impact. When you understand that what you sell lives far beyond a sales deck, the work carries more purpose, the grind makes sense, and the path forward has a way of revealing itself." **Matt Peterson, Vice President, Ticket Sales and Premium Seating, San Francisco Giants**

"One of the most important responsibilities we have as leaders in sports is creating real pathways for the next generation. This industry thrives when we're willing to share what we've learned, be honest about the challenges, and help young professionals navigate the reality, not just the highlight reel." **Lisa Feigenbaum, Vice President, Premium & Product Development, Portland Trail Blazers**

"There are a few critical components to being successful in sports business. First, one must be very curious, and that can manifest itself in a number of ways. Be curious about people, so that you're constantly learning from them, asking them questions, observing them and following up with them. These are the relationships that will serve as the spine and backbone of your success in sports business. Be present and focus on the people before you. Don't always be looking for others in the room. Stay in touch with them, drop them notes from time to time and keep them updated on you. They will appreciate that. Second part of being curious is to be informed. Read as much as you can about the people, the history and the day-to-day activities of the sports business. Nothing impresses more than demonstrating that you are a serious student of sports business and understand the critical issues and opportunities facing the industry. Be present, be curious, be prepared." **Abe Madkour, Publisher and Executive Editor, Sports Business Journal**

Chapter 4: Choosing the Right School or Program

Choosing where to study sports management feels like one of those decisions that could make or break your entire career. You've probably been told that the "right" program opens all the doors, that rankings matter, that prestige equals opportunity. But here's what actually happens: students graduate from top programs with zero practical experience and can't get hired, while others come out of schools you've never heard of with real connections and job offers waiting. This chapter breaks down what actually matters when picking a program (or making the most of where you already are), because spending four years and a fortune on the wrong education is a mistake you can't afford to make. By the end, you'll know exactly how to evaluate programs based on what leads to jobs, not what looks good in a brochure.

The Myth of the Perfect Program

Let me start by destroying a myth that costs people thousands of dollars and years of their lives: you don't need to attend a prestigious sports management program to break into this industry. I know that's not what you want to hear if you're stressing over college applications or considering graduate programs. You've probably been told that the "right" school opens doors, that brand names matter, and that rankings determine your career trajectory. Some of that is true, but far less than the admissions brochures want you to believe. What actually matters when choosing a sports management program is hands-on opportunities, alumni networks, and access to internships. Everything else is secondary. A top-ranked program in the middle of nowhere with professors who haven't worked in the industry in fifteen years will do less for your career than a solid program in a major sports market with professors who actively work in the field and an alumni network that actually helps graduates get jobs.

What Actually Matters: The Three Pillars

Hands-on opportunities are the single most important factor in choosing a program, yet they're often the most overlooked. You don't learn sports management from textbooks – you learn it by doing. The best programs integrate practical experience directly into coursework through projects with real teams, case competitions with industry judges, consulting work for local organizations, and hands-on event management where you're actually running operations, not just observing. When evaluating programs, ask specific questions: Do students work on actual games for local teams? Are there partnerships with professional or college athletic departments that provide real projects, not simulated exercises? Do capstone courses involve solving actual business problems for organizations? How many hours of practical experience does the average student accumulate before graduating? Programs that can't answer these questions with specifics are theoretically focused and will leave you underprepared for the realities of the industry. I've interviewed dozens of students with impressive degrees who couldn't explain basic game-day operations because they'd never actually worked one, and I've hired people from lesser-known schools who'd worked a hundred events and understood the business from the ground up.

Alumni networks determine whether your degree opens doors or just looks good on paper, and not all alumni networks are created equal. What matters isn't how many alumni a program has, but how active, connected, and willing to help they are. The best programs have alumni working across the industry who actively recruit from their alma mater, respond to cold emails from current students, provide informational interviews, and refer qualified candidates when positions open. Before choosing a program, look up 20-30 alumni on LinkedIn and see where they actually work. Are they in the roles and organizations you aspire to? Are they concentrated in certain markets or spread across the country? Then reach out to 3-5 alumni and ask about their experience, particularly how much did the program help them get their first job?

Do they stay connected to the program and help current students? How would they rate the practical preparation they received? Their answers will tell you more than any glossy brochure. Schools with strong sports management programs often have formal alumni mentorship programs, active LinkedIn groups, regional networking events, and career fairs where organizations specifically recruit from that program. If the program can't connect you with successful alumni or if those alumni don't respond to outreach, that's a massive red flag regardless of the school's reputation.

LinkedIn can be one of your most powerful tools for building connections in the sports industry, but you need to use it strategically. Start by clicking the search bar at the top of your homepage and selecting "People" from the menu. Once you run an initial search, look for the "All Filters" button to refine your results. Under the "Schools" filter, input the school you're interested in, or alma mater; this shared background often provides an immediate conversation starter. You can also type specific team names or organizations directly into the current company search bar, such as "Los Angeles Lakers" or "IMG Academy," and LinkedIn will show you people who list those organizations in their profiles. This targeted approach allows you to identify alumni working for specific teams, fellow graduates in sports management roles, or professionals at organizations where you're seeking opportunities. The key is being specific with your filters. The more you narrow your search, the more relevant and approachable your potential connections become.

Access to internships is where location and professor connections become critical, and this is often the deciding factor between similar programs. Programs in major sports markets – New York, Los Angeles, Chicago, Boston, Phoenix, Atlanta, Dallas, and

Miami – offer proximity to dozens of professional teams, leagues, agencies, and vendors, which means more internship opportunities, more networking events, more guest speakers who are actually working in the industry, and more part-time work you can do while taking classes. A program in a smaller market might be excellent academically, but if you have to relocate every summer to get quality internships, you're spending money and missing relationship-building opportunities that local students accumulate naturally. Equally important are professors with active industry ties, not people who worked in sports twenty years ago and now just teach, but professionals who currently work in sports, sit on boards, maintain relationships with teams and organizations, and can make introductions that lead to internships and jobs. When evaluating professors, look at their LinkedIn profiles and recent work. Are they publishing relevant research? Speaking at industry conferences? Working with organizations? Serving in advisory roles? The best professors treat their students like future colleagues and actively connect them to opportunities because their reputation in the industry depends partly on the quality of graduates they produce.

Sports Management Worldwide

If you're looking for structured education specifically designed for the sports industry, Sports Management Worldwide (SMWW) is worth knowing about. Founded by Dr. Lynn Lashbrook, who is quoted earlier in this book, SMWW has spent decades building what is widely recognized as the global leader in online sports business education. With over 30,000 alumni working across 164 countries, their reach is hard to ignore.

What makes SMWW different from a traditional sports management degree is the focus on practicality. They offer more than 40 courses, each built around a specific role or area of the industry, including sports agency, scouting, general management, analytics, sports administration, broadcasting, marketing, and more.

The courses are all eight weeks long, are fully online, and are taught by actual industry professionals – think former general managers, team presidents, scouts, and agents, people who have lived the jobs they're teaching. That matters more than you might think. There's a big difference between learning sports marketing from someone who has studied it and learning it from someone who has done it at the professional level.

The courses are also designed around real life. If you're working full time, still in school, or managing other commitments, SMWW's self-paced format lets you engage as much or as little as your schedule allows. University credit is available at select institutions, and SMWW also partners with Concordia University Chicago for a full online Master's in Sports Leadership for those looking to go deeper.

Beyond the coursework itself, SMWW's value is also in the network. They host sports career conferences at major events throughout the year, connecting students directly with executives across the industry. Their alumni network spans every major professional league, from the NFL and NBA to MLB, NHL, MLS, and beyond.

A certificate from SMWW won't hand you a job. Nothing will. But it can shorten the time it takes to get in the door, give you industry-specific knowledge your competition might not have, and add a credible, recognizable name to your resume. For someone who is serious about breaking into sports and looking for every possible edge, it's a resource worth exploring.

Why Springfield College Was the Right Fit for Me

I chose Springfield College's Sport Management program, and looking back, it was one of the best decisions I've ever made, though it almost didn't happen. When I started my college search, I had already taken Springfield off my list. With only 2,500 undergraduate students, it was way too small for what I thought I wanted. I had visions of the big party school experience, the massive campus, the endless options. Springfield felt like the opposite of that dream, so I dismissed it without a second thought.

Then something happened that changed everything. My dad was on a flight from Boston to Baltimore during my junior year of high school. He struck up a conversation with the person sitting next to him, and somehow my interest in studying sport management came up. The first thing out of this stranger's mouth was, "Springfield College." Turns out, the guy my dad randomly sat next to was an executive on the College Boards (which administers standardized tests like the SAT and AP exams). Of all the flights, all the seats, all the conversations that could have happened, that one put Springfield back on my radar. My dad came home insisting we at least visit, so we went back for a tour.

I stepped on campus and hated it. It didn't click. Everything felt wrong, too small, too quiet, not what I'd imagined for myself. I was ready to leave after ten minutes and cross it off the list for good. But then we went on the actual tour, and something shifted completely. I fell in love. This was it. I could tell immediately. Everything that felt wrong initially suddenly felt right. The size meant I wouldn't be just a number, the tight-knit community meant real relationships with professors and classmates, the focus on sport management meant everyone was as serious about this career path as I was.

The lifeblood of Springfield College runs straight through the history of sport, and that goes back to its founding in 1885 as the YMCA Training School, literally built to train people to go out and improve communities through physical activity and Christian values. The YMCA's core mission of Spirit, Mind, and Body? Yup, invented at Springfield. The YMCA Triangle? Also from Springfield. The school's DNA is so deeply tied to sports that two of the most important games ever invented came straight out of its gym: James Naismith invented basketball there in 1891, and William Morgan, a Springfield grad, invented volleyball four years later in the neighboring city. Amos Alonzo Stagg, one of the most influential figures in the history of American football, also came through Springfield and helped shape how the game was coached and organized at a foundational level. So when people say sports are part of Springfield's identity, they mean it literally - the school didn't just teach about sports, it invented them.

What sealed it was another student. We struck up a conversation with a current student, and he was a junior on the baseball team, a sport I wanted to play in college. What was supposed to be a quick conversation turned into a private, hour-long conversation where he showed us everything, answered every question, and genuinely seemed excited to share what made Springfield special. At the end, he asked for my cell phone number and told me he'd let me know when practices were so I could come participate. When I told him I was still in high school and just visiting, he was genuinely surprised. He thought I was moving in that day (it was move-in day for students). That moment told me everything I needed to know about the culture at Springfield. This wasn't a place where students went through the motions. People were engaged, welcoming, and treated prospective students like future teammates, not just numbers on an admissions list.

What I didn't fully appreciate until I was enrolled was how perfectly Springfield's size and structure set me up for success in sports management. The program wasn't just academically strong; it was built around practical experience and industry connections. Professors knew every student by name, which meant they could tailor advice, make specific introductions, and write references that actually meant something because they knew your work intimately. The alumni network, while not as massive as some larger schools, was incredibly tight-knit and responsive. Springfield graduates remember what it was like to break into the industry, and they go out of their way to help current students because the community is small enough that your success reflects on the program.

The hands-on opportunities were embedded throughout the curriculum in ways that larger programs simply can't replicate. We weren't sitting in 300-person lecture halls learning theory; we were working actual events, managing real operations, solving genuine business problems for local and regional organizations. The program required extensive practical experience, which forced me to get into the field early and often. By the time I graduated, I had a resume full of tangible experience, not just coursework. I'd worked dozens of events, built relationships with professionals who'd seen my work ethic firsthand, and developed the confidence that comes from having actually done the job, not just studied it in a textbook.

In school, we were required to work the Naismith Basketball Hall of Fame Hoophall Classic as part of our hands-on experience in sport management. The event features the top high school basketball teams and future college and NBA stars, making it one of the most prestigious showcases in the country. This is an event you'll hear about later on, but it's run by the Basketball Hall of Fame; however, Springfield College students manage the student volunteer staff of about 100 students per year, with ESPN coverage and top-tier talent. Over 120 Hoophall Classic participants have gone on to play in the NBA since 2004, including stars like Kevin Durant, James Harden, Kyrie Irving, Anthony Davis, Karl-Anthony Towns, Jaylen Brown, Jamal Murray, Jayson Tatum, Zion Williamson, and Cade Cunningham. The event has produced 12 of the last 15 number one overall NBA draft picks, including 11 straight from 2011-2021.

Springfield also offered something I didn't know I needed when I was 17 and dreaming of the big party school, as it was far enough from home that my parents couldn't surprise me with random dinner visits. I went six hours away, which gave me real independence and forced me to figure things out on my own. But it was close enough that I could get home for a long weekend when I needed to, which mattered more than I expected once I was actually in school. That distance was perfect, enough space to grow up, but not so far that I felt completely disconnected from my support system when things got hard.

Looking back, Springfield was exactly what I needed even though it wasn't what I thought I wanted. The small size that initially turned me off became my biggest advantage. I built deeper relationships, got more personalized attention, and had access to opportunities that would have gone to someone else at a larger school where I would have been competing with hundreds of other sport management students for the same internships and professor connections. The program's emphasis on practical experience over theoretical knowledge prepared me for the realities of the industry in ways that a more prestigious name on my diploma never could have. And that random conversation my dad had on a plane? It put me on a path that changed my entire career trajectory.

If there's a lesson in my Springfield story, it's that you shouldn't dismiss a program because it doesn't match your preconceived notions of what college should look like. The metrics that seem important when you're 17 size, reputation, party scene, campus aesthetics, matter far less than the quality of education, access to practical experience, strength of faculty relationships, and responsiveness of the alumni network. Visit campuses even if they're not on your original list. Talk to current students and see if they're genuinely engaged or just going through the motions. Pay attention to how you feel when you're there, not just what looks good on paper. Sometimes the right fit isn't the obvious choice, but it's the one that surprises you when you give it a real chance.

Dr. Heather Gilmour, Chair of the Department of Sport Management and Recreation, puts it this way: "What makes SC special is how we've always put authentic, personal relationships first. There's a culture of genuine care woven throughout the Sport Management program. We encourage students to be real with themselves, honest in their relationships, and clear-eyed about their professional goals. You had that openness when you first visited campus as a high school senior, and you've held onto it. That matters. Finding the right program is important, sure, but learning never stops after graduation. Choosing the right school is just as crucial as landing the right job. Stay open to possibilities and true to yourself, just like you were then and just like you are now."

When Dave Gettleman was looking at graduate programs, he chose St. Thomas University specifically because of the opportunities available in Miami and the opportunities to get experience on campus. Most of the courses were taught by adjunct professors who were actively working in the field. His negotiation class was taught by an attorney who ran their own practice. The public relations course was led by the Director of Sports Information at the University of Miami. This gave students direct access to people who were doing the work currently, not just talking about it. Other programs Gettlemen considered were staffed primarily by full time professors who weren't currently working in the industry.

If You Didn't Major in Sport Management

A truth that should relieve a lot of pressure is that you absolutely do not need a sport management degree to work in sports. Some of the most successful people I know in this industry studied business, communications, marketing, economics, data science, journalism, hospitality, or liberal arts. What matters isn't your major; it's whether you have relevant skills, practical experience, and a genuine understanding of how the business works.

If you didn't major in sport management, here's how you can still break in and compete effectively with people who did. You'll need to be your own loudest advocate, network more intentionally than you might otherwise, and actively seek out opportunities that build a resume strong enough to go toe-to-toe with sport management grads. This means being strategic about internships, volunteer work, and side projects that prove you understand the industry. It also means getting comfortable telling your story in a way that shows how your different background is actually an advantage, not a weakness.

Find people who made the jump from your industry into sports. These conversations are gold. Ask them how they actually did it. What opened the door? Which skills from their old job mattered most? What do they wish they'd known earlier? The specifics matter here. Don't just ask, "How'd you get in?" Dig into the details. Did they take a pay cut? How long did it take? What surprised them about working in sports versus their previous industry? You're looking for the real story, not the LinkedIn version.

School Evaluation Matrix

Whether you're currently choosing a program or already enrolled, create a comprehensive evaluation to maximize your educational investment. Build a spreadsheet with schools or programs you're considering (or your current program) as rows and these criteria as columns:

1. Hands-on opportunities available
2. Active alumni network strength
3. Access to internships and organizations
4. Professor industry connections
5. Geographic location advantages
6. Cost vs. value assessment
7. Job placement rates and outcomes

Research each criterion thoroughly using program websites, LinkedIn alumni searches, informational interviews with current students, and conversations with career services. Rate each criterion on a 1-5 scale with specific evidence supporting your rating. If you're already in a program, this exercise identifies gaps you need to fill independently through networking, seeking additional internships, or leveraging alumni connections more aggressively. If you're choosing between programs, this matrix provides objective data for your decision rather than relying solely on rankings or reputation.

Part II: Building Your Experience

(Before Your First Job)

A strategic approach to launching your sports career through experience-building: maximizing internships by understanding their true purpose beyond resume lines (Chapter 5), getting creative when traditional paths don't work through volunteering, self-created projects, and campus involvement (Chapter 6), and developing geographic flexibility to pursue opportunities across markets while building community in new cities (Chapter 7).

"I'm excited for Stuart's book as he really has experienced the life of building a career in the sports industry. Instincts are good, but Stuart gives proven advice on how to navigate such a dynamic business. His own personal experience serves as a compass for those just beginning the same journey. I've been in this industry for over 40 years, and it requires determination, perseverance, and help. Building a network is of utmost importance and should begin as soon as possible. This book will serve as a roadmap for that and other skills as you begin the exciting journey through the thrilling sports industry." **D.J. Kazmierczak, Sr. Vice President Operations, Panini America**

"*Breaking Into Sports: The Real Guide to Landing Your Dream Job* is a book I wish I had when navigating my undergraduate & graduate degrees in Sports Management. In this book Stuart tells it like it really is, straight from the experiences of a current sports industry executive who really lived it every step of the way. Being in a position now to share our knowledge & expertise with students looking to pursue a career in our industry is an honor & a privilege. One of the many unique & great things about our industry is that people are always willing to give back, share their experiences & be generous with their time for those that are passionate about breaking in & follow in their footsteps. We were all in those seats once & someone did the same for us, it's almost a rite of passage to pay it forward & help others achieve their dream of working in the best industry in the world, sports! Bet on yourself, say YES to every opportunity at least once, have a positive, unrelenting work ethic, be willing to relocate anywhere, find a mentor you want to emulate & be a sponge at every stop along the way! This career choice is a lifestyle, not a job. You must truly love it if you want to be successful & have longevity. The nights, weekends & Holidays, when others are off…you're working! However, the relationships you build, the memories & unforgettable moments you create for those same fans are priceless!" **A.J. Tomeny, Vice President, Ticket Sales & Service, Nashville Predators**

"The sports business industry requires incredible patience and sacrifice but can be highly rewarding if you are willing to remain persistent! There is rarely a linear career path, and no two paths are ever the same. As you forge your own path, continue to chase the roles that create the most opportunity in the long run." **JB Greer, Founder, Hustle Sports Group**

"A long-lasting career in the sports industry requires patience and a long-term mindset. Starting out, you may choose a role driven by passion rather than pay. By treating these early experiences as opportunities to learn and grow, you set yourself up to eventually earn well while working in a field you love." **Kyle Waters, Chief Sales Officer, WNBA Seattle Storm**

"Paying it forward to aspiring professional sports executives is not only important, but also imperative to those of us in leadership positions. Taking the time to share career experiences and addressing industry job opportunities are also items in which to counsel job seekers. Our industry is one of the more emotional and physically taxing, but so rewarding if a fit for one's talents and passions." **Martie Cordaro, President, Omaha Storm Chasers**

"You control your effort and determination! Get involved through building a network and accumulating experiences (internships & volunteering are great places to engage). It is easier than ever in today's world to reach out to those that have a career in sports & entertainment. Not all sports professionals will engage, but many of us will "pay it forward" as was once done for us. Ask questions of, and learn whatever you can, from those that engage. As you land opportunities to get involved, be the hardest worker and learn all that you can. Opportunities to be involved in every step of an event/initiative, from ideation through execution, will set you apart from others. By gathering as much relevant experience as possible, and cultivating a network that will sing your praises, you will put yourself at the top of most stacks of resumes for that first, full-time position in the sports & entertainment world." **Ryan Niemeyer, Vice President, Ticket Sales and Service, Pittsburgh Pirates**

Chapter 5: Internships and Experience That Counts

Let's talk about internships. Not the glossy, Instagram-worthy version where you're high-fiving mascots and sitting courtside. The real version. The one where you're sorting mail, making cold calls, and learning more than you ever thought possible. I did sixteen internships and professional experiences across various sectors of the sports industry during college. Sixteen. People thought I was crazy. My friends were traveling the world or soaking up the beach, and I was driving across the country to work for free (or close to it) at baseball stadiums, hockey arenas, and front offices. Looking back, those experiences were the foundation of everything that came after. They opened every door in my career.

What nobody tells you about internships in sports is they're not just about the work you do. They're about proving you can show up, learn fast, and make yourself useful. They're about building relationships with people who will remember your name years later. And most importantly, they're about figuring out what you actually want to do in this industry.

"A job at the end of the internship is not guaranteed," Gettleman says bluntly. "It's typically a 12-month opportunity, and at the end of it, you're most likely going home. We make no promises and want the intern to have no expectations. Every single day is a job interview. As an intern, you never know who you're going to meet. The person you meet on the next to last day might have been watching you the entire time. No job is too small. Not all internships are equal. Some places you're getting coffee. Other places you have real responsibilities. Understanding how you communicate is also critical. There's office politics in every workplace. It's not always about the message. It's about the delivery. I can deliver the same message five different ways to the same person, and they'll take it five different ways." Gettleman continues by saying, "It's about building a foundation and building a base. Because as you go higher, the winds get stronger. If you get rocked and your foundation isn't strong, you're going to fail and go down in flames."

Aidan Reilly, a Minor League Technology Operations with the Milwaukee Brewers, puts it directly: "Your first job in sports won't look like your dream job, but it will teach you the habits that get you there." That's the part everyone understands. What catches people off guard is what comes next. "Getting your foot in the door, landing the internship, seasonal role, or fellowship is only the beginning," Reilly explains. "Staying in is even harder." He's right. Internships rarely convert to full-time positions because teams might only have one or two openings each year and dozens of capable interns cycling through. You're competing not just against your intern class, but against every intern the team has had in the last five years, plus candidates from other organizations, former players, and graduates from top programs.

The margin for error is microscopic. Every task becomes a test of work ethic, adaptability, communication, and your ability to add real value. One mistake can follow you across the industry. One strong impression can open doors you didn't even know existed. Even after securing a full-time role, the grind intensifies. "Sports front offices are built on constant evaluation of players, staff, and processes," Reilly notes. "Turnover is common, departments restructure frequently, and job security depends on performance, organizational success, and your ability to evolve as technology and strategy advance."

One of the most valuable pieces of advice Reilly received during his first year that stuck with him was, "The grass is not always greener on the other side. A title is worth nothing compared to the work ethic and dedication that you put into your job for higher-up executives. Don't work for a job title, work for your job security. In the end it's all a business and there are many others who want to be in your position."

Why Internships Matter More in Sports

In most industries, internships are nice to have. In sports, they're practically required. Think about it from an employer's perspective. They have hundreds of applicants for every entry-level job. Most of them claim to be passionate about sports. Most of them have decent grades. How do you separate the real from the resume builders?

Think of internships like test-driving a car before you buy it, or dating before you get married. Would you rather spend three months in ticket sales and realize you hate being on the phone all day, or would you rather sign a two-year contract for a full-time sales job and be miserable? Once you're in a job, switching is complicated. You've got a salary, maybe benefits, and you're worried about how it looks on your resume if you leave too quickly. But as an intern? You can try partnerships and discover the corporate side isn't for you. You can work in community relations and realize you love the grassroots connection with fans. You can spend a summer in operations and learn that the organized chaos of event day is exactly where you thrive. Every internship is a low-stakes experiment that helps you avoid high-stakes mistakes later. The goal isn't just to get experience. It's to figure out what kind of career you actually want before you commit to it.

Internships are proof builders. They show you've already done the work. You know what a 12-hour game day feels like. You've handled angry fans, managed tedious spreadsheets, and survived the organized chaos of event operations. You're not walking in blind, expecting the job to be all glamour and glory. The sports industry runs on connections and credibility. Internships give you both. Every internship adds people to your network. Every reference letter adds credibility to your name. By the time you're applying for full-time jobs, you're not a stranger anymore. You're the person who impressed someone at the Baltimore Orioles, or learned the ropes with the Basketball Hall of Fame, or showed up early every day at Frederick Keys.

The Real Purpose of Internships

When I tell people I did sixteen internships and professional experiences, the first question is always, "Why?" Fair question. After three or four, wasn't I done? Didn't I already prove myself?

Not exactly. Each internship taught me something different. The first few taught me the basics of the industry. The middle ones helped me explore different departments and roles. The later ones helped me build deeper skills and stronger relationships. By the time I graduated, I had worked in marketing, operations, ticketing, and partnerships. I knew what I loved, what I was good at, and what I never wanted to do again.

That's the real purpose of internships. They're your chance to experiment without the pressure of a full-time commitment. You can try sales and discover you love the competitive energy. Or you can try sales and realize you'd rather be in marketing. Both outcomes are valuable. The worst-case scenario isn't failing at an internship. It's landing a full-time job in a department you hate because you never took the time to figure out what fits you.

Internships also teach you how sports organizations actually work. The organizational charts, the hierarchies, the unwritten rules. You learn that the ticket office and the corporate partnerships team might as well be different planets, even though they're in the same building. You learn how decisions get made, how budgets get allocated, and how people build careers over decades. None of this is in a textbook. You have to see it up close.

Building Your Internship Resume: Freshman to Senior Year

Your internships should tell a story. Not just any story, but one that shows you're getting more strategic and focused each year. Here's how to think about it.

Freshman and Sophomore Years: Get Your Reps In

Early on, you're exploring. You don't need to land at the Yankees or the Lakers right out of the gate. Actually, you shouldn't aim for that yet. Start smaller. Work for your college's athletic department. Volunteer with a local youth sports league. Help a minor league team with their summer camps. The goal here is simple: get experience working in sports, period.

These early internships teach you the basics. You'll learn how sports organizations actually function, what the day-to-day looks like, and whether you even enjoy this world. You're also building fundamental skills like showing up on time, following through on tasks, and working with a team. Sounds basic, but these matter more than you think.

Junior Year: Get Specific

By now, you should have some clarity about what you want to do in sports. Marketing? Operations? Analytics? Sales? Your junior year internship needs to reflect that focus.

This is when you start being selective. If you want to work in NBA team operations, go after college basketball operations roles. If you're into sports marketing, find an internship that actually lets you create content or run campaigns, not just observe. The experience should align with your target job.

You're also at a point where bigger organizations will take you seriously. You have some sports experience on your resume now. You're not starting from zero. Use that.

Senior Year: Make It Count

Your final internship is your audition. Ideally, it's with the type of organization where you want to work full time. Maybe it's a professional team, a league office, or an agency. This internship should look as close as possible to your dream first job.

If you do well, there's a real chance they'll hire you after graduation. Even if they don't, you're building a reference who can vouch for your work at a high level. And you're proving to other employers that you can handle real responsibility in a competitive environment.

Some students try to cram in multiple internships senior year or during their last summer. That can work, but quality beats quantity here. One meaningful experience where you make an impact is worth more than three where you're just filling a seat.

The Through Line

When someone looks at your resume, they should see progression. Each internship should be a step up in responsibility, focus, or prestige. You're showing you didn't just stumble into sports. You built toward it intentionally.

Bill Fagan, the President of Business Operations with the Cleveland Cavaliers, mentions, "Love the game and the business. Start early, say yes to opportunities, and stay open-minded, every experience will shape your path, and your network will grow with you. A career in sports business is most rewarding when you have a passion for both sports and business. It's never too early to gain experience, seek out internships, part-time roles, and volunteer opportunities in the industry. Don't limit your thinking. Stay open-minded, because every role you take will teach you something that shapes your path. And the best part: your network will quietly grow with every experience you say yes to."

The Journey Through 16+ Experiences

Let me be clear about something right up front: I didn't accumulate sixteen internships and experiences during my four-year college degree because I had some master plan or because I'm exceptionally brilliant. I did them because I was trying to figure out what I actually wanted to do, where I fit in this industry, and how to make myself valuable enough that someone would eventually pay me. Some of those experiences were incredible learning opportunities. Others were glorified busy work. A few I probably shouldn't have done at all. But every single one taught me something, about the industry, about myself, or about what I definitely didn't want to do for the rest of my life.

The number isn't what matters. What matters is that I treated every experience, no matter how small or unglamorous, like it was preparing me for something bigger. I showed up early, stayed late, volunteered for the tasks nobody else wanted, asked questions constantly, and built relationships with people who could eventually help me. That approach, not the quantity of internships, is what actually opened doors. You don't need sixteen professional experiences to break into sports. But you do need to be strategic about the experiences you pursue, intentional about what you learn from each one, and relentless about making every opportunity count.

The Lessons Hidden in Every Opportunity

The internships I pursued were never just résumé builders – they were classrooms, laboratories, and proving grounds. Each role exposed me to a wide range of responsibilities, often far beyond the job description, and required me to learn by doing in real, high-pressure environments. As you read through the experiences that follow, I encourage you to pay attention not just to the organizations, but to the responsibilities themselves, and ask which ones you would want exposure to in your own internships. Not all internships are created equal, but many become valuable because of what you're willing to ask for, take on, and learn. What follows is a breakdown of the roles I held, the work I did, and the lessons I took away, offered as a practical roadmap for how internships can be leveraged into meaningful skill development and career clarity.

Frederick Keys taught me the foundation of everything. This was my first real baseball internship, a single-A MiLB affiliate of the Baltimore Orioles, working in marketing, business operations, and game day operations. This is where I learned that minor league baseball is the best education you can get in sports business because there's no specialized role, you do everything. I executed pre-game, in-game, and post-game promotions, which taught me event production and thinking on my feet when things inevitably went wrong. I assisted in advertising and executing the Keys Youth Baseball Camp, which taught me program management and working with kids and parents. I represented the Keys at various community appearances, which taught me how to be a professional ambassador for an organization. I developed, prepared for, and participated in various theme nights, which taught me creative marketing and activation. I even had to be the mascot for a game. The lesson: minor league sports is where you should start if you want to learn the business comprehensively and quickly. You'll wear every hat imaginable, and that breadth of experience is invaluable.

The Springfield Falcons hockey internship taught me that skills transfer across sports. Working game day operations for a minor league hockey team showed me that the fundamentals of sports business, customer service, promotions, operations, and fan engagement are the same whether it's baseball, basketball, or hockey. I developed and refined customer service and selling skills by interacting with fans constantly. I coordinated with front office staff for daily tasks and assisted with game day promotions, which taught me cross-departmental collaboration and how different departments need to work together for events to succeed. The lesson is you shouldn't limit yourself to one sport. The business principles are universal, and diversifying your experience across multiple sports makes you more adaptable and valuable.

The Baltimore Orioles experience taught me what major league operations look like and how different it is from minor leagues. Working as a sales and fan services representative for an MLB team showed me the scale and sophistication that comes with major league sports. The staff is larger, the budgets are bigger, the technology is more advanced, and the expectations are higher. But I also learned that bigger isn't always better for learning; in some ways, I learned more doing everything at the Keys than I did in a more specialized role at the Orioles. The value was seeing both levels and understanding how organizations scale from minor to major leagues. The lesson: experience both minor and major league environments if possible because they teach you different things, and understanding both makes you a better operator.

The Naismith Basketball Hall of Fame Hoophall Classic taught me how to manage large-scale events and lead teams. This wasn't just working an event, but managing one. Over three years, I progressed from volunteer to media and liaison supervisor, which meant real management responsibility. I developed schedules for over 75+ volunteers and over 30 team liaisons, which taught me workforce planning and coordination at scale. I managed and supervised event operations over the course of the five-day tournament, which taught me crisis management, delegation, and keeping dozens of moving pieces synchronized. I coordinated court time logistics for teams, which required detailed planning and constant communication. I collaborated with other supervisors to handle seating, fundraising, and transitions to ensure the event ran smoothly. This was high-stakes event management with nationally televised games, top high school recruits, college coaches, NBA scouts, and media from across the country. Everything had to work perfectly. The lesson: seek out high-pressure, high-visibility events where failure would be obvious and painful. That's where you learn what you're actually capable of handling.

The Hall of Fame experiences taught me that iconic institutions offer unique learning and network access, and sometimes, unforgettable moments you couldn't plan if you tried. I volunteered for both the Basketball Hall of Fame Enshrinement in Springfield and the Baseball Hall of Fame Induction in Cooperstown, and these weren't just events; they were celebrations of sports history involving legends, media, and industry executives. Working the Basketball Hall of Fame Enshrinement put me in proximity to people I'd only seen on TV. I hung out with Dr. J, talked with Bill Walton, photobombed pictures with Shaq and Allen Iverson, and even got to try on Shaq's Hall of Fame ring (which, for the record, was absurdly massive). In Cooperstown, I helped Yogi Berra out of his car, said hello to Sandy Koufax, and congratulationed Randy Johnson, moments that reminded me I was working at the intersection of sports history and legend. These weren't just cool stories to tell later. They taught me that being around excellence raises your standards, that the best organizations execute at the highest level, and that treating every interaction professionally matters because you never know who you're meeting or who's watching. The network access was invaluable; I met executives and industry professionals at these events who remembered me years later when I reached out for advice or opportunities. The lesson: if you can work for prestigious organizations or iconic events, take those opportunities. The name carries weight, the standards are higher, the moments are unforgettable, and the people you meet can change your career trajectory.

Dream Bat Company taught me entrepreneurship and the business side of amateur sports. Working as a baseball operations intern for a travel baseball organization showed me a completely different part of the sports ecosystem. I secured sponsors to help fund travel teams while branding and marketing to local businesses and organizations, which taught me business-to-business (B2B) sales, sponsorship acquisition, and how to demonstrate value to potential partners. I served as field supervisor for a 25+ team invitational tournament, which taught me large-scale logistics, vendor coordination, and managing chaos when you have limited resources. I coached multiple travel baseball teams to prepare for the summer season, which taught me leadership, communication, and how to manage competitive young athletes. The lesson is that amateur and youth sports are a massive industry that most people overlook. The business fundamentals are the same, the experience is valuable, and these organizations are often more accessible for getting real responsibility early in your career.

Originally I had accepted an internship with the Philadelphia Flyers in partnership activation, but I made a last-minute decision to turn it down because I wanted to sell, not just activate existing deals. That single choice completely altered my career trajectory and taught me an invaluable lesson that one decision can determine which side of the sports business you end up on. I landed at Goodyear Ballpark, the spring training facility for the Cincinnati Reds and Cleveland Guardians, and they threw me into the deep end immediately. On my second day, we were cold calling. By the second week, I was running my own meetings and closing deals. There was no hand-holding, no gradual onboarding, just hands-on learning from day one, which turned out to be the best education I could have received. We worked 45 straight days, and it felt like Groundhog Day, from selling, activating partnerships, and writing contracts for MLB, each individual team, and the City of Goodyear. The pace was relentless, but it hammered home two critical lessons that have shaped my entire approach to the business. Every second is an opportunity to sell, and relationships are everything. By the end of that internship, I had sold the highest-value partnership of any intern in the facility's history, a testament to what you can accomplish when you're willing to jump in, learn by doing, and treat every conversation as a chance to build something meaningful.

The Leadership Laboratory: My Campus Experience

Internships were only part of how I built experience at Springfield College. What happened on campus – the clubs I joined, the leadership roles I took on, the events I worked on, the relationships I built – mattered just as much as what I did during summers and semesters away. Campus involvement is often overlooked because it doesn't feel as "real" as professional internships, but that's a massive mistake. Campus experiences are where you develop leadership skills, build your network among peers who'll become your future colleagues, and create a track record of initiative that makes you stand out when competing for opportunities. I held leadership positions across multiple student organizations, which taught me management and organizational skills. I served as Class Vice President, Vice President for Student Ambassadors, Sport Management Club Executive board, starting two clubs, having three jobs, involved in fourteen clubs, among many other involvements. These weren't resume padding; these were real management responsibilities. Every leadership role taught me something about delegation, communication, conflict resolution, and delivering results with limited resources. Despite being highly involved on campus, I consistently maintained a high GPA, earning a place on the Dean's List throughout my academic career.

I worked three jobs on campus simultaneously, which taught me time management and work ethic in ways the classroom never could. I juggled working at the campus union as a front desk worker, driving the campus shuttle (which was really just a minivan ferrying students around campus), and serving as the student representative on the Public Safety Board of Appeals for parking tickets. By default, I became popular because everyone wanted their parking ticket thrown out. Between three paid positions, a full course load, and leadership roles in multiple clubs, I was constantly balancing competing priorities and managing my time down to the hour.

Working three jobs while managing everything else taught me prioritization, efficiency, and how to deliver quality work even when stretched impossibly thin. Most importantly, it taught me I was capable of handling way more than I thought I could, a lesson that prepared me for the demanding schedules and multiple responsibilities that define early career sports jobs. The lesson is to not be afraid to take on multiple commitments simultaneously. Learning to manage competing priorities while maintaining quality is exactly what employers need, and proving you can juggle multiple responsibilities makes you far more valuable than someone who's only ever focused on one thing at a time.

My willingness to say "yes" and dive into new experiences was a defining part of my college years. I played three club sports, because why not? A friend convinced me to join the paintball team, and I figured it would be something different to try. I joined the ultimate frisbee team thinking it would be great cardio, but it ended up being some of the most fun I had in college, capped off with unforgettable spring break trips that created lifelong friendships. And then there was the ski racing team, where I competed at a high enough level to be regionally ranked in New England. Each sport taught me something different about competition, teamwork, and pushing myself outside my comfort zone. Looking back, those experiences reinforced the same philosophy that would serve me in sports business: be willing to try new things, build relationships in unexpected places, and commit fully once you're in. The lessons from cold New England ski slopes and muddy ultimate frisbee fields translated directly to the grind of selling partnerships and building a career in an industry where adaptability and relationships are everything.

And somehow, in the middle of managing three jobs and everything else, I helped start two clubs on campus, including club gymnastics, which is hilarious considering I can't even somersault. I handled the organizational side, paperwork, budgets, scheduling, and recruiting members, while others handled the actual gymnastics. This taught me that you don't have to be an expert in something to help build it; you just need organizational skills and willingness to do the administrative work that makes things happen.

College bars are underrated networking venues. You'd be surprised how many professional relationships start over a pitcher of beer after class or at whatever spot the students claim as their own. The conversations are more relaxed, more authentic, and less transactional than formal networking events. Just keep your head on straight, because your classmates today are your colleagues and references tomorrow.

The Skills That Transfer From "Non-Sports" Work

What people don't tell you is some of the most valuable preparation for sports careers happens outside sports entirely. The skills you develop working in restaurants, retail, customer service, operations, or other "regular" jobs often make you more effective in sports roles than people who've only worked in sports.

Restaurant and food service jobs teach you how to work under pressure and serve demanding customers. Though I've never worked in restaurants, many of my peers did, and those who worked food service developed skills that made them excellent in game day operations and fan services roles. Restaurants teach you how to multitask (managing multiple tables/orders simultaneously), stay calm during rushes (everyone wants everything right now), work as part of a coordinated team (kitchen and front-of-house must synchronize), recover when things go wrong (orders get messed up, customers get angry), and maintain professionalism even when you're exhausted. These are exactly the skills you need working game day operations when you're managing multiple promotions, coordinating vendors, solving problems in real-time, and keeping fans happy regardless of what's happening on the field.

Retail jobs teach you sales fundamentals, product knowledge, and customer psychology. My Vineyard Vines experience taught me skills I still use, such as how to approach customers without being pushy, how to ask questions that reveal what they actually want, how to handle "just browsing" without giving up, how to overcome price objections, how to suggest complementary products naturally, and how to close sales confidently. I learned inventory management, loss prevention, visual merchandising, and how to work efficiently during peak traffic periods. Every single one of these skills transferred directly to ticket sales — the psychology of selling a $10,000 season ticket package is remarkably similar to selling a $100 pair of pants. You're identifying needs, building value, addressing concerns, and asking for the purchase. The lesson is that retail experience is one of the most underrated preparations for sports sales roles. If you're struggling to find sports internships, get a retail job and treat it like sales training.

Making Every Experience Count, No Matter How Small

The common thread across all these experiences, from major league internships to retail jobs to campus leadership roles, is that I treated each one like it mattered. I didn't phone in the small opportunities while waiting for the big break. I didn't do the minimum at unglamorous jobs while saving my energy for prestigious internships. I showed up fully for everything, did exceptional work regardless of whether it was paid or prestigious, and built relationships with everyone I worked with.

Every experience is an audition for the next opportunity. The supervisor at your small campus event might know someone at a professional team. The colleague you help at an unpaid internship might end up hiring at their next organization. The professor whose research you assist might make an introduction that leads to your first job. You never know which experience or relationship will open the door you need, so you can't afford to treat anything as throwaway. Every time you show up, you're building your reputation. Every interaction is a chance to prove you're reliable, capable, and someone people want to work with. The people who succeed aren't always the most talented, but they're the ones who consistently show up, do quality work, and treat everyone professionally regardless of the situation.

Look for opportunities to add value beyond your assigned responsibilities. At every internship, I looked for ways to contribute beyond what was expected. If I finished my assigned tasks early, I asked what else needed doing. If I saw a problem, I proposed solutions rather than just complaining. If someone was overwhelmed, I offered to help. This wasn't about working nonstop, it was about demonstrating initiative and making myself useful enough that supervisors remembered me and wanted to work with me again. The interns who got hired were almost never the ones who just did their assigned tasks and left; they were the ones who found ways to make themselves indispensable.

Document your experiences and accomplishments as you go, not when you're applying for jobs six months down the road. After every internship or significant experience, I wrote down what I did, what I learned, and what results I achieved. I saved examples of work I created, tracked metrics when possible, and collected references while the experience was fresh. This made updating my resume and preparing for interviews infinitely easier because I wasn't trying to remember details from years ago, I had documentation of exactly what I'd accomplished. Start a simple document or spreadsheet where you track every experience: organization, dates, title, responsibilities, accomplishments, skills developed, and key contacts. Update it immediately after each experience ends. You'll thank yourself later when you're trying to write compelling cover letters or answer interview questions.

Build relationships intentionally, not just transactionally. I stayed in touch with supervisors, colleagues, and mentors from every experience. I sent thank-you notes after my internship ended. I reached out periodically with updates on my career and asked for advice when making decisions. I congratulated people when they got new jobs or promotions. I offered to help when they needed something I could contribute to. These weren't calculated networking moves; rather, they were genuine relationships with people I respected and wanted to stay connected to. But those relationships became my network, and that network has opened doors throughout my career. The lesson is to treat every person you work with as a potential long-term connection, not just someone who serves a purpose in your current role.

The experiences you accumulate early in your career, internships, campus involvement, part-time jobs, volunteer work, and leadership roles aren't just resume lines. They're the foundation of your professional skills, your network, your reputation, and your understanding of how this industry actually works. Treat them all like they matter, because they do. Show up fully, do exceptional work, build genuine relationships, and create a track record of reliability and initiative. That's how you turn experiences into opportunities, and opportunities into a career.

Reilly's perspective on advancement is refreshingly honest: "Being 'good' earns you an internship. Being 'irreplaceable' earns you a job. You have to create value that a team can see, measure, or feel. If you don't, someone else will." The people who rise fastest say yes to the tasks no one else wants, like logging data at midnight, filming bullpens, tagging video, and driving long scouting routes. "Say yes more often than not, your future self will thank you for the experience you gained," Reilly advises. "By saying yes, that word opens up so many doors for you to succeed and thrive. The word yes shows the dedication, the grind, and the love for that specific task."

This isn't a 9-to-5, 40-hours-a-week career. It's missing holidays, not seeing family, and taking the risk of moving across the country to expand opportunities for growth. "Players get the spotlight; staff get the long nights, tight deadlines, and nonstop pressure," Reilly says. "If you don't love the work itself, the industry will push you out quickly. I've seen this happen in just one year."

The work becomes its own reward, but only if you genuinely love the craft of roster building, player evaluation, and organizational strategy. If you're chasing glamour or status, baseball operations will expose that immediately.

Level The Playing Field

Two websites stand at the forefront of helping students break into the sports industry by posting job opportunities. TeamWork Online bills itself as the "#1 Way To Find Jobs In Sports & Entertainment," and for good reason. It's become the gold standard for sports careers. More than just a job board or job aggregator, TeamWork partners directly with teams and organizations to bring thousands of positions across professional teams, leagues, collegiate athletic departments, and sports agencies to a centralized platform. The site allows students to search by role type, organization, and location while also offering career advice, salary insights, and application tracking tools that help candidates stay organized throughout their job search. Beyond job postings, TeamWork Online helps students build their professional network through 100+ events nationwide each year, connecting them directly with industry leaders and creating opportunities to form the kinds of authentic relationships that often lead to actual jobs in this relationship-driven industry. Complementing this is WorkInSports, which not only features extensive job listings but also provides premium resources like resume reviews, industry webinars, and insider access to hiring managers and recruiters actively looking for emerging talent.

Both platforms have democratized access to sports business opportunities by making openings visible and accessible to anyone willing to put in the work, rather than limiting opportunities to those with preexisting connections. For students serious about breaking into sports, these websites aren't optional; they're essential tools that provide the competitive intelligence, direct access, and strategic advantage needed to identify opportunities quickly, apply effectively, and ultimately land that first critical role that launches a career in an industry where timing and persistence often matter just as much as talent.

Beyond traditional job boards, three additional platforms offer comprehensive career development ecosystems that combine job access with education and networking. Sports Business Ventures, which serves thousands of sports professionals, offers The Playbook, a premium membership that includes proven resume templates, networking scripts, LinkedIn contact databases across every NBA and NFL team, daily job listings, weekly masterclasses with industry executives, and on-demand video courses teaching real-world sports business skills. theClubhouse, now owned by General Sports Worldwide, provides a virtual destination where aspiring professionals can access mentorship from over 140 industry veterans, attend live and on-demand webinars, receive one-on-one interview prep and resume coaching, and connect with peers through an active community forum. What sets these platforms apart from simple job boards is their holistic approach. They recognize that breaking into sports requires more than finding open positions; it demands building relationships, developing industry-specific skills, and gaining insider knowledge about how teams and leagues actually operate. For students who learn best through structured education and direct mentorship rather than trial and error, these platforms provide curated pathways that compress years of learning into accessible, actionable resources that can accelerate career entry and advancement in ways that independent job searching simply cannot replicate. Sport Management Worldwide is an online education platform offering certificate programs and courses specifically designed for people looking to break into or advance in the sports industry. They provide practical, career-focused training in areas like sports agency, marketing, analytics, and business operations. The platform also offers networking opportunities and job placement resources to help students transition from education to employment in sports.

When it comes time to actually choosing an internship, not all opportunities are created equal. You need to be strategic about what you accept. "I'm a big believer in having a project and not shadowing, because that is a drain on the employer," explains John Doleva, the President and CEO of the Basketball Hall of Fame, who has supervised countless interns. He's seen the disaster scenario play out repeatedly: "The intern comes in and they don't have a task every day... there's nothing worse than seeing somebody playing games and that's not good for anybody." His advice is direct: "As a student, if you're a junior or a senior, tell me what I'm going to be working on. If it's like, 'well, come in and you can sit and watch some phone calls happening and some Zoom meetings', no thank you."

Experience Acquisition Plan

Develop a strategic 12-month plan to build meaningful experience regardless of your current situation. Create three columns:

1. Formal Internships I'll Apply For
2. Creative Alternatives I'll Pursue
3. Skills I'll Develop Independently

Under Column 1: Formal Internships, list 10-15 specific opportunities with application deadlines, required materials, and any connections you can leverage. Under Column 2: Creative Alternatives, identify 5-7 options such as volunteering for campus athletics, working local sports events, creating content about sports business, conducting informational interview projects, or developing your own initiatives. Under Column 3: Skills Development, list 3-5 specific capabilities you'll build through online courses, books, or practice (examples: Excel proficiency, social media management, graphic design, video editing, public speaking). For each item across all three columns, assign yourself deadlines for completion or application. This isn't a passive wish list. It's an action plan with accountability built in. Review this plan weekly and update it as opportunities materialize or circumstances change. The goal is ensuring you're constantly building experience through multiple channels simultaneously rather than waiting for one perfect internship to appear.

"Stuart's journey in the sports industry reflects what this business is truly about: learning through real experience, staying adaptable, and leading with a genuine commitment to helping others. What I admire most is how he has taken everything he's seen, learned, and lived, and poured it into a book designed to guide the next generation. His perspective doesn't come from theory; it comes from showing up, doing the work, and wanting others to benefit from the lessons he's earned along the way. In a field where giving back often gets overlooked, Stuart stands out for his passion to serve and his drive to help others break into the industry with clarity and confidence." **Brian Davison, Co-Founder, Sports Business Ventures; Former Vice President of Player Development, Milwaukee Bucks; Nike Basketball Executive**

"When I was early on in my career, I reached out to and learned from many sports business professionals about how to have success in the sports industry. These people shared advice about how to set myself up for success, get promoted and make a name for myself in a highly competitive industry. As I've progressed through my career, I've now tried to be that person for others looking to break into the industry. Having known Stuart for many years, he is doing the exact same thing for the next generation of sports business professionals. If you listen to the advice shared within this book, you're going to put yourself into a great position to have success and have a long career in sports." **Taylor Fisher, General Manager, New Hampshire Fisher Cats**

"Understand the connection between a fan and the team they support and follow over time, through the ups and downs. That bond is both the foundation and the ever-evolving energy that drives the sports industry." **Todd Wienke, General Manager, Learfield (Marshall Athletics)**

"The students who succeed in breaking into this industry aren't necessarily the ones with the most polished resumes or degrees from the elite colleges and universities. They're the ones who understand that every conversation matters, every interaction, however brief, makes an impression and teaches you something, and the willingness to pursue opportunities both nationally & internationally can open doors you didn't even know existed. Be flexible learning the business side of sports, become familiar with the CBA and salary cap mechanics if you're heading toward football operations, and remember that this industry rewards people who are both strategic thinkers and relationship builders. Stuart has lived every stage of the journey he's teaching, from grinding through 16 internships and professional experiences, to building a career across some of the most respected organizations in professional sports. He doesn't just understand the business side of breaking in, he understands the people-side, the relationships that open doors, the resilience required when doors close, and how to turn early opportunities into sustained success. He's lived it and his experience is what makes his guidance so valuable." **Chris Olsen, Sr. Director of Football Administration, Atlanta Falcons**

"I landed my first internship at 20 years old by knocking on the office door of a Minor League Baseball team and asking for a job. In hindsight that experience unlocked my career. My advice to aspiring sports professionals is to start now. Volunteer, get an Internship, interview sports professionals, and begin building your resume. Don't just send your resume and profile out and expect to get responses. Go and knock on doors." **Justin Gurney, Vice President, Ticket Sales, Diamond Baseball Holding**

Chapter 6: Getting Creative When You Can't Land an Internship

You've been applying to internships for months and you're getting nowhere. Every application disappears into a black hole, follow-up email gets ignored, and you're starting to wonder if breaking into sports is even possible without connections or a fancy school name. Here's what nobody tells you: formal internships are just one path, and they're not even always the best one. The people who actually make it in this industry aren't the ones who waited around for the perfect internship to save them. They're the ones who got scrappy, created their own opportunities, and found ways to build real experience even when nobody was offering it to them. This chapter shows you exactly how to do that.

"Baseball is a game of failure. The best hitters to ever play the game fail 60% of the time. It can be a very trying and mentally exhausting endeavor. Entering into a career in professional sports can be equally as difficult. It is an industry, like the sports themselves, that can be very unforgiving. You must not only be intelligent and open-minded, but also motivated and resilient. Stuart has spent years in this industry. Use his experiences and knowledge to help you blaze your own trail, and use his book as a cheat code." Brad Ausmus, the Bench Coach for the New York Yankees, and MLB Veteran (15+ Seasons)

When the Traditional Path Isn't Working

Let's address the elephant in the room: what do you do when you're applying to internships and getting nothing but silence and rejection? You've sent out dozens of applications, you've tailored your resume, you've written thoughtful cover letters, and you're still getting nowhere. Maybe you're at a school without strong sports connections, or maybe you're in a market with limited opportunities. Maybe you're competing against hundreds of other applicants for the same few positions. Whatever the reason, the traditional internship path isn't working, and you're starting to panic.

What you need to understand is that formal internships are not the only way to build experience, and sometimes they're not even the best way. Some of my most valuable experiences came from opportunities I created myself rather than positions I applied for. The students who succeed aren't always the ones who land the prestigious internships; they're the ones who get creative, stay scrappy, and find ways to build experience regardless of whether traditional opportunities materialize. This chapter is about how to build a competitive resume and develop real skills even when nobody's hiring you for formal internships.

The "Always Say Yes" Philosophy: Early in your career, your default answer to almost every opportunity should be "yes," especially the ones that seem small, unpaid, or beneath you. You have no idea which experience will lead somewhere important, which connection will matter five years from now, or which seemingly insignificant task will teach you something valuable. The opportunities that seem least important at the time often end up mattering most.

I said yes to working a fundraising table at the Naismith Basketball Hall of Fame Hoophall Classic when I was a freshman, which is not exactly glamorous work. That led to being noticed by supervisors who gave me more responsibility the next year, eventually making me media and liaison supervisor managing over 75 volunteers. I said yes to being a scorekeeper for Springfield's baseball team, translated as unpaid work that meant showing up for every game regardless of weather. That led to relationships with coaches and athletic department staff who later made introductions that led to internships. I said yes to working security at the spring concert, or basically standing around making sure drunk college students didn't cause problems.

The worst that happens when you say yes is you spend a few hours doing something that doesn't lead anywhere, but builds your work ethic and expands your network. The best that happens is that an "insignificant" opportunity becomes the turning point in your career. I've seen it happen too many times to dismiss any opportunity as not worth your time. When you can't land formal internships, saying yes to everything creates the volume of experiences that eventually leads to breakthrough opportunities.

Volunteer Your Way Into the Industry

Volunteering is one of the most underutilized strategies for breaking into sports. Almost every team, league, event, and organization needs volunteers, and while unpaid work isn't ideal long-term, it's an incredibly effective way to get your foot in the door, build skills, and prove yourself when you can't get hired for paid positions. Identify events in your area that need volunteers. Professional and college games, tournaments, championships, marathons, golf events, festivals, and sports events happen constantly, and almost all of them need volunteer support. Sign up for everything you can manage around your class schedule. The goal isn't just to add lines to your resume. It's to get exposure to different aspects of sports operations, meet people who work in the industry, and prove you're reliable and capable.

Work for the college's athletic department (even unpaid). If you're struggling to land professional internships, your college athletic department is sitting right there, probably desperate for help, and most students completely ignore it. The athletics department offers accessible opportunities to build real sports experience without competing against thousands of applicants or relocating for summers. Approach coaches, administrators, and operations staff directly. Don't wait for formal job postings, as most campus athletic departments don't formally advertise student help because they traditionally work more informally. Email coaches, the athletic director, marketing coordinators, operations managers, and compliance officers. Offer specific skills and availability: "I have video editing experience and would love to help create highlight reels for recruiting," or "I'm available Saturday mornings and would be happy to help with game-day setup and operations." Make it easy for them to say yes by being specific about what you offer and when you're available.

Work game days for as many sports as possible. Most athletic departments need student help for game-day operations, setup, ticketing, ushering, hospitality, statistics, security, and clean-up. Volunteer to work games for sports you don't even care about. Each game is exposure to event operations, crisis management, and fan service. You'll learn how events run, what can go wrong, and how to stay calm under pressure. You'll also meet coaches, administrators, and visiting team staff who might remember you later.

Create your own projects and opportunities. When opportunities don't exist, create them. Some of the most impressive resume items I've seen from students weren't formal internships, and instead were self-initiated projects that demonstrated initiative, creativity, and genuine passion for the industry. Start a sports blog, podcast, or YouTube channel analyzing your favorite team or sport. This accomplishes multiple things, like building a portfolio of content you can show employers; demonstrates you understand the sport and industry deeply enough to create thoughtful analysis; develops your writing or speaking skills; and shows initiative and self-motivation. You don't need thousands of followers for this to be valuable. You need quality content that shows you can think critically about sports business. When I'm hiring, a candidate with a well-written sports business blog analyzing ticket pricing strategies or marketing campaigns impresses me far more than someone with a generic internship where they just did busy work. Conduct informational interviews and turn them into content. Reach out to 10-15 professionals in roles you're interested in and request 15-minute informational interviews about their career paths. Then write blog posts, create LinkedIn articles, or produce podcast episodes sharing what you learned. You build your network by connecting with industry professionals, you learn genuine insights about career paths, you create content demonstrating your interest and initiative, and you stay on people's radar because you're featuring them in your content. Several students I know have turned informational interview projects into job offers because the professionals they interviewed were so impressed by their initiative that they referred them for opportunities.

In the course I teach, I require students to conduct an informational interview with ten sports professionals and submit a one-page reflection on each conversation; it's a graded assignment, not optional. One student reached out to a manager with the Milwaukee Bucks to fulfill this requirement. That conversation turned into an internship offer. The internship turned into a full-time position. His entire career trajectory shifted because of a conversation he was required to have for a grade.

Create social media content for local teams or organizations that aren't doing it well. Find a local youth sports organization, high school team, college club sport, or community league with weak or nonexistent social media presence. Reach out and offer to run their social media for free for a season. Create content, build their following, and document the results. This gives you portfolio pieces, demonstrates tangible results (example: "grew Instagram following from 200 to 2,000," "increased engagement 300%"), and provides a reference who can speak to your social media skills. When you apply for marketing roles, you'll have actual work to show rather than just saying you're interested in sports marketing.

The "Start Local, Think Smaller" Strategy

Most students make the mistake of only targeting the big names - the NFL, NBA, MLB, major college programs. They send applications to the Yankees, the Lakers, the Patriots, and wonder why they never hear back. Meanwhile, they're completely ignoring the minor league baseball team 30 minutes away, the indoor soccer team in their city, the college summer league, or the regional sports commission that would actually respond to their emails.

Smaller organizations are often better learning experiences than major league teams, especially early in your career. At a Single-A baseball team, you might be one of the 15 people running an entire organization. You'll do actual marketing work, handle real budgets, make decisions that matter, and see the direct results of your efforts. You'll get responsibility far beyond what any entry-level person gets at a major league organization. At the Yankees, you might be intern number seven in a department of fifty people, spending your summer making copies and sitting in on meetings where you don't speak. At a minor league team, you might be running the entire social media presence or coordinating all the in-game promotions by week three.

The people running smaller organizations also tend to be more accessible and more willing to take chances on hungry young people, because they remember what it was like to be in your position. The general manager of a minor league team will probably respond to your email. The president of a major league team may not. The marketing director at a mid-major college will meet you for coffee. The marketing director at Alabama may ignore you.

Plus, the sports industry is smaller than you think. The people working at smaller organizations today are often the same people who'll be at major organizations tomorrow. The GM at that Single-A team might be running a Triple-A team in five years and a major league front office in ten. The relationships you build at smaller organizations often matter more than the name on your resume. I've seen students turn down opportunities at minor league teams because they didn't think the name was impressive enough, then watch other students take those jobs, work hard, build relationships, and get referred into major league positions two years later.

My freshman year internship with the Frederick Keys, the Single-A affiliate of the Baltimore Orioles, was my first real look at how a professional sports organization actually runs from the inside. Working alongside supervisors, fellow interns, and managers across different departments taught me early on that the sports industry is smaller and more connected than most people realize. You never know who you're standing next to - the people I worked with that summer have since gone on to the Washington Commanders, San Diego Padres, Nashville Sounds, New Hampshire Fisher Cats, Reno Aces, and one is now a broadcaster calling MLB games. Start where you can actually get in the door. Build real skills. Make genuine connections. Worry about the prestige later.

The Transfer-of-Skills Approach

When you can't get sports experience directly, the next best thing is getting adjacent experience that demonstrates the same skills sports organizations need. The fundamental skills of marketing, operations, sales, event management, and customer service are the same whether you're working for a basketball team, a concert venue, or a local restaurant. If you can prove you're good at those fundamentals elsewhere, you can make the case that those skills transfer to sports.

Work for a local concert venue or performing arts center. Event operations are event operations, whether it's a playoff game or a concert. You're learning how to manage crowds, handle logistics under pressure, coordinate security and concessions, deal with last-minute crises, and create positive experiences for attendees. When you interview for sports event operations roles, you can talk about the time you managed entry for a 5,000-person concert or handled a medical emergency during a show, or reorganized the volunteer coordination system. The skills are identical.

Do marketing or social media for any small business. If you can help a local coffee shop, boutique, or restaurant grow their social media following and drive actual business results, you can do the same for a sports team. The fundamentals of content creation, audience engagement, brand voice, and measuring ROI don't change based on industry. When you're interviewing for sports marketing roles, and everyone else is saying, "I'm really passionate about sports marketing," you can say, "I ran social media for a local business and increased their Instagram following from 500 to 3,000 in four months, which directly led to a 25% increase in weekend traffic." You have actual results to point to, not just enthusiasm.

Help with your school's student activities programming or campus events. Planning a concert, comedy show, festival, or speaker series for your campus teaches you budgeting, vendor negotiation, marketing, logistics, and crisis management. You're coordinating multiple moving pieces, working with limited resources, trying to create memorable experiences, and measuring success through attendance and feedback. Those are exactly the same challenges sports organizations face. A student who successfully planned their school's spring concert and drew 2,000 students has more relevant experience than someone who just shadowed at a sports organization.

Get sales experience anywhere you can find it. Call center work, retail, fundraising for nonprofits – any job that requires you to get people to spend money teaches you skills that directly translate to sports sales. Sales is sales. If you can sell gym memberships, or insurance, or donations, you can sell season tickets. And sales roles are often the easiest entry point into sports organizations because there's constant turnover and they're typically always hiring. Students look down on ticket sales, but I've seen dozens of people start in ticket sales and move into marketing, partnerships, or operations within a few years.

The key is being able to articulate the transfer. Don't just list "worked at a concert venue" on your resume and hope someone makes the connection. In your cover letter and interviews, explicitly explain: "While this experience wasn't in sports, I developed skills in event operations, crisis management, and customer service that directly apply to game-day operations for your organization." Make it easy for them to see how your experience translates.

The "Become Indispensable at One Thing" Method

Instead of being generally interested in sports and hoping someone gives you a chance, become genuinely skilled at one specific, valuable thing that sports organizations need. Don't be a generalist when you have no experience. Be a specialist in something tangible. Pick one skill, get really good at it, and offer that skill everywhere until people know you as "the person who does [that thing]."

Maybe you learn graphic design. You get good at Adobe Creative Suite, you study design principles, you practice constantly, and you build a portfolio. Now, when you volunteer or reach out to organizations, you're not asking, "Can I help with anything?" You're saying, "I can create graphics for your social media, game-day programs, promotional materials, and ticket designs." You're offering something specific and valuable that they actually need. You're not just another eager student; you're solving a real problem they have. Small organizations especially are always looking for good design work because they can't sometimes afford to hire a full-time designer.

Maybe you develop data analytics skills. You learn Excel at an advanced level, you understand basic statistics, maybe you pick up some Python or R. Now you can analyze ticket sales data, create attendance reports, track social media metrics, or build dashboards that help organizations make better decisions. Most smaller sports organizations are sitting on data they don't know how to use. If you can turn that data into actionable insights, you become valuable immediately.

Maybe you become an excellent photographer, develop strong writing skills, learn Spanish, or get certified in CPR and emergency response. It almost doesn't matter what the skill is, as long as it's genuinely useful and you're genuinely good at it. The point is that you're not generic anymore. When people think of you, they don't think "college student who likes sports." They think, "Oh, that's the person who made those great graphics for our tournament," or, "That's the one who runs our video content." This approach also makes networking easier and more natural. Instead of awkwardly asking, "Do you have any internship opportunities?" you can say, "I noticed your Instagram is fantastic and I'd love to help create some content for you." You're leading with value instead of need. You're making it easy for people to say yes because you're offering to solve a specific problem they have.

Being great at one thing also makes you memorable. In a sea of students who all say they're "passionate about sports" and "hard-working team players," you're the one with an actual skill that stands out. When opportunities come up, people remember you because you're not just enthusiastic, you're useful.

The Alumni Backdoor

Your college's alumni network is one of the most underutilized resources for breaking into sports, and most students overlook it. People are unusually loyal to their alma mater. Someone who might ignore a cold email from a random student will often respond when that student goes to the same school they attended. It's an instant connection and conversation starter that makes people more willing to help.

Go to LinkedIn and search for alumni who work in sports. Use your school's alumni database if they have one. Filter by company, search for teams, leagues, agencies, or sports media companies. You'll probably find dozens or even hundreds of people from your school working in various sports roles. These are people who understand exactly where you are because they sat in the same classrooms, walked the same campus, and faced the same challenges trying to break into the industry.

When you reach out, lead with the shared connection. Don't send a generic "I'm interested in sports and would love to learn about your career" email that could be sent to anyone. Make it specific: "I'm a current student at [School] studying [major], and I came across your profile and saw you're working in [Department] for the [Team]. I'm really interested in learning more about how you made the transition from [School] to professional sports, and I'd love to hear about your experience if you have 15-20 minutes for a quick call."

You're not asking for a job. You're not asking them to hire you. You're just asking for advice and information, which is a much lower barrier. Most people are willing to spend 15 minutes talking about themselves and their career, especially to someone from their school. And what happens is you have a good conversation, you ask thoughtful questions, you follow up with a thank you note, and now you have a connection in the industry who knows who you are. When an opportunity opens up, you're not a stranger anymore. When they need to refer someone, they might think of you. When you apply for a job at their organization, you can mention, "I spoke with [Name] who suggested I apply," and suddenly your application gets more attention.

I've seen this work countless times. A student reaches out to an alum working for an NBA team. They have a 20-minute conversation about the alum's career path. Three months later, the team had an opening. The alum forwards the job posting to the student before it's publicly advertised, or mentions the student to the hiring manager, or agrees to be a reference. The student gets an interview that they might not have gotten through the normal application process. Sometimes the alum doesn't have an immediate opportunity but connects the student with someone else in the industry who does.

The key is being genuine and strategic about it. Don't just spam every alum you can find with the same generic message. Pick people whose roles genuinely interest you, do some research on their background, and personalize your outreach. Ask smart questions. Show that you've thought about your career and aren't just randomly reaching out to everyone. Follow up. Stay in touch. These relationships compound over time. Alumni are also more likely to be honest with you about the realities of their roles and career paths. They'll tell you what they wish they'd known, what skills actually matter, what the job is really like versus what people think it's like. That information is valuable even if the conversation doesn't directly lead to a job.

Don't limit yourself to alumni in senior positions either. Someone who graduated three years ago and is working in an entry-level role might be even more helpful because they remember exactly what it's like to be where you are right now. They know what worked for them recently. They might know about internship programs or entry-level openings. They're close enough to your situation to give current, relevant advice.

The Persistence Timeline

Breaking into sports often comes down to simple math and persistence. Most people give up too early. They send out 25 applications, get no responses, and decide it's impossible. Meanwhile, the person who makes 100 contacts, follows up consistently, and stays visible for months, or even years eventually breaks through. You need a system that ensures you're consistently putting yourself out there without burning out.

Set a specific, manageable weekly schedule for outreach and applications. Don't just randomly apply to things when you remember or when you're feeling motivated. Make it routine. For example, every Monday reach out to five new people for informational interviews. Not five when you feel like it. Five every single Monday. Use LinkedIn, alumni databases, team staff directories, whatever you need. Send personalized, thoughtful messages asking for 15-20 minutes of their time to learn about their career path. Five messages take maybe an hour if you're doing them thoughtfully. That's 20 new contacts per month, 240 per year. You think you won't get somewhere after having 240 conversations with people in the industry?

Every Wednesday, apply to three opportunities. Internships, volunteer positions, part-time jobs, whatever's available. Three applications per week is 12 per month, over 150 per year. You're not just sending out a few applications and hoping, you're systematically covering every opportunity that exists. Some will be reached, some will be good fits, some will be safety options. Apply anyway. You never know which one will respond.

Every Friday, follow up on previous outreach. Email people you haven't heard back from. Thank people who did respond. Update contacts on what you've been working on. Send articles or resources that might interest them. Stay on people's radar. Most opportunities don't come from the first contact - they come from the fifth or seventh or tenth time someone hears from you and finally has something to offer or remembers you when an opportunity opens up.

Track everything in a simple spreadsheet. Who you contacted, when, what you said, whether they responded, and when to follow up. This keeps you organized and ensures nothing falls through the cracks. It also lets you see your progress over time. When you're feeling discouraged, you can look back and see "I've had 47 conversations this semester" instead of just feeling like nothing's working.

The reality is that most people quit after a month or two. They send some emails, apply to some jobs, don't get immediate results, and give up. If you stick with this system for six months, you'll have made 120+ new contacts and applied to 75+ opportunities. Someone will respond. Something will break through.

Maybe it won't be the perfect opportunity, but it'll be a door opening, which leads to another door, which leads to the opportunity you actually want.

I've seen this work too many times to doubt it. The students who break into sports aren't always the most talented or connected; they're the ones who are systematically persistent. They don't take rejection personally. They don't give up after a bad month. They treat job searching like a part-time job itself, with consistent hours and consistent effort, and eventually the math works in their favor.

Set the schedule. Track your efforts. Stay consistent. Give it at least six months before you even think about whether it's working. Persistence isn't glamorous, but it's more reliable than talent or luck.

Alternative Experience Portfolio

When traditional internships aren't materializing, create your own opportunities and document them professionally. This week, take three specific actions:

1. Identify two upcoming local sports events (high school championships, college games, community races, youth tournaments) and email the organizers offering to volunteer in a specific capacity based on your skills (social media coverage, event logistics, fan experience support). Use the email templates from Chapter 11, emphasizing what you'll contribute rather than what you'll gain.

2. Choose one sports organization with weak social media presence (local youth league, club sport, community program) and create a one-page proposal offering to manage their social media for one season, including specific content ideas and posting schedule.

3. Start a sports business project. This could be a blog analyzing ticket pricing strategies, a podcast interviewing local sports professionals, a video series breaking down marketing campaigns, or a newsletter covering sports business news. Commit to producing content weekly for 90 days.

As you complete these projects, document everything: save examples of your work, track measurable results (engagement growth, attendance increases, content published), and collect testimonials from people you helped. This portfolio becomes proof of initiative and capability when formal internships aren't on your resume.

"So excited that Stuart has put this book together. Given his experience and insight, the book functions like a GPS and the directions are from someone who has actually driven the route." **Dr. Bill Sutton, Director Emeritus of the Vinik Sport & Entertainment Mgmt. Program at the University of South Florida, Former NBA**

"The sports industry is a tight-knit, elite circle where everyone is chasing the same gold standard. At its core, sales is a volume game, but the wins actually come down to two things: how well you build relationships and how hard you're willing to out-hustle the person next to you. Stuart picked up on that rhythm immediately. During our time together, his ability to translate that drive into massive, tangible revenue and do it so quickly was genuinely impressive." **Kyne Sheehy Assistant Athletic Director, Ticket Sales, Premium Seating, and Service, University of Notre Dame**

"Sports and entertainment is an industry all about service to others at every level. To really make an impact on this industry, keep your focus on serving people. Doesn't matter if you are an executive leader of a team, just starting out as a new co-worker, or whenever you're engaging with a customer - we are called to serve. Serving others with passion will give you purpose and daily motivation to make sure you see everyone win. When others are winning, you will constantly find yourself in a winning culture. A winning culture combined with humble, innovative, servant leaders that have a high tolerance for ambiguity and strive for excellence is the ultimate recipe for success." **Sean Penix, Sr. Associate Athletic Director, Commercial Revenue & Strategy, Southern Methodist University**

"I'm honored to contribute an acknowledgment to this book, a resource that will undoubtedly become a blueprint for anyone aspiring to build a career in the sports business. Stuart's voice is one worth listening to, not just because of his deep experience across the industry, but because of the way he shows up every day. He is a phenomenal sales leader, an exceptional salesperson, and one of the most relentless follow-up machines I've ever encountered. In an industry where persistence, preparation, and consistency separate the good from the great, Stuart embodies all three. His insights come from years of doing the work, leading teams, developing talent, and delivering results at the highest levels. When he speaks on the truths of the sports world, you can trust that they come from firsthand knowledge and a career built on integrity and execution. This book reflects that. It offers clarity, direction, and real-world wisdom, the kind of guidance I wish every young professional entering the sports industry could have in their hands. If you're reading this, you're learning from one of the best. I'm grateful for the chance to acknowledge his work and even more grateful for the impact he continues to have on our industry." **Jamie Hernandez, Executive Vice President & Co-Lead, Partner Success (Sports), Fevo**

"When I entered into the industry, the leadership team had the sales and service staff read Legacy by James Kerr. What stood out to me was the concept of sweeping the sheds and never being too big for any assignment or role. In the sports industry, we have to adapt and wear many hats. Whether you're a sales leader or an inside sales representative, never lose sight of the small things that got you where you are and always be ready to take on the tasks that no one else wants to. Hard work beats talent when talent doesn't work hard." **Zach Johnston, Vice President, Ticket Sales and Service, Dallas Pulse**

Chapter 7: Moving for Opportunities

The job you want probably isn't in the city where you currently live. That's the hard truth about working in sports. There are only so many teams, and they're scattered across the country, which means if you're only willing to work in your hometown or wherever you went to college, you're competing for maybe 1% of the available opportunities while everyone else is going after the other 99%. Geographic flexibility isn't just a nice bonus in this industry, it's often the difference between getting stuck in mediocre roles and actually building the career you want. This chapter walks you through how to relocate strategically, build a life from scratch in a new city, and turn what feels like a scary upheaval into one of the best decisions you'll ever make.

Why Geographic Flexibility Matters in Sports

Sports is a geographically distributed industry. There are only 30 NBA teams, 30 MLB teams, 32 NFL teams, and they're spread across the country. If you limit yourself to working only in your hometown or your college city, you're competing for a tiny fraction of available opportunities. Being willing to relocate, especially to smaller markets that other people avoid, immediately expands your options and often accelerates your career because you're competing against fewer people who are willing to make that move.

Early in your career, you might need to take a minor league job in a small market to get your foot in the door. A few years later, a better opportunity might open in a mid-size market across the country. Later still, your dream role might finally be available in a major market, but only if you've built the experience and network by being willing to move when others weren't. The people who advance fastest are often the ones who said yes to opportunities in places like Boise, Des Moines, Albuquerque, or Chattanooga while others held out for New York, Los Angeles, or Chicago and waited years for openings that might never come.

Geographic flexibility also gives you negotiating leverage. When employers know you're willing to relocate, you become a more attractive candidate because you're not limited to local opportunities. And when you're already working somewhere, being willing to move for the right promotion makes you more valuable because organizations know you're prioritizing career growth over geographic comfort.

Michos also mentions, "I've had to move from my hometown to break into the industry. From CT, RI, DC, MIA, NY. Because of this, I was able to grow professionally but more importantly, personally. I got out of my comfort zone, took on opportunities I never dreamed of, and created relationships that last a lifetime."

The Reality: To Move Up, You Must Move On

There's a saying in sports: to move up, you must move on. For many people pursuing careers in this industry, geographic flexibility isn't optional, it's essential. The best opportunities aren't always in your hometown or where you went to college. Sometimes your dream job is in a city you've never visited, for a team you never cared about, or in a market you know nothing about. And if you're not willing to relocate, you're immediately limiting your options in an already competitive industry.

While geography can be vital to personal and professional success, early on in your career the people and leadership should be priority. Tanner Natzke, the Founder of the *Attitude, Efforts, Results* podcast, reminds young professionals that people and leadership are the ones that are going to truly develop who you are as a person and professional. The second most important thing is career development and culture. Without a forward thinking and positive culture, moving to a new opportunity can hinder your professional success. When you get all of these, then you can choose geography as the decisive reason to move for a new role.

Ross Lippe, the Manager of Brand Alliances for the MLS, has this to say: "You limit yourself significantly when you narrow your job market. Expand where you're willing to work, and all sorts of doors will open for you."

Whether you're a college graduate starting your first role in sports and moving to a new city, or you're several years into your career chasing a promotion that requires relocation, the thought of moving away from home can be legitimately scary. Leaving behind your support system, your friends, and your familiar routines, or not knowing where the grocery store is, where to work out, and where to meet people is all daunting. This fear deters people from pursuing promotions and chasing their dreams. But for those who take the road less traveled and embrace the uncertainty of relocation, it can be extraordinarily rewarding both professionally and personally.

I've lived in eleven states and counting, and building new communities is something I'm constantly doing. My wife is a travel nurse, which means we move every three to four months to a new city and state, and honestly, we love it. It allows us the opportunity to see parts of the U.S. we only could've dreamed of visiting and make friends and memories along the way. Don't get me wrong, it's nerve wracking knowing we might not know anyone in the city and need to figure out where to do our daily shopping, where to find good food, and how to build a social life from scratch. But when we leave each place, we've built a community with new friends, discovered hidden gems, and created memories that wouldn't exist if we'd stayed comfortable in one place.

The reality is if you want to maximize your career trajectory in sports, you need to be willing to move. Not necessarily every three months like we do, but you need to be open to relocating for the right opportunities. The question isn't whether you'll move, but how you'll make those moves successful, both professionally and personally.

When Growth Stops, It's Time to Move On

One of the most important career decisions you'll make is recognizing when you've outgrown your current role. This isn't about chasing a fancier title or jumping ship because you're bored after six months. It's about honest self-assessment: Are you still learning? Are you being challenged? Is your manager investing in your development? Are there opportunities to take on new responsibilities? If you've been in a role for 18-24 months and you're no longer growing, if you've mastered your responsibilities and there's no clear path to expand your role or move up within the organization, that's when you need to start exploring what's next. Growth is the currency of your early career, far more valuable than a prestigious title or a slightly higher salary. When you stop growing, you stop building the skills and experiences that make you marketable for future opportunities. Don't mistake comfort for contentment. Just because a job is easy or you're good at it doesn't mean you should stay if it's not pushing you forward.

However, don't fall into the trap of moving on simply because another organization offers you a better title. Natzke talks about how too many people leave growth opportunities for roles that sound impressive but offer little actual development. A promotion to "Manager" at a disorganized, resource-poor organization might look good on LinkedIn, but if you're not learning from strong leaders, if you're not being mentored, and if you're not building skills that translate to future roles, you've traded growth for a title. Similarly, don't skip around every year just because you can. Job hopping purely for titles creates a resume that signals you're chasing prestige rather than building expertise. Employers value professionals who stay long enough to see projects through, who demonstrate commitment, and who can point to tangible accomplishments beyond just collecting different job titles. Before you move on, ask yourself: What have I actually accomplished here? What skills have I built? What can I point to that shows I made an impact? If the answer is "not much, but I got a new title," you're making lateral moves disguised as progress, and eventually, that catches up with you.

John Michos, the Premium Sales Manager for the New York Mets, reminisces, "I've been fortunate to work for great teams, but more importantly, great leaders. They say follow the people when deciding where to work. That rings true 100%. Your leadership team will give you the tools to succeed with the goal of growing internally. If there isn't an opportunity that lines up with your timeline, they will help guide you externally."

The Practical Reality of Relocating

Let's talk about the logistics of actually moving for sports jobs, because this is where people get overwhelmed and back out of opportunities. Moving is expensive, complicated, and stressful, but it's also manageable if you plan strategically and use the right resources.

Budget for moving costs realistically. Moving isn't cheap, and sports organizations rarely cover relocation expenses for entry-level or early-career positions. You need to budget for things like transportation (gas if driving or flights if flying), moving truck or portable storage rental, security deposits and first month's rent, utilities setup fees, furniture and household items if moving to an unfurnished place, and living expenses before your first paycheck arrives. Costs can vary depending on distance and whether you're moving furnished or unfurnished. Start saving as soon as you know you'll be relocating, and explore whether family can help with initial costs that you'll repay once you're earning.

Consider short-term housing options before committing long-term. One of the biggest mistakes people make is signing a year-long lease before they've even started the job or explored the city. You don't know the neighborhoods, you don't know your commute, and you don't know if you'll even like the job enough to stay a full year. Short-term housing, ranging 1-3 months, gives you time to figure out the city, confirm the job is the right fit, and find permanent housing strategically rather than desperately. Furnished Finders is your best friend for short-term housing. Furnished Finders specializes in short-term, furnished rentals, typically 1-3 months, which is perfect for sports professionals relocating temporarily or wanting flexibility before committing long-term. These rentals are fully furnished with kitchens, which means you don't need to buy furniture, kitchenware, or household items immediately. You can move in with just your clothes and personal items, which dramatically reduces moving costs and complexity. The rentals are often cheaper than extended-stay hotels and far more comfortable. Because my wife is a travel nurse and we move every three to four months, we've used Furnished Finders almost every time when relocating, and it's been invaluable for having a comfortable, affordable place to land while figuring out the city and my long-term housing situation.

Beyond Furnished Finders, explore Airbnb for monthly rentals (often discounted compared to nightly rates), corporate housing companies that cater to relocating professionals, subletting from people who are traveling or on work assignments (check Craigslist, Facebook housing groups, or university housing boards if there's a college in the city), and extended-stay hotels like Extended Stay America or Residence Inn if you need something immediately and don't have time to search for better options. Short-term housing costs more per month than signing a lease, but it's worth it for the flexibility and reduced stress while you're adjusting to a new job and city.

One of the most underutilized resources for securing housing is your institution's alumni office, a network that can prove invaluable when relocating for a new opportunity in sport management. These offices maintain comprehensive databases of graduates, including their current locations and contact information. When you reach out to your alumni office about an upcoming move, they can facilitate introductions to graduates who have previously hosted students or young professionals, or who may be interested in doing so. These arrangements often come at significantly reduced rates, and in some cases, alumni offer housing at no cost for short-term stays.

This approach offers several distinct advantages. First, you're connecting with fellow graduates who share your institutional bond and understand the challenges of starting a career in the field. Second, alumni who participate in these programs typically have an established track record of hosting students, and the alumni office has vetted them as trustworthy contacts. This built-in screening process provides an added layer of security and peace of mind during what can otherwise be an uncertain transition. Don't overlook this resource; a simple conversation with your alumni office could open doors to affordable, reliable housing arrangements that ease your entry into a new market. Often, these alumni are empty nesters whose children have moved out for college or entered the workforce. With bedrooms now vacant, they welcome the opportunity to host young professionals entering the workforce.

Morria Heilman, a Springfield College classmate, lived this firsthand during her internship with the Brewster Whitecaps of the Cape Cod Baseball League. Through the Springfield College alumni network, she was connected with alumni who were empty nesters looking to open their home to a young professional just starting out and just like that, the housing problem that stops so many people from taking a leap on a great opportunity was solved. It's a perfect example of how a strong alumni network isn't just about job connections, it's about the whole infrastructure of building a career.

When you're ready for long-term housing, do your research. Once you've been in the city a few months, you understand commute times, neighborhoods, cost of living, and where you want to actually live. Talk to colleagues about which neighborhoods they recommend. Use crime mapping tools to check safety. Test your commute during rush hour before committing. Visit neighborhoods on weekends to see what they're like when you're not working. Read online reviews of apartment complexes, but take them with skepticism, as people usually only review when they're angry. Tour multiple places, negotiate where possible, and don't rush into the first place that's available just because you're tired of temporary housing.

Budgeting for your new city realistically. Cost of living varies dramatically across cities, and your sports salary doesn't adjust proportionally. A $40,000 salary goes a lot further in Birmingham, Alabama, than in San Francisco, California. Before accepting a job, research actual costs in that city: average rent for a one-bedroom in safe neighborhoods, utilities, transportation (will you need a car or can you use public transit?), groceries, and general expenses. Use tools like SmartAsset or Nerdwallet's cost of living calculators to compare. Make sure the salary actually works for that market; sometimes a lower-paying job in a cheaper city leaves you with more disposable income than a higher-paying job in an expensive market.

Adjusting to a New City: Building Your Life From Scratch

Moving to a new city for work is exciting, but it's also lonely and disorienting at first. You don't know anyone beyond colleagues. You don't know where anything is. You don't have your routines, your favorite spots, or your support system. Building a life in a new place takes intentional effort. It doesn't happen automatically just because you show up for work every day.

Don't rely solely on work friends. When you move to a city for a job, it's easy to rely entirely on colleagues and work friends. They're the people you see daily, they're going through similar experiences, and socializing with them is comfortable and convenient. It's great initially that they help you get a lay of the land, recommend restaurants and neighborhoods, and provide social connection when you don't know anyone else. The problem is what happens when their careers come calling and they move away? What happens when they leave the organization and you don't see them anymore? What happens if you leave that job, do you suddenly have no social life in the city you're living in? Relying exclusively on work relationships means your social life is fragile and tied entirely to one job, which sometimes isn't sustainable or healthy. Not to mention that, by finding friends outside of work, it'll make the city feel more like home. When you're seeing the same people day in and day out, especially on those 14-hour gamedays, it can become repetitive. When your social network is just work colleagues, usually conversations revolve around work. Personally after a 50-hour work week, the last thing I want to talk about is my job. I challenge you to go outside your comfort zone and build a life beyond work from the beginning.

Find Your League

Most people working in sports played sports growing up or at least participated in athletics recreationally. Use that and find your league, literally. Finding recreational sports leagues or fitness communities in your new city is one of the fastest and most effective ways to build a social network and feel at home.

I participate in group workouts, hiking, running, skiing, and ultimate frisbee, depending on where I'm living and what's available. These activities keep me physically active, which helps with stress and mental health, but more importantly, they're how I meet people and build community quickly. When I moved to Scottsdale, Arizona, I was fortunate enough to be introduced to a fitness studio that became one of the most welcoming communities I've ever experienced. The workouts were great, but the friendships and connections I made there transformed my experience in that city.

How To Find Your League

Write down what sports and activities you enjoy or want to try. Be specific: consider team sports like basketball, soccer, softball, volleyball, flag football, kickball; individual sports like running, cycling, swimming, climbing; fitness classes like CrossFit, HIIT, yoga, barre, spin, boxing; or outdoor activities like hiking, skiing, kayaking. Once you have your list, start searching.

Use Facebook to find local groups and leagues. Search "[your city] [your activity]" and you'll find groups, leagues, and communities (examples: "Phoenix adult soccer league," "Seattle hiking group," "Austin ultimate frisbee," "Denver runners"). Join these groups, introduce yourself as new to the city, and show up to events and games. Most recreational sports communities are welcoming to newcomers because they're always looking for more players and participants.

Use Google to find top-rated gyms, studios, and facilities. Search "best CrossFit gyms in [city]," "top yoga studios in [city]," or "climbing gyms near me." Read reviews, check out their websites and social media to get a feel for the community vibe, and visit a few places before committing. Many offer free trial classes or week passes, which let you test whether it's a good fit. Look for places that emphasize community, not just individual workouts. Those are where you'll actually meet people and build friendships.

Check out Meetup.com for organized activities and social groups. Meetup is specifically designed for connecting people around shared interests. Search your city and browse categories like Sports & Fitness, Outdoor & Adventure, or Social Activities. You'll find running clubs, hiking groups, pickup basketball games, cycling crews, and countless other options. The beauty of Meetup is that everyone there is explicitly trying to meet new people, so it's less awkward than trying to break into established friend groups.

Use ClassPass or Mindbody to explore different fitness options. Both platforms let you try different studios, gyms, and classes without committing to memberships. This is perfect when you're new to a city and want to sample what's available before deciding where to invest your time and money. Try a yoga studio one day, a boxing gym the next, a climbing gym after that, and you'll quickly figure out what you enjoy and where the communities feel welcoming.

Show up consistently, not just once. The key to building community through sports and fitness is consistency. Going to one pickup basket-ball game or attending one yoga class won't build friendships. Going every week for months will. People start recognizing you, conversations deepen beyond small talk, and eventually someone invites you to grab food after the game or meet up outside the activity. Consistency transforms you from "that new person" to "part of the group."

Leverage your college alumni network. Your alma mater is a built-in network in every city, and most people underutilize it. College alumni groups provide instant common ground: you went to the same school, you shared similar experiences, you probably know some of the same people or places even if you were there at different times. That shared connection makes it significantly easier to build relationships in a new city. Reach out to your alma mater about local alumni groups and events. Most colleges have regional alumni chapters that organize networking events, social gatherings, game watches, and volunteer activities. Email your alumni office, check your school's alumni website, or search Facebook for groups. Attend events even if you feel awkward going alone. Everyone there is explicitly open to meeting fellow alumni, so it's far less intimidating than trying to break into random social groups.

If your school doesn't have an active local chapter, use LinkedIn to find alumni in your city. Go to LinkedIn's search bar, click "People," then use filters to select your city and your alma mater under "Schools." Now you have a list of everyone who works in your area and went to your school. Send personalized connection requests: "Hi [Name], I'm a fellow [School] alum who just moved to

[City] for a job with [Organization]. Would love to connect with other [School] grads in the area and hear about your experience in [City]." Many will accept, some will respond, and a few might offer to grab coffee or give you advice about the city. Even if they don't become close friends, they're part of your network and can make introductions to others.

Connect through religious or community groups. If you're a religious person and attend services, your church, synagogue, mosque, temple, or other faith community can be an immediate source of connection and support in a new city. Religious communities are often explicitly focused on welcoming newcomers and helping people build connections, which makes them ideal for people relocating.

Attend services consistently and get involved beyond just showing up. Going to services once or twice won't build community; you're just another face in the crowd. Going every week, introducing yourself to people, and getting involved in smaller groups, volunteer activities, study groups, or social events is how you actually build relationships. Most faith communities have affinity groups (young professionals, singles, families, etc.) or service opportunities (volunteering for community outreach, helping with events, joining committees) that make it easier to meet people with shared values and interests.

Other Strategies for Building Community in a New City

Beyond sports leagues, alumni networks, and faith communities, here are additional strategies for building social connections when you relocate. Say yes to invitations, even when you'd rather stay home. When colleagues invite you to happy hour, say yes. When someone at your gym mentions a group hike, say yes. When you see an interesting event on Eventbrite or Meetup, go even if you don't know anyone. Building a social life requires putting yourself out there repeatedly, even when it feels uncomfortable or you're tired from work. The more you say yes, the more opportunities you create for friendships to develop.

Explore your city intentionally and become a "tourist" in your new home. Visit the museums, try the famous restaurants, hike the popular trails, attend sporting events and concerts, and explore different neighborhoods. Becoming knowledgeable about your city helps you feel at home faster, gives you things to talk about with new people, and creates opportunities to meet others who are doing the same things. Plus, you'll actually enjoy living there rather than just existing between work and your apartment.

Volunteer for local organizations or causes you care about. Volunteering accomplishes multiple goals, such as contributing to your new community, meeting people who share your values, and building connections outside work. Look for volunteer opportunities related to sports (youth leagues, adaptive sports programs, community athletics), causes you're passionate about (environmental conservation, food banks, animal rescues), or events that need help (festivals, races, fundraisers). Volunteering gives you structured social interaction and shared purpose, which naturally lead to friendships.

Be patient with yourself, because building community takes time. You won't have a full social life after one month in a new city. It takes 3-6 months to start feeling somewhat established and 6-12 months to really feel at home. That's normal. Don't get discouraged if the first few months feel lonely or if friendships develop slower than you'd like. Keep showing up, keep putting yourself out there, and trust that consistency will eventually build the community you're looking for.

When Moving Doesn't Work Out

Sometimes moves don't work out the way you hoped. The job isn't what you expected. The city doesn't feel right. You're miserable and questioning whether you made a massive mistake.

That's okay, it happens, and it doesn't mean you failed. Give it at least six months before making major decisions. The first few months in a new city are almost always difficult because everything is unfamiliar, you're adjusting to a new job, and you haven't built a community yet. Don't make permanent decisions based on temporary discomfort. Give yourself at least six months to truly adjust before deciding whether the move was a mistake. Often, things that feel unbearable at three months feel manageable or even good at nine months once you've built some stability and connections.

If you genuinely still want to leave, leave strategically. If after giving it a fair chance you're truly miserable or the job is toxic or unsustainable, don't force yourself to suffer indefinitely. To leave strategically, start job searching while still employed, save money so you can afford to relocate again, give appropriate notice, and maintain professionalism even if you're unhappy. Work with your manager, who will more than likely assist you in your transition. They can make calls on your behalf, help you through interview processes, or maybe they worked in the city you want to move to. Your reputation follows you in this industry, so leave every organization professionally regardless of your experience there. Every move teaches you something about what you need to thrive. Even moves that don't work out provide valuable information. Maybe you learned you need to live near your family. Maybe you realized you prefer small cities to large ones or vice versa. Maybe you discovered certain job functions aren't actually fulfilling even though you thought they'd be perfect. Use that information to make better decisions about future opportunities rather than viewing the move as wasted time.

The Long-Term Benefits of Geographic Flexibility

Being willing to move for opportunities, especially early in your career, compounds over time in ways that aren't immediately obvious. You build a national network rather than just a local one. You gain diverse experience across different markets and organizations. You prove to employers that you prioritize career growth over geographic comfort, which makes you more attractive for promotions and opportunities. You develop adaptability and resilience that make you better at navigating change and uncertainty. And you create a life full of experiences, friendships, and stories that wouldn't exist if you'd stayed in one comfortable place.

Every move we've made has been challenging initially. Every move required building community from scratch, figuring out a new city, and dealing with the discomfort of being somewhere unfamiliar. But every move has also expanded my network, taught me something new, introduced me to incredible people, and created experiences I wouldn't trade for anything. The willingness to move has accelerated my career in ways that staying in one place never could have.

You don't have to move every three months like we do. But if you want to maximize your career trajectory in sports, you need to be open to relocating when the right opportunities arise. Use the strategies in this chapter to make those moves successful, find short-term housing through Furnished Finders, budget realistically, build community through sports leagues and alumni networks, and give yourself time to adjust before making major decisions. Moving for opportunities isn't easy, but for those willing to embrace the challenge, it's often the difference between a stalled career and an extraordinary one.

Geographic Flexibility Assessment and Preparation

Complete this two-part exercise to prepare for career-driven relocation.

Part One: Create your personal mobility matrix. List every city or region where you'd realistically consider working and rate each on these factors (1-5 scale):

- Willingness to live there
- Sports market strength (number of professional teams and sports organizations)
- Cost of living relative to entry-level salaries
- Existing connections or network proximity to family and support systems.

Calculate a total score for each location. This clarifies which markets you should target and which compromises you're willing to make.

Part Two: Build your relocation toolkit. Research and bookmark these resources for your top 3-5 target cities:

- Furnished Finder listings
- Alumni database contacts in those locations
- Typical rent costs for one-bedroom apartments,
- Recreational sports leagues and fitness communities
- Major sports employers and organizations.

Create a folder with this information so when an opportunity arises in one of these cities, you're not starting from zero; you already know how you'll find housing, build community, and navigate the transition.

Finally, calculate your minimum relocation fund: first month's rent, security deposit, moving costs, and 2-3 months of living expenses for your target cities. This number becomes your savings goal, making relocation financially feasible when the right opportunity appears.

Part III: Network Through Action, Not Just Words

Mastering relationship-building that opens doors throughout your career: developing authentic networking strategies beyond transactional contact-collecting (Chapter 8) and recognizing why struggling organizations often provide better learning experiences than championship teams (Chapter 9).

"Two things that are hard to understand when you are starting out in the sports industry are to trust the process from those that came before you and to recognize that it's not how you start but how you are able to maintain consistent performance and longevity. Being able to self evaluate and learn from others that are going through a similar journey are key traits to learning and developing your craft."
Erich Bacchus, MLB Umpire

"As an athlete, I learned that talent and passion are not enough. What separates people is preparation, resilience, and understanding how the game really works behind the scenes. The next generation deserves honest guidance, not guesswork, and when we share what it truly takes to break in and build a career, we give them a real chance to succeed." **Drew Storen, Former Professional Baseball Player**

"The road to professional baseball is not a one-path-fits-all journey. The roadmap, for those getting into any part of the sports industry, is not the same for everyone; however, it takes successful individuals like Stuart to help guide the future generations in the right direction. Working with Stuart through the Baltimore Orioles as well as Israel National Baseball Team, it is safe to say his professionalism and knowledge of this industry is exactly what is needed to provide meaningful insight for future leaders in sports." **Dean Kremer, Professional Baseball Player**

"Careers in the sports industry are all about making it happen yourself, and staying committed when the spotlight isn't on you. Stuart doesn't just understand the industry, he understands the hustle behind it. More importantly, he equips the next generation with the right steps to enter it with confidence, grit, and purpose."
Rico Garcia, Professional Baseball Player

"I first met Stuart prior to the 2023 WBC. I immediately noticed his work ethic and dedication to helping any way he could, ranging from equipment to logistics and more. Since that time, he's traveled all around the country growing every organization he's been with. Stuart will be successful in any sports venture he sets his sights on, and I'm glad he's been with Team Israel to help us take the next step in the international baseball world." **Matt Mervis, Professional Baseball Player**

"Sports has become a place overrun with innovation. If somebody has new ideas that work, it doesn't matter what their background is, they'll find a way into the sport. It's amazing to hear the variety of stories from people around the game and colleagues on how they found a way to use their passion and differing knowledge areas to breakthrough into the sports world." **Jake Bird, Professional Baseball Player**

"Sports changed my life, and giving young people the blueprint to step into this world is one of the most meaningful things we can do. Helping them navigate the grind, the rejection, and the opportunities sets them up for success far beyond the field." **Brett Hundley, Former Professional Football Player**

"Advice from someone who has been drafted by an MLB team, played for 10 MiLB seasons, managed for 5 MiLB seasons and now a coordinator for an MLB organization; follow up. Never forget to circle back for a follow up response. Never think if you're trying to break into sports that you 'got it.' Feedback loops within organizations must be tight with no leaks. Follow up." **Jake Lowery, Catching & Game Play Coordinator, Washington Nationals**

Chapter 8: The Art of Building Lasting Relationships

Your resume isn't what gets you hired in sports. It's who knows your name, trusts your work, and thinks of you when an opportunity opens up. That's uncomfortable if you hate networking, but it's also liberating once you realize that networking isn't about being fake or collecting business cards at events you don't want to attend. Real networking is just building genuine relationships with people whose careers you find interesting, learning from their experiences, and staying in touch over time. The students who break into this industry aren't necessarily the ones with the best credentials. They're the ones who've built real connections with people who actually want to help them succeed. This chapter is about networking that actually works, the tactics, mindset, and strategies that build real relationships leading to real opportunities. This isn't a theory. This is what I've done to build a network across the sports industry that's opened doors, created opportunities, and built friendships that extend far beyond professional utility.

Personal Branding: You're Already Building One (Whether You Know It or Not)

Think about the last time you looked someone up before meeting them. Maybe it was a professor, a date, or someone you were going to work with on a group project. You probably Googled them, checked their LinkedIn, and/or scrolled through their Instagram. Within about 90 seconds, you formed an opinion about who they are.

That's personal branding. And the thing is, everyone who might hire you in sports is doing the exact same thing to you right now.

Your personal brand isn't some fake, polished version of yourself that you create for the internet. It's simply the impression people get when they encounter you, whether that's in person, online, or through someone else's story about you. It's your reputation, your vibe, what you're known for.

In sports, where jobs are scarce and competition is intense, your personal brand can be the difference between getting a coffee meeting and getting ignored. Why? Because sports is a relationship business. People hire people they know, or people who come recommended by people they trust. And before anyone takes a chance on you, they're going to check you out.

Why This Matters More in Sports Than Almost Anywhere Else

Most industries have structured recruiting processes. Sports doesn't really work that way. There's no campus recruiting schedule for minor league baseball operations jobs. No job fair for NHL front offices. Instead, someone mentions your name to someone else, that person checks you out online, and they decide whether you're worth a conversation.

Your personal brand is doing work for you even when you're not in the room. It's what makes someone think, "Oh yeah, that's the kid who really knows baseball analytics," or, "She's the one who's been grinding with that college basketball team's video work." A clear, authentic personal brand helps people remember you and know what you bring to the table.

The good news? You don't need to be fake or transform yourself into some corporate robot. The best personal brands in sports are just people being genuinely themselves, but intentional about how they show up.

Why Building Relationships Is Important

The sports industry runs on relationships. Not transactions, not resumes, not even talent, but relationships. The internship you land, the job offer you receive, the promotion you earn, they all come down to people who know you, trust you, and want to help you succeed. I've watched countless qualified candidates get passed over for opportunities because they treated networking like a checklist rather than relationship-building. Meanwhile, I've seen people with less impressive resumes land dream jobs because someone in their network vouched for them, thought of them when an opportunity opened, or simply enjoyed working with them and wanted to do it again. This isn't about who you know in some cynical, back-door-deals kind of way. It's about building genuine connections with people who respect your work ethic, appreciate your character, and believe in your potential. Those relationships become the foundation of your entire career in sports. The difference between breaking in and getting stuck on the outside often comes down to whether you've built real relationships or just collected business cards.

Klein says, "Talent gets you noticed, but your relationships and behavior decide your future. Your path in sports is shaped by your work and your relationships. If you deliver under pressure and treat people with respect, opportunities follow you from one role to the next. Sports is a small circle where your name moves faster than your resume. People trust the ones who show up, perform, and stay steady. That's what builds a real career."

"Man plans and God laughs," Gettleman says about his path into the NFL. He met a part-time scout for the Kansas City Chiefs at a coaching clinic, and they stayed in touch for a while before losing contact. Years later, that scout became the Director of Pro Personnel for the Buffalo Bills. Dave reached back out. The guy said, "Let's talk." When Dave met him, the conversation went well enough that the director told him, "As long as I'm here, you have an internship." One conversation changed everything.

"Breaking into the sports industry is rarely about a perfect resume and almost always about relationships. Networking opens doors, but authenticity is what keeps them open. When young people show up curious, hardworking, and true to who they are, they don't just build connections; they build trust, and that's what creates real opportunity," says Emily Dumas, the Senior Director of Membership Services at the Arizona Cardinals.

Why Most Networking Advice Is Misleading

Let's start by acknowledging that most networking advice you've received is misleading and makes everyone involved feel used. You've been told to "work the room," collect business cards like Pokemon, send generic LinkedIn connection requests to anyone with "sports" in their title, and treat every conversation as an opportunity to extract value from people. That's not networking; that's using people. And people can tell when you're using them, which is why most networking efforts fail spectacularly. Real networking isn't about collecting contacts. It's about building genuine relationships with people you respect, learning from their experiences, and creating connections based on curiosity and mutual benefit rather than immediate self-interest. When you approach networking as relationship-building rather than transaction-hunting, everything changes. People actually want to help you. Conversations become enjoyable rather than awkward. Opportunities emerge naturally rather than through forced asks. And your network becomes a genuine asset rather than a list of people who ignore your messages.

Kelsey Wisner, the Manager of Premium Seating at the Baltimore Orioles, says, "A lot of people will tell you to 'just get your foot in the door' and 'it is all about who you know.' Although both partially hold true, breaking into sports takes so much more than that. It takes sincerity, genuineness, and lots of sacrifice. You need to intentionally build relationships and make positive impressions on everyone you meet through interviews, LinkedIn, networking events, and in passing. The sports industry is much smaller than people realize and you may be passed on a job you thought you had in the bag, but if the impression you leave them with is positive, you will have a cheerleader throughout your career to get you to the places you want to reach. Valuing the people in your corner and the impression you leave on everyone you meet will make or break a lot of success you find in this industry - carry this over in all that you do and you will find endless success in sports!"

The Mindset Shift: From "Can You Help Me?" to "Can I Learn From You?"

The single most important shift you need to make is moving from a taking mindset to a learning mindset. When you reach out to people asking, "Can you get me a job?" or, "Do you know of any opportunities?" you're immediately positioning yourself as someone who wants to extract value. That puts people on the defensive because helping you becomes a burden rather than a pleasure.

Instead, approach every interaction with genuine curiosity: "Can I learn from you?" When you're authentically interested in someone's career path, their experiences, what they've learned, and the advice they'd give, conversations become collaborative rather than transactional. People love talking about their experiences and sharing what they've learned. It's validating and enjoyable. When you approach networking from a learning mindset, you're giving people the opportunity to reflect on their journey and feel valued for their expertise. That creates goodwill, builds real connection, and makes people want to help you when opportunities arise. This isn't manipulation, it's genuine curiosity. Don't fake interest in someone's career just to get something from them. Actually be curious. Ask thoughtful questions. Listen actively. Learn genuinely. When you do that consistently, the professional benefits follow naturally because people remember who made them feel valued and who treated them like a means to an end.

There's a reason sales professionals are often the best networkers in sports. They understand that networking isn't about talking, it's about listening. They know the fundamental truth that people won't remember exactly what you said, but they'll always remember how you made them feel. When you're on a networking call, your goal isn't to impress someone with your resume or rattle off your accomplishments. Instead, focus on making the other person feel valued. Compliment their career path. Tell them their role is your dream job and explain specifically why. Ask them about the challenges they've overcome and the decisions they're most proud of. This isn't manipulation, it's genuine human connection. When you validate someone's career choices and show authentic interest in their journey, you create a memorable interaction. They'll walk away from that conversation feeling good about themselves, and by extension, feeling good about you. That's the foundation of a lasting professional relationship, and it's far more powerful than any perfectly crafted elevator pitch.

"The average person knows when they're being fed a line of crap," Gettleman says. "You can figure out pretty quickly where people are coming from. If you want to build a real network, you need to be genuine. And I don't mean be a kiss-ass either. Be genuine. Be real. It sounds basic, but it matters." He continues by saying, "You only get one chance to make a first impression. If that impression is of someone who's just kissing up, that's what they'll remember. If you come across as pompous and arrogant, that's what sticks. Some people think they're showing confidence, but they're actually coming off like jerks." Finally Gettleman mentions, "When you're building your network and meeting people, you have to be real, genuine, and humble. It doesn't cost you anything to be nice."

"You have to be a good listener," Gettleman emphasizes. "Seek to understand. Understand that every individual looks at life through their own unique lens. In order to get to the right answer, you need to ask the right questions."

"If you want to break into sports, bring great energy. Make first impressions count. Prepare for life the same way you prepare for a game or activity you are passionate about. Talent may get attention, but habits build careers, master your life skills, ask good questions, earn trust, and build real relationships long before you need them," says Jeff Munneke, the Vice President of Fan Experience at Minnesota Timberwolves and Lynx.

"Flip the script from 'What's in this for me?' to 'How can I support you?' When you genuinely want to help others, they'll want to help you too. That mindset shift is what turns one-off networking interactions into real relationships that last your entire career," says Adriene Bueno, the Co-Founder of Arena.

Fix Your LinkedIn Before You Network

Before you start reaching out to anyone in the industry, clean up your LinkedIn profile. This is non-negotiable. Your LinkedIn is often the first impression people have of you professionally, and a sloppy profile signals that you're not serious. Start with a professional photo, not a selfie, not a party picture cropped to remove your friends, not a photo where you're wearing sunglasses or a hat. Get someone to take a clean headshot of you in professional attire against a neutral background. If you don't have access to a professional photographer, ask a friend with a decent camera or smartphone to take dozens of photos until you get one that works. This matters more than you think.

Next, write a professional bio that clearly communicates who you are and what you're trying to do. Don't leave it blank. Don't write something vague like "Recent graduate looking for opportunities." Be specific: "Recent [Your University] graduate with experience in [relevant areas] seeking to break into sports business, particularly interested in [specific roles or areas]." Use the headline space strategically. It's prime real estate that appears every time you comment, connect, or message someone. Make it count.

Fill out your experience section completely, even if you think it's not directly relevant to sports. If you've been a server, barista, retail associate, camp counselor, or held any job, list it. Work experience demonstrates reliability, responsibility, and real-world skills that matter. Describe what you did, emphasizing transferable skills like customer service, teamwork, problem-solving, or leadership. Don't leave your experience section empty because you think your non-sports jobs don't matter. Hiring managers want to see that you've held jobs and shown up consistently. List your education, any relevant coursework, clubs, volunteer work, and skills. Make your profile complete and professional.

Finally, build your network to at least 500+ connections. Why 500? Because that's when LinkedIn stops showing your exact connection count and just displays "500+," which signals that you're an active, connected professional rather than someone brand new to the platform. Getting there isn't difficult if you're intentional. Start by connecting with people you actually know – classmates, professors, former coworkers, family friends, people from your hometown. Then expand strategically using the networking strategies we covered, connect with people after informational interviews, after meeting them at events, after meaningful interactions on posts or in groups. Personalize every connection request with a brief note explaining why you're connecting. Don't just mass-connect with strangers; build a real network of people who actually know who you are or have some connection to you. Once you hit 500+ connections, maintain and grow your network by staying active, engaging with content, and continuing to make genuine connections. A cleaned-up LinkedIn profile with 500+ connections positions you as someone serious about your career and ready to be taken seriously by people in the industry.

The LinkedIn Strategy: 10 Messages Per Week

LinkedIn is the most powerful networking tool available to you, but most people can use it better. They create a profile, add a few connections, maybe post occasionally, and wonder why nothing happens. LinkedIn works when you use it actively and strategically, and that means consistent outreach. Send 10 connection requests and personalized messages per week to people in the sports industry.

This isn't random spam; this is targeted, thoughtful outreach to people whose careers interest you, who work for organizations you admire, or who are in roles you aspire to have. That's 40 connections per month, nearly 500 per year. Over your college career, that's 2,000+ industry connections built systematically. When you apply for jobs, hiring managers will see mutual connections, which immediately makes you feel less like a random applicant and more like someone who's already part of the industry network.

An example can be: *"Hi [Name], I'm a [your situation: sport management student, recent grad, professional transitioning to sports] interested in [specific area]. I've been following [Organization]'s work in [specific initiative, campaign, or accomplishment] and impressed by [specific thing]. Would love to connect and learn from your experience in [their role/department]."*

Example: *"Hi Sarah, I'm a sport management student at Springfield College interested in partnership sales. I've been following the Trail Blazers' innovative approach to community partnerships and am impressed by how you've integrated social impact into sponsorship packages. Would love to connect and learn from your experience in corporate partnerships."*

This works because it's specific (you mentioned their organization and something they worked on), genuine (you're clearly interested in what they do), and respectful (you're asking to learn, not asking for a job). Most people will accept it because you've demonstrated you're not randomly spamming everyone with "sports" in their title.

After connections are accepted, don't immediately ask for something. Many people accept your connection request, then find you send a long message asking for an informational interview or job leads. That feels like a bait-and-switch. Instead, engage with their content for a few weeks first. Like and comment thoughtfully on their posts. Share relevant articles or insights. Build some rapport. Then, after 2-4 weeks, send a message requesting a brief informational interview:

Hi [Name], thanks for connecting a few weeks ago. I've really enjoyed following your insights on [topic they post about]. I'm currently [your situation] and working to learn as much as I can about [specific area]. Would you be open to a 15-minute call where I could ask a few questions about your career path and advice for someone trying to break into [specific area]? I'm happy to work around your schedule.

Notice this message references the time since connecting (showing you're not immediately asking for something), mentions their content (showing you've actually engaged), is specific about what you want to discuss, respects their time by suggesting a short call, and makes scheduling easy by offering flexibility.

Join and engage in LinkedIn Groups. LinkedIn Groups are underutilized goldmines for networking because they're communities of people with shared professional interests, and participation gives you visibility and credibility beyond just sending connection requests.

Join groups relevant to your career interests and identity. Search for groups related to sports business, specific roles you're interested in, and communities you're part of. Some valuable groups to consider:

- Women in Sports and Events (WISE): One of the largest and most active communities for women in the sports industry, offering networking, mentorship, and job opportunities.

- Jewish Sport and Entertainment Professionals Network: Connects Jewish professionals across the sports industry for networking, Shabbat dinners at industry events, and career support. I created this group as a way to connect a small portion of the industry.

- Black Sports Professionals: Community focused on advancing Black professionals in sports through networking, mentorship, and advocacy.
- Sports Business Classroom: Educational community sharing insights, case studies, and career advice for sports business professionals.
- Sport Management Alumni Groups: Many universities have LinkedIn groups for sport management alumni, providing instant connection to people who went through similar programs.
- League-specific groups: NFL Alumni, MLB Network, NBA Careers, etc. often have groups where current and former employees network.

"If you are a woman entering the sports industry, join a women-in-sports group. You can find them at your college, your company, and in your local sports market. The sooner you build a network of women in the industry, the better. You will find opportunities for mentorship, sponsorship, networking, and most importantly, you will feel a sense of community and belonging," says Kristin Gow, Founder of Women Who Coach.

Engage actively, don't just lurk. Joining groups does nothing if you never participate. Comment thoughtfully on discussions, share relevant articles with your perspective, ask genuine questions, answer questions when you have insights, and participate in conversations. This visibility positions you as engaged and thoughtful, and people in the group start recognizing your name. When you send connection requests to group members later, they're more likely to accept because they've seen you contribute value to the community. Use groups to find informational interview targets. Browse group members and identify people in roles or organizations you're interested in. Shared group membership provides context and common ground that makes connection requests feel less random. When you send connection requests, mention the shared group:

The alumni network: your built-in advantage. Your alma mater is one of your most powerful networking assets, and most people completely waste it. Alumni are predisposed to help other alumni; there's shared experience, shared identity, and often genuine desire to "pay it forward" because someone helped them when they were starting out. Use that. Start with your school's formal alumni network and career services. Most schools have alumni databases, regional chapters, career networking events, and mentorship programs specifically designed to connect current students and recent grads with established alumni. Register for these services, attend events (even virtually), and use the alumni directory to identify people working in sports. Your school's career center can often facilitate introductions or provide contact information for alumni who've opted into mentoring or networking with students.

Use LinkedIn to find alumni when formal networks don't exist or aren't active. Go to LinkedIn's search function, click "People," then filter by your school under "Schools" and your current city (or cities you're targeting) under "Locations." You now have a list of every alum working in your area. Further filter by companies (search for teams, leagues, agencies) or job titles to narrow to people in sports. Send personalized connection requests mentioning your shared alma mater:

Alumni connections have significantly higher acceptance rates than cold outreach because shared school creates immediate commonality. Many alumni genuinely enjoy helping younger grads because they remember what it was like starting out.

Attend alumni events even when they're not sports-focused. Regional alumni happy hours, homecoming gatherings, career panels, and networking mixers put you in rooms with alumni across industries. Not everyone there works in sports, but many know people who do, and building relationships with alumni in other fields expands your network in unexpected ways. I've gotten sports introductions from alumni working in finance, healthcare, and technology because they knew someone, mentioned my interest, and made a connection. Stay connected to alumni you meet, and don't let relationships go cold after one conversation. After informational interviews or networking conversations with alumni, send thank-you notes (more on this to follow), connect on LinkedIn, and follow up periodically with updates on your progress. When you land an internship or job, let them know and thank them for their advice. When you see they've changed jobs or gotten promoted, congratulate them. These small touches maintain relationships so that when you need advice or help years later, you're not re-introducing yourself, but continuing an ongoing connection.

Preparing for Informational Interviews: Do Your Homework

When someone agrees to an informational interview or networking call, you're asking for their most valuable asset: time. Time is a commodity they cannot get back. They are blocking out on average 30 minutes for you, so be respectful of this. Come prepared to make every minute valuable, not just for you but for them as well by being an engaged, thoughtful conversation partner. Research the person and their organization before the call. Look at their LinkedIn profile to understand their career path. Read their company's website to understand what the organization does.

Google recent news about their team or company, not what is happening on the playing field, but in the office (unless they're involved in player movement). Check their social media to see what they're interested in or posting about. This research ensures you won't ask questions easily answered by Google, and you can reference specific things that show you've done your homework.

Prepare 10-15 questions in advance. You won't ask all of them, but having a robust list ensures you never run out of things to discuss and can adapt based on how the conversation flows. Use the same core list for multiple calls – work smarter, not harder – but customize a few questions based on each person's specific background.

Questions to include in your standard list:

About Their Career Path:
- What roles or experiences were most valuable in preparing you for your current position?
- If you were starting your career today, what would you do differently?
- What skills have been most important to your success?
- How did you decide which opportunities to pursue and which to pass on?

About Their Current Role:
- What aspects of your job do you find most rewarding? Most challenging?
- What skills or qualities make someone successful in this type of position?
- How has your role evolved since you started?

About the Industry:
- What trends are you seeing in [their area of sports business]?

- What challenges is [their organization/department] currently facing?
- How has [specific aspect of the industry] changed during your career?
- Where do you see the biggest opportunities for growth in sports business?

Advice for You:
- What advice would you give someone trying to break into [specific area]?
- What experiences or skills should I prioritize developing?
- Are there people you'd recommend I connect with or learn from?
- What resources (books, podcasts, conferences) have been valuable for your professional development?

Make the conversation personal by finding common ground. Research what you have in common. Did you go to the same school, grow up in similar areas, play the same sport, share hobbies or interests? Mentioning these connections early in the conversation builds rapport and makes the interaction more comfortable and memorable. "I saw you also played college baseball, I'm curious how that experience influenced your approach to working in sports business" is far more engaging than jumping straight into generic questions. Take notes during the call. This helps you remember what they said, it shows you're taking the conversation seriously, and it gives you specific things to reference in your thank-you note.

The Lost Art of Handwritten Thank-You Notes

I can count on maybe two hands, in my years working in sports, the number of times I've received a follow-up handwritten thank-you note after informational interviews, networking calls, or even job interviews. Whether you have a five-minute conversation, an hour-long informational interview, or just finished a formal job interview, follow up with both a thank-you over email **and** a handwritten note. Yes, it costs a little money and time, but how badly do you want to be remembered and separate yourself from everyone else? Handwritten notes are a lost art. If you send one, you'll be remembered when you apply for that dream job. Trust me. In a world where everyone sends quick emails (if they follow up at all), receiving a physical card in the mail is shocking and memorable. It demonstrates thoughtfulness, effort, and professionalism that's increasingly rare. How to write effective thank-you notes: Keep them short, specific, and genuine. Here's the structure:

- Thank them for their time. Be specific about what you're thanking them for.
- Reference something specific from your conversation. This shows you were paying attention and the note isn't generic.
- Reiterate your interest or express what you learned. Make it clear the conversation was valuable.
- Offer to stay in touch or follow up. Leave the door open for continued relationships.

Example handwritten note after an informational interview:

"Hi Sarah,

Thank you so much for taking time to speak with me yesterday about your career in partnership sales with the Trail Blazers. Your insight about the shift toward purpose-driven sponsorships and how you measure social impact ROI was incredibly valuable. It's an area I hadn't fully considered but now want to learn more about.

I really appreciate your advice about starting in ticket sales to learn the business fundamentals. I'm going to follow up on the contacts you mentioned and explore opportunities in that area.

Thanks again for your generosity with your time and advice. I'll keep you updated on my progress, and I hope we can stay in touch.

Best,
Stuart"

Send the email within 24 hours. Mail the handwritten note the same day or next day. The email shows promptness and professionalism. The handwritten note shows extra effort and thoughtfulness. Together, they make you unforgettable. Invest in professional thank-you cards and keep them stocked. Buy simple, professional note cards (nothing with cartoon characters or overly decorative designs, just clean, neutral cards). If you wait to buy cards, you won't send them. Make it easy on yourself. Vistaprint is a great place to start.

Lippe mentions this about following up: "It's really an easy formula that most people have a hard time following. Network with authenticity and curiosity. Send thoughtful follow-ups (handwritten notes go a long way). Obsess over process, not outcome. Doing the little things right makes all the difference."

When You Don't Hear Back: Don't Be Discouraged

Something that needs to be talked about more is that professionals get busy. Really busy. Your email might get lost in their inbox, they might intend to respond and forget, or they might just be overwhelmed and unable to take on more conversations right now. Don't take it personally, and don't give up after one message. An average CEO receives between 100-200 emails per day, with executives in larger organizations often reporting even higher volumes. Do the math: your single email represents roughly 0.5% of their daily inbox. Now consider the competition for their attention, urgent messages from board members, time-sensitive business decisions, revenue-generating opportunities, and crisis management. Your networking email, no matter how well-crafted, is competing against all of that. In this battle for attention, you're going to lose more often than you win. And that's okay. It's not personal; it's simply the reality of communication in today's fast-paced sports business environment. This is precisely why following up isn't just acceptable, it's essential.

When I went to work for the Baltimore Orioles the summer of my junior year of college, I probably emailed around 100 employees across all departments asking for informational interviews. I think I heard back from maybe two. Two out of a hundred, and I already had signed my offer letter. That's a 98% non-response rate. But of those two who responded, I had lunch with them, learned from their experiences, and ended up choosing the sales route as a result of one of those conversations. Those two conversations shaped my career trajectory more than the 98 rejections or non-responses.

I was stuck in a place many young professionals find themselves: I had experience in the industry I loved, but I had no idea what I actually wanted to do long-term. Partnerships? Ticketing? Marketing? Operations? Every departent seemed interesting, and I couldn't commit to a path. I was spinning my wheels. Then I grabbed lunch with Ray, the Senior Director of Corporate Partnerships at the Orioles, one of the two who responded. I didn't know Ray well as we worked in different departments, but he agreed to meet, and that conversation changed everything. As Ray walked me through his journey, explaining how he got to where he was and what his day-to-day actually looked like, something clicked. He didn't sugarcoat the work. He talked about the grind of building relationships, the satisfaction of closing a deal, and the creativity required to solve problems for partners. By the time we finished lunch, I knew exactly what I wanted to do. Sales wasn't just one option among many anymore, it was *the* path. That single conversation gave me the clarity I'd been searching for, and it set the trajectory for everything that came after. Follow up if you don't hear back after a week. Send a brief, polite follow-up:

"Hi [Name], I wanted to follow up on my message from last week about potentially connecting for a brief conversation about [topic]. I completely understand if you're too busy right now, but I'd still love the opportunity to learn from your experience when your schedule allows. Thanks for considering!"

Sometimes the follow-up is what gets you the response because they genuinely missed your first message or it reminds them they meant to respond. If you still don't hear back after a follow-up, follow up one more time. Then, if you still don't hear back, move on gracefully. Don't keep emailing; it becomes pestering rather than persistence. Add them to a list to try again in 3-6 months when their situation might be different. Sometimes timing just doesn't work, and that's okay. Focus your energy on the people who do respond rather than fixating on those who don't. Understand that non-response isn't rejection, it's just silence. People don't respond for countless reasons that have nothing to do with you, such as being overwhelmed, they're traveling, they changed jobs, they don't check LinkedIn often, your message got buried. Don't let non-responses discourage you from continuing outreach. The people who do respond and help you matter infinitely more than the ones who don't.

Building Trust Before Asking for Job Help

When speaking with professionals for the first time, within the first call or two, don't ask for a job. Please. You want to build the relationship and seek advice first. After you've built trust and demonstrated genuine interest in learning rather than just extracting job leads, then you can ask for help with your job search, but phrase it strategically. Instead of, "Do you know of any jobs?" or "Can you help me get hired?" say: "Hey, I'm starting to apply for jobs in [area]. What recommendations would you have for my search?" Or if you're interested in their specific organization: "Hey, I'm looking at applying to [their organization]. What recommendations would you have for someone applying there?" This phrasing is crucial because it asks for advice rather than asking them to put their reputation on the line. The reality is that professionals might be hesitant to pass along your resume directly or make introductions because they are putting their reputation on the line when they recommend someone. If you turn out to be unreliable, unprofessional, or underqualified, it reflects poorly on them. This isn't a negative reflection on you if they don't immediately offer to pass your resume along. You might not have built up enough trust with them yet.

Build trust through multiple interactions over time. Have 2-3 conversations. Send thoughtful follow-ups. Share articles relevant to your previous discussions. Update them on how you applied their advice. Demonstrate that you're serious, professional, and genuinely interested in learning. When you've built that foundation, asking for job search help feels natural rather than transactional. When they do offer to help, make it easy for them. If someone offers to pass your resume along or make an introduction, immediately send them your resume with a brief summary of what types of roles you're targeting and why you'd be a good fit. Draft the intro email they could send on your behalf. The easier you make it for them to help, the more likely they'll actually follow through.

Organizing Your Network: Use Your Phone Strategically

As your network grows, you need a system for remembering people and maintaining relationships. Your phone's contact list is an underutilized tool for this. When you meet someone or have a meaningful conversation, immediately add them to your contacts with detailed information. Don't just save their name and number, use the notes field to record. When you save a contact with a phone, put in their "company" line: the current company they're at, where you met them and city they work in (if not in the company name). This makes searching your contacts easy and helps you remember context when they call or text months later. Maybe you're visiting a city, or attending a game, and want to remember who you know in the city and/or team. Use the notes field of the contact for anything memorable: they mentioned their kid plays lacrosse, they're training for a marathon, they went to your rival school.

Set reminders to follow up. After significant conversations, set a reminder for 3-6 months later to send a check-in message. "Hi [Name], we spoke back in January about partnership sales, and your advice about [specific advice] was really helpful. I wanted to update you that I [your progress] and thank you again for your time. Hope things are going well with [something specific to them]!" These periodic check-ins keep relationships warm and ensure people don't forget you between when you first connect and when you might need their help or advice later. During my time as a student, I used an Excel sheet to track professionals I've had previous conversations with and the previous date of communication.

Get Business Cards and Build Your Professional Presence

Even as a student, having business cards makes you appear more professional and makes it easier for people to remember you and contact you later. When you meet someone at an event, game, or networking opportunity, handing them a business card is memorable and practical.

What to include on your business cards:
- Your name (obviously)

- Your title or status: "Sport Management Student, University of [School]" or "Aspiring Sports Marketing Professional"
- Your phone number
- Your email (use a professional email address)
- Your LinkedIn URL (customize it to linkedin.com/in/yourname)
- *Optional:* Your professional website if you have one

Keep cards simple and professional. Clean design, readable font, no cartoon characters or overly decorative elements. Vistaprint offers affordable professional business cards. Order 250-500 so you never run out. Keep a stack in your wallet, backpack, or car so you always have them available. If you want to take it to the next step, create a professional website. Platforms like Wix, Squarespace, or WordPress make it easy to build simple, professional websites for free or minimal cost. Your website can include your resume, portfolio of work (projects, writing samples, content you've created), bio, and contact information. It gives you a professional online presence beyond just LinkedIn and provides a place to showcase work that doesn't fit neatly on a resume. Include your website URL on your business cards and email signature. You can check out my website at www.StuartSokoloff.com for an example.

The Relationship-Building Mindset: Play the Long Game

Real networking isn't about immediate returns. It's about building relationships over years that compound into opportunities you can't predict when you start. The person you have coffee with as a student might hire you five years later. The colleague you help with a project might refer you for your dream job. The mentor you stay in touch with might make an introduction that changes your career.

Focus on building genuine relationships, not collecting contacts. Quality matters infinitely more than quantity. Having ten people who genuinely know you, trust you, and would enthusiastically recommend you is far more valuable than having thousands of LinkedIn connections who barely remember your name. Invest deeply in relationships with people you respect and enjoy, rather than superficially connecting with everyone.

Give before you ask. Look for ways to help people in your network before you need anything from them. Share articles relevant to their interests. Make introductions between people in your network who should know each other. Congratulate them on accomplishments. Offer to help with projects or events. When you build a pattern of giving value, people naturally want to reciprocate when you eventually need help.

Keep professionals and mentors updated with what is going on in your life. Maybe you're starting a new internship or job, you recently got married, or anything else can be a good check in moment. It provides a natural reason to reach out to them, rather than an "I hope all is well"-type message.

Stay patient and trust the process. Networking feels slow and ineffective at first because you're investing in relationships that won't pay off for months or years. That's normal. Keep showing up, keep being genuine, keep building connections. Over time, those relationships compound into opportunities, advice, and support that accelerate your career in ways you can't manufacture through transactional networking.

The people who succeed in sports aren't necessarily the most talented or best educated. They're often the ones with the strongest networks built through years of genuine relationship-building. Start building yours now, invest in it consistently, and trust that the compound effect of real relationships will create opportunities you can't even imagine yet.

Braun reminds readers, "Network! Network! Network! Like a lot of industries, it's not always about what you know, it's about who you know. The more people you can help or impress, the more doors will open for you. Everybody knows somebody."

Using Google Alerts

One of the most effective yet underutilized networking tools is Google Alerts. Set up alerts for the names of key contacts in your network, the organizations they work for, and relevant industry topics. When someone you've connected with gets promoted, their team makes a major trade, or their organization announces a new initiative, you'll be among the first to know. This gives you a legitimate, timely reason to reach out. A quick email saying, "Congratulations on the promotion to VP of Operations, well deserved!" or "Saw the announcement about the new arena project. That must be an exciting challenge," shows you're paying attention and genuinely interested in their success. These touchpoints keep you top-of-mind without feeling forced or transactional.

In the sports industry, where news breaks constantly and organizational changes happen rapidly, Google Alerts can be your competitive advantage. You're not just another person sending a "just checking in" email every few months. Instead, you're providing value by demonstrating industry awareness and building authentic relationships. When a contact's team wins a championship, hires a new coach, or launches a community program, that's your opening. The key is to keep these messages brief and sincere. You're acknowledging their success or milestone, not asking for something in return. Over time, this consistent, contextually relevant communication positions you as someone who understands the industry and cares about more than just landing a job.

This is also a phenomenal tool if you do go into sales. When your client moves offices, makes a big acquisition, hosts a big event, or names a new CEO, you're able to be one of the first people to congratulate them. Non-sales touchpoints are just as important as sales touchpoints.

Turn Fan Attendance into Face Time

If you're attending a game or event as a fan, you're sitting on an untapped networking goldmine. Two to three weeks before the game, identify two or three professionals you'd like to connect with and send them a brief, thoughtful email asking if they're available to meet before or during the event. Be specific about why you want to meet them, reference a project they've worked on, a talk they've given, or an initiative their department launched. However, the reality of game day is that most professionals won't stick around after games unless their job requires it. The parking lot clears fast, and executives are typically heading home to decompress after 12-hour days. Instead, suggest meeting before first pitch or during a quieter moment mid-game. More than likely, they'll genuinely try to come say hi, but game days have a Murphy's Law quality to them: everything that can go sideways usually does. A crisis erupts in suite services, a sponsor needs immediate attention, or a staffing issue demands their focus. You might miss each other entirely, and that's not a failure, but actually a perfect setup for your next move. When plans fall through, you have a natural, pressure-free reason to follow up afterward: "I know game day got crazy, I'd love to grab coffee and hear about how everything went." You've already established the relationship, demonstrated initiative by showing up, and now you have an easy path to a more substantive conversation away from the chaos of event operations. The key is understanding that the task isn't just about the 15-minute conversation during the game. It's about opening a door that leads to something deeper.

Shadow a Game Day (And Make Yourself Indispensable)

One of the most underutilized strategies for breaking into sports is requesting to shadow a game day in the department you're targeting. This isn't about passively observing; it's about embedding yourself in the operation and proving you can handle the intensity. Reach out to one or two people in the department, (don't blast the entire staff directory) with a clear and professional request. You'd be surprised how many professionals are open to hosting shadows, especially if you frame it correctly. Game days are controlled chaos, and an extra set of competent hands is almost always welcome. The difference between annoying and helpful comes down to preparation and self-awareness. When you make the ask, immediately follow up by asking what you need to do to prepare ahead of time, what to wear, and when to arrive. Should you familiarize yourself with their ticketing system? Review their promotional calendar? Understand their seating manifest? Show that you're not looking for a backstage tour; you're offering to contribute. On game day, arrive early, stay alert, and read the room. Know when to jump in and when to stay out of the way. Volunteer for the unglamorous tasks like restocking merchandise, running credentials to will call, and helping with suite setup. These aren't beneath you; they're your audition. When a crisis hits and you calmly execute without needing hand-holding, you've just separated yourself from every other person who's sent that department a resume. By the end of the night, you've built a relationship with someone who's seen you perform under pressure, which is infinitely more valuable than a cover letter sitting in an HR portal. They know you can handle the job because they watched you do it. It's also a great place to naturally meet leadership, hiring managers, and fellow colleagues. Take note of everyone you meet and when you get home, write an email and a handwritten thank you note.

Once You're In, Everyone Picks Up the Phone

Once you secure your full-time role in sports, the entire networking landscape transforms. Suddenly, you can reach out to professionals at other organizations with an almost 100% response rate. It's not arrogance, it's the nature of the industry. Once you're inside the fraternity, the barriers dissolve. What makes sports unique is that while we're fierce competitors on the field, off the field we operate as a collaborative community. We're all facing the same challenges, such as filling seats, activating sponsors, managing difficult clients, and navigating organizational politics. There's an implicit understanding that sharing knowledge doesn't weaken your competitive position; it elevates the entire industry. It's common for departments to organize field trips to shadow peer organizations and study their operations. What's working in their ticket sales model? How are they structuring their premium seating? What technology are they using for CRM? These aren't trade secrets we guard jealously, they're best practices we share openly. As a salesperson, I made it standard practice to regularly call group sales representatives at other teams to discuss strategy. What theme nights are driving their group business? How were they handling challenging negotiation scenarios? What objections were they hearing most frequently, and how were they overcoming them? One of my closest professional relationships was with Chris Bongo, a former group sales representative for the Arizona Coyotes, while I was with the Phoenix Suns. Despite working for competing organizations in the same market, we made it a point to grab lunch at least once a month. We'd dissect what was working, what wasn't, and brainstorm solutions to each other's challenges. There were multiple occasions where we'd send each other leads – a company couldn't make their schedule work with my team's calendar, or our pricing didn't align with their budget, so I'd connect them with Chris to see if the Coyotes were a better fit. Six months later, he'd return the favor. It might seem counterintuitive to help a competitor, but it demonstrates a fundamental truth about the sports industry: relationships compound over time, and generosity creates currency. The lead I gave away today might result in a referral, a job opportunity, or a partnership years down the road. In an industry where everyone eventually crosses paths again, whether at a new organization, a conference, or a career transition, your reputation for being collaborative and helpful becomes one of your most valuable assets.

Conferences: Where Networking Meets Nostalgia

Industry conferences represent some of the highest-leverage networking opportunities in sports, and the Baseball Winter Meetings rank among my personal favorites. Imagine a five-day event where thousands of baseball professionals converge in one hotel. It's like a college reunion, a networking summit, and a masterclass all compressed into a week of controlled chaos. You're running into former colleagues, meeting executives you've only known through email, and occasionally standing in line for coffee next to your childhood heroes. The accessibility is remarkable. General Managers, team presidents, agents, and vendors are all walking the same hallways, eating at the same restaurants, and attending the same sessions. Typically, I don't get starstruck – working in professsional sports has a way of normalizing celebrity – but the first time I met Reggie Jackson in the hotel lobby, young Stuart couldn't believe it. Especially growing up a diehard Yankee fan. What struck me wasn't just meeting a Hall of Famer, but discovering he was one extremely down to earth and engaging. He didn't have to stop and chat, but he did, and that encapsulates what makes conferences valuable. These events strip away the corporate hierarchy and create environments where authentic connections happen naturally. Being able to ask Joe Torre career questions one-on-one changed how I look at my heroes and the relationship I have with those who are the best at their job (because that is what athletes and coaches are). Conferences aren't just about the scheduled programming, though the panels and workshops provide genuine value. The real magic happens in the unscripted moments, like the hallway conversation that turns into a job lead, the hotel bar discussion that evolves into a mentorship, the chance encounter in an Uber line that results in a business partnership. This is where deals get structured, positions get filled, and careers get accelerated. You're building relationships with people who understand your challenges because they're living them, too. They know what it's like to miss a quota, manage a difficult sponsor, or navigate organizational change. That shared context creates immediate rapport and trust. If you're serious about breaking into sports or advancing your career, conferences aren't optional professional development; they're essential infrastructure for career growth. The investment in registration, travel, and accommodations pays dividends for years through the network you build. Make it a priority to attend at least one major industry conference annually, and when you're there, be strategic. Review the attendee list in advance, schedule coffee meetings, attend social events, and follow up diligently afterward. The connections you make can fundamentally alter your career trajectory, but only if you show up and engage fully. Not to mention, Kevin Millar may deny you an invitation to play golf, but invite you behind the MLB Network desk.

The Winter Meetings aren't the only game in town. Depending on your sport and career focus, different conferences offer similar high-leverage networking in their own contexts. The National Collegiate Sports Sales Championship (NCSSC) is where the most talented college students compete to demonstrate their sales skills directly in front of leading figures in the sports industry. This isn't just a competition, it's a showcase designed to help participants land their dream job, with teams and organizations actively scouting talent. If you're studying sales, business, or sport management and want to prove yourself in front of actual decision-makers, this should be at the top of your list.

The National Collegiate Sports Analytics Championship takes a similar approach for the analytics crowd, bringing together the nation's most promising business analytics students to present cutting-edge analyses to a panel of seasoned industry professionals. It's a rigorous, real-world scenario where aspiring analysts can shine and connect directly with front offices looking for data talent. The MIT Sloan Sports Analytics Conference has become the premier gathering for the broader data-driven side of sports, attracting executives, analysts, researchers, and tech professionals who want to understand how analytics shapes decision-making across all sports. Expect deep-dive panels on everything from player evaluation to fan engagement metrics, and a crowd that skews heavily toward front office operations and strategy roles.

Beyond these, sport-specific events like the NFL Scouting Combine (if you're in player personnel), the Learfield IMG College Intercollegiate Athletics Forum (if you're in college athletics), and various league-sponsored summits offer targeted opportunities depending on where your interests lie. Research what conferences align with your career goals, check if your school offers student rates or group attendance, and make attending at least one annual event a non-negotiable part of your professional development.

One critical skill that separates rookies from veterans at conferences is understanding the unwritten dress code and behavioral norms. At the Baseball Winter Meetings, you'll notice something interesting; most established professionals don't wear their name badges. They know everyone, everyone knows them, and the badge screams, "I'm new here." If you're attending a conference where badge-wearing is optional or inconsistently enforced, leave it in your pocket. You want to look like you belong, not like you're at freshman orientation. That said, some conferences strictly require visible credentials for access to certain areas, and ignoring that rule makes you look clueless, not confident. The key is reading the room. Arrive early on day one, observe what the veterans are doing, and adapt accordingly. If 90% of people are badged up, wear yours. If badges are dangling from bags or mysteriously absent, follow suit. The same logic applies to what you're carrying. That massive backpack stuffed with every possible item you might need? Leave it at the hotel. Nothing broadcasts "amateur hour" louder than someone navigating a crowded reception with a bulky bag, bumping into executives while fumbling for business cards. Carry a slim portfolio or leather folio with essentials, like business cards, a pen, a small notebook, and your phone. You're there to network and look professional, not to demonstrate your preparedness for a wilderness expedition. The goal is blending in with the decision-makers, not standing out as the overeager intern who came equipped for a week-long camping trip.

The moment will happen faster than you expect. You're standing in line for coffee, sitting at a panel, or waiting for an elevator (naturally), and someone asks, "So what do you do?" or "Tell me about yourself." If you fumble through an awkward, rambling response, you've blown your shot. Executives don't have patience for people who can't articulate their own value in 30 seconds. Your elevator pitch isn't about reciting your resume or listing every job you've ever had. It's about connecting three things: who you are, what you're good at, and what you're looking for. Here's mine from my early career days: "I'm Stuart, currently a junior at Springfield College, and I've done sixteen internships and professional experiences across various departments within sports, and I'm passionate about building relationships that actually move the needle. I'm here to learn from people like you and explore opportunities in sales." That's it. Clean, confident, memorable. Notice what's not in there: unnecessary backstory, my entire job history, or vague statements about "loving sports." Practice your pitch until it feels natural, not rehearsed. Say it out loud in your hotel room. Record yourself. Adjust the wording until it sounds like you, not like you're reading from a script. But here's the crucial part: have different versions ready depending on context. The pitch you give a GM is different from what you tell a fellow sales rep. Tailor it to your audience, but keep the core structure consistent. When someone asks about you at a conference, they're giving you a gift: their attention. Don't waste it by being unprepared. Have your story tight, your values clear, and your ask specific. That 30-second conversation could be the difference between getting lost in the crowd and landing your next opportunity.

Most of the conferences I am going to list are primarily designed for working professionals rather than students. However, they can still provide valuable networking opportunities if approached the right way. Many of these events are expensive, private (often exclusive or invite-only), or geared toward a high-level audience, meaning a strong background is usually needed to fully understand and engage with the content. That said, if you live in or near the host city, it can still be worthwhile to attend informally. Many conferences are held in major hotels, and simply spending time in the lobby or common areas dressed professionally can create organic opportunities to network with industry professionals, strike up conversations, and make meaningful connections without needing full conference access.

Sport Business Journal (SBJ) Conferences: SBJ National Sports Forum

One of Sports Business Journal's premier events, the National Sports Forum brings together senior executives from professional leagues, teams, media companies, and sponsors. The conference focuses on the business operations of sports, including revenue growth, fan engagement, media rights, and leadership strategy. It is a high-level, executive-driven event that offers valuable insight into how major organizations operate and where the industry is headed.

Leaders Meet: Innovation

Leaders Meet: Innovation is a global conference centered on forward-thinking ideas shaping the future of sport. Hosted by Leaders in Sport, the event attracts executives, entrepreneurs, and innovators from across leagues, clubs, brands, and technology companies. Discussions emphasize innovation, digital transformation, sustainability, and new business models within the global sports ecosystem.

The Business of Soccer

This conference is dedicated specifically to the commercial and operational side of soccer in North America and beyond. Attendees include league executives, club leadership, investors, media partners, and sponsors. Topics often include league growth strategies, ownership models, media rights, fan development, and the evolving global soccer marketplace.

Sports Business Awards: Tech

This event recognizes and celebrates innovation and excellence in sports technology. It highlights organizations, start-ups, and leaders driving advancements in data, fan engagement, digital platforms, and performance technology. The awards bring together executives and innovators who are shaping the tech-driven evolution of the sports industry.

Tech Week

Tech Week is a multiday event series focused on technology, innovation, and entrepreneurship, with strong crossover into sports, media, and entertainment. The conference features panels, networking events, and showcases with founders, investors, and executives exploring how technology is transforming business and consumer experiences.

Sports Business Awards

The Sports Business Awards honor outstanding achievements across the sports industry, including teams, leagues, executives, agencies, and brands. The event serves as both a celebration and a networking opportunity, attracting senior leaders and decision-makers from across the sports business landscape.

Brand Innovation Summit

The Brand Innovation Summit brings together brand executives, marketers, and strategists to explore how brands connect with consumers through sports, entertainment, and culture. The event focuses on storytelling, partnerships, fan engagement, and creative innovation, making it especially relevant for those interested in marketing and sponsorship roles.

Thought Leaders

Thought Leaders is an invitation-only retreat designed for senior executives to engage in deep, strategic discussions about the future of sports business. The event emphasizes leadership, collaboration, and long-term industry challenges, with a format that encourages meaningful conversations rather than traditional panels.

Thought Leaders: Tech

Thought Leaders: Tech is a technology-focused extension of the Thought Leaders series, bringing together executives at the intersection of sports, media, and technology. The event centers on emerging tech trends, data strategy, innovation leadership, and how technology is reshaping sports organizations at the highest levels.

Forty Under 40

The Forty Under 40 event celebrates the most impactful young executives in the sports business industry. Honorees are recognized for leadership, innovation, and career achievement, and the event serves as a high-profile networking opportunity among rising industry leaders, established executives, and influencers.

Other Conferences:

SEAT Conference (Sports Entertainment Alliance in Technology)

A leading sports technology conference focused on data, digital innovation, fan engagement, and revenue operations across professional and collegiate sports. The event brings together executives, tech leaders, and solution providers shaping the future of the sports industry.

CAA World Congress of Sports

The World Congress of Sports is widely considered one of the most prestigious sports business conferences in the industry. Hosted by Sports Business Journal, it convenes top executives from leagues, teams, agencies, brands, and media companies. The event focuses on strategic decision-making, leadership, and major trends influencing the future of global sports business.

Hashtag Sports Conference

A modern sports marketing conference centered on digital content, social media, brand storytelling, and fan engagement, this event is popular with marketers, content creators, and brand strategists focused on revenue growth through digital channels.

Big Data Bowl (NFL)

A prestigious analytics competition sponsored by the NFL, challenging participants to solve football-related data problems. It is known as a résumé-defining experience for those pursuing careers in football analytics.

SABR Analytics Conference

A baseball-focused analytics conference with strong ties to Major League Baseball organizations, attracting analysts, researchers, and front office personnel interested in data-driven decision-making in baseball.

OptaPro Analytics Forums

Internationally recognized soccer analytics events bring together analysts, clubs, and data professionals that are highly respected within global football for advancing quantitative analysis and performance insights.

Learfield IMG College Intercollegiate Athletics Forum

A major gathering of college athletics administrators, sponsors, and media partners, focusing on revenue generation, NIL, media rights, and the evolving business of college sports.

National Association of Collegiate Directors of Athletics (NACDA) Convention

The largest annual gathering of athletic directors and senior college sports administrators covers leadership, operations, compliance, and strategic issues facing collegiate athletics.

Women Leaders in Sports Convention

A highly regarded conference dedicated to leadership development, mentorship, and career advancement for women in athletics. This event is known for its strong networking culture and supportive environment.

Sports Lawyers Association Conference

A specialized conference focused on legal issues in sports, including contracts, representation, and labor relations. It has strong overlap with agent work and sports law careers.

Networking Action Campaign

Transform networking from abstract concept to concrete action with this 30-day challenge.

Week 1: Fix your foundation. Complete your LinkedIn profile overhaul using the guidelines from this chapter, achieve 500+ connections by connecting with classmates, professors, family friends, and past colleagues, and join three relevant LinkedIn groups (WISE, sports business groups, alumni groups).

Week 2: Launch your outreach campaign. Send ten personalized connection requests to sports professionals whose careers interest you, using the templates provided. Don't ask for anything yet, just connect.

Week 3: Engage strategically. Comment thoughtfully on five posts from professionals in your network, share one relevant article with your perspective, and send three follow-up messages to people who accepted your connection requests, asking for brief informational interviews.

Week 4: Deliver value. Complete at least two informational interviews from your outreach, send handwritten thank you notes to everyone who gave you time, and make one introduction connecting two people in your network who should know each other.

Track everything in a spreadsheet: who you contacted, when they responded, what you learned, and next steps. This isn't networking theory, it's a systematic campaign that builds real relationships. After 30 days, you'll have expanded your network by dozens of meaningful connections, developed relationships with several industry professionals, and created momentum you can sustain with 2-3 hours of networking activity weekly going forward.

"Work hard, work collaboratively and have fun. When you stop having fun, seek change. Learn from every failure and never make the same mistake twice. Most importantly be the person your dog thinks you are." **Julie Boyd, Chief Financial Officer, San Diego Wave Fútbol Club**

"Stuart is someone who "walks-the-walk" as he embodies what this book is about; from how he worked his way into the sports business, to having an impressive career, and now to "paying it forward" by sharing his learnings with others looking to do the same. Plus, he is a highly sought after mentor on theClubhouse by those looking to get into the sports industry" **Lou DePaoli, President, General Sports Worldwide**

"It's encouraging to see a book written to guide students pursuing a career in this industry. Passion is expected and may get you in the door, but consistency, reliability, coachability, and a willingness to solve problems are what keep you in the room. Figure out what makes you tick and go all in your pursuit and mastery of it. This book speaks to those values and to the habits that turn opportunity into a lasting career." **Joe Rickert, President, Taymar Sales U**

"It is one thing to love sports, it's another to handle the grind required to break into the industry. Stuart delivers the perfect blueprint for making that transition. If you are serious about moving from a fan in the stands to a professional in the front office, this is the playbook you need." **Joe Rugo, Executive Vice President, Partner Development, FEVO**

"You don't earn a career in sports by wanting it - you earn it the same way you earn playing time: preparation, consistency, and being a great teammate." **Leo Cardenas, Vice President of Sales and Service, On Location**

"Growing and maintaining a strong personal network can really pay dividends throughout a career, but especially for those in the early stages of their journey. The old adage of 'it's not what you know, but who you know' falls short in my opinion as it's not actually who you know, but rather who knows you. Following up with contacts, checking in with them periodically with meaningful dialogue and exchanges keeps a healthy network which benefits both parties. It's through these relationships that bonds can be created that lead to industry insight and even potential opportunities. One thing I've always been impressed with is Stuart's ability to maintain contact and do so in a respectful, thoughtful, and insightful way. I first met Stuart in 2016 when he was an undergrad and throughout his ascension into the sports world he has done a wonderful job of staying in touch in a meaningful and insightful way. I've enjoyed hearing updates and following his career success along the way. Do it all. This message is directed at folks who may not know exactly what path they want to take, but can also apply to those who think they know what their goals may be. Experiencing everything from operations, to food service, to event production, and especially sales not only creates a well rounded candidate for any role but also may open your eyes to an area of the industry you didn't know existed or didn't know you'd enjoy." **Noel Blaha, Sr. Vice President, Jacksonville Jumbo Shrimp**

Chapter 9: Learn in the Struggle How Bad Teams Build Better Careers

Everyone wants to work for the championship team with the packed arena and the waiting list for season tickets. That makes sense until you realize that working for a losing team in front of half-empty stands will probably teach you ten times more about how this business actually works. When everything's going well, you're executing in easy mode. When the team is terrible and nobody wants to buy tickets, that's when you learn how to actually sell, how to stay creative with no budget, and how to build something real instead of just riding momentum that someone else created. This chapter is about why the unsexy jobs at struggling organizations often turn into the best career moves you'll ever make, and how to tell the difference between a bad team that will teach you everything and a bad organization that will just waste your time.

The Unsexy Truth About Where You Learn Most

Yes, it's sexy to work for the Golden State Warriors during their championship run. Everyone wants that job. But will you learn more working for a 24-win Phoenix Suns team? Probably. And here's why that matters more than the Instagram posts showing you courtside at championship celebrations. When you work for a winning team, everything is easier. Tickets are easier to sell, sponsors are more open to have conversations, fans are engaged, and the budget is healthy. You're executing strategies in an environment where momentum carries much of the work. That's valuable experience, but it's not the same education you get when everything is hard.

When you work for a struggling team, one that's losing games, attendance is down, sponsors are questioning their investment, and budgets are tight, you learn how to actually build something. You learn creative problemsolving when resources are limited. You learn how to sell when nobody wants to buy. You learn how to engage fans who are frustrated and disillusioned. You learn how to do more with less, think strategically under pressure, and find solutions that don't exist in any playbook. Those skills are what make you valuable for the rest of your career, not the ability to execute strategies in ideal conditions.

"Go work for people, not logos. The only people that care what team/league you work for are the people that don't work in sports. What this is trying to portray is that there is no correlation between how successful a team is on the court, field or ice with the salesmanship of their reps. Some of the best sales reps come from scrappy backgrounds like NASCAR, minor league baseball and teams that traditionally are 0.500 or below. Working for the biggest brands doesn't equal the biggest opportunities & learning experiences," says James "JB" Bryant, the Director of Inside Sales for the FIFA World Cup 2026.

Why Struggling Teams Accelerate Your Growth

When I joined the Phoenix Suns, we were coming off a 24-win season. This wasn't the glamorous job everyone dreams about. But that season taught me more about sports business than any championship organization could have. Here's what you learn working for struggling teams that you don't learn when everything's going well.

You learn real sales skills, not order taking. When the team is winning and excitement is high, people call you wanting tickets. That's order taking, not selling. When the team is losing and nobody's interested, you have to actually sell, overcome objections, create value, build relationships, and educate people to invest in something that doesn't look promising on the surface. Those are the skills that translate everywhere. Anyone can take orders when demand is high. Not everyone can create demand when it doesn't exist. You learn resource-fulness and creativity under constraints.

Winning teams have budgets for marketing campaigns, premium giveaways, and expensive activations. Losing teams have to work with less. You have to get creative: grassroots marketing, guerrilla tactics, partnerships that don't cost money, leveraging relationships instead of budgets. Learning to deliver results without resources makes you far more valuable than learning to execute when money isn't an obstacle.

You learn how to engage and retain fans when they're frustrated. Keeping fans engaged during losing seasons is one of the hardest challenges in sports. You're not selling wins; you're selling community, experience, hope, and connection to something bigger than this season's record. Learning how to maintain relationships and loyalty when the on-field product isn't delivering teaches you fan engagement at a level that winning teams never have to master. You see what happens when things go bad, and you're prepared when it inevitably happens again. Every team, every organization, every career goes through difficult periods. If you've only worked in ideal conditions, you're not as prepared for adversity. Working through struggles early in your career means you've already developed the resilience, problem-solving, and persistence required to navigate challenges later. When you encounter difficulty in future roles, you're not panicking; you've been there before and you know how to work through it.

You get more responsibility faster because there's more need and less competition. Struggling teams need people who can contribute immediately, and there's less competition for opportunities because most people are chasing the sexy jobs with winning teams. You'll get responsibilities and visibility that would take years to earn at a championship organization. That accelerated growth compounds throughout your career.

Not all struggling teams are equal learning opportunities. Some are poorly run organizations where you'll learn bad habits. Others are well-managed organizations going through a rebuild where you'll learn from excellent leaders navigating difficult circumstances. Here's how to identify the difference – look at leadership, not record. Research the front office executives. Are they respected in the industry? Do they have track records of building successful organizations? Are they investing in the business side even while the team struggles on the field? Good leadership in a bad situation is a better learning environment than poor leadership in a good situation.

Assess whether the organization is investing in a turnaround or just managing decline. Some struggling teams are actively rebuilding, hiring new executives, investing in infrastructure, and implementing new strategies. Others are just trying to minimize losses until something changes. You want to join organizations that are building toward something, even if they're currently struggling, not organizations that have given up. Talk to current and former employees about culture. Struggling teams can have terrible cultures where everyone's miserable and blaming each other, or they can have resilient cultures where people are committed to turning things around together. Reach out to people who work or worked there and ask about the culture, leadership, and whether they felt supported during difficult times.

Consider the market and resources. A struggling team in a major market with good ownership is different from a struggling team in a small market with financial constraints. Both are valuable learning experiences, but understand what you're walking into and whether the organization has the resources to eventually turn things around.

Follow the Young Disruptors Changing the Game

While established executives offer invaluable wisdom from decades of experience, some of the most innovative thinking in sports business is coming from young professionals who are reimagining how the industry works. These are people in their 20s and 30s who haven't been in the business long enough to accept "that's how we've always done it" as a valid answer. They're leveraging technology, challenging traditional revenue models, rethinking fan engagement, and building new pathways that didn't exist five years ago. Following these emerging leaders gives you insight into where the industry is headed, not just where it's been.

Take someone like Jentry Mullins who's building innovative approaches to sports business while still in his 20s. Young executives like Jentry represent a generation that grew up digital-native, understands evolving fan behaviors instinctively, and isn't afraid to experiment with unconventional strategies. They're working at startups disrupting ticketing, creating new media companies, launching emerging leagues, and finding opportunities in spaces traditional sports organizations haven't prioritized. Following these innovators, commenting on their content, engaging with their ideas, and learning from their approaches positions you to understand and capitalize on industry shifts before they become mainstream. The executives running teams today are valuable to follow, but the young disruptors experimenting today might be running the industry tomorrow. Pay attention to both.

Follow 10-15 leaders whose careers or thinking interests you. Engage with their content, comment thoughtfully, share with your perspective, and ask genuine questions. This builds visibility and demonstrates you're thinking seriously about the industry.

Use Social Media to Learn, Not Just Scroll

Set an intentional time for professional development on social media. Spend 20 minutes daily engaging with industry content, read posts from leaders you follow, comment thoughtfully on 3-5 pieces of content, or share insights. This isn't mindless scrolling; it's structured learning. Try creating your own content sharing what you're learning. Write posts about insights from internships, interesting trends you're following, or lessons from experiences. You don't need thousands of followers, you need to demonstrate you're actively thinking about the industry. Engage consistently over time. Showing up once doesn't build visibility. Commenting regularly on leaders' posts makes you recognizable. Over months, you're not just another random follower; you're someone who engages intelligently with their content.

The combination of working for struggling teams where you learn through adversity and following leaders who share their wisdom creates accelerated growth that seeking only prestigious, winning organizations never provides. Choose the unsexy opportunities. Learn in the struggle. Follow people who've navigated challenges successfully. That's how you build skills that last beyond any single job or season.

Opportunity Evaluation Framework

Develop a systematic approach to evaluating job opportunities that looks beyond prestige and winning records. Create a decision matrix for any opportunity you're considering (internship, entry-level job, or career move) with these evaluation criteria:

- Learning potential: will this role expose me to diverse challenges and force skill development? Rate the specific skills you'll build.
- Responsibility and autonomy: will I get meaningful responsibility quickly, or will bureaucracy slow my growth?
- Leadership quality: research the people who lead the organization or department. Are they respected in the industry? Do they develop talent? What's their leadership reputation?
- Organizational trajectory: is this organization investing in turnaround, or managing decline? Look for evidence of new hires, strategic initiatives, and resource allocation.
- Network expansion: who will I meet and work with? What relationships will this enable?

- Career positioning: how does this role position me for my next move? Does it build capabilities that transfer?

For each criterion, assign a weighted score based on what matters most to your current career stage. Calculate total scores for opportunities you're comparing. This framework prevents you from automatically chasing prestigious organizations while overlooking roles that might offer better growth. Use this matrix every time you're evaluating opportunities throughout your career, adjusting the weights as your priorities evolve.

Part IV: Standing Out From the Crowd

Mastering the application and interview process that converts opportunities into offers: crafting resumes that start conversations rather than list responsibilities (Chapter 10), writing emails that get responses and build relationships (Chapter 11), interviewing with professionalism from parking lot to follow-up (Chapter 12), and maintaining an active pipeline of opportunities instead of waiting on one organization (Chapter 13).

"I believe every job that you get is a stepping stone for the next - of course, that is hard to see at the moment but each challenge helps build resiliency and character - setting up the next chapter to be even greater." By under promising and over-delivering, you can go from good to great. If you can sell yourself, outwork everyone else in the room and be a kind person, the opportunities are truly limitless." **David Braun, Partner and Co-President, GSM Marketing**

"Breaking into the sports industry is about understanding how the business really works and taking intentional steps that move you forward. What this book offers is a clear, practical look at the path from interest to opportunity, showing readers how to build real relationships, create value, and navigate an industry that rewards persistence and authenticity. It gives aspiring professionals the kind of actionable, inside-the-business guidance that most people wish they had when starting out." **Gabby Munoz, Director, Corporate Partnership Development, Miami Dolphins and Hard Rock Stadium**

"I think the most important step is to recognize the opportunities around you (on your campus, in your city, etc) to get started in gaining professional experience in any capacity (say yes!). There's no substitute for real-world experience and understanding. Few know this better than Stuart, who made it a point to recognize opportunities and maximize his understanding of the industry and how he wants to grow in it. And as we ourselves grow in the game, we have a responsibility to pay forward the mentoring and assistance that we got from others as we were looking to get our start in sports." **Gabriel Alvarez, Assistant Director, Player Development, Operations at San Francisco Giants**

"I've had the pleasure of working with a lot of individuals aspiring to break into and advance in the sports world. I know few who were more effective in their networking and broad scope of development and experience than Stuart. He's been there, done that and got the t-shirt in a variety of organizations and roles within the sports industry. His insights are from personal experience as well as a well-developed network of individuals from across the sports world." **Keith Bryant, former Director, United States Olympic and Paralympic Committee and former CEO and Executive Director, USA Judo**

"Building a career in the sports industry doesn't happen by accident. It takes a strategic approach that involves networking yourself, building genuine relationships with industry colleagues/leaders and doing things others are not willing to do. Stuart's step-by-step guide puts these "industry professional" tips in one place and provides a practical, easy to apply "cheat code" for anyone who's willing to do the work. No one makes it in sports alone. With Stuart's new guide, you won't have to be alone." **Mike Robbins, Director, Suites & Group Sales and Service, New York Yankees**

"The only way to be truly successful in sports, is to obsess over your work. The same way the very best athletes obsess over their craft, you need to do the same. Whether it's sales, marketing, event operations; whatever. Wherever you find your passion it needs to be on your mind all the time. I haven't set an out of office email in 13 years. When I'm on vacation, I'm just working less. You're never off." **Justin LaLone, Director, Ticketing & Business Operations, Chicago Cubs Spring Training**

Chapter 10: The Resume: More Than a Piece of Paper

Your resume will not get you the job. Let's just get that out of the way right now. What it will do, if you build it right, is get someone interested enough to have a conversation with you, and that conversation is where you actually get hired. The problem is that most people treat their resume like a comprehensive record of everything they've ever done, cramming in every responsibility and task from every job they've held, hoping something sticks. But hiring managers spend about six seconds scanning your resume on the first pass, which means you're not trying to tell your whole story. You're trying to make them curious enough in those six seconds to want to hear more. This chapter shows you how to build a resume that actually does that job instead of just looking impressive on your side of the screen.

What a Resume Actually Is (And Isn't)

Let's start by squashing the myth that's been drilled into your head since high school: your resume will not get you a job. And your resume is not a comprehensive record of everything you've ever done, and it's not a checklist of experiences you're trying to prove. It's not a document where you cram every responsibility, skill, and accomplishment into bulleted lists hoping something catches a hiring manager's attention. Your resume is a conversation starter. That's it. Its job is to get someone interested enough in you that they want to have a conversation, a phone screen, an informational interview, or a formal interview where you can actually tell your story, demonstrate your value, and show why you're the right person for the opportunity. If your resume gets you that conversation, it's done its job perfectly, even if it doesn't list every single thing you've ever accomplished.

The reality is that hiring managers spend six seconds scanning your resume on the first pass. Six seconds. In that time, they're not reading every word, they're scanning for signals that you might be worth their time. Are you in the right field? Do you have relevant experience? Does anything jump out as interesting or impressive? If the answer is yes, they'll spend more time reading. If not, you're in the rejection pile before they reach the bottom of the first page. This changes everything about how you should build your resume. You're not trying to be comprehensive; you're trying to be compelling in six seconds. You're not listing every responsibility; you're highlighting the most relevant and impressive things you've done. You're not writing for yourself; you're writing for someone who's looking at 200 resumes and needs a reason to care about yours specifically.

Quagliata states. "I look for clear, concise resumes that answer the question, 'Do I trust that this person can do the job at hand?' If you can, start each bullet point with a verb that explains your tasks so hiring managers can start drawing connections between your experience and how you might fit within the open position. In short, don't make the hiring manager work too hard to see how qualified you are!"

The Purpose of Your Resume: A Tool to Get to Know You

Your resume is serving one primary purpose, and that is to give hiring managers enough information about who you are, what you've done, and what you're capable of so that they want to learn more. It's the trailer, not the full movie. It's the appetizer, not the entire meal. It should leave them curious, interested, and ready to have a conversation where you can provide the depth and context that a one-page document can't capture. This means your resume should answer a few fundamental questions quickly and clearly: Who are you? What's your current status (student, recent grad, professional), what field are you in, and what are you trying to do?

This should be immediately clear from your header, summary (if you include one), and the way you've organized your experience.

What have you done that's relevant? What experiences, skills, and accomplishments demonstrate you can succeed in the role you're applying for? This is where most of your resume real estate should go, to experiences and achievements that directly relate to what the job requires. Why should they care? What makes you different from the other 199 people applying? What's interesting, impressive, or unique about your background? This might be the volume of experience, unique opportunities, measurable results, or skills that set you apart.

Can you do this job? Do you have the baseline qualifications, education, experience level, and technical skill that the role requires? Hiring managers need to quickly confirm you meet minimum requirements before they invest time learning more about you. If your resume clearly answers these questions in six seconds of scanning, it's working. If someone has to study your resume for two minutes to figure out who you are and whether you're qualified, you've already lost.

Resume Layout and Structure: Make It Easy to Scan

Format matters more than you think. A well-formatted resume that's easy to scan will get read. A poorly formatted resume with cluttered layouts, inconsistent formatting, or hard-to-read fonts will get tossed regardless of how impressive your experience is. Hiring managers are looking for reasons to narrow the pile; don't give them formatting as an easy excuse to eliminate you. Use a clean, professional template with a clear hierarchy. Your name and contact information should be prominent at the top. Section headers (education, experience, and skills) should be bold and easy to identify. Each experience should be clearly separated with consistent formatting. Use white space strategically – cramming text to fit everything makes it unreadable. Try to make each experience have the same number of bullet points.

Stick to one page for students and recent grads, maximum two pages for experienced professionals. If you're a student or within five years of graduation, your resume should be one page. You don't have enough experience to justify two pages, and forcing it to two pages makes it look like you're padding. If you have 5-10+ years of experience, two pages is acceptable, but make sure page one is strong enough to make them turn to page two. Use consistent, professional fonts and formatting. Stick to standard professional fonts: Calibri, Arial, or Times New Roman. Font size should be 10-12pt for body text, slightly larger (14-16pt) for your name. Use bold, italics, and bullet points consistently throughout, don't bold some job titles and not others, and don't use different bullet styles in different sections.

Order sections strategically based on your strongest assets. For students, lead with education because it's your strongest credential. For professionals, lead with experience. If you have particularly impressive skills (certifications, technical proficiencies, languages), consider placing a skills section high on the page where it gets noticed. Include clear contact information, but keep it minimal. Name, phone number, email, LinkedIn URL, and optionally your city/state. You don't need your full address (privacy concern, and it can trigger location bias). I personally do not put a city, nor state, but this is my personal opinion. You don't need "References available upon request", as that's assumed. Plus, if they want it, they'll request them later on in the interview process. Make your LinkedIn URL a custom short link (linkedin.com/in/yourname), rather than the long default URL and/or add your personal website.

Writing Bullets That Actually Matter

This is where most resumes fail. People write bullets that describe responsibilities and what they were supposed to do rather than accomplishments and what they actually achieved. Hiring managers don't care what your job description says. They care about what you delivered, what results you produced, and what you learned that makes you valuable to their organization.

Start bullets with strong action verbs, not weak passive language. Compare these:

Weak: "Responsible for managing social media accounts"

- Strong: "Managed social media accounts for minor league baseball team, growing Instagram following 40% and engagement 65% over one season"

The second bullet tells them what you did and what resulted from your work. Always push toward specificity and results. Quantify results whenever possible. Numbers make accomplishments concrete and impressive. Compare:

- Vague: "Sold season tickets for a professional sports team"
- Specific: "Generated $75,000 in season ticket revenue over 12-week internship, ranking 2nd among an 8-person sales team"

Numbers don't have to be revenue; they can be growth percentages, attendance increases, number of events managed, size of audiences reached, number of people supervised – anything that demonstrates scale or impact. Focus on accomplishments and learning, not just tasks. Don't just list what you did, explain what resulted or what you learned. Compare:

- Task-focused: "Assisted with game day operations for 25 home games"
- Accomplishment-focused: "Coordinated game day operations for 25 home games, managing 15-person

volunteer staff and troubleshooting real-time issues to ensure seamless fan experiences"

The second version shows responsibility, scale, problem-solving, and impact. The XYZ method makes your accomplishments impossible to ignore. One of the most powerful frameworks for writing resume bullets is the XYZ method: Accomplished [X] as measured by [Y] by doing [Z]. This formula forces you to think about your work in terms of measurable impact rather than vague responsibilities. Organizations hire people to solve problems and generate results, not complete tasks. The XYZ method ensures every bullet demonstrates not just what you did (Z), but what resulted from your work (X) and how you prove it (Y). Compare these examples:

- *Weak:* "Responsible for social media management for college athletic department."
- *Strong:* "Grew Instagram following by 47% and engagement by 83% (Y measuring X) by creating consistent content calendar and leveraging student-athlete stories (Z)."

- *Weak:* "Worked on ticket sales for a minor league baseball team."
- *Strong:* "Generated $82,000 in group ticket revenue (X), ranking 2nd among 10-person sales team (Y), through targeted outreach to local businesses and youth organizations (Z)."

When you can't quantify with hard numbers, use scale (managed 15-person team), scope (coordinated 40 events), rankings (top performer), or recognition (promoted after 6 months). Go through your current resume and convert task-focused bullets into XYZ format by asking: What actually resulted from this work? How can I measure that result? What specific actions did I take? This exercise reveals accomplishments you'd forgotten and makes your value obvious and measurable.

Customize bullets for each application. Don't send the same generic resume to every job. Read the job description, identify the 3-5 most important skills or experiences they're seeking, and make sure your resume prominently features bullets demonstrating those exact things. If they want someone with sponsorship activation experience, make sure your most impressive sponsorship bullets are prominent. If they want data analysis skills, highlight your analytical work. Use the PAR method: Problem, Action, Result. Strong bullets often follow this structure:

- Problem/Context: What challenge existed or what were you trying to achieve?
- Action: What did you specifically do?
- Result: What happened because of your actions?

Example: "To reverse declining student attendance (Problem), developed targeted marketing campaign leveraging social media influencers and student organizations (Action), resulting in 35% increase in student ticket sales over previous season (Result)."

Take time to analyze the job description and identify the key words and phrases that appear repeatedly, such as terms like "revenue generation," "stakeholder engagement," or "game day operations." Then strategically weave these exact terms into your resume and cover letter where they genuinely apply to your experience. Most sports organizations use Applicant Tracking Systems (ATS) that scan applications for these specific keywords before a human recruiter ever reviews them. If your resume doesn't include the right terminology, it may be filtered out automatically, regardless of how qualified you are.

You don't need to use this format for every bullet, but when you have impressive accomplishments, this structure tells a compelling story in one sentence.

Common Resume Mistakes to Avoid

Typos and grammatical errors: This should be obvious, but resumes with typos get immediately rejected. Proofread multiple times. Have others proofread. Use spell-check. One typo might be forgiven; multiple typos signal carelessness.

Generic, one-size-fits-all resumes: Sending the same resume to every application shows you're not serious about any specific opportunity. Customize your resume for each application, emphasize relevant experiences, use language from the job description, and show you understand what they're looking for.

Lying or exaggerating: Don't list skills you don't have, inflate your role in projects, or claim accomplishments you didn't achieve. The sports industry is small; people will find out, and your reputation will be tainted. Be honest about what you've done and let your real accomplishments speak for themselves.

Including irrelevant information: Your high school achievements don't matter once you're in college. Your college involvement doesn't matter much once you're five years into your career. Cut relentlessly if it's not impressive or relevant to the job you're applying for and remove it to make room for what actually matters.

Poor formatting that makes scanning difficult: Dense paragraphs, inconsistent formatting, tiny fonts, and lack of white space all make your resume hard to read and more likely to be rejected. Remember to focus on accomplishments instead of responsibilities. Your job description isn't impressive, everyone with that job title had similar responsibilities. What's impressive is what you specifically achieved, how you exceeded expectations, and what results you produced.

Including "References available upon request": This is outdated and wastes valuable resume space. It's assumed you'll provide references if asked. Use that line for something that actually adds value.

Finally, always send your resume as a PDF named "FirstName LastName JobTitle Resume.pdf" so hiring managers can easily identify whose resume they're reviewing. Always submit your resume as a PDF unless the job posting specifically requests otherwise. PDFs preserve your formatting across all devices and operating systems, ensuring that the careful layout and design you created looks exactly the same on the hiring manager's screen as it does on yours.

Your Resume is a Living Document

Your resume should evolve constantly as you gain experience, develop skills, and refine your career focus. After every internship, job, or significant experience, update your resume immediately while the details are fresh. Every few months, review your resume and ask: Is this still representing me accurately? Are there better examples I could use? Is the emphasis right for what I'm pursuing now? Don't wait until you're actively job searching to update your resume; by then, you've forgotten important details and accomplishments. Keep a running document where you track everything you do, every accomplishment, every metric, every skill developed. When you update your resume, you'll have a comprehensive record to pull from rather than trying to remember details from years ago. Your resume is not a static document you create once and use forever. It's a living tool that should grow and improve as you do. Invest time in making it excellent, customize it thoughtfully for each opportunity, and use it as the conversation starter it's meant to be – the first step in telling your story and demonstrating why you're the right person for the opportunity.

Your Cover Letter: Address It Head-On

Your cover letter is the best place to address overqualification concerns before they become deal-breakers. Don't ignore the elephant in the room or pretend your MBA doesn't exist. Instead, acknowledge it briefly, then pivot to why this specific role makes sense for you right now. Be clear about your priorities and explain how this job aligns with your career goals. Maybe you managed a team for three years and realized you miss the hands-on work. Maybe you're relocating and this organization's mission resonates with you. Maybe you're pivoting from corporate to sports and you're willing to start at an entry point to learn the industry from the inside. Whatever your reason is, make it genuine and specific to this job, not just, "I'm passionate about sports." Then, match your skills directly to what they're asking for. Choose accomplishments from your background that directly address the problems mentioned in the job description. If they need someone who can manage social media campaigns, talk about the time you increased engagement by 35% in three months. If they need someone who can wrangle complex schedules, describe how you coordinated logistics for a 50-person event. Be concrete about what you can contribute from day one, whether that's bringing systems that streamline their workflow, connections that open doors, or simply the ability to hit the ground running without a long ramp-up period. Frame yourself as the best fit not because you have the most experience, but because your specific experience solves their specific problems right now. The goal is to sound like someone who's thought this through and wants this exact job, not someone who's taking whatever they can get while they keep looking.

Resume and Cover Letter Transformation Workshop

Transform your resume from a task list into a compelling accomplishment document. First, inventory your current resume: print it out and highlight every bullet point that describes responsibilities versus accomplishments. If most bullets describe what you were "responsible for" rather than what you achieved, you've identified the problem. Next, complete the XYZ conversion exercise: for every experience on your resume, write 3-5 bullets using the formula "accomplished [X] as measured by [Y] by doing [Z]." Force yourself to quantify impact with numbers, percentages, rankings, or scale. If you can't quantify, use scope (managed team of 15), duration (coordinated 40 events), or recognition (promoted after 6 months). Then, create three versions of your resume customized for different types of roles: one emphasizing sales and revenue skills, one emphasizing operations and event management, one emphasizing marketing and content creation. This forces you to think about how your experiences translate to different contexts.

Your cover letter isn't a summary of your resume, it's your chance to tell the story your resume can't. Think of a job you're interested in applying for, or a job description that got you excited in the past, and think about the cover letter you would write for it. Start with why this specific job at this specific organization matters to you right now, not generic enthusiasm about sports. Then connect 2-3 of your strongest accomplishments directly to the problems mentioned in the job description. Use the same XYZ formula, but in narrative form: "When our department needed to increase engagement, I tested five different content strategies over two months and identified the approach that grew our Instagram following by 35%, exactly the kind of rapid experimentation your posting mentions needing for game day content." End with what you'll focus on in your first 90 days. This shows you've thought past getting hired to actually doing the work. Keep it to one page, match their tone (formal for league offices, conversational for startups), and make every sentence earn its place. If you're overqualified for the role, address it head-on in one or two sentences, then pivot immediately to why this role makes sense for you and what you bring that no one else does.

Finally, get brutal feedback: send both your resume and cover letter to three people (a professor, a working professional in sports, and a peer) with this specific request: "Does this resume make you want to interview me? Does this cover letter make you believe I actually want this job? What's confusing? What's most impressive?" Implement their feedback and repeat this exercise every 3-4 months as you gain new experiences. Your resume and cover letter should be living documents that evolve constantly, not something you update once and forget.

"Landing a career in sports can be one of the most challenging feats a recent graduate can encounter. Considering the sheer number of jobs available vs. the total number of career seekers, you must find a way to position yourself to be a "can't miss" candidate. Even in sales departments where the department size is typically one of the largest in an organization, candidates can face as low as a 1-2% chance of getting hired. There is a tremendous amount of noise for a hiring manager to work through. How can you be the noise they hear? What I recommend is adhering to the "P to the Sixth Power" principle. Prior Preparation Prevents Piss Poor Performance. Ask yourself, what are you doing today to position yourself for your future career? Take a deep dive into who you are, what you value, the lifestyle you want to live, the core principles you want to live by, and fully understand your "why" behind all of it. This will help you determine your purpose. We often hear candidates talk about "passion" in their interview. Passion is great, but without purpose, you have a tank full of gas with no map to guide you. Eventually you will run out of gas because this industry will test you, break you, work you harder than you ever thought possible. This industry is a lifestyle, not a hobby. To survive, thrive, and succeed long-term, you must know why you are doing this in the first place. Next, stop waiting until you need a job to begin building relationships. Athletes don't wait until gameday to practice their craft! While you are in college, volunteer as much as possible, find jobs that put you in challenging human facing positions where you must think on your feet, and say "Yes" to as many opportunities as possible. Reach out and connect with leaders who are currently working in sports. Ask them smart questions about their journey, take notes, adhere to their advice, and stay in contact. You are selling yourself. No salesperson makes one call or outreach and stops there. Then, send a handwritten thank you note to the person who blessed you with their time. People in this industry are generous and will give you their time, you simply need to ask for it. Last, you are building a brand with everything you do. The content you share, the social posts you make, the activities you participate in, and the interactions you have. What is your brand? When hiring managers bring someone into their company, that person is now a representation of the hiring manager/leader, the department, and the organization. Your brand means far more than you can understand. Build it wisely, humbly, and with character. Be coachable, intentional, work on your mindset daily, and take ownership of your actions. Don't get ahead of yourself. Stop chasing titles and money. Chase people, leaders, and purpose. When you do that, the right opportunities will find you and success will chase you." **Nick Richardson, Vice President, Ticket Retention & New Business Development, Texas Rangers**

"I believe in paying it forward by adding perspective and honoring the ongoing cycle of giving and receiving. My growth came from exposure to many experiences and viewpoints, not adherence to a single philosophy, because there is no universal path to success in this industry. Having benefited from that openness from others, I feel a responsibility to continue the cycle by sharing insight that gives the next generation context, clarity, and confidence, and reminds them they do not need to climb the entire ladder at once, only take the next step." **Ryan Davenport, Sr. Vice President, Ticket Sales & Service, Miami Marlins & loanDepot park**

"It takes courage to jump into the unknown. It takes further courage and care to document, share and express all your firsthand wins and learning points. Thank you for crafting a book that helps chart a thoughtful course for tomorrow's industry leaders." **Andrew Seymour, General Manager, Mississippi Mud Monsters**

"I'm grateful to Stuart for inviting me to be part of this project. Breaking into professional sports as a physical therapist is challenging, but it's a path filled with growth, relationships, and moments that remind you why you chose this field in the first place. To the students reading: stay driven, stay patient, and keep showing up. Every opportunity I've had came from consistency, humility, and a refusal to not get to where I wanted to be." **Kyle Belski, PT, DPT, SCS, FAAOMPT, Former Physical Therapist, San Francisco Giants**

"Books like this weren't available as I tried to break into sports. Having a guiding light to help navigate the grind and land your dream job would have been helpful in the early part of my education and career. Now we have this roadmap to help remove some of the guesswork and fear of whether you are doing it right or not. When in doubt, make that contact, establish an internship, follow your dreams" **Brad Epstein, Head Athletic Trainer, Milwaukee Brewers**

"Breaking into professional sports is challenging. It takes a little break and a lot of hard work. But if I could give one piece of advice it's that people will always remember how you made them feel rather than what you do for them. There's a human element to sports. One that often gets lost on the casual fan. The athletes I work with wake up and put their pants on one leg at a time, just like you. Maintaining professionalism while leaving the "star struck" aspect at the door is wildly important. Treating people as if they are family to you goes a long way. Sometimes long enough, that when all is said and done, they become your extended family." **Ari Cowen, Sports Medicine Professional**

"Whichever organization you break in with should have leadership that is invested in your success and growth. Your first job (and boss) will have the opportunity to shape your career far more than you realize at the time. Your first chance may not be with your favorite team or local team. It may not come with the biggest or most prestigious club. It may not be the most glamorous market or may not be the biggest. But quality management and leadership make all the difference early in your career by developing you for the role you are interviewing for, PLUS once there, preparing you for roles in the future. Go anywhere for dynamic quality leadership. You must be relentless in this pursuit. Even if it seems inconvenient or requires you to go outside your comfort zone." **Kai Murray, Director, Season Ticket Sales & Business Development, Kansas City Royals**

"Breaking into sports isn't about having the perfect resume or the 'right' first job. It's about consistently showing up with humility, work ethic, and a deep desire for continual learning and development. The most successful careers are built by people who find what they're passionate about and approach every role as an opportunity to add value while enhancing their skillset." **Jordan Elkary, Assistant Director, Player Development, Boston Red Sox**

"Network Authentically - Building genuine connections is the cornerstone of success. Early in my career I learned it's not just about who you know, but more importantly, about who knows you. Start by being intentional with your outreach and consistently ask your network to introduce you to one or two people from their circle. Over time, this approach will yield exponential growth in your connections. Building authentic relationships can open doors you never knew existed and can significantly shape your career path." **Shelby Jacobs, Director, Partnership Sales, LA Clippers**

Chapter 11: The Art of the Email – Every Message Matters

Most people think getting hired in sports is about having the perfect resume or knowing the right people. While there is some truth to this, here's what actually happens: you send an email that gets ignored because it's generic and forgettable, or you nail the interview but never follow up properly, or you reach out to someone who would've helped you except your email made you look unprofessional. Email is how you get opportunities in this industry, from the cold outreach that leads to informational interviews to the follow-up after an interview that keeps you top of mind. The difference between candidates who break in and candidates who don't often comes down to who knows how to write emails that actually get responses. This chapter breaks down the specific types of emails you'll send throughout your job search and career, with annotated examples showing exactly what works and why. Master these templates, understand the principles behind them, and adapt them to your voice and situation. The investment you make in learning to write excellent emails will pay dividends throughout your entire career.

Why Email Skills Separate You From Everyone Else

In an industry where hundreds of people apply for every position, your ability to write clear, compelling, professional emails is one of the most undervalued skills that can set you apart. Most people send unprofessional emails – generic, poorly formatted, riddled with errors, or awkwardly pushy. When you consistently send excellent emails, you stand out immediately because you're demonstrating communication skills, attention to detail, and professionalism that most candidates don't show.

Every email you send is an audition for working in this industry. When you reach out cold to a professional requesting an informational interview, you're showing whether you can communicate professionally with people you don't know. When you email before an interview, you're demonstrating whether you can present yourself effectively and build rapport. When you follow up after meetings or interviews, you're showing whether you understand professional communication norms and basic courtesy. Hiring managers are evaluating your emails just as carefully as your resume and interviews, because email is how you'll communicate with colleagues, clients, and partners if they hire you.

The Cold Outreach Email: Breaking Through to Strangers

Cold outreach – emailing people you don't know to request informational interviews, advice, or introductions – is how you expand your network and create opportunities that don't exist through formal channels. Most people don't send cold outreach emails because they are either scared to get started or nervous about rejection. That's a mistake. People in this industry generally want to help. They remember what it was like starting out, and many are willing to spare 15 minutes if you approach them professionally and make it easy to say yes. Here's what a strong cold outreach email can look like:

Subject: Springfield College Student Seeking Advice on Partnership Sales

Hi [First Name],

My name is Stuart Sokoloff, and I'm a junior at Springfield College studying Sport Management with an interest in corporate partnerships. I came across your profile while researching professionals in partnership sales at NBA teams, and I was particularly impressed by your work on [specific partnership, initiative, or accomplishment you found through LinkedIn/news].

I'm currently exploring partnership sales as a career path and working to learn as much as I can from people actually doing the work. Would you be open to a brief 15-20 minute phone call where I could ask a few questions about your career path and advice for someone trying to break into partnerships?

I'm happy to work around your schedule and would be grateful for any time you can spare. Thank you for considering, and I completely understand if your schedule doesn't allow for it.

Best,
Stuart Sokoloff

Why this works is because the subject line is clear and specific. "Springfield College Student Seeking Advice on Partnership Sales" immediately tells the recipient who you are, what you want, and that this isn't spam. Generic subject lines like "Quick Question" or "Networking" can get ignored; Then, you've immediately identify yourself and provide context. The first sentence tells them who you are (student, school, focus area) so they understand your situation without having to guess. You demonstrate you've done research. Mentioning something specific about their work shows this isn't a mass email, but instead you chose to reach out to them specifically for a reason. This makes people far more likely to respond because it's personalized and respectful of their expertise.

You make a clear, reasonable ask. A "15-20 minute phone call" is specific and time-bound. People are more likely to say yes to a defined commitment than an open-ended "can I pick your brain sometime?" You make it easy to say yes and easy to say no. "Happy to work around your schedule" removes friction. "I completely understand if your schedule doesn't allow" gives them an out without guilt, which paradoxically makes them more likely to respond because you're not being pushy.

Once someone agrees to a networking call or informational interview, take the initiative to send a calendar invite immediately.

Include their phone number in the invite, which you can often find in their email signature. This shows that you'll be calling them, don't rely on them to call you. Something I used to do is attach my resume to the calendar invite. I never knew who had internships or jobs opening up in the near future where my qualifications would fit. They can get busy and caught up, and ultimately forget and get busy. This simple gesture accomplishes several things at once. First, it shows professionalism and respect for their time by making the meeting official and easy to track. Second, it demonstrates initiative and follow-through, qualities that are essential in sports management roles. Third, it removes friction from the process, as they don't have to add it to their calendar themselves or search for your contact information when it's time for the call. You're making it as easy as possible for them to connect with you. This small act of organization signals that you're someone who takes ownership of details and doesn't wait for others to manage logistics. In an industry where game day operations and event coordination require proactive planning, showing this trait early in a networking relationship sets you apart from candidates who simply wait for instructions.

When to Break the "Don't Contact" Rule

Many job postings explicitly state "do not contact hiring managers" or "no phone calls please." Most candidates follow this instruction blindly. You shouldn't, at least not entirely. Here's when and how to strategically ignore that guidance. After you've applied, send a brief, thoughtful email to the hiring manager (if you can identify them) expressing genuine interest and asking about culture fit. If you cannot find them, you can search LinkedIn to easily find the interviewer's email, or by using RocketReach.co. RocketReach.co gives you a few free credits to get contact information for the person you are searching for. Frame it as wanting to ensure it's the right fit for both parties, not as asking for special treatment or status updates on your application. Example:

"Hi [Name], I recently applied for the [Position] role and wanted to reach out regarding the vacancy. I'm genuinely excited about [Organization]'s approach to [specific thing], and I wanted to learn a bit more about the team culture to ensure this would be a strong mutual fit. Would you have a few minutes to share what you're looking for in the ideal candidate? I completely understand if you prefer I go through the formal process, but I wanted to express my genuine interest directly. Best, [Your Name]"

This works because:

- You're not asking for special treatment, you're asking about fit.
- You're demonstrating initiative and genuine interest.
- You're giving them an easy out if they prefer you follow the process.
- You're distinguishing yourself from the 200 other candidates who followed the "don't contact" rule without thinking.

Don't abuse this strategy. Use it sparingly for roles you're genuinely excited about where you have strong qualifications. If you email every hiring manager for every job you apply to, you'll annoy people and hurt your reputation. Be strategic, be genuine, and be respectful.

The candidates who get hired aren't always the most qualified; they're often the ones who found ways to stand out, build relationships, and demonstrate genuine interest in ways others didn't. Email is one of your most powerful tools for doing exactly that. Master it, use it strategically, and watch how it transforms your job search and career.

The "Before Interview" Email: Setting Yourself Apart

A strategy most candidates don't use, but that can dramatically increase your chances, is to send a thoughtful email to your interviewer 24-48 hours before the interview, introducing yourself and expressing genuine enthusiasm. Most job postings say "do not contact hiring managers directly" or "no phone calls please." Do it anyway, strategically. You're not calling to ask about your application status or push for special treatment. Asking about culture shows you're being thoughtful about where you work, not desperate for any job. Here's what this email looks like:

Subject: Excited for Our Interview on [Date] – [Your Name]

Hi [Hiring Manager Name],

I wanted to reach out before our interview on [Day, Date at Time] to introduce myself and let you know how excited I am about the [Position Title] opportunity with [Organization].

A bit about me: I'm currently [your situation, recent grad from Springfield College, working in sales at XYZ team, etc.], and I've spent the last [timeframe] building experience in [relevant area]. What drew me to this role specifically is [mention something specific from the job description or your research about the organization, could be their approach to fan engagement, a recent initiative, their culture, their growth trajectory].

I'm particularly excited about this opportunity because:
- *[Specific aspect of the role that aligns with your interests/skills]*
- *[Something about the organization's mission, culture, or approach that resonates]*
- *[How this role fits into your career goals]*

274

Beyond my experience in [relevant areas], I believe I'd be a strong fit because [mention 2-3 qualities, skills, or experiences that directly match what they're looking for].

If there's anything I should prepare or bring beyond what we've discussed, please let me know. I'm looking forward to learning more about the team and how I can contribute to [specific goal or initiative relevant to the role].

Best,
[Your Name]

Why this works is because the subject line references the scheduled interview. This immediately provides context and shows you're organized and prepared. You introduce yourself with relevant context. The "about me" section gives them a preview of who you are without rehashing your entire resume. Keep this to 1-2 sentences. Also, you demonstrate you've researched the organization. Mentioning what specifically drew you to the role shows this isn't a generic application; you understand what they do and why it matters

The numbered list of excitement points is specific and genuine. Generic enthusiasm ("I love your team!") doesn't impress anyone. Remember, you need to be a fan of the business before you're fan of the sport. Specific enthusiasm about aspects of the role or organization that align with your interests and goals shows thoughtful consideration. You clearly articulate why you'd be a good fit. This preview of your value proposition primes them to see you as a strong candidate before the interview even starts. You offer to prepare further and express forward-looking enthusiasm. This positions you as someone eager to contribute, not just get a job. You're setting yourself apart by doing what others don't. Most candidates show up to interviews cold. You're building rapport before you even meet, which gives you an immediate advantage.

The Post-Interview Thank You Email: Speed and Substance

After every interview, phone screen, in-person interview, panel interview, or casual coffee meeting, send a thank you email within 24 hours. This is non-negotiable. The thank you email serves multiple purposes. It demonstrates professional courtesy, keeps you top of mind, allows you to reiterate your interest and fit, and gives you a chance to address anything you wish you'd said differently in the interview. Also, mail a hand-written thank you note the same day. While the email shows promptness, the handwritten note demonstrates extra thoughtfulness and effort that almost nobody bothers with anymore. It's this combination that makes you truly unforgettable. Here's what a strong post-interview thank you looks like:

Subject: Thank You – [Position Title] Interview

Hi [Interviewer Name],

Thank you for taking the time to meet with me today about the [Position Title] role. I really enjoyed learning more about [specific thing discussed, could be a project, the team structure, their approach to fan engagement, etc.] and how the [Department] is approaching [specific challenge or initiative mentioned].

Our conversation reinforced my excitement about this opportunity. I'm particularly energized by [mention 1-2 specific aspects of the role or organization discussed in the interview that genuinely excited you], and I believe my experience with [relevant experience or skill] would allow me to contribute immediately to [specific goal or project they mentioned].

I also appreciated your insight about [mention something specific they said, advice they gave, perspective they shared, or interesting point they made]. It gave me a better understanding of [what you learned or how it shaped your thinking].

Please don't hesitate to reach out if you need any additional information from me. I'm very interested in this opportunity and would welcome the chance to join the team.

Thanks again for your time and consideration.

Best,
[Your Name]

Why this works is because it's sent quickly. Sending within 24 hours shows you're organized, enthusiastic, and professional. Waiting several days suggests you're not that interested or forgot. It references specific conversation points. Generic thank yous feel obligatory. Specific references to what you discussed show you were engaged and paying attention. It reiterates your fit and interest. This isn't just courtesy, it's another opportunity to position yourself as the right candidate by connecting your experience to their specific needs. It shows you were listening and learning. Mentioning something specific they said demonstrates active listening and thoughtfulness, qualities every employer values. It keeps the door open for continued conversation. "Don't hesitate to reach out" and "very interested" without being desperate keeps you in consideration without seeming pushy.

The Follow-Up Email: Persistence Without Pestering

You sent a cold outreach email and didn't hear back. You interviewed, and the timeline they gave you has passed. You were told they'd make a decision "by end of week" and it's been two. Now what? Follow up. Most people don't, which is why following up professionally sets you apart. People get busy, emails get buried, timelines slip. Following up shows genuine interest and persistence, both qualities employers value. The key is following up in a way that's professional and helpful rather than annoying and desperate. When following up, reply to the same email thread you originally sent rather than starting a new one. This keeps the conversation in one place so the recipient can easily see your original message without having to search through their inbox. Here's what a follow-up email looks like after no response to initial outreach:

Hi [First Name],

I wanted to follow up on my email from last week about potentially connecting for a brief conversation about your career in partnership sales.

I completely understand if you're too busy right now or if this isn't a good time. If you do have 15 minutes in the coming weeks, I'd still love the opportunity to learn from your experience. If not, no worries at all, I appreciate you even considering it.

Thanks again,
[Your Name]

Here's what a follow-up looks like after an interview when the timeline has passed:

Hi [Hiring Manager Name],

I wanted to follow up on the [Position Title] role we discussed on [date]. I know hiring timelines can shift, and I remain very interested in the opportunity. You mentioned hearing by [date] and it's been a few days since it's passed. When should I be expecting to hear back about next steps?

If there's any additional information I can provide or if you'd like to discuss my background further, please let me know. I'm happy to make myself available whenever works best for your schedule.

Thanks again for your consideration, and I hope to hear from you soon.

Best,
[Your Name]

Why this works is that you're brief and respectful of the recipient's time. You're not rehashing everything from the original email, you're just gently reminding them you're still interested. You acknowledge reality without being negative. "I understand if you're too busy" or "I know timelines can shift" shows you're reasonable and understand they're dealing with competing priorities. You reiterate interest without desperation. "I remain very interested" is professional enthusiasm. "Please respond, I need this job" is desperation. Stay on the professional side. You make it easy to respond. You're not demanding answers or putting them on the spot, you're simply keeping the door open. If you don't hear back after one follow-up, follow up again. If you still don't hear back, move on gracefully. Don't follow up multiple times. One follow-up is persistence. Multiple follow-ups become annoying. Remember, your time is just as valuable as theirs. If they don't respond after a follow-up, accept that it's not happening right now and focus your energy elsewhere.

Email Best Practices That Apply to Everything

Regardless of what type of email you're sending, these principles apply universally, like to proofread ruthlessly. Typos and grammatical errors in emails are even worse than on resumes because emails are supposed to be quick communication. If you can't proofread a short email, why would anyone trust you to communicate with clients or colleagues? Read your email out loud before sending. Use spell-check. Have someone else read important emails before you send them.

Keep it concise. Busy people don't read long emails. Get to the point quickly. If your email is more than 3-4 short paragraphs, it's probably too long. Use the stoplight test to check your email's scannability. If someone glanced at your email for three seconds while stopped at a red light, could they understand what you're asking and why? If not, it's too long or unclear. Edit ruthlessly until your main point is immediately obvious. Use professional formatting. Proper capitalization, punctuation, and paragraph breaks. No text-speak, no emoji (unless the relationship is very established and casual), no all caps. Your email should look like professional communication, not a text to a friend.

Have a clear subject line. Vague subject lines like "Question" or "Hello" get ignored. Specific subject lines like "Springfield College Student Seeking Partnership Sales Advice" or "Thank You, Marketing Coordinator Interview" tell the recipient immediately what the email is about. Include a professional email signature. Every email should have your signature at the end with your name and contact information, phone, email, LinkedIn URL. Make it easy for people to reach you or learn more about you. Match your tone to the relationship and situation. An email to a close mentor can be warmer and more casual. An email to a hiring manager you've never met should be professional and polished. Read the room (or in this case, read the relationship) and adjust accordingly. Respond promptly to emails you receive. If someone takes time to respond to your outreach or follow up after an interview, respond within 24-48 hours, acknowledging their message and addressing whatever they asked. Slow responses suggest you're not actually that interested.

Email Like a Boss

Effective email communication is about projecting confidence and respecting both your time and the recipient's. When you need to follow up after a delay, avoid the apologetic "sorry for the delay." Instead, acknowledge the passage of time with "thanks for your patience," which assumes good faith and maintains your authority. When discussing scheduling, replace the deferential "what works best for you?" with the more collaborative "could you do...?" which suggests options while still being flexible. Your enthusiasm should be professional, not desperate. Change "yeah, you are welcome" for "always happy to help," which conveys capability without over-eagerness. When expressing uncertainty, confidence matters: rather than tentatively writing "I think maybe we should..." use the decisive "it'd be best if we..." to demonstrate conviction in your recommendations. Acknowledge difficult situations without making excuses. "Working this is hard" becomes the solution-oriented "it'd be easier to discuss in person," which moves the conversation forward. Never write vague check-ins like "where the heck are we on this" or "just wanted to check in." Instead, ask directly "when can I expect an update?" which establishes clear expectations. When you make an error, own it cleanly: replace the rambling "ahh sorry my bad totally missed that" with the concise "thanks for letting me know." And regarding your availability, don't ask permission with "could I possibly leave early?" but rather inform with clarity: "I will need to leave for at..." Finally, avoid phrases that undermine your message like "hopefully that makes sense?" and instead close with the confident "let me know if you have questions," which assumes your communication was clear while remaining open to dialogue. Every email is an opportunity to demonstrate profes-sionalism, decisiveness, and respect for everyone's time.

The Handwritten Note: The Lost Art That Still Matters

We covered this in the networking chapter, but it's worth repeating here: after significant interactions, interviews, informational interviews, or someone making an introduction on your behalf, send a handwritten thank you note in addition to your email. Mail it the same day or next day after the interaction. Handwritten notes are so rare now that they're shocking and memorable when they arrive. They demonstrate thoughtfulness, effort, and professionalism that almost nobody bothers with anymore. I can count on two hands the number of thank you notes I've received after informational interviews or even formal job interviews in the past few years. The candidates who sent them are the ones I remember and think of first when opportunities arise. Keep thank you notes short and genuine:

"Hi [Name], Thank you again for taking time to speak with me yesterday about partnership sales. Your advice about [specific advice they gave] was incredibly valuable, and I'm already [how you're applying it]. I really appreciate your generosity with your time and insights. Best, [Your Name]"

Buy professional note cards (simple, clean design, nothing cutesy), keep them stocked with stamps, and make sending them a habit after every significant professional interaction, or even after a networking event. If you're unsure where to mail it, send it to the organization's corporate office address or venue, as it will eventually find its way to the right person and shows you went the extra mile. This small investment of time and money creates outsized returns in how people remember and think about you.

In a world of endless emails, standing out requires going old school. Doleva shared, "Emails are nice, but why don't you send a written thank you? We don't get a lot of mail anymore. So when something comes in, it's like, wow, they wrote me a handwritten thank you note." He's brutally honest about email effectiveness: "Out of 100 emails I get a day, do you know how many I delete? Probably 75%." The investment is minimal but the impact is significant: "It takes five minutes. You can buy a bunch of thank you cards on Vistaprint with your name and 75 cents to mail them off, and it's a lasting impact that is understated these days."

Email Mastery Challenge

Emails are how you'll get most opportunities in sports, so master this skill deliberately. This week, complete these five exercises:

- Write and send three cold outreach emails to professionals whose careers interest you, using the templates and principles from this chapter. Focus on making them specific, genuine, and easy for the recipient to say yes.

- Draft a "before interview" email for a hypothetical interview with your dream organization. Make it specific enough that you could send it with minimal customization when a real opportunity arises.

- Purchase professional thank-you note cards and write three practice thank-you notes as if you'd just completed informational interviews. Get feedback on these from a professor or mentor: are they specific? Genuine? Memorable?

- Create an email template library with your customizable versions of the following scenarios: cold outreach, follow-up after no response, thank you after informational interview, thank you after job interview, and checking in after accepting a connection request. Save these in a document you can access quickly.

- Review the last ten professional emails you've sent. Identify patterns in your mistakes: are you too wordy? Too vague? Too apologetic? Not specific enough? Awareness of your tendencies helps you self-correct.

Finally, establish a 24-hour response standard: from now on, respond to all professional emails within 24 hours, even if just to say, "Got this, will respond fully by [date]." Responsiveness is a competitive advantage that costs nothing but discipline.

"My best advice to students is to form genuine relationships with everyone you connect with. Have a goal of 20 minutes a day for strictly relationship building. Folks in this industry love to network, but it's very hard to stick out and be memorable. Research their paths and ask genuine questions. People love to talk about themselves, so dig deeper and ask 2nd and 3rd level questions. One of the biggest networking mistakes is young professionals only try to connect with people at the top of the organization. Team President, AD, Director, etc. These professionals get 100's of inbound requests and messages daily. Network with people in the roles you are applying for. These people typically have more time and are more willing to connect because they were just in the same boat of trying to break into the industry. Connect with people that would be peers to you in roles and organizations you'd love to work for. That way when a job is posted, you now have an in." **Howard Ticker, Group Vice President, Playfly Aspire**

"The old saying "It's not what you know but who know", is only partially correct. Yes, it helps to be networked to get in the door but you also need key knowledge to navigate the sports business as a college student, recent graduate or early career professional. This book would have been a must read and reference for me if it was available when I was in that position. Kudos to Stuart for putting pen to paper with these truths, insights and advice for the future of our industry!" **Denise Sicheneder, Sr. Vice President, Sales and Service, Spinzo**

"Effort & Attitude are the two things you can control in life. Continue to be an advocate for yourself, be a sponge, & take every opportunity even if it doesn't fall into your job description." **Nick Spano, Vice President of Ticket Sales, Columbia Fireflies**

"Careers in sports are built by showing up with heart. Being humble enough to keep learning, empathetic enough to truly understand others, authentic in how you show up and lead, resilient when the path isn't linear, and thoughtful in every interaction. My advice to students and young professionals is to focus less on titles and more on how they show up every day. For those already in the industry, we have a responsibility to open doors, share what we've learned, and help the next generation feel seen and supported. When we lead this way, we build stronger careers and a stronger future for sports." **Jamie Roberts, Sr. Director, Membership Sales & Service, Diamondbacks**

"It's great to see someone who's seen the ins and outs of sports provide one of the most glaring absences for those aspiring to join the sports and entertainment world, which is a roadmap and peek behind the curtain. This will help give those future professionals transparency into the industry and hopefully help them prepare" **Chris Bongo, Director Ticket & Premium Sales, San Diego Wave Fútbol Club**

"For those starting out in the sports business, I think it's most important to find out what you don't want to do, more than what you do. Your career will be a journey, one with lots of twists and turns. Finding out what you enjoy doing daily will help you find your passion and purpose and keep you in the industry for as long as possible. Once you find that out, seek meaningful people to place in your life, and keep them in your life for a reason, a season, or a lifetime. And always believe the best is yet to come!" **Jonathan Norman, Director of Partnerships, Tepper Sports & Entertainment**

Chapter 12: Interview Prep Like a Pro

Interviews are two-way conversations. You should be interviewing the company just as much as they're interviewing you. You want to ensure this is an organization you can grow and learn with, just as much as the company is ensuring you're the right fit for not only the job description, but also the culture and long-term growth. Too many candidates treat interviews as interrogations rather than conversations. "One thing about interviews, it's always one way, right? I think it would be interesting for younger people to come with some pretty pointed questions about the job," Doleva suggests. He encourages candidates to flip the script: "Not only what can I do for you, but what can I expect from the organization for support?" The confidence to ask about your career path shows maturity: "If I want to grow in the organization, tell me what I need to do, or what my career path would be. Understanding that I'm starting at the bottom, but I'm ready to perform, and I know I can do a good job for you."

Doug Holtzman, the Senior Vice President of Sports at Sportsdigita, reminds those interviewing, "You've got to make it a full-time job...to get a full-time job! Think of yourself as your own CEO, CMO, COO of YOUR own company. Everything that you do will either positively or negatively affect your company. I think about that every single day! Be extremely proactive and do not be afraid to reach out to people. Take notes on every single person that you speak with so when you speak with them again, you can reference what you talked about. Do not be afraid to set a 'next steps' while on your call with the person too! Do lots of homework! Finally, remember that yes, they are interviewing you… But, you are interviewing them too. You want to make sure that not only are you a fit for them, but they are a fit for you!"

This chapter breaks down everything you need to know to interview like someone who belongs in this industry, from the tactical details most people overlook to the questions you should ask and how to tell stories that make you memorable.

Phone Screening Interviews: Your First Real Test

Phone screenings are the first real filter in the hiring process, and understanding their purpose will help you approach them correctly. The person on the other end, often someone from HR or talent acquisition, isn't trying to determine if you're the perfect candidate. They're simply vetting you to make sure you meet the basic qualifications and aren't raising any immediate red flags. Can you communicate clearly? Do your salary expectations align with the budget? Are you actually interested in this specific role, or are you just applying everywhere? Their job is to eliminate candidates who don't fit, not necessarily to identify the best one. Pass this initial screening, and you'll move forward to the people who actually make hiring decisions.

What most candidates miss about phone interviews is that your energy translates through the line. You might think that because they can't see you, your body language doesn't matter. When you're sitting slouched in a chair, staring at your computer screen, that flatness comes through in your voice. The solution is simple: smile while you talk and move around during the call. Stand up. Walk around your room or pace in your hallway. Motion creates emotion, and that energy will be audible in your tone, pace, and enthusiasm. The hiring manager on the other end can't see your smile, but they can absolutely hear it. This is especially critical in sports, where passion and energy are prerequisites for nearly every role.

Treat the phone screen with the same preparation you'd give an in-person interview. Have the job description in front of you, research the organization beforehand, and prepare 2-3 questions to ask at the end. Find a quiet space with good cell service. Nothing kills your credibility faster than "can you hear me now?" moments or background noise. And remember, this isn't the time to negotiate salary or ask about vacation days. Your only goal is to sound competent, enthusiastic, and worth bringing in for the next round. Make it easy for them to say yes.

One of the smartest questions you can ask is, "Who will I be speaking with in the next round, and what are their roles?" This isn't just polite curiosity, it's strategic preparation. Knowing whether you'll be talking to the hiring manager, a department head, HR, or a panel of multiple people allows you to tailor your approach and research accordingly. Each person cares about different things. An HR representative wants to know you're a culture fit and won't be a liability. A department head wants to know you can do the work and solve their problems. A C-suite executive wants to know you understand the business and can think strategically. If you don't know who's in the room, you can't prepare effectively.

Once you have their names, do your homework. Look them up on LinkedIn. Read their bio on the company website. Google them to see if they've been quoted in articles, spoken at conferences, or have any public-facing work. What's their background? Did they play sports? Have they been with the organization for 15 years or just joined 6 months ago? These details give you context for the conversation and potential talking points. If you notice your interviewer played college basketball and you did too, that's a natural connection. If they recently led a major initiative that was covered in the trades, reference it thoughtfully. This level of preparation shows initiative and genuine interest, two qualities that separate candidates who want *a* job from candidates who want *this* job.

The practical benefit is that knowing who you're meeting with reduces anxiety. Walking into an interview blind is unnecessarily stressful. When you know you're speaking with the Director of Ticket Sales and the VP of Revenue, you can anticipate the types of questions they'll ask and prepare relevant examples from your experience. You'll feel more confident, more prepared, and more in control. If the recruiter doesn't volunteer this information during the phone screen, simply ask, "Can you tell me who I'll be meeting with and a bit about their roles?" It's a completely reasonable question that signals professionalism, not pushiness.

The Interview Starts Before You Walk in the Room

Most people think the interview begins when they sit down across from the hiring manager and the first question is asked. The interview starts the moment you schedule it, how you prepare, how you present yourself, and how you handle every detail, from parking to attire to small talk, signals whether you're a professional or just someone who wants a job in sports.

The small details matter far more than most candidates realize. Doleva explains that the interview begins the moment you walk through the door: "I often go down to the reception area and bring candidates in myself. As we walk down the hallway, I'm watching. Are they staring at the floor like they're headed to prison, or are they looking around, trying to absorb everything? Do they engage with people we pass? Do they say anything?" Your demeanor before you ever sit down in the conference room speaks volumes. Doleva continues, "If both candidates have enthusiasm and preparation, then you've got yourself a mini Mighty Mo situation, but that doesn't happen very often. Usually, someone rises to the top pretty clearly." The message is simple: enthusiasm and preparation are the differentiators. Show genuine interest in your surroundings, engage naturally with everyone you encounter, and demonstrate that you've done your homework. These seemingly minor moments often determine who gets the offer.

Interviewing well is a skill you can learn and improve with practice. The candidates who get offers aren't necessarily the most qualified on paper; they're the ones who prepare thoroughly, present themselves professionally, tell compelling stories, ask thoughtful questions, and make interviewers feel confident they'd be excellent colleagues.

The Details That Separate Amateurs From Professionals

Before we even get to what you say in interviews, let's address the details that communicate professionalism without you saying a word. These might seem minor, but they compound into an impression that either works in your favor or against you. Show up 20-25 minutes early, but wait in your car or nearby until 10 minutes before. This gives time in case of unexpected traffic or travel delays. Arriving too early puts pressure on the interviewer and makes you seem desperate or like you don't understand professional norms. Arriving exactly on time or late is obviously bad. The sweet spot is walking in 5-10 minutes before your scheduled time, early enough to show you're punctual, not so early you're awkward.

Choose a parking spot toward the back of the lot. While this might seem like an odd suggestion, it serves two purposes. It shows you're considerate rather than prioritizing your own convenience, and it gives you time to compose yourself before anyone sees you. Instead of arriving flustered while juggling your jacket, phone, and padfolio, you can make a polished first impression. It's a small move that demonstrates thoughtfulness and self-awareness.

For men, invest in a well-fitting suit and quality dress shoes. You don't need to spend thousands of dollars, but your interview outfit should fit properly (not too baggy, not too tight), be clean and pressed, and look professional. Stores like Indochino and Suit Supply offer affordable, modern-fitting, and made-to-measure suits. Get your pants hemmed and your jacket sleeves adjusted; fit matters more than brand. For shoes, invest in quality oxfords (not square-toed, not overly trendy) that are polished and in good condition. Your appearance shouldn't be the most memorable thing about you, but it shouldn't distract or work against you either.

Wear pastel-colored dress shirts, but when in doubt, stick with white. Pair these with a navy or charcoal grey suit. Here's why: pastel shirts (light blue, lavender, soft pink) show personality and approachability while remaining professional, but white is the safest choice when you're unsure of the context or want to project maximum formality. A great website to get quality shirts is Charles Tyrwhitt – this is where I get my shirts from. It's pretty common to find their famous 3-for-$99 deal (three dress shirts for $99). Navy and charcoal grey suits are versatile classics that work for virtually any business setting. They're less severe than black, more professional than lighter colors, and they complement both pastel and white shirts beautifully. This combination strikes the perfect balance between being memorable and being appropriate. Wear shirt stays and a v-neck undershirt. Shirt stays keep your dress shirt tucked in properly throughout the interview so you're not constantly adjusting. A v-neck undershirt (not crew neck) stays hidden under your dress shirt and, when not wearing a tie, prevents the undershirt from showing. These details ensure you look polished from start to finish. Don't wear shirts with breast pockets, and definitely don't put pens in them. Breast pocket shirts with pens sticking out scream "salesperson" or "dad at a hardware store," not as polished and professional. Don't put a pen in your breast pocket; if it leaks, you'll have an ink stain front and center on your chest, instantly ruining your professional appearance and signaling carelessness. For your tie, choose a solid or subtly patterned tie in burgundy, navy, or a complementary shade that picks up tones from your shirt. Avoid novelty ties, overly bold patterns, or anything that could be polarizing or distracting from the conversation. Your shoes should match your suit. Brown leather dress shoes pair with navy, while black leather works with charcoal grey. Either color works with both suits, but brown with navy and black with charcoal are the classic combinations. Match your belt to your shoes – brown belt with brown shoes, black belt with black shoes, and ensure both are polished and free of scuffs.

For women, business casual is equally safe – dress pants or a knee-length skirt with a blouse or sweater, paired with closed-toe flats or low heels. A blazer adds polish and professionalism if you want to elevate the look. Avoid anything too casual (like jeans or sneakers), too revealing, or overly trendy. Stick with classic colors like navy, black, grey, or pastels that look professional without being distracting. Like with men's attire, fit matters more than brand, so make sure everything fits properly and is clean and pressed. Your appearance should communicate that you take the opportunity seriously without overshadowing the conversation itself.

Carry a professional padfolio with extra copies of your resume on quality paper. Bring 3-4 copies of your resume printed on resume paper (thicker, higher-quality than regular printer paper). Carry them in a leather or professional padfolio with a notepad for taking notes. Bring two pens, in case one dies or for some reason the person opposite you doesn't have one, as it shows you're prepared. Don't bring a backpack, as it makes you look like you're coming from class, not showing up as a professional. Carry nothing in your pockets if possible. Bulky pockets ruin the lines of your suit and make you look sloppy. Leave your wallet in your car or bring only essentials (ID, one credit card, car key). Carry a handkerchief or napkin in your dominant hand pocket, not for blowing your nose, but for discreetly wiping sweaty hands before handshakes.

Another small but valuable piece of advice that nobody tells you is when you arrive for an interview, take the elevator up and the stairs down. It sounds trivial, but think about it. You want to walk into that interview room composed, breathing normally, looking professional. If you just climbed four flights of stairs to prove you're energetic, you're now sitting across from the hiring manager sweating and trying to catch your breath while answering questions about your strengths. Not ideal. Take the elevator up. Arrive calm and collected. But after the interview? Take the stairs down. This solves the awkward post-interview elevator wait where you're standing next to the person who just interviewed you in complete silence, or worse, trying to make small talk when the conversation is clearly over. The stairs give you a clean exit. You shake hands, thank them for their time, walk out with confidence, and disappear down the stairwell. It's a tiny detail, but tiny details compound into professional presence.

Don't bring drinks into the interview, and politely decline water or coffee they offer. Your hands should be free for handshakes, gesturing naturally, and taking notes. Holding a cup means you're managing a drink throughout the interview, you risk spilling, and you look less polished. If they insist, accept graciously, take one sip, and set it aside.

Notice what's in their office and use it to break the ice. Diplomas, sports memorabilia, family photos, and awards are conversation starters that build rapport before formal questions begin. "I noticed your degree from [School], I've heard great things about their program. What was your experience there?" or, "Is that a signed jersey from [Player]? How did you get that?" These small connections humanize the interaction and make you memorable. Avoid conversations about religion, politics, or other controversial topics. Even if the interviewer brings these up (which they shouldn't), deflect gracefully. You're there to demonstrate you can do the job, not debate worldviews.

Take notes during the interview. Bring your padfolio with a pen and take brief notes when they share important information: key priorities for the role, names of team members, projects they mention. This shows you're engaged, you value what they're saying, and you're organized. Ask permission at the start: "Do you mind if I take a few notes during our conversation?" Nobody will say no, and it positions you as thorough and professional. But don't sit there journaling every word like you're a court reporter; maintain eye contact and stay engaged in the conversation.

Virtual Interview Excellence

Virtual interviews are now standard, and many candidates treat them too casually because they're at home. Virtual interviews require the same professionalism as in-person, plus additional technical preparation. Test your camera, microphone, and internet connection 30 minutes before. Join the meeting link early to confirm everything works. Check your audio levels, make sure your camera is positioned at eye level (not looking up your forehead), and confirm your internet is stable. Technical difficulties make you look unprepared. Join the meeting five minutes early and wait in the virtual lobby. Just like arriving early in person, this shows you're punctual without being awkwardly early. Use this time to take a few deep breaths and center yourself.

Blur your background or use a neutral virtual background. Your interviewer should focus on you, not your messy apartment or unmade bed. Webconferencing systems like Zoom and Teams both offer background blur or professional virtual backgrounds. Have notes in front of you strategically. One advantage of virtual interviews is that you can have notes visible that you couldn't bring to in-person interviews. Use sticky notes around your monitor with key points you want to mention, questions you want to ask, or reminders ("smile," "slow down," "pause before answering"). Don't read from scripts, but having prompts visible keeps you on track. Look at the camera, not the screen. This is hard and takes practice, but looking at the camera creates eye contact with the interviewer. Looking at their face on screen makes it appear you're looking down or away. Practice this before interviews so it feels natural.

Smile more than feels natural. Warmth and energy don't translate as well through video, so you need to slightly exaggerate positive expressions to come across as engaged and enthusiastic. A neutral expression on video reads as bored or uninterested. Dress professionally from head to toe even though they can only see your torso. Yes, wear dress pants and shoes even though you're sitting at home. It affects your mindset and ensures you look professional if you need to stand up for any reason.

The Two-Way Interview

Remember, you're interviewing them as much as they're interviewing you. This isn't just something people say to make you feel better; it's a critical mindset shift that changes how you show up in interviews. You're evaluating whether this organization's culture aligns with your values, whether the role actually matches what was advertised, and whether this is somewhere you can see yourself thriving for the next few years. Pay attention to how they treat you during the process. Do they respond promptly? Are they organized and respectful of your time? How do they talk about their team and their challenges? Ask questions that reveal what it's really like to work there: "What does success look like in this role after six months?" or, "Why did the last person leave this position?" These aren't confrontational questions, they're smart ones. The worst career mistake you can make is being so desperate to get hired that you ignore red flags and end up in a toxic environment or a role that doesn't fit. You're not just trying to get any job in sports; you're trying to find the right job with the right organization. Approach every interview with confidence that you bring value, and use that time to determine if they deserve your talent and energy.

While you need to be selective about finding the right organization for your first step into the industry, you can't afford to be too picky. When evaluating new opportunities with other sports sales teams, Tanner Natzke emphasizes this balance carefully. He gives the example that across all 122 Big Four professional sports teams (MLB, NBA, NFL, NHL), the average organization may hire approximately 10 sales-specific roles annually. That's roughly 1,220 positions opening up each year. On the surface, that might sound like plenty of opportunity. But when you compare those 1,220 openings to the thousands of aspiring professionals competing for sports industry careers, the numbers tell a different story. The competition is fierce, and the available positions shrink dramatically when viewed against the demand. The takeaway? Be strategic, but stay realistic. Sometimes getting your foot in the door matters more than landing the perfect first role. "The good news is that there are more jobs than ever in sports. The bad news is that there is more competition than ever." reminds Scrivines.

Doleva puts it bluntly, "You've got to see yourself as a product. You're a product, and your competition is the other 100 people that sent in a resume or response to a job request." His strategy is clear: "Position yourself as a brand, and be able to articulate that brand. What makes you different from those other 100 people?" Doleva emphasizes the importance of being specific about your experience: "Don't just answer questions with generic responses. If someone asks about your interests and you say, 'Well, I like marketing,' that's not enough. Be effusive. Say, 'I've done this, I've got this experience, and I want to share it with you.'" The difference between candidates who land offers and those who don't often comes down to this: can you clearly communicate what makes you valuable? Treat yourself like a product you're selling, because in the interview process, that's exactly what you're doing. Know your unique value proposition and deliver it with confidence and specificity.

Common Interview Questions and How to Answer Them

Certain questions come up in almost every interview. Preparing strong answers in advance ensures you don't fumble when asked. Use the STAR method (Situation, Task, Action, Result) to structure your stories. This keeps answers concise while demonstrating impact.

Situation: Briefly set the context (where, when, what was happening)

Task: Explain what needed to be done or what challenge existed

Action: Describe specifically what YOU did (not what the team did, what was your role?)

Result: Share what happened because of your actions, quantifying when possible

"Tell me about yourself." This isn't an invitation to recite your entire resume. It's asking: who are you professionally, what's your background, and why are you here? Keep this to 60-90 seconds. Any longer and you lose them. Structure your answer in three parts:

- Where you are now: "I'm currently [your situation, recent grad from Springfield College, working in inside sales with the Phoenix Suns, etc.]"

- How you got here: "I got into sports through [brief origin story], and over the past [timeframe] I've built experience in [relevant areas]."

- Why you're excited about this opportunity: "I'm here today because [specific reason this role/organization interests you and aligns with your goals]."

"Why do you want to work here?" Don't say "I love [team]" or "I'm a huge fan." Remember, you need to be a fan of the business before you can be a fan of the team. Show you've researched the organization and understand what makes it unique: "I'm drawn to [Organization] specifically because of [mention 2-3 specific things: recent initiatives, approach to fan engagement, leadership, growth trajectory, culture, innovative programs]. What particularly excited me was [mention something specific you learned through research], and I believe my experience in [relevant area] would allow me to contribute immediately to [specific goal or project]." This answer demonstrates research, specificity, and that you're thinking about how you can contribute, not just what you want from them.

"What's your greatest strength?" Don't say "I'm a hard worker" or "I'm a team player." Everyone says that. It's too vague and there's not enough proof. Instead, name a specific skill and back it with a real example: "I'd say my greatest strength is [specific skill like building relationships, data analysis, project management, problem-solving]. For example, in my role with [Organization], I [brief, concrete example of what you did]. That resulted in [specific outcome]. I think that ability to [restate the skill] would be particularly valuable in this role because [connect it to what they need]." This gives them something concrete to remember you by and shows you understand how your strengths actually translate to results they care about.

"What's your greatest weakness?" Don't give the cliché "I'm a perfectionist" or "I work too hard." That's obviously false. Instead, share a real weakness you're actively working on improving: "Early in my career, I struggled with [real weakness - delegating, public speaking, data analysis, whatever is true; for me it is saying "yes" to everything... as you can tell]. I've been working on this by [specific actions you've taken], and I've seen improvement in [specific results or feedback]. It's still an area I'm developing, but I'm much stronger than I was a year ago." This shows self-awareness, commitment to growth, and honesty – all things employers value.

"Tell me about a time you failed." They're not trying to disqualify you, they're assessing how you handle setbacks, learn from mistakes, and take responsibility. Use the STAR format: "In my internship with [Organization], I was responsible for [situation]. I [what went wrong, be specific]. Looking back, I should have [what you'd do differently]. What I learned from this experience was [specific lesson], and I've since applied that by [how you've improved]. It was a valuable lesson that made me better at [relevant skill]." Own the failure, show what you learned, demonstrate you've improved. That's what they're looking for.

"Where do you see yourself in 5 years?" Don't say "in your job" or "running the organization." That's either threatening or unrealistic. Show ambition and career thinking without being presumptuous: "In five years, I want to have progressed from [entry role] to [realistic next step, coordinator to manager, inside sales to account executive, etc.], developed deep expertise in [specific area], and taken on increasing responsibility in [relevant function]. Ultimately, I want to be someone the organization trusts with important projects and who's contributed measurably to [relevant organizational goals]." This shows you're ambitious and thinking long-term, but focused on earning progression through performance rather than expecting it. They're looking for candidates who would want to grow internally for years to come.

"Why should we hire you?" This is your chance to clearly articulate your value proposition. Structure it around fit: "You should hire me because I bring [2-3 specific strengths that match the role requirements], I'm genuinely excited about [specific aspect of the organization or role], and I've demonstrated I can [mention specific relevant accomplishment]. Based on our conversation, it sounds like you need someone who can [restate key priority they mentioned], and my experience [specific relevant experience] positions me to deliver that immediately." You're showing you listened, you understand what they need, and you can deliver it.

"How do you handle conflict?" Don't say "I just avoid it" or claim you never have conflict. That's unrealistic and makes you seem either dishonest or unable to work with different people. Instead, show you can navigate disagreements productively: "When I have a conflict, I try to focus on the actual problem, not emotions or who's right. In my internship with [Organization], a teammate and I disagreed about [specific situation]. Instead of arguing, I suggested we sit down and clarify what we were each trying to accomplish. It turned out we agreed on the goal but had different ideas about how to get there. We found a solution that worked for both of us. I've learned most conflicts come from miscommunication, and if you can get everyone focused on the shared objective, you can usually work it out." This shows you're mature enough to handle the inevitable disagreements that come up in any job without damaging relationships or letting it affect your work.

Behavioral Questions: Telling Stories That Stand Out

Many interviews include behavioral questions: "Tell me about a time when..." These assess how you've handled situations in the past to predict how you'll handle similar situations in the future. Example behavioral questions:

- "Tell me about a time you had to deal with a difficult customer/fan."
- "Describe a situation where you had to work with a difficult team member."
- "Give me an example of a time you failed and what you learned."
- "Tell me about a time you had to meet a tight deadline under pressure."
- "Describe a situation where you had to persuade someone to see things your way."

For each, prepare 2-3 stories from your experiences that demonstrate problem-solving, team-work, leadership, resilience, customer service, sales ability, and creativity under constraints. Have these stories ready so you're not scrambling to think of examples mid-interview.

Questions You Should Ask (Because Not Asking Is Worse)

Interviews are two-way conversations. You're evaluating whether this is the right opportunity just as much as they're evaluating whether you're the right candidate. Always, and I mean **always**, ask questions. Not asking questions signals you're not curious, not engaged, or just desperate for any job. Here are questions that make you look thoughtful and give you valuable information:

About the role:

- "What does success look like in this role in the first six months? What would make you say I'm doing a great job?" *This helps you understand the expectations and priorities from the start so you can align your efforts with what matters most.*

- "How is performance measured? What metrics or outcomes am I being judged on?" (For sales this will almost always be revenue and hitting key performance indicators (KPIs), aka the daily call numbers, weekly appointments set and completed, etc.) *Knowing the exact metrics gives you clarity on how success is quantified and how to focus your time effectively.*

- "Who held this role previously and where are they now? What led to this position opening?" *This gives you context about the position's history, whether it's a growth opportunity or if there have been challenges in the role.*

- "What are the biggest challenges someone in this role will face in the first few months?" *Understanding the early obstacles helps you gauge the learning curve and show you're proactive about overcoming them.*

About the team and organization:

- "Can you describe the team I'd be working with? What are the dynamics like?" *This shows interest in collaboration and helps you assess whether the team culture aligns with your working style.*

- "What opportunities exist for advancement? What does the typical career path look like for someone starting in this role?" *This demonstrates long-term thinking and helps you evaluate if the company supports internal growth.*

- "What made you choose [Organization] over other opportunities? What's kept you here?" *Hearing the interviewer's personal perspective gives authentic insight into what's great about the company.*

- "What's been the biggest surprise, positive or negative, about working here?" *This often leads to honest, less rehearsed answers that reveal the company's true culture.*

- "How would you describe the culture here? What types of people thrive in this organization?" *This helps you gauge if your personality and values will fit the company's environment.*

- "Tell me about the last change you implemented based on employee feedback and the impact it had." *This tells you insight into the culture and management style.*

About next steps:

- "What are the next steps in the interview process?" *This shows you're interested and organized, and it clarifies what to expect moving forward.*

- "What's the timeline for making a decision?" *Understanding timing helps you manage expectations and follow up appropriately.*

- "Is there anything about my background or experience that gives you hesitation about my fit for this role?" (This is bold but gives you a chance to address concerns directly.) *This gives you a rare chance to address concerns directly and demonstrate self-awareness and confidence.*

The picture question (one of the most powerful):

- "Let's say I'm six months into this role and you're telling me what a great hire I was. What did I accomplish that made you feel that way?" *This question makes the interviewer visualize you succeeding in the role and forces them to articulate what success actually looks like. It positions you as forward-thinking and results-oriented, and the answer gives you incredibly valuable information about what actually matters in the role.*

Ask 3-5 questions, not every question on this list. Choose questions most relevant to what you learned during the interview and what you genuinely want to know. Quality over quantity.

The Dinner or Coffee Interview: Different Rules Apply

Sometimes interviews happen over meals or coffee rather than in offices. These require different etiquette and preparation.

For dinner interviews, look at the menu ahead of time online. Know what you want to order before you arrive so you're not studying the menu while trying to have a conversation. This also prevents sticker shock if it's an expensive restaurant. Order something in the middle price range, easy to eat, not messy. Don't order the cheapest thing (looks like you're uncomfortable), don't order the most expensive thing (looks presumptuous), and don't order anything requiring your full attention to eat (spaghetti, ribs, whole fish). Rather order grilled chicken, steak, or salmon — straightforward options. The senior person will almost certainly pay. Don't fight it. When the check comes, offer once ("Can I contribute?"), and when they decline (they will), thank them graciously and move on. Don't make it awkward by insisting. Drink what they drink. If they order alcohol, it's acceptable (but not required) to order one drink. If they don't drink, don't be the only one ordering alcohol. Match their energy.

When attending a networking dinner or similar engagement where you've established strong rapport, you can demonstrate leadership and generosity by prepaying discreetly. Arrive 10-15 minutes early, provide your credit card to the server, and explain that you'd like to settle the bill in advance. They'll hold your card and process the payment when appropriate; rest assured, servers are professionals who handle this regularly. This approach allows you to pick up the tab seamlessly without the awkward negotiation that often occurs when the check arrives. It's a subtle power move that shows confidence, thoughtfulness, and respect for your guest's time, leaving a lasting positive impression that extends well beyond the meal itself. Use the meal to show you can build relationships and make small talk. The dinner isn't just about formal interview questions; it's assessing whether you're someone they'd enjoy working with. Be personable, ask questions about them, find common ground, and show personality beyond your resume.

For coffee interviews, arrive early and prepay for your drink. Get there 10-15 minutes before they arrive, order your coffee, and pay for it. When they show up and order, you've already handled yourself and aren't making them wait or wonder about payment. Alternatively, give your card to the barista ahead of time. Tell them you're meeting someone and you'd like to cover both drinks. This signals professionalism and generosity without making a scene about paying. Choose a table away from noise and distractions. Scout the coffee shop when you arrive and grab a quiet table in a corner where you can have a conversation without yelling over espresso machines. Before arriving, check online photos of the venue to confirm there's ample seating available. Nothing undermines a professional meeting faster than wandering around awkwardly searching for a table or standing uncomfortably because the place is packed. Knowing the layout in advance ensures you can walk in confidently and settle into a productive conversation without distraction.

Position yourself with your back against the wall. This way, the other person faces the wall with nothing else to look at, keeping their attention focused entirely on you. It's a small but effective way to maintain engagement and control the dynamic of the conversation. Don't bring a full meal. Coffee and maybe a small pastry at most. This is a conversation, not brunch. Research parking availability ahead of time; if they struggle to find parking, you'll lose valuable conversation time and start the meeting flustered instead of focused. "The same rule applies off the field as it does on it: the hardest worker wins." mentions Joey Meredith, the Senior Director, Ticket Sales at the Tennessee Titans.

What Not to Do in Interviews

Just as important as what you should do is avoiding fatal mistakes that disqualify otherwise strong candidates. Don't bring up salary, benefits, or time off in first interviews. These conversations happen after they've decided they want you. Bringing them up early signals you're focused on what you get rather than what you contribute. Don't send gimmicks like pizzas or coffee to the office. Some candidates think sending food or gifts makes them memorable. It doesn't help and can actually hurt; it reads as gimmicky or trying to buy favor rather than earning it through qualifications and fit.

Don't badmouth previous employers, bosses, or colleagues. Even if you had terrible experiences, frame them neutrally or focus on what you learned. Complaining about past situations makes interviewers wonder if you'll complain about them next. Don't lie or exaggerate. The sports industry is small. People know each other. References get checked. Even if they don't ask for your references, odds are they know someone at that organization and will call them anyway. Exaggerating accomplishments or making up experiences will get caught, and your reputation will be destroyed. Don't be late. If you're running late due to genuinely uncontrollable circumstances (accident, emergency), call ahead immediately and apologize profusely. Otherwise, being late is unforgivable and signals you don't respect their time.

Follow-Up: The Interview Doesn't End When You Leave

Within 24 hours of your interview, send a thank you email following the template from Chapter 11. Reference specific things discussed, reiterate your interest and fit, and express gratitude for their time. Additionally, send a handwritten thank you note the same day or next day. Mail it immediately so it arrives within a few days of your interview. The combination of a prompt email and a thoughtful handwritten note makes you memorable and demonstrates professionalism that almost nobody else shows. If they gave you a timeline for next steps and it passes without hearing from them, follow up once with a brief, polite email (see Chapter 11 for template). If you still don't hear back after a follow-up, move on gracefully and focus your energy on other opportunities.

Interviewing well is a skill that improves with practice. Every interview, even ones that don't result in offers, teaches you something about how to present yourself, answer questions, and build rapport with potential employers. Prepare thoroughly, present yourself professionally, tell compelling stories, ask thoughtful questions, and follow up graciously. Do this consistently, and you won't just get one offer, you'll get multiple offers and the luxury of choosing the opportunity that's truly the best fit for your career.

Interview Preparation System

Most people "prepare" for interviews by worrying about them. Build a systematic preparation process instead. Create an interview prep template you'll complete for every interview:

- **Organization research section:** leadership team, recent news and initiatives, competitive positioning, organizational culture indicators, financial health and trajectory. Spend 2-3 hours researching each organization thoroughly.

- **Role analysis section:** key responsibilities from job description, skills and experiences they're prioritizing, how your background aligns (with specific examples ready), questions you have about the role.

- **Story bank:** write out 10-12 STAR-format stories covering different competencies (sales success, handling rejection, teamwork, leadership, problem-solving, learning from failure, working under pressure). Practice telling these stories out loud until they flow naturally.

- **Question preparation:** detail your answers to common questions (tell me about yourself, why this organization, why this role, greatest weakness, biggest failure, where you see yourself in 5 years), plus 8-10 thoughtful questions you'll ask them.

- **Logistics checklist:** plan your interview location and parking, what you're wearing (laid out the night before), materials you're bringing (resume copies, padfolio, pen), arrival timeline.

Finally, do three mock interviews: one with a professor, one with a career services counselor, and one with a working professional who can give you honest feedback. Record yourself answering common questions on video and watch it back – you'll identify verbal tics, lack of energy, or unclear answers that you can't hear in the moment. This preparation level isn't overkill; it's what separates candidates who get offers from candidates who get "we'll keep your resume on file."

"Breaking into the industry isn't easy. In many cases, it means showing your commitment long before anyone is willing to hire you. Almost everyone trying to get their foot in the door talks about their passion for sports, but passion alone doesn't set you apart. Commitment shows up in what you do. Plenty of people like the idea of working in professional sports, but far fewer are willing to put in the work to make it happen. Taking initiative, whether by launching your own projects or building experience that proves your dedication, can make all the difference. That effort is what separates those who are serious from those who are simply interested." **Chris Slivka, Director, Player Development, Arizona Diamondbacks**

"I had the privilege of working directly with Stuart for several seasons in Phoenix, and he consistently embodied the qualities you look for in a true sports professional. In an industry where it's easy to find people chasing titles or business cards, Stuart stood out for the right reasons, his passion, dedication, and genuine commitment to the work. The people who thrive in this field are the ones who treat each day as an opportunity to grow, contribute, and elevate those around them. Stuart approached every challenge with that mindset. In a constantly evolving environment, we rely on individuals who are willing to jump in without hesitation and lead by example. Stuart is one of those people, and professionals like him are what keep our industry strong." **Josh Strumlauf, Director, Premium & Ticket Sales, Seattle Sounders & Reign FC**

"Fall in love with the process and sell what happens off the field rather than what is on the field. The key to establishing yourself in the industry and growing is creating a scalable process that can be replicated across multiple areas rather than ticket sales, marketing, or operations." **Jake Lucas, Sr. Director, Ticket Sales, D.C. United**

"Breaking into sports isn't easy. Even in a world where information is everywhere and connections feel closer than ever, it's still easy to misstep when trying to find your path. What Stuart has created with this book is a much-needed resource, one I truly wish I'd had back in college. Read this book. Be genuine. Be different. And never lose your enthusiasm for learning, if you do, it's time to find something else." **Paul Bee, Director of Sales, Cosm**

"Working in the sports ticket sales industry, and thinking back to when I was looking for my first role, it would have been extremely helpful to have a guide like this. Any student can look the part and interview well for their first inside sales role, but having the knowledge and passion to do the job at the highest level makes all the difference. I truly urge students to understand what they need to do, but also think about whether this is the right role for them to truly be successful. It's easy to want to work for a sports team, but the employees who enjoy the revenue generation and competition that come with the role are truly successful." **Jon Ketzlach, Sr. Director, Membership Services and Events, Brooklyn Sports & Entertainment**

"My best advice is to be ready to work. No matter what role you start out in, you're not going to work regular hours. You will work a lot of hours. Be present and eager. Many entry-level employees that I've seen over the years value the concept of working in sports, and the cool logo on the business card, more than the work required to succeed in sports business." **Pat Ayling, Director, Membership Services, Philadelphia Flyers**

Chapter 13: Don't Wait Around, Keep Your Options Moving

The conference room at the New York Mets felt electric. I was sitting there with the other candidates, palms sweating, trying to look confident. This was it, my dream setup. New York City, a professional baseball team, subsidized housing in NYC, and friends already living nearby. Everything about this organization had clicked during my research: the people, their development process, and where their alumni ended up in their careers.

I'd aced the phone screen, flown in, crashed on my cousin's couch, and now I was here for the group interview. When they handed us each a phone number and a name, my heart rate spiked for a second. "You'll be cold calling out loud, one at a time," they explained. The other candidates looked terrified. We all thought we were about to call real buyers, real decision-makers who could shut us down in seconds. But I had an advantage they didn't know about: I'd just finished a corporate partnerships internship for the Cleveland Guardians and Cincinnati Reds Spring Training facility where I'd been cold calling for months. I wasn't scared to dial; my ego was bulletproof from rejection. I crushed it. Did everything they asked. Later we found out we'd been calling other account executives within their own organization, but it didn't matter. I'd performed under pressure. I hit all the key performance indicators (KPI's) they wanted, such as getting the prospect's name, potential game package they were interested in, and a follow up meeting set. "We'll be in touch within a week," they said as we filed out. That was the last clear communication I received from them for longer than I wanted.

One week passed. Then two. I followed up via email – nothing. Called, voicemail – same thing. The organization that had seemed so perfect, so aligned with everything I wanted, had gone completely radio silent. And I was just sitting there, waiting, like a loyal dog expecting his owner to come home. That's when I learned the most important lesson about breaking into sports: *nobody is coming to save your career. You have to save it yourself.*

I was mindlessly scrolling LinkedIn one afternoon when a post stopped me cold: an inside sales position with the Phoenix Suns & Mercury. Basketball. A sport I honestly didn't care to watch in my leisure time, but I knew the NBA was one of the best in the business. Phoenix, Arizona, I promised myself I wouldn't go back to and where I only knew two people. Everything about it screamed "wrong fit." But you know what it also screamed? *Opportunity.* I applied immediately and sent a direct email to Jentry Mullins, one of the inside sales managers who'd posted it. I didn't wait. I didn't overthink. I didn't stay loyal to the Mets who were currently ghosting me.

The next morning, I got an email back from Jentry asking to schedule an interview *that day.* I was at home, completely unprepared, but I pivoted fast. We did the phone interview, and I performed well. He told me I'd need to speak with Cara Leis, the other hiring manager, and she'd reach out with times within 24 hours. The next afternoon came and went. No word from Cara. I started getting nervous, not just about Phoenix, but about my entire future. Was I about to graduate without a job? Had I bet everything on sports, and was I about to lose? I decided to take an afternoon nap to clear my head. Poor timing. My phone started buzzing and woke me up. Groggy, confused, I picked it up. It was Cara. "Did I catch you at a good time? Can you interview right now?" Of course I could. I literally popped up off the couch like I'd been shocked with a defibrillator. I ran to the kitchen counter to grab a pen and paper. Every ounce of tiredness evaporated as I shifted into professional mode. We talked. And she mentioned since it was Friday, so I wouldn't hear anything until the following week.

Monday morning, my phone rang. Kyle Pottinger, the Senior Director of Business Development. A senior director was calling *me,* a college kid who was about to graduate. Kyle officially offered me the position and wanted to answer any questions I had, to congratulate me on getting the role, and to make sure I was confident in my decision. We talked for as long as I needed. He made me feel like I mattered. That's when I knew. This was the organization that wanted me. They moved fast. They communicated clearly. The higher-ups invested time in making sure I felt valued.

Tuesday morning, my phone rang again. It was the Mets. "We'd like to offer you the position." Three weeks of silence, and now suddenly they were ready. If I'd just waited around like they'd asked me to, if I'd been "loyal" to the organization that couldn't even return my follow-up emails, I would have been thrilled. I would have said yes immediately. But I was ready to accept Phoenix.

Here's what I learned that will serve you throughout your entire career in sports: Organizations will not keep themselves accountable to you. You must keep yourself accountable to your own career.

The Mets weren't malicious. They weren't trying to ghost me. They were just busy, timelines had shifted, moving at their own pace with dozens of other priorities. I was important to myself, but I was just another candidate to them.

If I had waited, if I had put all my eggs in that one basket because it felt like the "perfect fit," I would have spent three weeks in limbo, anxiety spiraling, opportunities passing by. Or worse, I might have gotten no offer at all. Instead, I kept moving. I kept applying. I kept my options open. And when an organization showed me through their actions (not their words, not their brand name, nor their location) that they valued me and wanted me on their team, I knew where I belonged.

Phoenix wasn't my first choice on paper. But they earned my commitment through how they treated me in the process. That tells you everything you need to know about what it's like to work there. Your dream job isn't the one with the best brand or the best city or the best amenities. Your dream job is the one where people treat you like you matter before you've even started. Watch how organizations move. Watch how they communicate. Watch whether senior leaders invest time in you.

So please, don't wait around. Keep interviewing. Keep applying. Keep your pipeline full until you sign an offer letter. Because organizations won't watch out for you. You have to watch out for yourself.

By the time decision week rolled around, I wasn't choosing between staying unemployed or taking whatever came my way. I had four offers on the table with the New York Mets, the New Jersey Devils, the Phoenix Suns and Mercury, and a 12-month contract to work operations for the Israel Baseball League in Israel.

On paper, each one had something compelling. The Mets were the original dream. New York, baseball, everything I thought I wanted. The Devils were in New Jersey, close to home, familiar territory. Israel was the wildcard, a chance to live abroad and do something completely different for a year. And then there was Phoenix, the organization that had moved fast and made me feel wanted from day one.

I eliminated the Mets first. Not just because of the three weeks of silence, but because of what that silence revealed. If that's how they operated during the hiring process when they were supposed to be recruiting me, what would it be like once I was actually working there? I needed to be somewhere that communicated, that valued urgency, that treated people like they mattered.

The Devils were trickier. On the surface, it looked solid. Professional hockey, a major market, a recognizable brand. But when I talked to my mentors, the ones who'd been in sports sales long enough to know which organizations developed talent and which ones just burned through it, they all said the same thing. The Devils' inside sales team was massive. It was a factory. High volume, high turnover, churn and burn. You'd get your reps in, sure, but you'd also be one of dozens doing the exact same thing, fighting for

314

attention, hoping someone noticed you long enough to promote you before you burned out.

That left Israel and Phoenix.

The Israel Baseball League was tempting in a way I didn't expect. Twelve months living abroad, working in operations, and being part of building something international. It sounded like an adventure, the kind of experience that would make for great stories later. But here's the thing – it was operations, not sales. And if I wanted to break into sports and build a real career trajectory, I needed to start in sales. That's where the path was clearest. That's where teams were hiring every single year. Operations would've been cool, maybe even unforgettable, but it would've delayed the start of my actual career by a year.

Looking back now, part of me wishes I'd taken it. Sometimes the unconventional path, the one that doesn't fit the LinkedIn timeline, is the one that shapes you the most. But at the time, I made the practical choice. I went with Phoenix.

Not because it was in the best city, I actually told myself it was too hot, and after my internship ended, I swore I would never return. Not because basketball was my least favorite sport (however, I know the NBA is one of the best business organizations). But because of everything in the moments leading up to that decision. They moved fast. They communicated clearly. Kyle Pottinger, a senior director, called me just to make sure I felt confident. They showed me, through their actions, that I mattered to them before I'd even signed anything.

That's the lesson here. You're going to have moments where you need to choose between the brand name and the organization that actually wants you. Between the opportunity that looks better on paper and the one that treats you better in practice. Between the adventure and the strategic move.

There's no perfect answer. I know that teams are always hiring, especially in sales. If you pick the place that invests in you, develops you, and treats you like you matter, you'll get other chances down the road. The perfect city will still be there. The dream team will hire again. But the organization that shows you who they are during the interview process? That's telling you exactly what it'll be like to work there.

I chose Phoenix. And I chose right.

When "Overqualified" Really Means "We're Worried"

Here's something that might catch you off guard: you can actually have too much experience for a sports job. Or at least, that's what the rejection email will say.

The reality is that when a hiring manager says you're overqualified, they're usually not questioning your ability to do the work. They're worried you'll get bored, leave when something better comes along, or that you don't truly want the role. It's a risk assessment, not a skills assessment. They're thinking about their own problems: the cost of hiring and training someone who might bail in six months, or the awkwardness of managing someone who has more experience than they do.

This happens a lot in sports because career paths aren't always linear. Maybe you spent three years in analytics at a Fortune 500 company and now you want to break into a team's analytics department. Maybe you have an MBA but you're applying for a coordinator role because that's the entry point. Your background isn't the problem. How you're framing it is.

Here's how to flip that script:

Stop leading with your full resume. Instead, lead with relevance. When you're telling your story in interviews or writing your cover letter, don't try to showcase everything you can do. Focus on the specific problems this role needs solved and show how your background prepares you to solve them immediately. If it's a social media coordinator job, talk about the time you grew engagement by

40% in three months, not about your leadership experience managing a team of twelve. Save the depth of your experience for when it matters.

Signal commitment, not just interest. Hiring managers need confidence that you're not using the role as a short stop. Be explicit about why you want this specific job, right now. Maybe you're pivoting industries and you're willing to take a step back to learn the sports business from the inside. Maybe you're relocating and this organization aligns with where you want to build your career long-term. Whatever your reason is, make it clear and genuine. Vague answers like "I'm passionate about sports" won't cut it.

Show you're not above the grunt work. One fear hiring managers have is that you'll coast or complain because the job feels beneath you. Counter that by sharing examples of times you rolled up your sleeves and did unglamorous work. Talk about a time you stayed late to help a teammate finish a project, or when you took on administrative tasks that weren't in your job description because the team needed it. That kind of humility signals you're a culture fit, not a flight risk.

Paint a picture of your first 90 days. This is one of the most effective ways to reframe yourself from "risky hire" to "sure thing." In your interview, walk them through what you'd focus on in your first few months on the job. Be specific. What would you learn? Who would you talk to? What quick wins could you deliver? This shows you've thought seriously about the role and helps them visualize you actually doing the work, not just passing through.

Your experience isn't a liability. But if you're not intentional about how you present it, it can feel like one to a nervous hiring manager. The goal is to make them feel safe hiring you, to show them you're not overqualified for the job, and that you're exactly qualified for what they need right now.

Active Pipeline Management

Treat your job search like a sales pipeline, because that's exactly what it is. Create a spreadsheet tracking every opportunity you're pursuing with these columns: Organization, Position, Application Date, Status, Next Action, Deadline, Priority Level (A/B/C), and Notes. Commit to this rule: you must have at least 5-10 active opportunities in your pipeline at all times. When one moves forward or gets rejected, immediately add a new one to replace it. Never let yourself become emotionally dependent on one opportunity while neglecting all others.

This week, complete these actions:

1. Apply to five positions, even if you think they're long shots.
2. Send follow-up emails to three organizations where you've applied but haven't heard back in 2+ weeks.
3. Identify your "dream job" opportunity and simultaneously identify three backup options that are nearly as appealing. Research them thoroughly and prepare applications.
4. Set calendar reminders to follow up on every application two weeks after submission if you haven't heard anything.
5. Join TeamWork Online, WorkInSports, and other sports job boards, setting up alerts for relevant positions. Update your spreadsheet daily with any status changes and weekly with new opportunities. This system prevents you from putting all your eggs in one basket and sitting around waiting for one organization to respond. It keeps momentum going when rejections happen. And most importantly, it ensures you're making decisions from a position of options rather than desperation, which inevitably leads to better career choices.

Part V: You're Hired! Now What?

Navigating your first role and building sales excellence that launches your career: understanding the reality of entry-level positions from fundamentals to managing up (Chapter 14), and mastering sales roles that most careers begin in, from ticket sales to premium partnerships, with frameworks for succeeding in rejection-heavy environments and leveraging sales experience into future opportunities (Chapter 15).

"My advice is to focus on self-discovery - understanding what makes you unique and learning how to articulate that to the people around you. What differentiates you from the person next to you is a combination of your upbringing, education, strengths, and past experiences, both positive and challenging. It's your unique journey that has brought you to where you are today, and now the question is how you choose to use it. Talk to former employers, family members, and friends. Ask them what they see as your strengths. Reflect on your experiences and consider this: based on everything you've learned so far, what are three career pathways you'd like to explore further, and why? Working in sports isn't about chasing one perfect job title, it's about understanding who you are, where you add value, and being intentional about how you use your story."
Kristin Durning, Director, Ticket Sales & Commercial Development, New York Red Bulls

"I always come back to the three C's: connections, character, and communication. Everyone is knowledgeable at some level and believes they work harder than anyone else, so what really separates you? Connections help get your foot in the door and show that someone is willing to vouch for you. Character is what draws interest once you're in the room. Communication is what keeps you there. Not just speaking well, but listening, taking feedback, and being able to adjust how you communicate based on who you're talking to. When those three work together, they leave a lasting impression. If students focus on that, they'll separate themselves pretty quickly."
James "DJ" Johnson, Major League Strength Coach, Miami Marlins

"Everyone in sports is a fan, what separates professionals is the ability to perform when emotion stops and preparation starts."
Marco Patrie, Premium Sales, FIFA World Cup 2026

"It's all about relationships and showing up. Relationships matter and they follow you everywhere you go. Find a way to get your foot in the door, and once you are there, show your worth." **Sam Zapatka, Men's National Team Manager at U.S. Soccer Federation**

"For any student looking to break into the industry, my best advice is to embrace the 'boots-on-the-ground' reality of this journey. You must be willing to master the grind of entry-level sales, leverage geographic flexibility, and view every rejection as a data point rather than a defeat. The most successful people I've seen in this business are those who didn't just wait for an opening; they built genuine, non-transactional relationships long before they needed a favor. This book serves as the essential playbook for that transition. It moves past the academic theory and gets into the real-world mechanics of how to stand out, how to network with authenticity, and how to turn an entry-level role into a lifelong career launchpad in the most rewarding industry there is." **Stuart Spiers, Manager, Ticket Sales, Atlanta Hawks**

"If you've ever wanted to work in sports, you need this book. Stuart is like that older brother who actually knows what he's talking about, he'll tell you the real deal that your professors and guidance counselors leave out." **Rachael Feldberg, Game Presentation and Events Manager, LA Galaxy**

"Most careers in sports aren't shaped by big breaks or perfect timing, they're built by staying focused on the work in front of you. Early on, I learned that understanding the process mattered more than impressing people. This book reflects that reality and reinforces that progress comes from consistent effort, patience, and doing the next task well." **Noel Guevara, Senior Manager, Community Partnerships & Programs**

Chapter 14: First Job Lessons

Landing your first job in sports feels like you've made it, like you've finally broken through after all the networking and applications and rejection. But getting hired is just the opening kickoff. The real game starts when you show up on day one and realize that nobody cares about your degree or how passionate you are about sports. What they care about is whether you can actually do the work, handle the grind, and not mess up the small things that seem irrelevant until they're not. Rather than diving into theory or case studies, this chapter examines the hands-on, sometimes gritty realities of starting out in the sports business. We'll cover everything from what to pack in your backpack to how to handle the inevitable rejection and burnout that comes with this demanding industry. Consider this your guide for not just surviving, but thriving in your entry-level role.

Welcome to the Show

Landing your first job in sports feels like winning the championship. You've networked, polished your resume, aced the interview, and finally got the offer. But the reality check is that getting the job is just the opening tip-off. The real game begins on your first day, and how you play those early quarters will shape your entire career in the sports industry.

Doleva states that the fastest way to advance isn't just doing your job, it's doing the work nobody else wants to do. "Be ready to start at the bottom and be ready to differentiate yourself quickly by doing work beyond what your job description is." He explains the strategy: "Consistency in your own role is the most important thing, but adding on little things, even the smallest stuff. Your manager knows exactly what's going on and knows who the high performers are." The key is supporting, not encroaching: "The person over here is ready to step up and step in, and has shown it. And you know, as long as you don't encroach, but you support, a manager is surely going to notice."

The Business of Memories

Strip away the statistics, the highlight reels, and the championship banners, and sports is fundamentally in the business of creating memories. Not selling tickets. Not moving merchandise. Not filling luxury suites. Those are merely the transactions that grant access to something far more valuable and enduring. Moments that people will carry with them for the rest of their lives. A father bringing his daughter to her first game. A group of college friends reuniting for their annual rivalry matchup. A company's salesperson closing the deal of a lifetime courtside. A couple celebrating an anniversary in the same seats they sat in on their first date 20 years ago. These aren't customers, they're memory-makers, and if you're in a customer-facing role in sports, you're not just providing a service. You're a supporting character in some of the most important stories people will ever tell.

This perspective fundamentally changes how you approach every interaction. The parent who can't find their seat isn't an interruption to your evening, they're someone whose child is about to experience the magic of live sports for the first time, and your patience and warmth in that moment becomes part of their origin story as a fan. The frustrated season ticket holder calling about a billing issue isn't a problem to solve quickly and move past; they're someone who has invested thousands of dollars and decades of loyalty into your organization, and how you make them feel in that five-minute conversation can determine whether that relationship continues or ends. The corporate guest who approaches you with a question during a suite event isn't taking you away from more important tasks, they are your most important task, because their experience directly impacts whether their company renews a partnership worth hundreds of thousands of dollars.

Understanding that you're in the memory business demands a level of intentionality that separates good customer service from exceptional customer service. It means recognizing that people don't remember the score of every game they attend, but they'll remember forever how you made them feel when something went wrong, or when you went above and beyond to make something right. It means acknowledging that, in an era where people can watch games in the comfort of their homes with better views, cheaper food, and cleaner bathrooms, they're choosing to come to your venue for an experience they can't replicate on their couch. Your job is to justify that choice. Every interaction, no matter how brief or seemingly mundane, is an opportunity to create a moment of delight, to solve a problem with grace, to make someone feel valued and heard. Do this consistently, and you're not just providing customer service you're building the emotional foundation that transforms casual fans into lifelong advocates who don't just attend games, but bring their friends, their families, and their colleagues because they trust that your organization will treat them with the same care and respect that made them feel special. That's the real product sports organizations sell, and if you're customer-facing, you're on the front lines of delivering it.

One of my first B2B sales was to a company in Scottsdale, Arizona. The CEO happened to be a huge Suns fan, which certainly didn't hurt during the pitch. A few months into the season, he casually mentioned he'd be taking his son to a game for his birthday. They already had premium seats, so I knew they'd have a good time. But I wanted to make it unforgettable.

I started making calls. I worked with our operations team to get them courtside access during warmups so his son could watch the players up close, see them go through their routines, and feel the energy of the arena before the crowd arrived. I arranged for the Gorilla, the Suns' mascot, to stop by their seats mid-game. I got his son's name up on the jumbotron for his birthday, bright lights and all. And I had a bag of Suns gear, jerseys, hats, the works, delivered to their seats during the second quarter.

The CEO texted me photos throughout the night. His son, grinning ear to ear, standing courtside. The Gorilla gave him a high five. The scoreboard birthday wish. He called me the next day just to say thank you, and told me it was the best birthday his son ever had. He couldn't stop talking about it around the office. At the end of the season, he upgraded his seats.

That's the thing about going the extra mile. It doesn't always require a massive effort or a huge budget. It just takes paying attention, remembering what matters to people, and doing something thoughtful with the resources you have. That one gesture turned a satisfied customer into someone who actively wanted to deepen the relationship. He didn't upgrade because the seats were better. He upgraded because we made him feel like more than just an account number.

During my time with the Suns, I received an email that I still think about regularly. A family was traveling from Australia, not for a vacation, but for a single basketball game. The father's favorite player was Devin Booker, and after being confined to a wheelchair with a terminal diagnosis, he had one wish: to see his hero play in person. We coordinated their entire experience. We got them courtside access during warmups, loaded them up with Suns merchandise, and made sure they were recognized on the scoreboard. The father's face during warmups, watching Booker just feet away, is an image I'll never forget. After the game, he looked at me and said, "This was the greatest day of my life." Those words hit differently when you know someone's time is limited. It made me realize what we actually do in this industry. We don't just manage events or coordinate logistics. We create the days people will remember forever. The stories they'll tell their grandchildren. The moments that can define their lives. That's what working in sports really means.

But going above and beyond doesn't always end the way you hope. I sold a pair of second-row courtside seats to a gentleman who owned a chain of local stores. He bought two tickets for personal use, one for him and one for his son. From the first game, you could spot him in the crowd. He was animated, passionate, the kind of fan who lived and died with every possession. It was actually exciting to watch someone care that much, to see the game through his eyes. A few games into the season, a pair of feet-on-the-floor seats opened up, the absolute best seats in the house. He jumped at the opportunity and upgraded immediately.

That's when things started to go sideways.

He got a little too animated. Started yelling at the referees, not just passionate fan stuff, but over the line. NBA security got involved during one game, then another. The NBA Commissioner's office called. They weren't calling to compliment our sales numbers. They were calling to tell us we needed to pull his season tickets.

We had to make that call. We had to tell someone who loved the team, who had just upgraded to the best seats in the arena, that he couldn't come back. It was an unpleasant conversation that needed to happen. He was upset, but understanding. He felt blindsided, even though he had been given warnings. And honestly, I understood why. From his perspective, he was just being a fan.

But there are lines, and he'd crossed them. Going above and beyond for customers matters, but so does protecting the experience for everyone else in the building, the players, the referees, and the integrity of the game itself. Sometimes doing right by one person means disappointing another, and that's just part of the job.

Title vs. Responsibility

The truth about job titles in your first role? They matter far less than you think. Whether you're called a "Coordinator," "Associate," "Representative," or "Assistant," the actual words on your business card are largely irrelevant at the entry level. What matters is the responsibility you're given and, more importantly, the responsibility you create for yourself. Two people can have identical titles in the same organization but wildly different career trajectories based on how they approach the work. The person who sees their role as strictly defined by their job description will have a very different experience than the person who sees their title as a baseline and actively seeks ways to add value beyond it. When you're early in your career, you're not defined by your title; you're defined by your reputation for getting things done, solving problems, and making the people around you better. Focus on building that reputation, and the titles will take care of themselves. Chase impressive titles while delivering mediocre work, and you'll find those titles don't open the doors you hoped they would. In sports, people remember what you did and how you did it, not what your email signature said while you were doing it.

When looking at your first few years of a job, O'Conner reminds professionals, "You've been in the industry five years. Do you have five years of experience, or do you have one year of experience five times? Five years of experience is what you want. One year five times means you have no progression, no growth. You're not building layers or learning. You're just in wash, rinse, repeat mode."

Marina Foté, the Senior Manager of Publicity at the Los Angeles Memorial Coliseum, says, "Throughout your sports career journey, walk consistently in the pursuit of opportunities to set yourself apart. I got my first job in sports after answering a trick question in an interview correctly. The rest is history! Bring unique and creative ideas, perspectives, and insights to the table, and before you know it, you'll set yourself up for sustained success."

Jillian Waitkus, the former Director of Sales at the Kentucky Derby and Churchill Downs, and Louisville Bats, continues, "Breaking into sports isn't about "making it" or being chosen, it's about learning how organizations actually work. This industry rewards those who can read dynamics, navigate change, and protect their long-term credibility, not just those willing to do whatever it takes. Titles don't equal power. Visibility doesn't guarantee security. And talent alone won't protect you from politics, budgets, or leadership turnover. If you don't develop discernment early, how decisions are made, who influences them, and why, you'll work twice as hard for half the leverage."

The Entry-Level Reality and the Fundamentals That Matter

You've probably heard the phrase "once you're in, you're in" when it comes to the sports industry. There's truth to this, but let's be clear about what it actually means. Breaking into sports is notoriously difficult because everyone wants to work in this field. However, once you've proven yourself in one organization, doors start opening more easily. You become a known quantity. You have contacts. You understand the unwritten rules of the industry. You've proven yourself against thousands of others to get previous jobs, and other teams trust you to get the job done.

Here's one of the most underrated advantages of being inside an organization: access. If you're an employee, you can walk up to a Vice President in the hallway and ask if they have 15 minutes for coffee sometime this week to learn about their career path, and there's a decent chance it happens that day or the next. You're colleagues. You're on the same team. You share the same badge access and sit in the same offices. But if you're an outsider trying to break in? That same conversation requires a LinkedIn message that might get ignored, a follow-up email, maybe a referral from a mutual connection, and weeks of back and forth just to schedule a 20-minute phone call. Being "in" collapses time and removes barriers. You're in the building. You're at the staff meetings. You see the President grabbing lunch in the cafeteria and can strike up a conversation. This proximity and legitimacy is why your first job, even if it's not your dream role, is so valuable. It puts you on the inside where relationships form organically, where learning happens through osmosis, where opportunities emerge from casual conversations. That's what "once you're in, you're in" really means. But that first role? It's probably going to be humbling.

Something that shifts once you start working in sports is you stop watching games the way fans do. When you're at the arena or stadium for work, you're not locked into every play or checking fantasy stats. You're observing how the sales team is hosting clients in suites, noticing which in-game promotions get the biggest crowd reactions, watching how operations staff manage the flow during timeouts, studying what advertisements are running on the video board and when, seeing how the corporate groups in premium seating are being serviced, and mentally cataloging what's working and what isn't. You're scanning the building for attendance patterns, noting which concession stands have the longest lines, and watching how your colleagues in different departments execute their roles. Even when you go to games at other venues on your own time, you can't turn it off. You're analyzing their game presentation, comparing their fan experience to yours, and thinking about what ideas you could bring back to your organization. This shift from fan to professional is gradual but inevitable, and it's not a loss, it's gaining a deeper appreciation for the machinery that creates the experience everyone else gets to simply enjoy.

Let's address the elephant in the room: yes, you might be doing a coffee run or two. You might be making copies, organizing promo closets, or handling tasks that have nothing to do with your degree in sport management. The coffee runs don't last forever, but the reputation you build while doing them does. Every entry-level task is a test: Are you reliable? Do you have a good attitude? Can you be trusted with bigger responsibilities? The quicker you can execute the small tasks flawlessly, the faster you move beyond them. Beyond the coffee runs and administrative tasks, here's what entry-level roles in sports typically involve. As Jentry Mullins, the Senior Vice President of Ticket Sales and Service at Brooklyn Sports & Entertainment, reminds young professionals that you can only control the controllables, your attitude and your effort. You can't control what tasks you're assigned, who gets promoted, or how quickly you advance. But you can control how you show up every single day and how hard you work. That's where your power lies.

"Control your controllables and focus on the intangibles above all else. Have a strong work ethic, be open to learning, be coachable, be passionate about your craft and crave getting better each and every day. If you do those five things, there is no doubt that you're going to be ahead of 99% of your peers and the sky will be the limit," says P.J. Davidson, the Vice President of Ticket Sales and Service for the Brooklyn Football Club.

"Breaking into sports usually means doing unglamorous work for people who get the glory. If you can be reliable, low-ego, and good at solving problems without complaining, you'll stick around. Everyone can work hard for a season. The people who last are the ones who stay reliable when they're tired, stressed, and not being watched. This industry runs on relationships. When you build real ones, your support system ends up being bigger than your job title, and the best advice often comes from someone working at a completely different level," says Dave Jones, the Athletic Operations & Certified Athletic Equipment Manager at Montclair State University.

Klein reminds young professionals, "Expect long hours, little sleep, and little appreciation. Plenty of people want your spot and they will take it the moment you ease up. Stay engaged. Show initiative. Be a solid respected teammate people can count on. Talent stands out, but it won't take you where you want to go on its own. Your ability to build relationships, think on your feet, perform, and be a good person carries you through a career in sports. If you're difficult to work with or you fail to build strong relationships, you'll find yourself out fast. This business moves like a roller coaster with fast steep climbs and steeper, faster drops that feel like they go on too long. Keep things on an even keel. When you ride the highs too hard, the lows hit twice as hard. If you stay steady through both, you stay ready for whatever comes next." Sports look glamorous from the outside, but your career depends on how you work when nobody is watching. The people around you remember your attitude, your reliability, and your results. Those three things open more doors than passion ever will."

Jake Bye, the Senior Vice President of Ticketing and Premium Experience at the New York Mets, states, "Don't be outworked as that's the one thing you are fully in control of. And in an industry such as this, be interesting. Read, travel, be well-rounded and likable. People do business with people they like."

Dan Gartner, the Vice President of Ticket Sales for the Portland Timbers & Thorns FC, goes on to say, "I'm a firm believer that effort and attitude can set anyone apart from their peers. Others may have more experience or more resources, but ultimately how you choose to carry yourself is the biggest indicator of how far you can go and how much you can accomplish, especially in the sports industry."

Some of the most common entry level roles and what they entail are:

Game Day Operations: You'll arrive before fans and leave after everyone's gone home, handling everything from checking credentials at gates to managing crowd flow to solving problems nobody anticipated. You're the person making sure 20,000 people get in safely, find their seats, and leave without incident. That means coordinating with security, managing volunteers, trouble-shooting equipment failures, and handling the inevitable chaos that comes with live events. The reality is that game days are exciting and fun, but they're also exhausting. By the end of a seven-game home stand, you'll have worked 80 hours in eight days. You'll stand for 12-hour shifts. You'll miss your friends' birthdays and family dinners because games happen when normal people have free time. But you'll also develop an incredible ability to think on your feet. When the power goes out in a section, when a fan gets belligerent, when the visiting team's bus is late, you figure it out. The adrenaline of pulling off a smooth event is real, and the skills you build here translate everywhere in the sports business.

Sales and Service: You'll make cold calls, manage small account bases, and handle customer service issues. Entry-level sales roles often mean 50-60 hour weeks during the season, with nights and weekends standard. You'll face daily rejection and demanding clients. The mental toughness required here is real. The reality is that people start here because the pay ceiling is higher than most departments. Base salary plus commission means top performers can out-earn their peers, and the upward trajectory is faster. Sales teaches you revenue generation and resilience, two skills that open doors to leadership roles across the organization. This is where many successful sports executives got their start, not by accident, but because proving you can generate revenue makes you valuable anywhere in the business. You'll get told "no" far more than "yes." You'll learn to handle angry season ticket holders and convince skeptical prospects. But if you can survive and thrive here, you'll have options throughout your career.

Sports Marketing: You'll assist with promotional campaigns, manage social media accounts, support sponsor activations, and help develop marketing strategies. Most of your time goes to creating content calendars, writing copy, analyzing engagement metrics, and coordinating promotional events. You might help plan a theme night one week and track the ROI of a billboard campaign the next. The reality is you'll produce a staggering amount of content. During the season, you might create 10-15 social media posts per day, write game notes, design graphics, and still need to think strategically about what's working and what's not. The metrics never sleep. You'll learn what resonates with fans at 2 A.M. when a post goes viral, and you'll cringe when something you thought was clever falls completely flat. The best part? You see immediate results. Post something good, and you'll watch the engagement roll in within minutes. The challenging part? The ideas need to keep coming, day after day, win or lose.

Content Creation and Marketing: You'll generate a high volume of content, managing social media accounts, writing game notes, creating graphics, and constantly thinking about engagement metrics. The pace is relentless, especially during the season. You might create 10-15 social media posts per day, write game recaps, design promotional graphics, and still need to think strategically about what's working and what's not. The reality is that the metrics never sleep. You'll figure out what fans actually care about when a post blows up at 2 in the morning, and you'll feel that stomach drop when something you were sure would hit just... doesn't. The upside? You see results instantly. Create something good and the engagement starts flooding in right away. The hard part? You need fresh ideas every single day, whether your team wins or loses. The team gets blown out by 30? You still have to find an angle. A star gets traded? You're making content about it before the news even settles. It's creatively exhausting and never stops, but if you genuinely love telling stories and connecting with fans, it's one of the most rewarding jobs out there.

Athletic Trainer Assistant: You'll support athletic trainers with injury prevention, treatment, and rehabilitation under direct supervision. This means preparing treatment areas, maintaining equipment, assisting with therapeutic exercises, documenting treatments, and helping athletes through their recovery protocols. You'll learn to tape ankles, apply modalities like ice and stim, and recognize when something needs the head trainer's attention. The reality is that the hours are long and the schedule is unpredictable. You're there before practice starts and you stay until the last athlete is treated. If someone gets hurt during a game, you're working late. If there's a tournament weekend, you're working the weekend. You'll build genuine relationships with athletes because you see them at their most vulnerable, frustrated and in pain, working to get back to what they love. The job requires both technical knowledge and emotional intelligence. You need to know your anatomy and treatment protocols, but you also need to know when an athlete needs encouragement versus when they need a reality check about their recovery timeline. It's physically and emotionally demanding, but if you're drawn to the medical side of sports, there's nothing quite like helping someone return to competition.

Administrative Support: You'll support a department or executive by managing schedules, coordinating meetings, tracking expenses, and handling correspondence. This role is less glamorous but offers incredible learning opportunities if you keep your eyes and ears open. You're in the room where decisions get made, even if you're just taking notes. The reality is that you'll learn how the business actually works. You'll see how deals get negotiated, how decisions get made, and how successful executives manage their time and priorities. You'll also do a lot of unglamorous work like expense reports, travel arrangements, and inbox management. But if you're strategic about it, you can turn this role into a master class in sports business. Pay attention during the conference calls you're scheduling. Read the contracts you're filing. Ask questions when things slow down. The executives who started here didn't just keep their heads down; they absorbed everything happening around them and built relationships that lasted their entire careers.

Understanding the demands upfront isn't meant to discourage you; it's meant to ensure you're choosing this path with your eyes wide open, ready to embrace both the grind and the magic that makes it worthwhile.

Now let's talk about the small things that actually matter more than you think. This sounds absurdly simple, but invest in a good backpack. Your backpack is part of your professional presentation, and in sports, you're often carrying a lot: your laptop, chargers, a change of clothes for game days, snacks for long shifts, and various materials you need for your role. Skip the ratty college backpack with your university logo plastered across it. Choose something durable in a neutral color that looks polished. Brands like Tumi, Briggs & Riley, or even a well-made JanSport in simple black can work. When you're walking into a stadium or arena every day, you want to look like you belong there as a professional, not as a fan or student. Similarly, think about the other physical tools of your trade. Get a quality portfolio for taking notes in meetings. Have a professional-looking water bottle. Keep breath mints in your bag. These small details contribute to how seriously people take you. Pack toothbrush and deodorant. On your twelfth hour of a gameday, you'll thank me.

Every organization has its own culture around attire, but the general rule for entry-level employees in sports is to dress slightly better than you think you need to. On non-game days, business casual is usually safe, depending on the organization. When I first started with the Suns, we had to be clean shaven, suit and tie everyday, even non-gamedays. You could lose the necktie when you get your tie cut (getting promoted to Account Executive in sales). On game days, you might be in a polo and khakis or the organization's branded apparel. Pay attention to what others at your level and one level above you are wearing. Match or slightly exceed that standard. Always have a blazer or sport coat accessible. Unexpected meetings with ownership, sponsors, or executives happen regularly in sports organizations. Being able to quickly look more polished has value. These fundamentals – the quality of your work on small tasks, your professional presentation, your attention to detail – create the foundation for everything else. You can't network your way out of a bad reputation for sloppiness, and you can't talk your way into opportunities if people don't take you seriously as a professional.

O'Conner says that honesty and hard work are the two cornerstones of getting into this business and staying in it. My grandmother used to tell me there are two four-letter words you can say every day: "'Hard work.' I'll admit I was never the sharpest knife in the drawer, but I'll contend there aren't too many people in this business who out-worked me in the last 40 years. That matters more than you think."

The Triple Threat and Reading the Fine Print

The challenge of your first job in sports isn't just doing your assigned tasks well. It's simultaneously proving yourself, learning the industry, and building relationships that will carry your career forward. Balancing these three priorities requires intentionality, and most people struggle with it because they focus too heavily on just one dimension.

Your first priority is always excellence in your actual job duties. You cannot network your way out of poor performance, and you won't get learning opportunities if you can't handle your current responsibilities. Underpromise and overdeliver, especially early on. If you think something will take you three hours, tell your supervisor it'll take half a day, then deliver it early. Ask clarifying questions up front rather than wasting time redoing work because you were afraid to ask. When you receive an assignment, confirm the deadline, the desired format, who the audience is, and what success looks like. Create systems for routine tasks, build templates, checklists, and workflows that make repetitive responsibilities efficient. This frees up mental energy for higher-level work. And document your wins by keeping a running list of your accomplishments, projects completed, and positive feedback received. This becomes invaluable during performance reviews or when seeking promotions.

But performance alone isn't enough. Your entry-level role is an education, and the best young professionals in sports are obsessive learners. They understand that every meeting, conversation, and project is a chance to understand how the business works. Volunteer for cross-functional projects whenever opportunities arise to work with other departments; this broadens your skill set and your network simultaneously. Once you've been in your role for a few months and have proven yourself reliable, start asking colleagues in other departments if you can take them to coffee to learn about their roles. Most people are flattered by this request and happy to share their career path. Attend everything you can; if your organization offers professional development sessions, all-staff meetings, or training opportunities, be there. Even if it's not directly related to your role, you're learning about the business and showing you're invested. Read everything by subscribing to industry publications like Sports Business Journal, Front Office Sports, and Sportico. Follow league news. Understand the business dynamics of your sport. Come to work informed about what's happening in the industry.

The third dimension is networking, and the relationships you build in your first job are often the most valuable of your career. These are your peers who will rise through the industry with you. Your first boss might be a mentor for life. The people you connect with now will remember you as someone who was hungry, hardworking, and helpful. But networking isn't about what people can do for you – it's about building genuine relationships by being helpful, reliable, and pleasant to work with. Help your colleagues when they're slammed. Share useful information. Be the person others want to work with. When colleagues leave for other opportunities, congratulate them and keep in touch. Your network expands exponentially when you maintain relationships with people across multiple organizations. Invest in relationships outside your immediate department because sales-people, operations staff, and content creators can teach you about aspects of the business you might never see otherwise. Plus, when opportunities arise in other departments, they'll think of you. Remember that character matters, because sports is a small industry and your reputation follows you.

Be someone known for integrity, work ethic, and treating people well regardless of their position or status.

Volunteer for the organization's charitable foundation or community relations initiatives; these events naturally bring together people from across all departments in a relaxed, mission-driven environment where relationship building happens organically over shared purpose rather than forced networking.

Now let's talk about evaluating job offers, because when you receive that first offer in sports, your excitement might make you want to accept immediately. Take a breath. While salary is important, it's not the only factor that determines whether a job is right for you. Some of the following questions you want to ask before accepting your job offer. Figure out which of the following is important to you now and what do you think will be important. Does the organization offer a 401(k) plan? If so, is there an employer match? Even in your early twenties, retirement planning matters. An employer who matches your 401(k) contributions is essentially giving you free money. If two jobs offer similar salaries but one matches up to 4% of your 401(k) contributions and the other offers no retirement benefits, the real compensation difference is significant over time. Ask specifically:

- What retirement plan does the organization offer?
- Is there an employer match, and if so, what's the percentage and vesting schedule?
- When can you enroll?

Understanding health insurance is equally critical. What health insurance plans are available? What's the premium cost for employee coverage? What's the deductible? Does the organization contribute to an HSA (Health Savings Account)? For many entry-level employees, health insurance premiums can take a significant bite out of your paycheck. Understanding these costs upfront is essential. Ask specifically:

- What health insurance options are available?

- How much will be deducted from my paycheck for premiums?
- What's the deductible and out-of-pocket maximum?
- Does coverage include dental and vision?

Some organizations offer additional benefits that have real value, like tuition reimbursement or continuing education allowances, complimentary or discounted tickets to games, gym memberships or wellness programs, commuter benefits or parking passes, and bonuses, which are particularly common in sales roles.

Let's talk about paid time off (PTO), because this is where many young professionals make a critical mistake. They see a low PTO number, maybe 10 days for your first year, and think, "That's fine. I'm young and energetic. I don't need much time off." You're wrong. You need PTO. Burnout is real in sports. The industry is notorious for demanding schedules, especially during the season. If you work in a sport with an 82-game season or a 162-game season, you're looking at months of intense work with very few days off. Without adequate PTO, you will burn out. It's not a matter of if, but when. PTO is also a sign of organizational culture. Companies that offer competitive PTO understand that rested employyees are more productive, creative, and loyal. Organizations that offer minimal PTO often have cultures where taking time off is discouraged or seen as a weakness. You need time to recharge because sports is a passion industry, which means it's easy to let it consume your entire life. Taking time off isn't lazy or uncommitted; it's essential for maintaining your physical health, mental well-being, and relationships outside of work. The best sports executives understand this. They take vacations. They disconnect. They come back refreshed. And life happens. You'll get sick. Family members will need you. Your best friend will get married. Without adequate PTO, these normal life events become sources of stress and conflict with your employer.

When evaluating a job offer, anything less than 14 days of PTO for an entry-level role should be a yellow flag. Industry standard is typically 14-20 days, plus holidays. If an organization offers significantly less, ask about it directly: "I notice the PTO is lower than the industry standard. Can you help me understand the philosophy around time off here?" Also ask if PTO is available to use immediately, or is there a waiting period? Can unused PTO roll over? Is there a "use it or lose it" policy? What's the culture around actually taking PTO?

Culture is difficult to quantify but impossible to ignore. It's the difference between a job you tolerate and one where you thrive. During the interview process and when evaluating offers, pay close attention to work-life integration. Notice I didn't say work-life balance, because in sports, true balance is rare, especially at entry levels. But integration matters. Does the organization acknowledge that employees have lives outside work? Are people sending emails at 10 P.M. expecting responses? Do people take vacations? Ask, "Can you describe what a typical week looks like in this role?" "How does the organization support employee wellbeing?" "What does work-life integration look like here?" Look at professional development by asking whether the organization invests in growing its people. Are there clear paths for advancement? Do they promote from within? Ask, "What does the career trajectory typically look like for someone starting in this role?" "What professional development opportunities are available?" "Can you tell me about someone who started in this role and where they are now?"

Pay attention to diversity and inclusion by looking around. Who's in leadership? Who's in the room during interviews? What does the staff directory look like? Organizations serious about diversity don't just talk about it; they demonstrate it through their hiring, promotion, and retention practices. Ask, "Can you tell me about the organization's approach to diversity, equity, and inclusion?" "What does the leadership team look like?" Watch for turnover patterns because if people are constantly leaving, that's a red flag. If the organization is proud of long-tenured employees, that's a green flag. Ask, "What's the typical tenure for people in this department?" "Why did the last person in this role leave?" Finally, understand management philosophy by thinking about who you'll report to and what their leadership style is. Your first boss in sports can shape your entire career trajectory. A good manager will develop you, advocate for you, and teach you the business. A bad manager will stunt your growth and make you miserable. Ask during conversations with your potential manager, "What's your management philosophy?" "How do you approach developing early-career professionals?" "What does success look like in this role after six months? After a year?" Trust your gut. If something feels off during the interview process, it probably is. If people seem miserable, burnt out, or unwilling to answer direct questions about culture, pay attention to those red flags.

Reading the Room Before You Enter It

Something I wish I thought about sooner is the fact that not all sports organizations are created equal, and the culture you land in will matter more than the logo on your business card.

I got incredibly lucky with the Suns. I didn't realize how lucky until I started hearing stories from friends at other organizations. The truth is, I should have cared more about organizational culture when I was sifting through opportunities. I was so focused on just getting my foot in the door that I didn't stop to ask the questions that actually determine whether you'll thrive or just survive.

At the Suns, if you missed your revenue target for a month, you didn't immediately get put on a performance improvement plan (PIP). Your manager sat down with you to figure out what wasn't working. Were you not prospecting enough? Did you need help with your pitch? Was something happening in your personal life that was affecting your focus? They treated you like a human being who was still learning, not a replaceable part in a machine. That approach created loyalty. People wanted to get better because the organization was invested in their development, not just their production. However, I've heard stories from colleagues at other teams where missing your number for a single month triggered a formal PIP. Where managers operated from fear rather than trust. Where the assumption was that you weren't trying hard enough, not that you might need coaching or better resources. That's not development. That's punishment disguised as accountability.

The same goes for internal politics. Every organization has politics to some degree. That's just the reality of working with humans. But there's a difference between navigating normal workplace dynamics and working somewhere where politics trumps performance. I've heard about organizations where it doesn't matter how good your work is if you're not aligned with the right executive faction. Where getting credit for your ideas depends on who your manager knows upstairs. Where game day assignments are determined by favoritism rather than competence, and you're stuck working every single event, whether it makes sense for your role or not.

At the Suns, the culture rewarded results and teamwork. If you did good work and treated people well, you got opportunities. That sounds basic, but it's not universal. Some organizations have cultures where the partnerships department is cutthroat, where account executives compete against each other instead of collaborating, where someone else's success feels like your failure. That kind of environment might push some people to perform, but it burns most people out.

The hard part is that you can't always see this clearly from the outside. Organizations aren't going to advertise that they're dysfunctional during the interview process. But there are questions you can ask and signals you can catch.

During interviews, pay attention to how people talk about their colleagues. Do they speak positively about their teammates, or is there subtle negativity? When you ask, "What do you like most about working here?" Do people light up talking about the people and the mission, or do they give vague corporate answers?

Ask directly about performance management. "How does the organization support people who are struggling to hit their targets?" A healthy culture will talk about coaching, training, and resources. A toxic culture will talk about accountability and consequences.

Ask about turnover. "What's the average tenure for people in this role?" If people are leaving after a year or two, that's a red flag. If people have been there five, seven, ten years, that tells you something about the environment.

Ask about work-life integration during the season. "What does a typical week look like when we're in the thick of games?" If they can't give you a straight answer or if the answer sounds unsustainable, believe them.

Look at who's in the room. If you're interviewing for a sales role and you meet people from other departments, that's a good sign. It means collaboration is valued. If you only meet your direct manager and maybe one colleague, ask yourself why.

I realize now that getting the Suns job wasn't just luck in terms of breaking into the industry. It was luck that I landed somewhere that treated people well, invested in development, and created a culture where you could actually build a career instead of just surviving until you burned out or got fired.

If I could go back and talk to myself as a college senior applying for jobs, I'd say this: you're going to be so focused on just getting an offer that you'll ignore the signs telling you whether it's the right offer. Don't do that. Ask the hard questions. Trust your gut when something feels off. Remember that your first job shapes how you view this entire industry. Start somewhere that makes you better, not somewhere that just makes you tired.

The Suns made me better. I stayed there longer than I initially planned because the culture made me want to stay. That's what you should be looking for. Not just an organization that will hire you, but one that will invest in you, challenge you fairly, and treat you like you matter.

That's worth more than a bigger title or a slightly higher salary at a place that views you as disposable.

Sustainability, Rejection, and When to Change Course

The sports industry will take everything you're willing to give. If you let it consume you completely, you'll burn out, not in ten years, but in two. Sustainability isn't selfish; it's strategic. The most successful executives in this industry aren't the ones who burned brightest in their first few years, then flamed out. They're the ones who found ways to sustain their passion and energy over decades. That requires intentional choices about how you manage your energy from day one.

Burnout doesn't happen overnight. It builds gradually, and you need to watch for the warning signs. You dread going to work, even on game days that used to excite you. You're constantly exhausted, even after a full night's sleep. You're more cynical and negative about the work. Your physical health is suffering from frequent illness, weight changes, or poor sleep. Your relationships outside work are strained or neglected. You're less productive despite working longer hours. If you're experiencing multiple symptoms, you need to make changes immediately. The first step is using your PTO. We've discussed why it matters; now let's talk about actually using it. Plan vacations, take long weekends, use your days off, and – here's the critical part –truly disconnect. Don't check email. Don't respond to Slack messages. Trust that your team can handle things without you for a few days.

You need to create boundaries, and this is hard in sports where the culture often glorifies being constantly available. But you need boundaries. Maybe that means not checking email after 9 P.M., maybe it means having Sundays be completely work-free, maybe it means not bringing your laptop on vacation; whatever boundaries you set, communicate them clearly and stick to them. Find outlets outside of sports because your entire identity cannot be wrapped up in your job. Maintain hobbies. Cultivate friendships outside the industry. Exercise regularly. These aren't luxuries; they're necessities for longevity in this business. When you're working 60-hour weeks during the season, basic health practices like sleep, nutrition, and exercise often slip. But they're precisely what you need to maintain performance. Prioritize 7-8 hours of sleep. Eat actual meals, not just whatever's available at the concession stand or the staff room. Move your body regularly. These aren't separate from your professional success; they're foundational to it. Remember that your career in sports is a marathon, not a sprint.

If you work in sports, you will face rejection constantly. From fans, clients, colleagues, hiring managers, people who think they could do your job better because they watch a lot of games. Learning to handle rejection without letting it destroy your confidence is a critical skill. If you're in ticket sales or sponsorship sales, you'll hear "no" far more than you'll hear "yes." Cold calling for ticket sales might result in hundreds of rejections before you get one sale. This is normal. The best salespeople don't take it personally. They understand that rejection is simply part of the numbers game. You'll apply for promotions you don't get. You'll interview for jobs that hire someone else. You'll pitch ideas that get shot down. Each one stings. But here's the truth: rejection in your career is often about fit, timing, or internal politics, all factors largely outside your control. It rarely reflects your worth or potential. If you work in a fan-facing role like social media, communications, or customer service, you'll receive criticism from fans. Some will be valid. Much of it will be harsh, personal, and disproportionate. Remember: fans are emotionally invested in outcomes you often can't control. Their anger usually isn't really about you.

The key is separating the person from the outcome. A "no" on a sale doesn't mean you're a bad salesperson. Not getting promoted doesn't mean you're not talented. A fan's angry tweet doesn't define your worth. The outcome is information, not identity. When you face professional rejection, seek specific feedback by asking, "I appreciate you considering me for this opportunity. Would you be willing to share what skills or experiences I could develop to be a stronger candidate in the future?" Most people will respect this question and give you useful information. Maintain perspective by remembering that every successful person in sports has a history of rejection. The GM who just won a championship was probably passed over for multiple jobs earlier in their career. The head coach was probably fired at some point. Rejection is universal in this industry. You're not uniquely cursed; you're normally challenged. Build resilience through small exposures, understanding that the more you face rejection and survive it, the easier it gets. Sales roles are valuable early in your career partly because they teach you to hear "no" repeatedly without taking it personally. This skill transfers to every aspect of a sports career. Have support systems by maintaining relationships with people who remind you of your value when you're facing rejection. Mentors, peers, friends outside the industry – these people can provide perspective when you're struggling.

Burnout is different from rejection. Rejection is external. Burnout is what happens when the demands of your job exceed your capacity to meet them for a sustained period. In sports, with long seasons, demanding schedules, and a culture that often glorifies overwork, burnout is a genuine risk.

Burnout is characterized by three primary symptoms: **emotional exhaustion**, where you feel drained, depleted, and used up; **cynicism**, where you become detached from your work and increasingly negative about it; and **reduced efficacy**, where, despite working hard, you feel ineffective and unaccomplished. If you're experiencing all three, you're likely burned out. This isn't something you can power through with determination. It requires real changes.

Consider whether it's the role or the organization. Sometimes you're in the wrong seat on the bus. The role itself might not align with your strengths or interests. Other times, the bus itself is the problem, the organizational culture is unhealthy. Distinguish between the two, because the solutions are different. Know when to leave because sometimes, despite your best efforts, the situation isn't fixable. If the organization's culture is toxic, if your manager is unsupportive, if the demands are unreasonable and unchangeable, it might be time to find a new opportunity. Leaving isn't failure. Sometimes it's the smartest career move you can make.

Most people in sports don't follow a linear career path. You might start in ticket sales and end up in business operations. You might begin in minor league baseball and move to college athletics. You might work in professional sports, then pivot to the agency side or sports tech. Career pivots are normal, even expected. They happen because you discover new interests as your first role gives you exposure to different aspects of the business. You might realize you love the strategic planning side more than the execution side. You might find you're more interested in data analytics than day-to-day operations. These discoveries should inform your career direction. Your priorities shift over time. Early in your career, you might be willing to work 70-hour weeks and travel constantly. As your life evolves, those priorities often change. You might want more stability, better work-life integration, or to stay in one city. These are legitimate reasons to pivot. Opportunities arise unexpectedly when someone reaches out with a job you hadn't considered, a new league or team launches, or a mentor offers you a role in a different sector. Stay open to unexpected paths. Sometimes the role isn't what you expected, you take a job and realize it's not a good fit, the work doesn't align with your strengths, the culture is problematic, or the role was misrepresented during the interview. You're allowed to change direction. A phrase my father taught me is, "I'm never looking, but I'm always listening." It doesn't hurt to take an informational interview to see what unexpected opportunities are vacant.

To pivot successfully, focus on building transferable skills regardless of your specific role. Communication, project management, relationship building, data analysis, and problem-solving – these skills make pivoting easier. Network across departments and organizations because the relationships you build create pathways for pivots. If you've developed a reputation for strong work and you know people in different areas of the business, opportunities emerge naturally. Be honest about what you're seeking. When you realize you want to make a change, communicate that clearly, first to yourself, then to mentors and your network: "I've been in ticket sales for two years and discovered I'm really interested in the sponsorship side of the business. Who should I talk to about opportunities in that area?" Don't burn bridges. Even if you're leaving a bad situation, exit professionally. Give appropriate notice. Make sure to tell your manager when you start looking at new opportunities, because more than likely they'll help you transition and even uncover new roles in the marketplace. If you're under a good manager, they'll want the best for you. Document your work. Help with the transition. The sports industry is small. Your reputation matters more than any single job. Reframe perceived setbacks because getting laid off, getting fired, or having your team relocate might feel like disasters in the moment, but they often become pivot points that lead to better opportunities.

Your first job in sports is important, but it's not everything. It's the beginning of a long journey in a complex, challenging, and rewarding industry. Give yourself grace during these early years. In your first year, and especially as an intern, you're expected to make mistakes. This is your first full-time role, you aren't supposed to know what you're doing. You'll make mistakes. You'll face rejection and setbacks. You'll question whether you're cut out for this business. You are. The fact that you're reading this chapter, preparing for the realities of the industry, shows you're approaching this thoughtfully. That self-awareness and willingness to learn from others' experiences will serve you well. Work hard, treat people well, take care of yourself, stay curious, build relationships, and remember that everyone successful in this industry started exactly where you are – uncertain, excited, and trying to figure it all out. Your first job is just the first chapter of your career story. Make it a good one, but don't let it define you. The best is still ahead.

Managing Up

If you want to advance in sports, or any industry, you need to understand one fundamental truth: your boss impacts your trajectory more than anyone else in the organization. They decide what projects you get, what opportunities come your way, whether you get promoted, and how you're perceived by senior leadership. That's why managing up is one of the most important skills you can develop. Managing up means proactively shaping your relationship with your supervisor in a way that benefits both of you. It's understanding their communication style and adapting to it. It's knowing what their boss cares about and helping them look good upward. It's bringing solutions, not just problems. It's giving them the information they need when they need it, without requiring them to chase you down. Too many talented people plateau in their careers because they focus exclusively on doing their job well while neglecting the relationship with the person evaluating that work. Your boss should never be surprised by what you're working on, confused about your impact, or unsure whether you're the right person for a bigger role. Managing up ensures they always have clarity, and that clarity translates directly into career growth.

A Cautionary Tale: When Opportunity Becomes Temptation

I was working at the Phoenix Suns when this happened, and it still sticks with me as one of the most sobering lessons about taking your job for granted.

A ticket manager who had been with the organization for 15 years got caught selling team tickets through StubHub without authorization. This wasn't some new employee who didn't know better. This was someone who had built a career there, worked his way up, and had the trust of the entire organization.

Between 2017 and 2019, he sold more than 2,800 tickets through a third-party platform. Because of the way ticketing systems work, the Suns could not see where tickets were posted other than Ticketmaster (our primary ticketing platform). The Suns didn't sell tickets on StubHub, so this was completely unauthorized. He had multiple accounts on Stubhub and would post open inventory for sale. He would send the buyer tickets as complimentary and keep the profits.

When it all came out, he was indicted on four felony charges, including filing false tax returns to hide what he was doing. He eventually pled guilty and had to pay back over $450,000 in restitution to the Suns. Add in what he owed the state, and the total came to over $471,000. He also got sentenced to a year in county jail and three years probation.

Think about that for a second. Fifteen years with one organization. Gone. A career in sports that many people would kill for. Gone. And now a felony record that makes it nearly impossible to work in professional sports again.

He had everything most people entering this industry dream about. A stable job with an NBA team. Years of experience. Relationships throughout the building. The respect that comes from being there through multiple eras of the franchise. And he threw it away.

I'm not sharing this to pile on someone who already paid a heavy price. I'm sharing it because it's the clearest example I've ever seen of what happens when you take your position for granted and convince yourself the rules don't apply to you. Working in professional sports is a privilege, not a right. These jobs are competitive because everyone wants them and hundreds of qualified people would love to take your spot. The moment you start thinking you're irreplaceable or that you can cut corners without consequences, you're putting everything at risk.

The access you get in sports, whether it's tickets, merchandise, relationships with players, or inside information, comes with enormous responsibility. Teams trust you with assets worth millions of dollars. They trust you to represent the brand professionally. They trust you not to abuse your position for personal gain. Break that trust, and you're done. Not just at that organization, but likely in the entire industry. Sports is a small world. People talk. Word gets around. And nobody wants to hire someone who violated that trust somewhere else.

This isn't about being paranoid or walking on eggshells. It's about understanding that the opportunity you've been given is valuable and treating it that way. Show up. Do your job with integrity. Don't take shortcuts. Don't convince yourself that a little side hustle using company resources is harmless.

Because when it all comes crashing down, and it will, you'll lose far more than just a paycheck. You'll lose your reputation, your network, your career trajectory, and potentially your freedom. Fifteen years of building a career, gone in an instant. That's the real cost of taking your job for granted.

Building Relationships Beyond Your Department

Your network inside your organization matters as much as the one outside it. Doleva offers practical advice: "Get out, maybe not the first day, maybe not the first week, but when it's comfortable, and understand more about the organization." He shares his own approach: "Get up from your desk. Maybe it's at lunchtime. Go wander around the organization and the arena. Walk the back hallways. See what the maintenance crew is up to. Say hello."

Doleva explains the payoff: "If somebody from VIP sales happens to know the catering people, they're going to say, 'Oh, you know, I know John. He's been down here. He's very pleasant.' Those kinds of things don't cost you much time, and they certainly don't cost you any money." These simple interactions build goodwill across departments. When you need a favor, have a question, or want to collaborate on something, you're not a stranger; instead, you're someone people actually know and want to help. In the sports industry, where so much depends on teamwork across functions, these relationships become in-valuable to your success.

Jose Moreno, the Chief Marketing Office of USA Pickleball, mentions, "Hustle and grit will help you stand out early, but integrity is what builds a lasting career. The sports industry is small, and people remember how you show up, how you treat others, and whether they can trust you. It can take years of doing the right thing to build your reputation, and only minutes to damage it. Lead with a servant mindset. Be willing to help, learn, and add value before expecting anything in return. If you work hard, stay humble, and take care of people along the way, the opportunities will come."

First 90 Days Success Plan

Whether you're starting your first job soon or want to prepare for when you do, create your 90-day onboarding plan. Divide a document into three sections, Days 1-30, Days 31-60, Days 61-90, and set specific goals for each period.

- Days 1-30 goals: master the basics of my role; identify and introduce myself to ten key people across different departments; understand how my work connects to organizational priorities; establish daily/weekly routines that set me up for success; identify one small way to add value beyond my job description.

- Days 31-60 goals: take on one project or responsibility beyond my core duties; schedule informational coffees with three colleagues in different departments; identify one process improvement I can suggest; get feedback from my manager on my performance so far and areas to develop.
- Days 61-90 goals: deliver one visible win that demonstrates my value; establish myself as reliable and coachable; begin thinking about skills I need to develop for my next-level role; and build relationships outside my immediate team.

For each 30-day period, identify specific actions you'll take to achieve these goals. This level of intentionality during your first 90 days sets the trajectory for your entire tenure at an organization. Most people show up and reactively do what they're told. You'll be strategic about building relationships, adding value, and positioning yourself for growth from day one. Review and update this plan weekly during your first three months, tracking what's working and adjusting what isn't.

"Landing a job in sports isn't about trying to be the perfect candidate, it's about consistently showing up wherever you are, consistently showing curiosity, humility, kindness, and treating everyone, regardless of their status, with honor and respect. People will notice. Your career in the industry will be built on relationships. You'll find your way if you work hard, stay honest and respectable, and take care of people along the way. Once you're in, you have a responsibility to uphold your integrity, and hold the door open for the next person." **Chelsey Falzone, Manager Youth Engagement, Minnesota Twins**

"Everyone needs a Stuart on their winning team! The first to volunteer, first in & last out, always wanting to see another teammate win, selfless, and never settling. Stuart is the blueprint of what it takes to thrive in the sports industry. He does not give up after hearing no, and he doesn't take his foot off the gas after a win. Growing up, my parents always told me, "Do what you love, and you'll never work a day in your life!" For me, working in sports isn't a job, it's what I love. Now that doesn't mean we don't work long nights, haven't sacrificed moving away from family, or celebrated holidays at work. But it does mean that every morning I get out of bed with purpose, and that in itself is my definition of being rich. It is truly an honor to work in this industry and that's something that should never be taken for granite. For anyone looking to break into the industry, be honest with yourself when answering why you want to work in sports, don't get complacent after the yes, and once you climb the ladder, don't forget to pay it forward!" **Adrienne Markham, Senior Manager, Partnership Marketing, Las Vegas Aces**

"Few people understand the grind of breaking into sports like Stuart. This book is the roadmap every aspiring sports professional has been waiting for." **Jonathan White, Sports Business Executive**

"While Stuart and I met through Springfield College, we connected largely through the world of baseball. A mentor, he has always been a helping hand with doors always open for conversation. This book is going to be a great resource for students and professionals alike to use as a direction and guide as they begin their journey through the sports industry." **Aidan Reilly, Minor League Technology Operations, Milwaukee Brewers**

"Breaking Into Sports: The Real Guide to Landing Your Dream Job - is a home run! Stuart is an expert in the field, someone who understands the industry and is able to cut through the noise often shared in textbooks to provide real, applicable insights. I'm thankful for his friendship, collaboration, and professional insight. My hope is that readers are encouraged by his transparency and honesty from a real-world perspective." **Hannah Conlisk, Guest Services Coordinator, AT&T Stadium**

"This book is the playbook every aspiring sports professional needs. It provides real strategies with no fluff. If you're serious about turning your passion into a career, this guide will show you how to do just that." **Tanner Natzke, the Founder of the Attitude, Efforts, Results podcast**

"A road map to a career in sports is something that I wish I had when I was completing internships and applying for jobs in sports and there's no better person to learn from than Stuart. I'd encourage anyone to listen to his advice and apply it to their own career path." **Sam Leventhal, Assistant Director, Creative Media & Branding, University of Florida Athletics**

Chapter 15: Sales, Service, and Relationship Roles

Most people don't want to hear that their first job in sports will probably be in sales. You spent four years studying the industry so you could work with athletes or plan events or create content, not so you could make cold calls and get rejected a hundred times a day. Sales feels unsexy compared to the roles you imagined, and the myths about what salespeople actually do make it seem even worse. But here's the truth that every successful executive in this industry will tell you: sales is some of the best education you can get, and the skills you develop there will serve you for your entire career regardless of where you end up. This chapter isn't about convincing you to love sales. It's about helping you understand why so many careers start there, what makes someone successful in these roles, and how to leverage the experience into whatever career path you ultimately want to pursue. Whether you spend two years or twenty years in sales, the skills you develop will serve you for the rest of your professional life.

The Path Most Traveled (And Most Resisted)

Let's be honest, most people starting their careers in sports will begin in sales, and most people don't want to hear that. You didn't get a degree in sport management to make cold calls and you didn't spend four years studying the industry to hear "no" a hundred times a day. You imagined yourself working with athletes, analyzing game footage, crafting marketing campaigns, or managing operations on game day. Sales feels unsexy compared to those roles. It conjures images of pushy car salesmen, boiler rooms full of people dialing for dollars, or that person at the mall kiosk trying to straighten your hair while you're clearly trying to avoid eye contact. Here's the truth that every successful executive in sports will tell you: sales is some of the best education you can get in this industry, and the skills you develop there translate to every role you'll ever have. The VP of Marketing? Probably started in sales. The Chief Revenue Officer? Probably started in sales. The President of Business Operations? You guessed it, probably started in sales. Even people who end up in analytics, content creation, or operations often spent time in sales early on because it teaches you how the business actually works.

Before we can talk about what sales actually is, we need to address what it isn't. There are pervasive myths about sales roles in sports that keep talented people from even considering them or cause people to quit before they've given themselves a real chance to succeed.

Myth #1: Sales is just bothering people who don't want to talk to you. This is the most damaging myth because it contains a kernel of truth that gets wildly exaggerated. Yes, when you're making outbound calls or working a lead list, many people won't be interested. But what changes your perspective is that you're not selling garbage. You're selling an experience that brings people joy. You're selling memories that families will talk about for years. You're selling community connection and belonging. When someone says yes to season tickets, they're not just buying seats; they're buying identity, tradition, and shared experiences. A sponsorship isn't just a logo on a sign; it's a partnership that helps a business reach its goals while supporting something meaningful in the community. When you believe in what you're selling, the conversation changes from "bothering people" to "finding the people who want what we have to offer." The difference is profound.

Myth #2: You have to be an extroverted, naturally charismatic "salesperson type." This myth costs the industry some of its best potential salespeople. The truth is that some of the most successful salespeople in sports are introverts who succeed precisely because they're better listeners than talkers. They ask thoughtful questions. They pick up on subtle cues. They build deep, lasting relationships rather than working the room superficially. What matters in sales isn't your personality type; it's your work ethic, your coachability, your resilience, and your genuine interest in solving problems for other people. Some of the worst salespeople are the smooth-talking extroverts who love hearing themselves talk but never actually listen to what the client needs.

Myth #3: Sales is a dead-end job. Look at the organizational chart of any sports organization and trace backward. This breaks down how the overall organization flows, who resorts to who, and who leads departments. The people in the C-suite, the senior vice presidents, the directors – a disproportionate number of them started in sales. Why? Because sales teaches you about revenue generation, which is the foundation of every business decision. It teaches you to think like an owner: What drives profitability? How do we create value? What are customers willing to pay for? These aren't entry-level questions; they're executive-level questions. Sales gives you that framework early. Moreover, sales success is quantifiable. You either hit your numbers or you don't. When promotion opportunities arise, having a track record of measurable success makes you a compelling candidate. Sales isn't where careers go to die; it's often where they're launched.

Myth #4: It's all about being aggressive and closing deals. The hard-charging "always be closing" stereotype is outdated and ineffective, especially in sports where relationships matter enormously. The best salespeople in sports think long-term. They're building relationships that might not result in a sale this season but will three seasons from now. They're creating advocates who refer other customers. They're establishing trust that makes renewals easier year after year. Aggressive tactics might generate a one-time sale, but they destroy the relationship equity that creates sustainable revenue. Modern sports sales is about consultation, problem-solving, and partnership, not arm-twisting.

What Sales Actually Teaches You (And Why It Matters Long-Term)

When people talk about sales being valuable, they often speak in vague terms about "transferable skills" without explaining what that actually means. Let's get specific about what you learn in a sales role and why those lessons apply to literally every job you'll ever have in sports, or any industry, for that matter.

Communication under pressure. In sales, you're constantly communicating value to people who are skeptical, busy, distracted, or outright hostile. You have maybe 30 seconds to earn someone's attention on a cold call. You have one meeting to convince a potential sponsor that your partnership is worth their investment. You're learning to be clear, concise, and compelling when it matters most. This skill transfers everywhere. When you're pitching a new marketing campaign to leadership, you're selling your idea. When you're negotiating a contract with a vendor, you're selling the partnership. When you're interviewing for your next role, you're selling yourself. The ability to communicate effectively under pressure is perhaps the single most valuable professional skill you can develop, and sales forces you to develop it daily. If you're a collegiate coach, you're constantly selling your school and program to prospective athletes.

Handling rejection without internalizing it. You're going to hear "no" constantly in sales. You'll make 100 calls and get 95 rejections. You'll spend hours preparing a sponsorship proposal that gets declined after one meeting. Someone will commit to season tickets, then ghost you completely. In the beginning, this feels personal and demoralizing. Over time, you develop the mental framework that separates you from the outcome. Their "no" isn't about your worth as a person or even necessarily about your pitch.

It's about timing, budget, priorities, and circumstances you can't see or control. This psychological resilience becomes invaluable in every aspect of your career. When you don't get the promotion, when your project gets cancelled, or when your idea gets rejected in a meeting, you've already developed the tools to process that disappointment and move forward productively. Most people take years to develop this resilience. Sales accelerates the timeline dramatically.

Active listening and reading people. Bad salespeople talk too much. Good salespeople ask better questions and actually listen to the answers. Great salespeople can read between the lines, picking up on hesitation, understanding underlying concerns, and recognizing buying signals. You learn to shut up and let silence do the work. You learn to ask follow-up questions that get to the real objection behind the stated objection ("smoke-screen objections). You learn to pay attention to tone, body language, and what's not being said. These skills make you a better manager because you can understand what your team actually needs rather than what they're comfortable saying. They make you a better colleague because you can navigate organizational politics and understand competing priorities. They make you a better human because you're genuinely interested in understanding others' perspectives.

Understanding the business fundamentals. Sales forces you to understand revenue, where it comes from, how it's generated, what drives growth. You start thinking about margins, lifetime value, acquisition costs, and retention rates. You understand the profit and loss in a natural way because you're directly responsible for part of it. When you move into other roles, this foundation is invaluable. The marketing person who understands revenue thinks differently about campaigns. The operations person who understands sales thinks differently about the fan experience. The content creator who understands business thinks differently about what stories to tell. Sales gives you business acumen that informs every decision you'll make for the rest of your career.

Resilience and work ethic. Sales in sports are demanding. You're working long hours, facing constant rejection, dealing with difficult clients, and carrying the pressure of hitting targets that determine whether you keep your job. It's hard. And that hardness is valuable because it calibrates your sense of what "difficult" means. After you've survived the grind of sports sales, very few professional challenges will feel insurmountable. You've already proven to yourself that you can handle pressure, persist through adversity, and maintain performance when things are hard. That confidence becomes foundational.

Relationship building at scale. In sales, you're not just building one or two key relationships. You're managing dozens or hundreds of accounts, each requiring attention, cultivation, and genuine care. You're learning systems for staying in touch, remembering details, following up consistently, and making people feel valued even when you're juggling a massive workload. These relationship management skills transfer directly to every role. When you're managing up, managing across, or managing down, you're drawing on these same capabilities.

Why Athletes Make Elite Salespeople

Athletes bring a unique perspective to sales that stems from years of balancing personal accountability with team objectives. On the field or court, every athlete knows their specific assignment, the block they need to make, the route they need to run, or the defensive position they need to hold. They execute these tasks with precision because failure to do so lets down their teammates. Yet the best athletes never lose sight of what truly matters: the scoreboard. They understand that perfect execution of their individual role means nothing if the team doesn't win. This duality, the discipline to handle your responsibilities while maintaining unwavering focus on the collective goal, translates seamlessly into sales.

In a sales environment, this athletic mind-set becomes a powerful advantage. Former athletes approach their quotas, calls, and meetings with the same rigor they once brought to practice drills and game preparation. They do the unsexy work – the cold calls, the CRM updates, the follow-up emails – because they know these are their assignments. But unlike sales professionals who get lost in activity metrics, athletes instinctively understand that these tasks are merely means to an end. The goal isn't to make 100 calls; it's to close deals that drive revenue and help the company win in the marketplace. They've spent their entire athletic careers learning to subordinate ego and personal statistics to team success, making them naturally aligned with organizational objectives rather than individual glory. Where others might celebrate hitting their call volume, athletes ask the more important question: did we win? Perhaps most valuable of all, athletes are inherently coachable. They've spent their entire careers receiving immediate, often direct feedback from coaches and adjusting their performance in real-time. Where others might become defensive when a manager corrects their pitch or questions their approach, athletes instinctively lean in; they've been conditioned to see coaching not as criticism, but as the fastest path to improvement.

"There is no substitute for hard work. The people I've seen make the greatest impact in the sports business world share the same mindset as the best athletes on the field, ice, and court: they show up every day ready to put in the work, constantly striving to improve, because success is the only option." says Joshua Nanavaty, the Vice President of Ticket Sales and Service for the San Jose Sharks

The Reality of Different Sales Roles in Sports

Not all sales roles are created equal, and understanding the differences helps you make informed decisions about which path might be right for you. Let's break down the most common types of sales positions you'll encounter in sports and what each one actually entails.

Inside Sales is where most people start, and it's exactly what it sounds like. You're selling tickets, usually season tickets or mini-plans to start, with the goal of eventually moving people to season tickets. But depending on the organization, this can vary greatly. Some organizations, like the Suns, start full menu (selling everything). Inside sales means you're primarily working the phone and email rather than meeting people face-to-face. Again, this will depend on the organization; at the Suns we were able to set face-to-face appointments right away. You're given a lead list, maybe people who attended a game last year, bought tickets once, or signed up for information on the website. Your job is to contact them, qualify their interest, overcome objections, and close sales. The volume is high. You might make 80-100 calls a day. Your success is measured by metrics and how many calls you make, how many conversations you have, and how many tickets you sell. The base salary is usually low with commission potential that can significantly increase your earnings if you're successful. The hours are long, especially during the season. You're often making calls early in the morning, or in the evening when people are home from work, and you're working every game day because that's when you can engage with people who showed up.

This role is valuable because it's a crash course in sales fundamentals with immediate feedback. You learn what messaging works and what doesn't. You develop phone skills and objection handling. You build resilience because you're facing rejection constantly. And if you're successful, you can earn decent money and position yourself for promotion relatively quickly. Many organizations have clear advancement paths where successful inside sales reps move to group sales, membership (season ticket) sales, an experience/retention role, or even a premium role in 9-12 months.

Group Sales reps focus on selling blocks of tickets to businesses, youth sports teams, churches, schools, and social organizations, typically 15-25 tickets minimum per order. You're working the phones heavily, but also attending community events, networking with youth sports leagues, and building partnerships with local businesses. The sales cycle is sometimes shorter than season tickets but longer than single-game sales, often taking weeks from initial contact to close. Your compensation is usually base salary plus commission per ticket sold, with bonuses for hitting monthly or seasonal targets. The volume is high; you might be managing 50-100 active opportunities at once while constantly prospecting for new leads.

Let's use the NBA as an example. The Boston Celtics have approximately three group sales representatives, while when I worked with the Phoenix Suns, we had twelve. For calculation purposes, let's say the average NBA team employs ten group sales reps. With 30 NBA teams, that's only 300 NBA group sales positions in the entire world. Across all major professional sports (MLB, NBA, NFL, NHL, MLS), you're looking at roughly 1,500-2,000 sales positions total in North American major league sports, and when you consider how many people want to work in sports, these numbers are staggeringly small.

This role is valuable if you're learning how to sell to organizations rather than individuals, which means understanding decision-making processes and navigating gatekeepers. You're developing pipeline management skills because you're juggling many deals at different stages simultaneously. You're building relationships across the community that extend beyond sports, which create a valuable local network. Many successful account executives and premium sales reps started in group sales because it teaches volume management and organizational selling without the pressure of massive deal sizes.

Season Ticket Sales reps are focused on the holy grail of ticket sales: converting single-game buyers and partial plan holders into full season ticket members. You're primarily selling to businesses, with the occasional single game buyer sale sprinkled in.

You're working longer sales cycles, sometimes six months to a year of relationship building before someone commits. You're having deeper conversations about value, investment, and identity because a season ticket package might cost $3,000-$15,000+ depending on the sport and seat location. You're managing a smaller book of accounts than group sales, but with higher touch and more personal relationships. Compensation typically includes a higher base salary with substantial commission on new sales and renewal bonuses.

This role is valuable when you're learning consultative, high-consideration selling where emotional connection matters as much as logical value propositions. Season ticket holders are the lifeblood of most sports organizations; they provide predictable revenue, fill seats consistently, and become brand ambassadors. Understanding how to create and maintain these relationships teaches you about customer lifetime value and loyalty in ways that transactional sales never can. Success in season ticket sales often leads directly to premium seating roles or account management positions because you've proven you can handle complex, high-value relationships.

Membership or Retention roles flip the script; instead of hunting for new customers, you're farming existing relationships to keep them active and engaged. You're managing a book of current season ticket holders or members, ensuring they're satisfied, solving problems before they become cancellation reasons, and looking for opportunities to upgrade their packages or add benefits. Your success is measured by retention rate and upsell revenue rather than new sales. You're making regular check-in calls, hosting member events, sending personalized communications, and acting as the primary relationship owner between the organization and its most valuable customers. Compensation often includes base salary plus bonuses tied to retention percentages and upsell targets.

This role is valuable because you're learning that keeping a customer is often more profitable than acquiring one, and you're developing the skills to do it at scale. You're handling the full spectrum of customer experience, from enthusiastic fans who just need someone to talk sports with, to frustrated members threatening to cancel, who need real problem solving. You're learning service recovery, relationship deepening, and how to have difficult conversations that preserve relationships. These skills transfer directly into account management, customer success, and leadership roles because every business needs people who can maintain and grow existing relationships, not just chase new ones.

Premium Sales focuses on the highest value products: courtside seats, club seats, suites, loge boxes, and other VIP experiences that can cost $50,000-$500,000+ annually. You're selling to corporations, wealthy individuals, and business owners who view these purchases as business tools, client entertainment, or lifestyle investments. The sales cycle is long, often six months to two years, and involves multiple stakeholders, complex negotiations, and detailed proposals. You're not just selling seats; you're selling hospitality, exclusivity, networking opportunities, and business value. You're spending significant time entertaining prospects at games, attending high-end business events, and building relationships with people who make major financial decisions. Compensation is heavily commission-based with the potential for significant earnings if you're successful.

This role is valuable if you're operating at the highest level of sports sales, interfacing with C-suite executives, entrepreneurs, and ultra high-net-worth individuals. You're learning how to navigate complex directly to businesses (B2B) sales processes, build business cases for premium investments, and manage relationships with sophisticated buyers. The skills you develop – strategic selling, executive communication, negotiation, and relationship management with influential people – translate directly to sponsorship sales, partnerships, and senior revenue leadership positions. The network you build in premium sales can be the most valuable asset of your entire career because these relationships are with people who have resources, influence, and decision-making power across industries.

Mainly in season ticket and premium sales, and often in group sales, you are selling B2B. This gives you valuable insight and ability to cross sell across departments, giving you the ability to re-sell a company multiple times throughout the year. You can bring a group out multiple times, or spread season tickets to different departments.

Regardless of whether you're in groups, season tickets, premium, or retention, it's valuable because it's where you learn the fundamentals of the sports business in the most direct way possible. You're not theorizing about revenue or studying fan behavior in the abstract; you're living it daily through hundreds of real conversations with real customers making real buying decisions. You're learning what actually motivates people to spend money on sports, what objections they have, what value propositions resonate, and what causes them to say yes or walk away. This customer insight becomes invaluable regardless of where your career goes because every decision in sports, from ticket pricing to marketing campaigns to facility design to in-game entertainment, should ultimately serve the goal of making it easier for customers to buy and stay engaged. People who've done ticket sales understand this intuitively. They've felt the impact of a price increase on their close rate, they've heard customers complain about parking or concessions, they've learned which giveaways actually drive attendance and which are wasteful, and they understand that every seat filled or left empty represents a real conversation, a real decision, a real relationship. This ground-level understanding of how the business actually works, customer by customer, ticket by ticket, creates a foundation that informs better decision making at every level of an organization for the rest of your career.

Sponsorship and Partnership Sales is typically not an entry-level role, but it's where many successful ticket sales reps aspire to move. You're selling corporate partnerships, everything from naming rights to category sponsorships to custom activation programs. The deals are complex, often six or seven figures, with long sales cycles that can take a year or more from initial contact to signed contract. You're working with marketing directors, CMOs, and agency partners. You need to understand not just your organization's assets, but also the client's business objectives, their competitive landscape, and how sports partnerships can drive measurable value for them.

This role is valuable if you're operating at a strategic level, thinking about business objectives and return on investment (ROI) in sophisticated ways. You're managing major accounts with significant revenue impact. You're often working cross-functionally with marketing, content, and operations teams to deliver on partnership agreements. The relationships and business acumen you develop in sponsorship sales translate directly to senior leadership roles.

One of the underrated benefits of sales roles, especially ticket sales and sponsorship positions, is access to experiences other departments never get. When you're hosting clients, you're not sitting in the upper deck; you're in premium suites with catered food, taking clients to high-end steakhouses on the company card, attending exclusive events that aren't open to the public, and sometimes traveling to away games or league events as part of relationship building. You're schmoozing with business owners and executives in settings that feel more like lifestyle than work. A 25 year old in ticket sales might find themselves courtside at a playoff game or in a luxury box at the Super Bowl, not as a fan who saved up for months, but as part of their job. These aren't just fun perks; they're education. You're learning how high-level professionals conduct themselves, how deals get made in informal settings, and how to be comfortable in rooms where you're the youngest person by 20 years. You're building a network of successful people who see you as a peer, not a kid. And let's be honest, when your friends are grinding it out in corporate cubicles and you're texting them photos from behind home plate or from a suite at the arena, the perks don't make the rejection and long hours disappear, but they certainly make them more palatable. Just remember, you're there to work and build relationships, not to be a fan. The moment you forget that and start treating these experiences as personal entertainment rather than professional opportunities, you've lost the plot.

What Actually Predicts Sales Success

If sales success isn't about being naturally charismatic or aggressively closing deals, what does separate good salespeople from mediocre ones? After watching hundreds of people go through sales roles in sports, certain patterns emerge. Here's what actually predicts success:

Coachability trumps experience. The best predictor of success in entry-level sales is not whether someone has done it before, but whether they're willing to learn and implement feedback. Sales roles typically provide extensive training, scripts, objection handling, product knowledge, and process. The people who succeed are the ones who actually use what they're taught rather than thinking they know better. They role play even when it feels awkward. They record their calls and listen back critically. They ask their manager for feedback and then actually change their behavior based on it. Natural talent matters less than willingness to be coached and commitment to continuous improvement.

Discipline beats motivation. In sales, motivation comes and goes. Some days you feel energized and unstoppable. Other days, after the tenth rejection in a row, you want to quit. The people who succeed have developed the discipline to execute regardless of how they feel. They make their required number of calls even when they don't want to. They show up to morning sales meetings with energy, even when they're exhausted. They maintain their pipeline management and follow-up cadence even when it would be easier to let things slide. This discipline, the ability to do the work even when you don't feel like it, is what separates the people who wash out in six months from the people who succeed and advance.

Genuine curiosity about people. The best salespeople are actually interested in the person on the other end of the conversation. They ask questions because they want to understand, not just because the script tells them to. They remember details about people's lives. They follow up on things that mattered to the client. This genuine interest can't be faked long-term, and it's what transforms transactional relationships into genuine connections. When someone can tell you actually care about solving their problem rather than just hitting your quota, the entire dynamic changes.

Comfort with numbers and metrics. Sales are quantified constantly. You need to track your activity metrics, your conversion rates, your pipeline, your close rate, and your average deal size. People who succeed embrace this rather than resist it. They use data to understand what's working and what isn't. They test different approaches and measure the results. They know their numbers cold because those numbers tell the story of their performance. If you're allergic to metrics and measurement, sales will be frustrating. If you enjoy the clarity of knowing exactly where you stand, sales provides that in spades.

Emotional intelligence and adaptability. No two customers are the same. The approach that works perfectly with one prospect falls completely flat with another. Good salespeople can read the situation and adapt their approach accordingly. They know when to push and when to back off. They can navigate difficult conversations without getting defensive. They can handle an angry client without taking it personally. This emotional intelligence, the ability to understand and manage both your own emotions and others', is perhaps the most important skill in sales and the hardest to teach.

Persistence without desperation. There's a fine line between persistent follow-up and annoying someone into saying no just to get you to go away. Good salespeople understand this line intuitively. They follow up consistently but not oppressively. They add value with each touchpoint rather than just checking in. They respect when someone says "not now" but keep the door open for "maybe later." They're persistent because they believe in what they're selling and they know that timing matters, but they're not desperate because they have enough pipeline that any individual deal doesn't make or break them.

Systems thinking and organization. When you're managing hundreds of accounts at different stages, organization isn't optional. Good salespeople develop systems for tracking conversations, scheduling follow-ups, noting important details, and managing their time. They use customer relationship management software (CRM) systems effectively. CRM's are used by almost every company across the world. It's a place to house all your customers' information, track what they've purchased, gain insight into conversations, keep a pipeline of deals, and many other customizable tools. Some of the biggest CRM companies are Salesforce, Microsoft Dynamics, and Hubspot. They have daily and weekly routines that ensure nothing falls through the cracks. This organizational capability becomes increasingly important as you advance in your career and your responsibilities expand.

Understanding Commission: What You Actually Take Home

Let's talk real numbers, because commission structures in sports sales can dramatically impact your earning potential, and sometimes this isn't explained clearly enough. Commission rates typically range from 2% to 15% depending on the organization, product type, season timing, and active incentives. A courtside seat package in a major market might run $150,000 for a full season. If you're earning 10% commission on that sale, you just made $15,000 on one deal. Sell three of those in a season, and you've added $45,000 to your base salary. Suites work similarly but with different math. A premium suite might cost $250,000 annually. At 8% commission, that's $20,000 in your pocket. The catch? Commission rates aren't uniform. New ticket sales during the offseason might earn you 12% because the team needs commitments before the season starts. Renewing an existing account in March? You might only see 3% because the heavy lifting was already done. Selling upper-level season tickets versus club seats can mean the difference between 5% and 12% commission rates. Premium inventory can carry higher percentages because it's harder to move and generates significantly more revenue. If you're earning a $45,000 base salary and you sell $2 million in season tickets and suites at an average 8% commission, you're taking home $160,000 in commission, bringing your total compensation to $205,000. That's why top performers in NBA sales can clear $250,000+ annually while their teammates are on track for $60,000. The product matters, the commission structure matters, and your ability to close premium deals matters exponentially more than grinding out volume on cheap seats.

Finding Your Pocket

When evaluating new opportunities with other sports sales teams, Natzke offers crucial advice: "Find Your Pocket." Start by examining the pricing landscape. Is it stable or constantly shifting? Price increases can create challenging conversations with loyal, long-time season ticket holders who've stuck with the organization through thick and thin. Next, assess the team's trajectory honestly. Are they genuinely emerging from a rebuild, or have they been selling the same "better days ahead" narrative for years? If it's the latter, fans have already tuned out that message. Consider the inventory reality. What's actually available to sell? With limited inventory, especially premium products, where will your commission come from? Yes, selling out is the ultimate goal, but you still need to earn a living in the meantime. The sweet spot? Joining a team two to three years before their hockey stick moment. A hockey stick moment is when a team finds tremendous success in a finite amount of time. This timing gives you enough runway to deeply understand the organization and venue while positioning yourself to capitalize on the upswing. Think about sales executives who joined the Golden State Warriors just before their mid-2010s championship dynasty. Another career-defining opportunity is being part of a new stadium build. Sales professionals have catapulted their careers by riding these once-in-a-generation moments.

Sales is Like Dating

If you've ever experienced the nervous energy of a first date, the careful attention to what you wear, the deliberate choice of venue, the mental rehearsal of interesting things to say, then you already understand the essence of sales. Consider the fundamental rule of dating: you don't drop to one knee and propose marriage before the appetizers arrive. Yet countless eager professionals enter the sports industry and do exactly that, pitching premium partnerships or season ticket packages before they've learned their prospect's name, let alone their needs. The parallel isn't coincidental. Sales, at its core, is the art of building relationships, and like dating, it requires patience, genuine curiosity, and the emotional intelligence to recognize that the best conversations happen when you're listening twice as much as you're talking.

That first date, or first meeting, isn't about closing the deal. It's an audition for both parties, a low-stakes exploration to determine whether a second conversation is worth anyone's time. When you meet someone for coffee, you're not evaluating whether they'd make a good spouse; you're simply asking yourself, "Do I enjoy this person's company enough to see them again?" Your prospect is asking the same question about you, except their version sounds like, "Does this person understand my business? Do they listen, or just wait for their turn to talk? Can I trust them with my budget and my reputation?" The pressure isn't to be perfect, it's to be present, prepared, and genuinely interested in solving their problems rather than simply hitting your quota. Miss that opportunity to make a meaningful connection, and there won't be a second meeting. But nail the fundamentals of active listening, thoughtful questions, and authentic engagement, and you've earned something far more valuable than a signature; you've earned the right to continue the conversation.

The most successful salespeople I've encountered in nearly a decade of sports business don't succeed because they've mastered the perfect pitch or can recite their product's features in their sleep. They thrive because they've internalized what every person who's been in a healthy relationship knows instinctively – connection precedes commitment. You remember the first dates that felt effortless, where conversation flowed naturally and time seemed to evaporate. Those moments happened because both people were genuinely invested in understanding each other. Corporate partners and season ticket holders aren't buying your inventory; they're buying into a relationship with you and your organization. Show up desperate, talk only about yourself, or fail to demonstrate that you've done your homework about who they are and what they care about, and you'll get the same result you'd get on a bad date: a polite excuse and a quick exit. But approach each interaction with authentic interest, do the work to understand their world, and create genuine value for their specific situation? That's when sales stops feeling like sales and starts feeling like the beginning of something both parties are excited to build together.

Surviving and Thriving in Your First Sales Role

Knowing that sales is valuable and actually succeeding in a sales role are two different things. Here's practical advice for not just surviving, but excelling in your first sales position in sports.

Master the fundamentals before you get creative. Every sales organization has a process, and that process exists because it works. Use the scripts you're given, at least initially. Follow the sales methodology they teach you. Make the required number of calls. Do the role-playing exercises even though they feel awkward. Too many people want to reinvent the wheel before they've proven they can execute the basics. Once you've demonstrated that you can hit your numbers following the standard approach, you'll have earned the credibility to experiment and personalize your approach. But start by doing what works.

Track everything and understand your metrics. Know your numbers cold. Your calls per day, your contact rate, your conversion rate at each stage of the funnel, your average deal size, and your close rate. Understand what activities lead to results and do more of those activities. If you're struggling, your metrics will tell you where the breakdown is happening. Are you not making enough calls? Are you not converting conversations to appointments? Are you not closing deals you should be closing? The data tells you where to focus your improvement efforts.

Build genuine relationships with your manager and team. Your manager has likely done the role you're doing and has seen hundreds of people go through it. They know what works. They can see patterns you can't see yet. Build a relationship where they feel invested in your success. Ask for feedback regularly. Implement what they suggest. Similarly, your peers are your best resource. The person who sits next to you and crushes their numbers every month? Take them to coffee and learn everything you can from them. Sales can feel isolating, but building a strong team culture makes the hard days more bearable and accelerates your learning.

Develop a pre-call routine. The best salespeople don't just pick up the phone and start dialing randomly. They have a routine that gets them in the right mindset. Maybe that's reviewing their talk track, or listening to music that pumps them up, or reviewing successful calls from previous days. Find what works for you and be intentional about your mental preparation. Your energy and attitude come through the phone, and managing your state is part of the job.

Learn to love the no. This sounds counterintuitive, but every "no" brings you statistically closer to a "yes." If your close rate is 10%, then nine nos mean the next call is likely a yes. There's a general rule in sales: 33% of people will always buy, 33% will never buy (even if you're selling $1 for $0.50), and 33% are undecided. This is where the salesperson comes in. Reframe rejection as progress rather than failure. Some salespeople literally track their nos as proudly as their yeses because they understand it's a numbers game and the only way to get more yeses is to get more nos along the way.

Focus on activities you can control. You can't control whether someone buys, but you can control how many calls you make, how prepared you are, how you follow up, and how you show up every day. Focus your energy on the inputs that are within your control, and trust that if you consistently execute those activities well, the results will follow. Getting obsessed with outcomes you can't control is a recipe for frustration.

Celebrate the small wins. Sales can be grinding, especially when you're in a slump. Celebrate everything worth celebrating: a good conversation even if it didn't close, positive feed-back from a client, hitting your call goal for the day, or a teammate's success. Building momentum matters, and recognizing progress, even small progress, helps maintain the positive mindset required for this work.

Take care of yourself. Sales is mentally demanding, and burnout is real. Use your time off. Maintain interests outside of work. Exercise regularly. Get enough sleep. The grind is unsustainable if you don't build in recovery. The best salespeople treat themselves like athletes: they understand that peak performance requires rest, nutrition, and mental health maintenance.

Remember this is a chapter, not your whole story. Most people don't stay in entry-level sales forever, nor should they. Set goals for what you want to learn, how long you want to stay, and where you want to go next. Maybe it's 18 months to prove you can succeed, build your skills, and then move into a different role. Maybe it's two years to maximize your earnings and your network before transitioning. Having a timeframe helps you stay motivated because you're treating this as part of a larger career plan rather than feeling stuck in a job you don't love. But while you're there, commit fully. Half-assing sales doesn't work, and you're only hurting yourself by going through the motions without giving it a real effort.

The 80/20 Rule: Why Your Ears Matter More Than Your Mouth

There's a formula that separates mediocre salespeople from exceptional ones, and it has nothing to do with how persuasive you sound. It's that you should listen 80% of the time and talk 20% of the time. And if you're new to sales, you're probably doing the opposite.

The instinct when you're starting out is to fill every silence with words. You've memorized your pitch, you know the features of your product, and you're eager to prove you know what you're talking about. So you talk, and talk, and talk. You explain the benefits of club seats, the value of a season ticket package, and the ROI of a sponsorship. You answer questions they haven't asked. You overcome objections they haven't raised. You're performing, and it feels productive because you're demonstrating knowledge and enthusiasm.

The problem is that while you're talking, you're learning nothing. You're not discovering what actually matters to this specific person. You're not hearing the hesitation in their voice that tells you price isn't really the issue, timing is. You're not catching the moment when they mention their kid plays travel hockey, which is your opening to talk about youth sports group packages. You're not building a relationship, you're delivering a monologue. And people don't buy from monologues. They buy from people who understand them and from people they like.

The 80/20 rule forces you to do something that feels counterintuitive: make the conversation about them, not you. When you're listening 80% of the time, you're asking questions that uncover what they actually care about. You're giving them space to talk themselves into the value rather than you having to convince them. You're paying attention to tone, word choice, and what they emphasize versus what they gloss over. All of that information is diagnostic. It tells you how to position your pitch, what objections to address, and whether this person is a real prospect or just being polite.

Let's get tactical about what this actually looks like. You're on a call with a potential season ticket holder. Here's the wrong approach: "Hi, I'm calling about our season ticket packages. We have incredible seats available in the lower bowl, and if you commit today, we're offering a 10% discount plus access to our exclusive member lounge." You've just used up your 20% in the first 15 seconds, and you have no idea if this person cares about discounts, lounge access, or lower bowl seats.

The right approach: "Hi, I'm calling about season tickets, but before I get into anything, I'm curious, how long have you been following the team?" Then you stop talking. Let them answer. Really listen to what they say. If they've been a fan for 20 years, that's different from someone who just moved to town. If they mention going to games with their dad as a kid, you're talking about legacy and tradition, not just seats. If they talk about bringing clients to games, you're selling business value, not fandom.

After they answer, you ask another question: "What's kept you from getting season tickets before now?" Or, "When you do come to games, what makes it a great experience versus just okay?" Each question peels back another layer. Maybe they mention parking is a nightmare. Maybe they say their schedule is unpredictable. Maybe they're worried about committing to 41 games when they can only attend 20. Now you actually know what you're solving for. Now when you talk, and you will talk, your 20% is surgical. It addresses their specific situation rather than spraying generic value propositions and hoping something sticks.

Here's what happens when you get this right: the prospect feels heard. They feel like you're actually trying to help them make a good decision rather than just closing a deal. And when people feel that way, they trust you. They open up more. They tell you the real objection, the one beneath the surface objection. They start selling themselves because you've asked questions that make them articulate why this might make sense for them.

The best part? When you listen more than you talk, you also avoid one of the most common rookie mistakes in sales – talking past the close. Someone is ready to buy, they've mentally committed, and instead of shutting up and moving to paperwork, you keep pitching. You bring up another feature. You mention another benefit. And in doing so, you introduce doubt. You make them second-guess. You snatch defeat from the jaws of victory because you didn't recognize the buying signal and stop talking. When you're listening 80% of the time, you hear those signals. You hear, "That actually sounds pretty good," or, "Let me talk to my wife, but I think we're interested." Those are green lights. Your job at that moment is to say, "Awesome, let me send over the details and we can get you set up," not to launch into a five-minute explanation of parking pass options.

This doesn't mean you never talk or that your pitch doesn't matter. It means you earn the right to pitch by first understanding the person you're pitching to. Your 20% should be high-impact: clear, concise, and tailored to what you've learned in the other 80%. Think of it like this: if you're talking 80% of the time, you're *guessing* what matters to them. If you're listening 80% of the time, you *know* what matters to them. And when you know, you don't need to talk as much because everything you say is relevant.

One of my mentors in sales used to say, "You have two ears and one mouth. Use them in that ratio." It's simple advice, but most people ignore it because talking feels like doing something and listening feels passive. It's not. Listening is active. It's strategic. It's how you gather the intelligence that makes your pitch actually land. If you walk away from a sales call and you talked more than the prospect did, you probably didn't learn enough to close the deal. If you walk away and your throat hurts from talking, you definitely screwed up.

The 80/20 rule is hard to execute at first because silence feels uncomfortable. You ask a question, and there's a pause while they think. Your instinct is to fill that pause with more words, to clarify the question or offer your own answer. Resist that instinct. Let the silence sit. Give them space to think and respond. Some of the most valuable information you'll ever get comes after a pause, when someone finally says what they were hesitant to admit.

Practice this deliberately. Role-play with a colleague and have them time you. Record your sales calls and listen back. Calculate the ratio of time you spent talking versus listening. If you're anywhere close to 50/50, you're talking too much. Aim for 80/20, and if you overshoot and hit 90/10, that's not a bad problem to have. The prospect will tell you everything you need to know to close the deal if you just give them the space to do it.

And here's the beautiful irony: when you talk less, people think you're smarter. They think you're more thoughtful. They feel like you actually get them. The loudest person in the room is rarely the most effective salesperson. It's the person asking the best questions and actually listening to the answers. Be that person. Your close rate will thank you.

Think about the last time you went to the doctor. The good ones don't walk in and immediately start prescribing medication.

They ask questions. What are your symptoms? When did this start? Does anything make it better or worse? They're diagnosing before they're prescribing, because the prescription is worthless if they don't understand the actual problem. Sales works exactly the same way. You can't prescribe a solution until you've diagnosed the problem, and you can't diagnose the problem without asking questions.

This is why the 80/20 rule isn't just about being polite or letting someone talk. It's about being effective. Every question you ask is gathering diagnostic information. When someone says they used to have season tickets but gave them up, you need to know why. Was it the cost? The time commitment? A bad customer service experience? A move to a different city? Each answer points to a completely different solution, and if you're too busy talking to ask, you're prescribing the wrong thing. The best salespeople are like the best doctors. They ask follow-up questions. They dig into the details. They don't accept surface-level answers because they know the real issue is usually one layer deeper. And just like you'd trust a doctor who takes time to understand your situation over one who rushes to write a prescription, prospects trust salespeople who actually diagnose their needs before pitching a solution.

The Three Most Powerful Words in Sales

If you learn nothing else from this section, memorize this phrase: "Tell me more." These three words are the nuclear option of sales conversations, and most people underestimate them completely. When a prospect says something even remotely interesting, responding with "tell me more" does two things simultaneously. First, it proves you're actually listening, not just waiting for your turn to talk. Second, it gets them to elaborate on exactly the thing you need to understand to close the deal. They mention they're frustrated with their current season tickets? "Tell me more." They casually drop that they're thinking about corporate hospitality options? "Tell me more." Do they express concern about the team's performance? "Tell me more." You're not being lazy by using the same phrase repeatedly. You're being strategic. You're giving them permission to go deeper, to reveal the real issue behind the surface statement, to talk themselves into understanding their own needs. The best part is it works in almost any context and never sounds scripted because it's genuinely curious. Most salespeople hear something important and immediately jump in with a solution. Instead, you're going to hear something important, say "tell me more," and let them hand you the exact roadmap for how to sell to them. It's the closest thing to a cheat code that exists in sales.

The High-Earning Exit: Why Sports Sales Opens Doors to Enterprise Sales

A secret that sports sales professionals discover when they look outside the industry is if you can sell sports, you can sell anything, and often for significantly more money. Think about what you're doing in sports sales. You're selling people to spend thousands of dollars on a product nobody actually needs. Businesses won't lose money if they don't sponsor your team. Families won't suffer if they don't buy season tickets. The product you're selling is pure discretionary spending, emotional connection, and perceived value. There's no utilitarian argument. Nobody needs sports. But you're still closing deals, overcoming objections, and building relationships strong enough that people choose to invest in your product instead of a million other things they could do with that money. Now compare that to enterprise software sales, medical device sales, or B2B technology sales. Those salespeople are selling products that actually solve business problems, increase efficiency, reduce costs, or generate revenue for their clients. The value proposition is logical and measurable. The need often already exists, you're just convincing them your solution is the best one. If you can sell something nobody needs, imagine how effective you'll be selling something they actually do need.

This realization has led countless sports sales professionals into enterprise sales roles where base salaries start at $80,000-$120,000 with uncapped commission structures that can add $100,000-$300,000+ annually for top performers. Companies like Salesforce, Oracle, SAP, Stryker, and software-as-a-service (SaaS) startups actively recruit from sports sales because they know the resilience, relationship-building skills, and sheer grinding work ethic required to succeed in sports translates directly to high-value B2B sales. The transition typically happens after 3-5 years in sports when you've proven you can sell, built confidence in your abilities, and realized you want the compensation that matches your skill level. It's not selling out, it's recognizing that the foundation you built selling sports has prepared you to compete at the highest levels of professional sales, where the product might be less exciting but the paycheck is substantially larger and the work-life balance is often better. Many who make this move stay in touch with sports through personal fandom rather than professional grind, and they don't regret the transition.

During COVID, I left the sports industry entirely and went into the medical device sales world. This directly taught me to refine my sales skills and not take no for an answer. I continually kept in contact with my network, ensuring that if and when I wanted to get back into the industry near and dear to my heart, it was an easier transition. Although my time in medical device sales lasted just under a year, it was a period of immense learning. The financial rewards were extraordinary, but as I reflected on my life priorities, I realized the lifestyle wasn't sustainable. With 150 flights and 220 days spent in hotels over the course of 10 months, I came to a clear conclusion: this wasn't the life I wanted.

Making the Jump from Sales to Your Next Role

Sales is valuable as a launching pad, but at some point, you'll want to move into a different role. Here's how to successfully make that transition.

Build relationships outside your department. While you're in sales, invest in relationships across the organization. Volunteer for cross-functional projects. Get coffee with people in departments you're interested in. Understand what other teams do and how the organization works beyond your immediate role. When opportunities arise, these relationships become pathways. The marketing director who knows your work and likes working with you will think of you when a role opens up.

Document your impact. Keep a running record of your achievements: revenue generated, retention rates, customer feedback, and process improvements you implemented. When you're applying for internal positions or external opportunities, you need to articulate the value you created. "I was in sales" is generic. "I generated $500K in new revenue, maintained a 92% retention rate, and developed a referral program that generated 30% of new accounts" tells a much more compelling story.

Translate your skills to the new context. When you're interviewing for a marketing role, don't just say, "I was successful in sales." Explain how the customer insights you gained from thousands of sales conversations make you a better marketer. When you're pursuing an operations role, talk about how understanding the sales process helps you think about the fan experience differently. Make it easy for the hiring manager to see how your sales background is an asset rather than a pivot they need to take a chance on.

Be patient with timing. Internal moves often require putting in your time and proving yourself first. If you've been in sales for six months and you're already trying to move to a different department, that might raise questions about your commitment and follow-through. Most organizations expect you to stay in a role for at least a year, often closer to 18-24 months, before transitioning. Use that time to excel in your current role while building the relationships and skills that will make your next move possible.

Don't burn bridges in your exit. When you do move on, whether internally or externally, leave your sales role in good shape. Help train your replacement. Document your accounts and processes. Maintain your performance through your notice period. The sports industry is small, and how you exit matters. Your sales manager might become a reference for future opportunities or might end up working somewhere you want to work someday. Professional exits create options; messy exits close doors.

When Experience Doesn't Equal Professionalism

During my time in Inside Sales with the Phoenix Suns, I worked alongside a woman who served as a masterclass in how not to approach your first role in sports, despite having legitimate sales experience on her resume. On paper, she should have been an asset to the team. She had worked in sales before. She understood prospecting, objection handling, and closing techniques. She knew the fundamentals. But knowing how to sell and understanding how to succeed in the hyper-competitive world of sports are two entirely different things.

Her fatal flaw wasn't a lack of ability, it was a catastrophic misunderstanding of culture, work ethic, and professional standards. She operated with a rigidity that alienated everyone around her, insisting that her previous sales experience made her methods unquestionable. It was her way or the highway, and she made sure everyone knew it. Constructive feedback was met with defensiveness. Collaboration was treated as an inconvenience. Team norms were suggestions that didn't apply to her. But the moment that crystallized her complete disconnect from the reality of breaking into sports came every afternoon when she decided her workday was finished. She would turn to the office computer, the same computer the organization provided to drive revenue and build relationships with potential ticket buyers, and print coloring sheets. And not discreetly. Then she would sit at her desk, in full view of colleagues who were still grinding through call lists and following up with leads, and color. Like a child in a waiting room.

The coloring was embarrassing. Her ultimate downfall was inevitable. During a sales training session in front of the entire staff and leadership team, the kind of high-visibility moment where you should be hyper-aware of how you're representing yourself, she made comments that crossed the line from unprofessional to terminable. The details matter less than the outcome: she was fired immediately. Not put on a performance improvement plan. Not given another chance. It was a stark, uncomfortable reminder that the sports industry has zero tolerance for people who demonstrate they don't understand the privilege of working in it.

Let me be abundantly clear: don't do this. Ever. Not in any professional setting, but especially not in sports, where hundreds of qualified candidates would gladly take your position without a second thought. The sports industry doesn't owe you anything, regardless of your previous experience. It doesn't care that you've hit quota somewhere else or that you're accustomed to different workplace norms. Entry-level roles in sports are auditions for bigger opportunities, and every person around you – your manager, your colleagues, executives walking past your desk – is evaluating whether you have the hunger, humility, and work ethic to earn the next opportunity. My former colleague failed that audition spectacularly. Her tenure was short, her reputation damaged, and the lesson she left behind was invaluable. Talent without professionalism is worthless, and previous success means nothing if you can't read the room, respect the culture, and conduct yourself with the maturity the industry demands. If you want to color, do it at home. If you want a career in sports, act like someone who deserves one, because the moment you don't, there are a thousand people ready to take your place.

Your first sales role in sports is probably not going to be your dream job. It's going to be hard, often frustrating, and occasionally demoralizing. You'll question whether you made the right choice pursuing sports. You'll see friends in other industries making more money with better work-life balance. You'll be tempted to quit. But if you stick with it, execute consistently, stay coachable, and maintain perspective that this is a chapter in a longer story, you'll develop skills that open every other door in this industry. The VP who interviews you five years from now will respect that you paid your dues in sales. The startup founder will value that you know how to generate revenue. The colleague will appreciate that you understand the business fundamentals. Sales isn't where careers end; it's where they begin. And the skills you build there – resilience, communication, business acumen, relationship building – don't depreciate. They compound. Every conversation, every rejection, every closed deal is an investment in capabilities that will serve you for decades. So embrace the grind. Learn everything you can. Build relationships. Hit your numbers. And when you've proven what you can do, leverage that experience into whatever comes next. The path through sales might not be the one you wanted, but it's the one that works. And on the other side of it, you'll be better equipped for success than you ever could have been without it.

Sales Skills Development Plan

Whether you're in sales now, starting soon, or trying to prepare for future sales roles, develop these capabilities deliberately. Create a 90-day sales skill-building plan focusing on four core competencies:

1. Communication and storytelling. Practice the STAR method by writing out ten accomplishment stories and

recording yourself telling them out loud. Get feedback from a mentor on clarity, confidence, and conciseness.

2. Handling rejection and building resilience. Set a goal of experiencing 20 rejections this month. Apply for stretch opportunities, make cold calls for a friend's business, ask for things where "no" is likely. Desensitize yourself to rejection deliberately.

3. Active listening and reading people. In every conversation this week, practice asking three follow-up questions before making any statement about yourself. Notice when you're waiting to talk versus actually listening. Record and reflect on what you learn.

4. Product knowledge and value articulation. Choose any product or service (doesn't have to be sports-related) and practice explaining its value in 30 seconds, 2 minutes, and 5 minutes. Get feedback on whether you're leading with features (what it is) or benefits (what it does for the customer).

For each competency, identify one specific resource (book, course, mentor conversation) you'll use to improve, one specific practice activity you'll complete weekly, and one metric for measuring improvement. Sales skills aren't innate, they're developed through deliberate practice. Commit to this development plan regardless of your current role, because these skills transfer to every aspect of your career.

Part VI: Playing the Long Game: Growth, Grit, and Giving Back

Sustaining long-term growth through continuous learning and purposeful contribution: giving back through mentorship, volunteering, and professional community involvement that opens unexpected doors while creating meaning beyond titles (Chapters 16 & 17).

"My advice to students would be to network, network, network! Building relationships across departments (not just within the one your internship is based in) is essential. You never know who knows somebody that can connect you to an opportunity. Networking is such a valuable tool for me personally, as it helped me land my role at the USL." **Riley Coleman, Human Resources Generalist, United Soccer League**

"I highly recommend Stuart's book as a "must read" for those looking to enter the sports industry. It provides the truth behind the sports industry and what it takes to enter the industry. The book is a homerun!" **David Scrivines, 25+ Year Professional Baseball Scout**

"Sports journalism isn't easy, and no path is linear. This book provides real insight and guidance on the different routes you can take, which is so important for anyone navigating this industry." **Nayo Campbell, Digital Content Reporter and Producer for the Utah Jazz**

"Breaking into sports is similar to breaking into any profession. Get experience, start at the bottom, be humble, ask lots of questions, find mentors, build relationships and get the soft skills right - show up on time, do what you are asked really well (no matter trivial it seems), respond promptly to requests. The compounding power of experience is powerful. Thank you Stuart for shining a light on what it takes to build a career in sports." **Eric Shuffler, Sports Entrepreneur, Co-Owner, Staten Island Ferryhawks**

"Sure, working in sports can be fun. After all, it's the reason so many of us fall in love with the game as kids and never quite let go. That passion is exactly why breaking into the industry feels like such an impossible dream for so many people. But here's the thing: actually getting your foot in the door is one of the toughest challenges any job seeker will face. That's what makes Stuart's guidance so valuable.

We're incredibly lucky that someone like Stuart, who has lived this journey and built a successful career on the other side, is willing to share what he's learned. As someone who has been through the grind myself, I can tell you: Stuart absolutely nailed it." **Rob Bradford, Boston Red Sox Beat Writer**

"Trying to navigate today's ever changing media landscape is like walking on quicksand. Thankfully, Stuart is stepping up to pay it forward and share his incredible wealth of knowledge about how to not only land a job, but forge and sustain a career. I've always said sports are the best form of reality television around, because you literally never know what will happen once the game begins. Stuart's book is the perfect guide to help you get in the door, control the controllables around the games and enjoy the incredible ride." **Cindy Brunson, TV Play by Play voice for Athlete's Unlimited Pro Hoops, TNT Sports, NBC Sports, and the University of Arizona Women's Basketball.**

"I'm constantly asked by students and young people how to break into the business of television sports. I'm thrilled to direct them to Stuart's wonderful book, a real world guide that goes into great detail of how to get there and how to stay there!" **Bob Rathbun, Atlanta Hawks TV Play-by-Play**

Chapter 16: Continuous Learning and Reading

You've already landed your first job in sports, but that's just the beginning. The executives running teams and leagues don't stop learning once they have a job title. They read constantly, stay curious about business and human behavior, and treat education as a lifelong practice rather than something that ended with a diploma. This chapter isn't a generic pitch about why learning matters. It's about building actual habits around reading, podcasts, and continuous development that separate people who plateau early from people who keep advancing throughout their careers.

The Education That Actually Matters Starts After Graduation

The uncomfortable truth is that your sport management degree is just the entry ticket. It proves you were interested enough to study this field and disciplined enough to complete a program. But the real education, the learning that actually determines how far you go in this industry, happens after you walk across that graduation stage. The executives who reach the top aren't the ones who stopped learning when they got their degrees. They're the ones who treat learning as a lifelong practice, who read voraciously, who study industries beyond sports, who constantly seek to understand things more deeply. The difference between people who plateau at coordinator or manager level and people who reach director and VP roles often comes down to intellectual curiosity. The people who advance are constantly learning about business strategy, leadership, psychology, economics, technology, and culture. They read books that have nothing to do with sports and apply those insights to sports problems. They're students of human nature, organizational behavior, and what drives success across contexts. They understand that sports is a business, and the best lessons about business often come from outside sports entirely.

This chapter is about building a learning practice that extends beyond your formal education. It's about the books that shaped how I think about this industry, career development, leadership, and life. These aren't just titles to add to your Goodreads list, they're books that will change how you see the world if you actually read them and wrestle with the ideas. Some are about sports. Most aren't. All of them have made me better at navigating this industry and building a career that matters. You can find a recommended reading list at the back of the book.

Why Reading Still Matters in a World of Podcasts and Videos

You can learn from podcasts, YouTube videos, online courses, and social media threads. All of these formats have value. But reading books, actual books that require sustained attention and deep engagement, develops cognitive capabilities that other media don't. Reading builds your ability to follow complex arguments across hundreds of pages. It strengthens your attention span in a world designed to fragment it. It forces you to sit with ideas long enough to truly understand them rather than just consuming surface-level takes. It exposes you to vocabulary, sentence structure, and ways of thinking that make you a better communicator and thinker.

The people who reach senior leadership in sports are almost universally readers. They talk about books that influenced them. They recommend books to their teams. They reference ideas from books in strategy conversations. Reading signals intellectual seriousness in a way that consuming media doesn't. When you can reference insights from books in conversations with mentors, hiring managers, or colleagues, you're demonstrating depth of thinking that sets you apart. This isn't about showing off, it's about genuinely developing the mental frameworks that make you more effective at every level of your career.

Make reading a habit now, while you're in school and have some flexibility in your schedule. Build the practice of reading 20-30 minutes before bed, during your commute, or first thing in the morning. Start with one book per month. That's twelve books per year, which is more than most people read. Over a decade, that's 120 books, a completely different level of knowledge and perspective than you'll have without this practice. The investment is small. The return compounds forever.

Build that practice now. Make reading non-negotiable. Protect 20-30 minutes a day for reading, even when you're busy - *especially* when you're busy. The busiest, most successful people I know are also the most disciplined about reading because they understand it's not a luxury, it's an investment that compounds. Your sport management degree gives you the baseline. The recommendations in the back of this book and the thousands of others you'll read across your career give you the depth, perspective, and wisdom to actually lead. Don't just collect titles. Read deeply. Think critically. Apply what you learn. Share insights with others. And never stop being curious. The students who treat learning as something that ends at graduation plateau quickly. The students who treat graduation as the beginning of their real education build careers that matter. Be the latter. Start with the book recommendations in the back. Then find your own. The learning never stops, and that's exactly the point.

Learn By Listening: Essential Sports Business Podcasts

One of the easiest ways to stay educated about the sports industry is listening to podcasts. You can learn while commuting, working out, doing laundry, or running errands. Podcasts expose you to current trends, insider perspectives, and real conversations with executives who are actually doing the work you want to do. They're free, they're accessible, and if you're serious about breaking into sports, you should be listening regularly. Here are the essential podcasts you need in your rotation:

Attitude, Effort, Results (AER Podcast) hosted by Tanner Natzke is an industry-leading show designed specifically for people trying to break into and become elite in the sports industry. Natzke brings on high-level guests, executives, leaders, and high performers, who share their expertise and provide real-time, actionable advice on starting and accelerating your career. He also provides solo episodes focused on mindset, networking, industry trends, and career strategies. *AER* has one-on-one coaching available, as well as a sales academy that is specifically designed to get you into the industry. The podcast emphasizes the importance of attitude, effort, and results in personal and professional growth, making it essential listening for students seeking real-world guidance on getting started and standing out in sport management.

Start Here (Listen to these first):

- ***Attitude, Effort, Results (AER Podcast)*** - Hosted by Tanner Natzke, this is a must-listen for anyone serious about breaking into and advancing in the sports industry. AER features executives, sales leaders, and high performers who share practical, real-time advice on getting hired, standing out, and accelerating your career. In addition to guest interviews, solo episodes focus on mindset, networking, industry trends, and sales development. AER also offers one-on-one coaching and a Sales Academy built specifically to help aspiring professionals land roles in sports. If you're looking for tactical guidance rooted in attitude, effort, and measurable results, start here.
- ***52 Weeks of Hustle*** - Travis Apple brings on working professionals from every major league who share real tactics for breaking in and moving up, especially in sales roles where most people start.
- ***The Joe Pomp Show*** - Quick 15-minute episodes that break down the money and business side of sports in a way that's

easy to digest. Perfect for your commute, and Joe has a knack for explaining complex deals clearly.

- **SBJ Morning Buzzcast** - A daily 10-minute briefing on what's happening in sports business right now. This keeps you current and gives you smart things to say in networking conversations and interviews.

Essential Weekly Listens

- **The SportBusiness Podcast** - Gets you thinking globally about media rights, sponsorship deals, and how the international side of sports works. The production quality is high and the content is substantive.

- **Navigating Sports Business** - High-level executives sharing their actual career paths and the decisions they made along the way. This is gold for understanding how people really climbed the ladder.

- **Sports Business Radio** - Goes deep on specific topics like agent negotiations, media deals, and brand partnerships. The interviews are thorough and you'll learn how deals actually get done.

For Staying Ahead

- **Sports Business Conversations** - Won the Sports Podcast Award for best sports business podcast. Focuses on where the industry is heading rather than just recapping what already happened, which helps you think strategically.

- **Unofficial Partner Podcast** - Richard Gillis gets executives to open up and speak honestly about their careers and the industry. The conversations feel real, not like PR interviews.

- **Front Office U** - Specifically designed for college students and young professionals, so it speaks directly to your situation with practical networking advice.

- ***SportsPro Podcast*** - Great for international perspectives and understanding how the global sports industry operates differently across regions.

- ***Sports Geek*** - If you're interested in digital marketing, social media strategy, and how teams connect with fans online, Sean Callanan was one of the first doing this well.

- ***Bloomberg Business of Sports*** - When you want to understand the financial and economic side of major sports stories. They pick one topic and really break it down.

My honest advice: start with three podcasts max. I'd go with *52 Weeks of Hustle* for career tactics, *SBJ Morning Buzzcast* to stay current, and *Attitude, Efforts, Results* to learn from some of the best. Once those become a habit, add one or two more based on what interests you most. The consistency matters more than trying to listen to everything.

To actually use these podcasts, pick one episode per week from any of these shows and listen during your commute, workout, or while doing errands. Use them to supplement what you're learning in class. When you study sponsorship, media rights, or athlete branding, you'll hear real-world examples and current case studies through these podcasts. Keep a notebook or notes app where you jot down interesting insights, strategies you hadn't considered, names of companies or executives you want to research further, or concepts you want to explore more deeply. When you're working on projects or papers, you can reference specific episodes to demonstrate that you're staying current with industry trends and learning from practitioners, not just textbooks. The key is consistency. Listening occasionally won't help you much, but making podcasts a regular part of your routine will keep you informed, inspired, and conversational about what's actually happening in the sports business right now. Some of the best networking you can do is reach out to the guest speakers on these podcasts. It makes for a natural reason to reach out.

Master's Programs

Let me give you my personal take on master's degrees, and it's going to be blunt: unless you're pursuing a profession that requires certification to practice, like becoming a doctor, lawyer, medical professional, or accountant, a master's degree is not worth the time nor money. In fields like medicine and law, advanced degrees aren't optional. A doctor can't practice without completing medical school and residency. A lawyer can't represent clients without a Juris Doctor (JD) and passing the bar. Those credentials are gatekeepers, and there's no way around them. But sports management? For the most part there's no licensing requirement. No governing body says you need a master's to work in ticket sales, partnerships, or operations. What you need is experience, and you'll gain more applicable knowledge in six months working for a team than you will in four years sitting in a classroom. Graduate programs can teach you theory, but they can't teach you how to handle an angry season ticket holder, close a sponsorship deal under deadline, or navigate office politics. Those skills only come from doing the job. Meanwhile, the person who skipped grad school and started working is two years ahead of you in experience, relationships, and earning potential. That's a gap you may never close.

Learning System and Reading Plan

Build a sustainable learning practice that extends beyond graduation. First, audit your current learning inputs: how many books did you read last year? What podcasts do you listen to? What industry publications do you follow? Are you actively learning or passively consuming? Be honest about the gap between where you are and where you want to be.

Next, create your learning system:

1. Reading commitment: choose a realistic target (one book per month is 12 per year, which puts you ahead of 90% of people). From the recommended reading list, select three books you'll read in the next 90 days. Schedule 20-30 minutes of daily reading time and treat it as non-negotiable.
2. Podcast routine: subscribe to 3-5 industry podcasts from the recommended list. Block time during your commute, workouts, or weekly routine to listen. Take notes on key insights.
3. Industry news: subscribe to Sports Business Journal, Front Office Sports, and two other sports business publications. Spend 15 minutes every morning reading industry news.

Create an application practice. For every book you read or podcast you hear, identify one specific idea you'll implement within one week. Learning without application is entertainment, not development. Create a simple tracker (spreadsheet or notebook) where you log what you read, key takeaways, and how you applied the lessons. Review this quarterly to see your intellectual growth over time. Finally, find an accountability partner, a classmate, colleague, or mentor who's also committed to continuous learning. Share what you're reading, discuss ideas, and hold each other accountable to your learning goals. This system transforms learning from something that happens accidentally into a disciplined practice that compounds over your entire career.

Chapter 17: Giving Back

"I still remember the people who took the time early in my career to guide my journey and give me advice on how to break into and succeed in the world of sports. That's a big reason why I try to take time every week to pay it forward to the next generation who will work in an industry that's almost entirely different from the one we are currently experiencing. That said, a few things will never change, the importance of passion and work ethic, making genuine relationships, thinking creatively and welcoming new ideas. I can't wait to see what things look like when I can just sit back and enjoy it from the couch." **Josh Rawitch, President, Baseball Hall of Fame**

The best career advice nobody tells you is that helping others will do more for your trajectory than any title change ever will. Mentoring students, volunteering for causes you care about, and staying connected to people trying to break in creates opportunities you can't manufacture through networking alone. You don't need to wait until you're a VP to start giving back. The moment you land your first job, you know things that someone six months behind you desperately needs to learn. This chapter breaks down the practical ways to give back throughout your career, why it matters more than you think, and how to do it without burning out while you're still building your own path.

The Paradox of Getting Ahead by Helping Others

Your sport management degree is merely an admission pass. It shows you cared enough to pursue this field and had the determination to finish the program. But genuine education, the kind that truly shapes your trajectory in this business, begins the moment you accept your diploma. What they don't mention while you're hustling through those first jobs, working tirelessly to demonstrate your value and move up, is the quickest path to elevating your career is frequently to quit obsessing over your own climb and begin investing in other people's success. This sounds counterintuitive, maybe even naive. You're working 60-hour weeks, you're underpaid, and you're still trying to figure out your own career path, so why would you spend precious time and energy helping other people? Because giving back, through mentorship, volunteering, joining professional organizations, and sharing what you've learned, opens more doors than chasing titles ever will. It expands your network in ways that feel authentic rather than transactional. It keeps you connected to fresh perspectives and emerging trends. It reminds you why you got into this industry in the first place. It builds a reputation as someone who invests in others, which makes people want to invest in you. And perhaps most importantly, it gives your career meaning beyond just climbing the organizational chart.

This chapter is about the various ways you can give back throughout your career, why it matters more than you think, and how to do it in ways that are sustainable and genuinely valuable. I'll share my own experiences with organizations like Suns Charities 88 with the Phoenix Suns, along with mentoring students, guest lecturing, and staying connected to the next generation of sports professionals. Because the truth is, the most fulfilled people in this industry aren't the ones who got the biggest titles, they're the ones who helped the most people along the way. The biggest mistake people make about giving back is waiting until they've "made it" to start. They think they need to be a VP or have 20 years of experience before they have anything valuable to offer. You have something valuable to offer the moment you land your first job in sports, because you just did something that thousands of students are trying to figure out how to do. You know things that the person six months behind you desperately wants to know.

I started mentoring students when I was maybe two years into my career, still figuring things out myself, still making mistakes, still unsure about my own path. I thought, "Who am I to give advice?

I barely have this figured out." But what I learned is that the person one or two steps behind you doesn't need wisdom from someone at the top of the mountain. They need practical guidance from someone who just navigated the terrain they're about to cross. They need to hear that it's normal to feel overwhelmed, that rejection is part of the process, that everyone struggles early on. You remember what it was like to be in their position in a way that someone 20 years into their career doesn't. Start giving back early. You don't need permission. You don't need a formal title. You just need to be willing to help people who are where you were recently. Answer their questions honestly. Review their resumes. Do informational interviews. Share what worked and what didn't. This doesn't require massive time commitments, even 30 minutes a month talking to students makes a difference. Helping others clarifies your own thinking. When you articulate lessons you've learned to someone else, you understand them more deeply yourself. Mentoring isn't just generous, it's strategic in the best way.

"When people ask for my help, I'll do my best to open the door," Gettleman explains. "But once that door is open, the rest is on you. I don't want to hear excuses if you don't get the job. I got you in. You have to get the job."

"Too many students today are graduating with degrees but no clear direction. I've always felt a responsibility to give back because when I was in school —trying to understand my passions and identify my strengths – I relied heavily on mentors and the wisdom of others who were willing to guide me. Now, as an industry professional myself, I feel a deep desire to do the same for those chasing their dreams," says Brett Dougherty, the Senior Manager of Premium and Formation Sales at the Dallas Cowboys.

Mentorship: The Relationship That Goes Both Ways

Formal mentorship programs exist in many organizations and professional groups, but the most valuable mentoring relationships often form organically. Someone reaches out for advice, you have coffee, the conversation is valuable enough that you stay in touch, and over time, a relationship develops where you're invested in their success and they're learning from your experience. They don't need you to have all the answers or to have a perfect career trajectory. They need you to be honest about your experiences, the successes and the failures. They need you to make introductions when you can, to review their work when they ask, and to provide perspective when they're making difficult decisions. They need you to challenge them when they're settling or making excuses, and to encourage them when they're doubting themselves. Most importantly, they need you to care genuinely about their development, not just go through the motions of mentorship because it looks good on your resume.

This isn't a one-way transaction. Good mentees push you to stay current because they're asking about things happening right now in their experiences. They expose you to new perspectives, how the next generation thinks about work, what they value, what they're willing to tolerate and what they're not. They keep you honest by asking questions that force you to examine assumptions you've held for years. They often become some of your strongest advocates, spreading your reputation as someone who invests in others. And years later, when they've succeeded, they remember who helped them along the way. Some of my best professional relationships and opportunities have come through people I mentored early in their careers who later were in positions to return the favor.

Show up consistently. If you commit to meeting monthly, actually meet monthly. Don't ghost when you get busy. Ask more questions than you give answers, help them think through problems rather than just telling them what to do. Make introductions when you can, but don't promise connections you can't deliver. Be honest about your own mistakes and limitations; perfection isn't inspiring, authenticity is. Celebrate their wins genuinely. And know when to let the relationship evolve or end naturally. Not every mentoring relationship lasts forever, and that's okay. You don't need a formal program, though those help with structure.

Respond when students or early-career professionals reach out on LinkedIn asking for advice. Say yes when professors ask if you'll talk to their classes. Volunteer to participate in informational interview programs at your alma mater or local universities. Join professional organizations that connect experienced professionals with students. Look for opportunities with-in your own organization to mentor people in other departments or at earlier career stages. The opportunities are everywhere once you're looking for them.

"Anyone who tells you they got where they are all by themselves is lying, not only to you, but to themselves. Networking requires give and take. You have to take calls and make calls. You have to give advice and listen. And here's the thing about paying it forward: if I help you move through this industry, you don't owe me. You owe the next person coming up behind you," states O'Conner.

Volunteering: Giving Time and Skills to Causes That Matter

Volunteering your time and professional skills to causes you care about might seem disconnected from career development. It's not. The skills you develop through volunteer work, such as event planning, fundraising, board governance, or marketing on a shoestring budget, translate directly to your career. The people you meet through volunteering often become valuable professional connections. And aligning yourself with causes that matter signals your values in ways that pure career advancement doesn't.

My Experience with Suns Charities 88

I was involved with Suns Charities 88 after my time with the Phoenix Suns, and it was one of the most meaningful aspects of my professional life beyond the day job. Suns Charities 88 is the Phoenix Suns' nonprofit foundation dedicated to improving the lives of children and families in Arizona through education, health and wellness, and youth sports programs. Their mission is to create positive change in the community by providing resources and opportunities to underserved populations, and getting involved with people across sports, executives, coaches, broadcasters, and athletes who share a commitment to giving back to the Phoenix community.

One experience that stands out was working at an annual event at Dick's Sporting Goods with Cam Johnson and Alvan Adams. Cam was playing with the Suns at the time, and Alvan is a former long-time Sun (he is the only player in NBA history to win Rookie of the Year, make an All-Star Team, and reach the Finals all in the same year - 1976) and current Vice President, Facility Management at the Suns. We took local kids in need of school clothes shopping, giving them the opportunity to pick out everything they needed for the school year. Watching these kids light up as they selected new shoes, backpacks, and clothes – things many of us take for granted – was incredibly humbling. Cam and Alvan were fully engaged, helping kids pick out gear, talking with families, and making every child feel special. It wasn't a photo op or a quick appearance; it was hours of genuine connection and giving back. Seeing the impact that a few hours and some resources could have on these families' lives put everything in perspective about what actually matters.

I volunteered at fundraising events, helped coordinate community outreach programs, supported youth basketball clinics, and stayed connected to the organization's work throughout my tenure with the Suns. What I got from this went far beyond professional networking, though that happened too. It gave me perspective about what actually matters, kept me grounded when I was stressed about work stuff that was ultimately trivial, and connected me with people I genuinely respected and wanted to be around. When you're grinding through a tough week at work, remembering the kid who got emotional picking out his first pair of basketball shoes reminds you why sports matter – not because of wins and losses, but because of the platform they provide to impact lives.

My Ongoing Work with Jewish National Fund

Currently, I'm deeply involved with Jewish National Fund (JNF-USA), an organization that's been transforming lives in Israel and building connections between Israel and North America for over 120 years. JNF-USA works on environmental sustainability, water solutions, community development, education, and critical infrastructure projects that strengthen Israel and create opportunities for its people. What drew me to this organization was the intersection of my professional background in sports and their commitment to building community through athletic infrastructure and youth development programs.

When I first got involved, I joined the Project Baseball and Softball Task Force, an initiative focused on building baseball and softball infrastructure in Israel. This wasn't just about constructing fields, it was about creating spaces where Israeli youth could learn, compete, and grow through sports. Baseball and softball aren't traditionally major sports in Israel, but the task force recognized their potential to teach teamwork, discipline, and leadership while also building cultural bridges with North America where these sports are deeply embedded in the culture. We worked on developing fields, securing equipment, training coaches, and establishing leagues that would give Israeli kids the same opportunities to fall in love with the game that American kids have had for generations.

The work was challenging and incredibly rewarding. We had to navigate logistical complexities, fundraising requirements, and the unique challenges of building sports infrastructure in a country where these sports were still gaining traction. But seeing those fields come to life, watching Israeli kids step onto a properly maintained diamond for the first time, and knowing that we'd created sustainable programs that would impact thousands of young people made every obstacle worth it. The task force brought together people from across the United States, all united by a belief that sports can transform communities and create opportunities where they didn't exist before.

Beyond the task force, I've stayed actively engaged with JNF-USA's broader mission. I've participated in fundraising campaigns, attended events connecting diaspora Jews with Israel's development needs, and used my platform in sports to raise awareness about the organization's work. What I've learned through this involvement is that the skills you develop in sports, like project management, relationship building, strategic thinking, and fundraising, are directly transferable to nonprofit work. And conversely, the perspective you gain from nonprofit involvement makes you better at your day job. When you've spent time working on projects that genuinely change lives, the day-to-day stresses of ticket sales or partnership negotiations feel less overwhelming because you have a clearer sense of purpose and impact beyond the immediate business outcomes.

The skills I've developed coordinating events, supporting fundraising campaigns, working with diverse stakeholders across continents, and managing complex infrastructure projects have made me better at my professional work in ways I didn't anticipate. More importantly, this work has kept me connected to something larger than myself and reminded me that the sports industry's real value isn't just entertainment, it's the platform it provides to build communities, create opportunities, and impact lives in meaningful ways.

Find causes you actually care about. Don't volunteer just because it looks good or because you think it'll help your career. Choose organizations whose missions resonate with you personally, whether that's youth sports, education access, health research, community development, or something else entirely.

For me, that organization is the Jewish National Fund. My connection to Israel isn't abstract or philosophical. It's deeply personal, rooted in my family's history and the people who shaped who I am. My grandfather was the Associate Executive Vice President of the American Jewish Joint Distribution Committee (JDC) and later worked as a social scientist with the World Health Organization. In 1991, he helped oversee Operation Solomon, the dramatic airlift that brought over 14,000 Ethiopian Jews to Israel in just 36 hours. During that operation, one Boeing 747 carried 1,088 passengers, setting the record for the most people ever transported on a single flight. The seats had been removed to fit more people, and two babies were born mid-flight. That's the kind of work my grandfather dedicated his life to, bringing Jews home when their lives were in danger.

My family member, Gerda Weissmann Klein, was a Holocaust survivor and humanitarian who spent her life speaking about tolerance, resilience, and the importance of standing up against hatred. Gerda survived three years in Nazi labor camps, a three-month death march, and lost her entire family in the Holocaust. When American soldiers liberated her camp in 1945, she weighed 68 pounds. She later married Kurt Klein, the American soldier who liberated her camp that day, and they spent over 50 years together sharing their story and working to promote human dignity. Her story of survival became the basis for her memoir *All But My Life* and the HBO documentary *One Survivor Remembers*, which won an Academy Award and an Emmy. In 2010, President Obama awarded her the Presidential Medal of Freedom, the nation's highest civilian honor, for her tireless work promoting tolerance and Holocaust education.

If you've ever been to the United States Holocaust Memorial Museum in Washington, D.C., you've probably seen Gerda. Her testimony plays on a loop at the end of the museum's permanent exhibition. After walking through room after room documenting the horrors of the Holocaust, visitors encounter Gerda speaking directly to them, sharing what she learned from her experience and urging people to recognize the humanity in everyone. She dedicated the rest of her life to education and ensuring people never forget what happened, speaking to students, writing books, and reminding anyone who would listen that hatred starts small before it becomes systematic.

And my great-grandparents and grandmother fled Germany in the 1930s because of Nazi persecution. They left everything behind to survive.

These aren't just stories I learned about in history class. These are the people who made it possible for me to exist. Israel represents something tangible for me, a place that exists so that no Jewish family ever has to flee with nowhere to go. The Jewish National Fund works to build and strengthen that place, and being part of that work honors the sacrifices my family made and the values they lived by.

Once you find your cause, offer skills that are actually valuable. Find your place within an organization. I like to go by the three "T's": time, treasure, and talent. If you can give all the time in the world, offer to help with anything and everything. If you have disposable income, donate money. Just about every non-profit will always be looking to raise money. And lastly, talent. If you're good at marketing, offer marketing help. If you know how to manage events, help with events. Don't just show up to fold chairs, offer the professional capabilities you're developing. Organizations need skilled volunteers who can contribute expertise, not just bodies filling space.

You'll develop skills in low-stakes environments where mistakes aren't career-ending. You'll build relationships with people outside your immediate professional circle. You'll gain experience with different types of organizations and leadership structures. You'll get exposure to senior leaders in informal settings where they see you contributing rather than just networking. And you'll build a reputation as someone who shows up for things beyond their job description. All of these compounds over time in ways that are hard to predict but consistently valuable. This also helps you build a community outside of work to make your new city feel like home.

Elevate Phoenix: When the Mission Becomes Yours

When a colleague left for another job opportunity, I inherited one of his accounts, Elevate Phoenix. This wasn't just any non-profit. They had a multi-year relationship with the Phoenix Mercury that ran deep. The partnership value alone far exceeded my yearly sales goal. This wasn't an account I could afford to mess up. This was a relationship I needed to nurture.

Annie Meyers Drysdale, a basketball legend and Hall of Famer, sat on their board. For those who don't know the name, Annie was the first woman to receive a full athletic scholarship to UCLA, the only woman to try out with an NBA team, Olympian and Hall of Famer, and a trailblazer for women in sports. This organization wasn't just another line item on her resume. It was close to her heart.

Elevate Phoenix's mission was simple but powerful: to introduce urban students to a positive and caring teacher/mentor who helps ensure they don't have to navigate life's toughest challenges alone. They provided mentorship, educational support, and opportunities to kids who needed them most. And our partnership with the Mercury gave us a unique way to deliver on that mission.

We provided students with unforgettable experiences. Courtside seats to watch some of the best athletes in the world; meet-and-greets with players who looked like them, who came from similar backgrounds, who proved that dreams were possible; and behind-the-scenes access that made them feel seen, valued, and inspired. These weren't just perks. For many of these kids, it was the first time anyone had invested in them like that.

I didn't just manage the account. I showed up. I attended their events. I built relationships with the people on the ground doing the work. And I made sure they had everything they needed to keep changing lives. Because at the end of the day, this wasn't about hitting my sales numbers. It was about being part of something bigger than a contract.

Professional Organizations: Your Extended Network and Learning Community

Joining professional organizations feels optional, especially when you're paying dues out of an entry-level salary. But membership in the right professional groups is one of the highest ROI investments you can make early in your career. Here are some of the benefits that professional groups can offer:

- Access to industry events and conferences where you meet people beyond your organization.
- Educational programming, webinars, workshops, and certification programs that develop your skills.
- Job boards where members post opportunities before they're public.
- Mentorship programs that connect you with experienced professionals.
- Volunteer leadership opportunities that build your resume and visibility.
- And perhaps most valuably, a community of people at similar career stages facing similar challenges, plus access to senior leaders who are active in the organization.

The specific organizations depend on your focus area, but here are some that matter in sports:

- Sports Business Association for broad industry networking and programming.

- Stadium Managers Association for facilities and operations professionals.
- National Sports Forum for business-side professionals across teams and leagues.
- Sports Lawyers Association for anyone interested in legal and business affairs.
- Association of Luxury Suite Directors (ALSD) for premium seating professionals.
- Women in Sports and Events (WISE) for women building careers in sports.
- Black Sport Professionals to connect, empower and advance diverse professionals in the sports industry in all areas and levels of business.
- League-specific groups, university alumni sports networking groups, and local chambers of commerce with sports industry focus.

Don't just pay dues and ignore everything, that's wasted money. Attend events, even when you don't feel like it, even when you're tired after work. Volunteer for committees or task forces, as this is how you meet people and get noticed. Participate in online forums or discussions. Present at conferences if the opportunity arises. Use the job board. Take advantage of educational programming. The members who get the most value are the ones who actively participate, not the ones who passively hold membership cards.

You join an organization at 24, feeling like you're on the outside looking in. You volunteer for a committee, which introduces you to people you'd never have met otherwise. You stay active for a few years. By 30, you're connected to hundreds of people across organizations, markets, and functional areas. By 35, you're speaking at their conferences and serving in leadership positions. By 40, you're the person early-career professionals are reaching out to, and you're hiring people from the network you built. That's how this compounds over a career. But it starts with joining when you're 24 and feeling like you don't belong yet.

Guest Lecturing and Speaking: Teaching as Learning

One of the most valuable things I do regularly is guest lecture at universities, my alma mater and others, talking to sport management students about career paths, industry realities, and practical advice for breaking in. I started doing this because professors asked and I wanted to give back. I continue doing it because I get as much out of it as the students do.

Why guest lecturing matters: It forces you to organize your thinking. When you have to explain something to 30 students, you have to clarify it for yourself first. What do I actually think about this topic? What advice would I give? What lessons have I learned that are worth sharing? This process makes you a better thinker and communicator. You also get challenged by smart questions from people who see things from different perspectives. Students ask questions that expose assumptions you didn't realize you were making. They push back on conventional wisdom in ways that make you reconsider whether that wisdom still holds. And you stay connected to how the next generation is thinking about careers, work, and the industry, which keeps you from becoming out of touch.

How to start speaking or lecturing: Reach out to professors at your university or local schools. Tell them your background and offer to come speak to classes about your career path, your functional area, or specific topics relevant to their curriculum. Most professors are thrilled to have guest speakers because it breaks up the semester and gives students a real-world perspective. Don't wait for someone to ask you. Be proactive. If you cannot make it in person, offer to speak virtually. You can also volunteer to speak at student organization meetings, sport management clubs, career panels, or industry events. Start small with a 30-minute talk to one class, and build from there. The more you do it, the more comfortable and effective you become.

What to talk about: Students don't need another lecture about theory, they get that from professors. They need practical wisdom from someone in the trenches. Talk about your career path, the decisions you made, the mistakes, and the things that worked and didn't. Talk about the realities of your role that textbooks don't cover. Give actionable advice about resumes, networking, interviewing, surviving entry-level jobs. Answer their questions honestly, even when the honest answer is, "I don't know," or, "that part of this industry is really hard." They're starving for authenticity, not perfection.

The reputation you build: When you consistently show up to help students, word spreads, professors remember, students tell their friends, and you become known as someone who invests in the next generation. This reputation opens doors, professors reach out with opportunities, students who are now working in the industry remember you and make introductions, and administrators ask you to serve on advisory boards. All because you showed up and shared what you know.

Staying Connected to Students and Early-Career Professionals

Beyond formal mentorship, volunteering, and speaking, there are countless small ways to stay connected to people earlier in their careers. These small touches compound into relationships and reputation.

Be responsive on LinkedIn. When students or early-career professionals reach out asking for advice or informational interviews, respond. Even if you can't meet, send a thoughtful message. Point them toward resources. Make an introduction. It takes five minutes and means everything to someone trying to break in. If you're getting too many requests to handle individually, create a link you can easily send out. Tools like Calendly let you set up office hours or short consultation slots, or you can create a document with resources, advice, and contact information that you share with everyone who reaches out. This way you're still being helpful without doing custom work for each person. I try to respond to every genuine outreach I get, even if it's just to say, "I'm swamped right now but here are three people you should connect with," or, "here's an article that addresses your question," or, "here's my Calendly link if you want to grab 15 minutes next week." Most people ignore these messages. Being someone who actually responds makes you memorable.

Do informational interviews. When someone asks for 15-20 minutes of your time to learn about your career path or role, say yes whenever possible. These conversations rarely take more than 30 minutes, they're often energizing, and you never know who you're helping. Some of the students I talked to years ago are now in positions where they've been able to help me, making introductions, flagging opportunities, or just being great people to know in the industry. I never did those informational interviews expecting anything in return, but the relationships that developed have been valuable beyond measure.

Share opportunities. When you see job postings, internships, or opportunities that might help students or early-career professionals, share them. Post them on LinkedIn and send a DM to the people you think of. Send them to people who might be interested. Forward them to student organizations, career services offices, and the department professors. This costs you nothing and helps people immensely. You become known as someone who's looking out for others, which builds social capital that eventually comes back around.

Stay humble about your success. When you talk to people earlier in their careers, don't position yourself as having it all figured out. Share your ongoing struggles, the things you're still learning, and the mistakes you're currently making. Authenticity builds better relationships than performative success. People don't need you to be perfect, they need you to be real.

The Doors That Open When You Stop Chasing Them

The thing about giving back is you can't do it cynically. If you're mentoring people or volunteering just to build your network or enhance your resume, people sense it and it doesn't work. You have to genuinely care about helping others and supporting causes that matter. But when you do that, when you show up consistently, when you invest in people without expecting immediate return, when you give your time and skills to things beyond your job description, doors start opening that you weren't even knocking on.

People want to work with people who invest in others. When hiring managers are choosing between candidates with similar qualifications, they choose the person they've seen show up to help students, volunteer at events, participate in professional organizations, and make others around them better. Because those traits predict the kind of colleague and leader someone will be. Organizations promote people who make everyone around them better, not just people who are individually successful.

My career has been shaped as much by relationships formed through giving back as by anything I did in my actual job – the people I mentored who later became colleagues or made key introductions, the connections formed through volunteering that led to opportunities I never would have discovered otherwise, the reputation built by showing up consistently for students and causes I care about, which led people to think of me when opportunities arose. None of this was strategic in the moment. I wasn't volunteering or mentoring as a career move. But in retrospect, investing in others has been the highest ROI activity I've engaged in professionally.

Making Giving Back Sustainable

The risk with all of this is burning out. You're already working long hours in demanding roles. Adding mentoring, volunteering, and professional organization involvement on top of that can feel overwhelming. Here's how to make it sustainable:

Set boundaries. You don't have to say yes to everything. Choose the activities and commitments that matter most to you and are genuinely sustainable. It's better to do one or two things well than to spread yourself so thin you're ineffective everywhere and resentful about all of it.

Build it into your routine. Rather than treating giving back as something extra you do when you have time, build it into your regular rhythm. Maybe that's one informational interview per week, or one guest lecture per semester, or volunteering at one major event per quarter. When it's part of your routine rather than an add-on, it's more sustainable.

Set expectations clearly. When you commit to mentoring someone or volunteering for an organization, be clear about what you can and can't do. Don't overpromise. It's better to under promise and over deliver than the reverse. People respect honesty about your capacity more than grand commitments you can't keep.

Know when to step back. There will be seasons of your career – when you're changing jobs, getting married, dealing with personal challenges – when you don't have capacity for the same level of giving back. That's okay. Step back when you need to, then reengage when you can. The point isn't to be a martyr, it's to build a sustainable practice over decades.

Remember why you're doing this. When you're tired and you have another informational interview request or another volunteer committee meeting, remind yourself why this matters. You're helping people who were exactly where you were a few years ago. You're supporting causes that genuinely make the world better. You're building relationships that make your career more meaningful. This isn't an obligation, it's an opportunity.

The Long View: Building a Career That Matters

At the end of your career, you probably won't remember every promotion, every title change, every organization you worked for. But you'll remember the people you helped, the students you mentored who built successful careers, the causes you supported that made a difference, and the community you built through showing up consistently for things that mattered. Giving back isn't separate from building your career, it's enhancing your career, just in ways that are harder to measure than salary increases and title changes. It's building a reputation as someone who invests in others. It's building a network of people who know you genuinely care about their success. It's building skills and perspective that make you better at your actual job. And it's building meaning into work that can sometimes feel transactional or superficial.

Start now. Don't wait until you've "made it." Reach out to one student this week and offer to talk about their career questions. Sign up for one professional organization and actually participate. Volunteer for one cause you care about. Guest lecture in one class.

Answer one LinkedIn message you might normally ignore. These small acts compound over time into a career that's not just successful by external measures, but meaningful by internal ones.

The sports industry has given you opportunities. Give back. Pay it forward. Help the next person trying to break in. Support causes that matter. Stay connected to students and early-career professionals. Build a community, not just a resume. Because at the end of the day, the people who find the most fulfillment in this industry aren't the ones who climbed the highest. They're the ones who helped the most people along the way.

Giving Back Action Plan

You don't need to wait until you've "made it" to start giving back. Choose one specific action from each category and commit to it this month:

1. Mentorship: send LinkedIn messages to three students or early-career professionals, offering a 20-minute informational call to discuss their career questions. Schedule and complete these conversations within 30 days, using the relationship-building principles from Chapter 8.
2. Volunteering: identify one cause or organization you genuinely care about (youth sports, community development, a nonprofit aligned with your values) and volunteer for one event or commit to one ongoing role. Don't overthink it, just show up and contribute.
3. Professional community: join one professional organization relevant to your career interests (WISE, Black Sports Professionals, Sports Business Association, alumni groups) and commit to attending one event in the next 60 days. Don't just pay dues, actively participate.
4. Knowledge sharing: write one LinkedIn post sharing a lesson you've learned in your sports management journey,

do a guest talk for one class or student organization about your career path and internship experiences, or respond to five LinkedIn messages from people asking for advice that you've previously ignored.

Track the impact of your giving back: who did you help, what resulted from your involvement, how did it make you feel, and what relationships developed. Set a recurring calendar reminder quarterly to evaluate whether you're maintaining these commitments or if they've fallen away in the busyness of your career. Giving back isn't something you do once, it's a practice you sustain throughout your career. Start building that practice now, while the memory of trying to break in is still fresh and you genuinely understand what people one step behind you need.

Conclusion: The Game Starts Now

You're holding this book because you want to work in sports. Maybe you've wanted this since you were a kid watching games with your family. Maybe you discovered this passion recently. Either way, you're at the beginning of something that's going to be harder, more rewarding, more frustrating, and more meaningful than you can imagine right now. And here's what I need you to understand before you close this book and start executing everything we've talked about: enjoy this part. Enjoy being in school where your biggest stress is exams and group projects. Enjoy having summer breaks to intern, explore different roles, or just recharge, because once you're working full-time in sports, summers don't exist, and they're just the busiest part of the season or when you're grinding through offseason projects. Enjoy the freedom of not yet being locked into a career path, of having options still wide open, of being able to explore without consequences. Enjoy the flexibility to take a random Tuesday off or change your mind about what you want to do without disappointing an employer or derailing a career trajectory. Enjoy the friendships you're building with people who share this dream. Enjoy game days as a fan before you're working them as a professional. Because once you're in the industry, once you're grinding through 60-hour weeks during the season, once you're dealing with difficult bosses and office politics and the reality that even dream jobs are still jobs, you'll look back on these years with nostalgia. Don't rush through them wishing you were already somewhere else. Be present. Learn everything you can. Build relationships. Make mistakes while the stakes are low. This is the foundation you're building everything else on.

And some perspective to carry with you is that sports isn't life or death. We're not performing surgery. We're not saving lives. We're not curing diseases, or building infrastructure, nor teaching children to read. We're in the entertainment business. Yes, sports matter to people; they bring joy, builds community, creates memories, and gives people something to rally around. That's the real value. But when you're stressed about a campaign that didn't perform, a sale you lost, a promotion that went to someone else, or a mistake you made on game day, remember the stakes. Nobody dies because you didn't hit your ticket sales quota. The world keeps spinning when your marketing campaign underperforms. This perspective isn't about not caring or not working hard, it's about maintaining sanity in an industry that can consume you if you let it. Work hard. Care deeply. But don't lose yourself in the process. At the end of the day, we're helping people enjoy a game. That's a privilege, not a crisis.

Your career isn't going to look like mine. It's not going to look like your classmate's, or your professor's, or that executive you admire on LinkedIn. And that's exactly how it should be. There's no single path into sports, no formula that guarantees success, no checklist you can complete that earns you the career you want. You're going to zigzag. You'll take jobs that seem like steps backward but position you for bigger moves later. You'll pivot between departments, between organizations, and between markets. You'll leave sports for a while and come back. You'll question whether this is worth it, whether you made the right choice, whether you should have just gone into a "normal" industry with better pay and saner hours. All of that is normal. All of that is part of building a career that's yours, not someone else's template. But what will always matter, regardless of which path you take, is effort, curiosity, and kindness. Those three things stand out in every organization, at every level, in every role. Effort, showing up consistently, doing the work even when you don't feel like it, and executing the unglamorous tasks with excellence are the foundation of everything. No amount of talent or connections compensates for not working hard. Curiosity, staying interested in learning, asking questions, reading beyond your job description, studying how things work, is what separates people who plateau from people who advance. The curious ones keep growing. And kindness – treating people well regardless of their position, helping others succeed, remembering that everyone in this industry is human – builds the reputation and relationships that determine your opportunities. Politics, who you know, being in the right place at the right time, all of that matters. But effort, curiosity, and kindness matter more, and they're the only factors entirely within your control.

So here's your final challenge: close this book and reach out to someone today. Maybe it's a professional whose career you admire – send them a message on LinkedIn explaining specifically what you respect about their path and asking one thoughtful question. Maybe it's a professor you haven't talked to in a while – thank them for something specific they taught you and tell them how you're applying it. Maybe it's a classmate who's struggling – offer to help them prepare for an interview or review their resume. Maybe it's someone one step behind you, a younger student or someone trying to break into sports – offer to share what you've learned. Start your own story by contributing to someone else's. Build the habit of reaching out, of asking for help, of offering help, and of staying connected. Because this industry runs on relationships, and relationships start with someone making the first move. You have everything you need to build a career in sports. You have the knowledge from this book, from your classes, from the countless hours you've spent studying this industry. You have the passion that drove you to this field in the first place. You have the opportunity to start building now: networking, gaining experience, developing skills, creating a presence. What happens next is up to you. Will you execute, or will you just think about executing? Will you stay curious and keep learning, or will you assume this book gave you everything you need? Will you help others along the way, or will you only focus on your own advancement?

The sports industry needs people like you, people who care enough to read books like this, who are willing to work hard for less money than they could make elsewhere, who genuinely love what sports mean to people and communities. It needs your energy, your ideas, your perspective. But it won't wait for you to feel ready. It won't hand you opportunities just because you want them. You have to go create them. So get started. Reach out to that person today. Apply for that internship you've been procrastinating on. Join that professional organization. Clean up your LinkedIn profile. Read one of the books recommended at the end of this book. Take one action, right now, that moves you closer to where you want to be. And then tomorrow, take another action. And the day after that, another. Because careers aren't built in grand gestures. They're built in small, consistent actions compounded over years.

Welcome to the industry. Welcome to the grind, the joy, the frustration, and the privilege of working in sports. Your story starts now. Make it a good one.

About the Author

Stuart Sokoloff is a dual American-German citizen and sports business professional from Germantown, Maryland, with over a decade of experience across sales, operations, and revenue generation in professional sports. Throughout his career, Stuart has worked with organizations, including Athletes Unlimited, Phoenix Suns & Mercury, Baltimore Orioles, the San Francisco Giants, and the Cleveland Guardians & Cincinnati Reds Spring Training facility, building experience in ticket sales and service, corporate partnerships, and fan engagement strategies.

Stuart's journey in sports began at Springfield College, where he completed an extraordinary 16 internships and professional experiences across various sectors of the sports industry, a foundation built on relentless drive and commitment to learning the business from the ground up. He holds a Bachelor of Science in Sport Management, with minors in Sports Analytics and Coaching, and served as Vice President of his class, Vice President for the Sport Management Club, while actively leading multiple student organizations.

A passionate educator and mentor, Stuart serves as an adjunct professor at his alma mater, Springfield College, where he teaches a 300-level course in Sports Sales and Service, preparing the next generation of industry professionals with real-world insights and practical tools gleaned from years of hands-on experience.

Beyond his domestic work, Stuart has contributed to international sports, working with the Israel National Baseball Team, including preparation for the 2020 Tokyo Olympics and at the 2023 & 2026 World Baseball Classic. He has served on several nonprofit boards, including the Jewish National Fund, reflecting his commitment to giving back and supporting causes he believes in.

When he's not building revenue strategies, mentoring future sports leaders, or teaching the next generation, Stuart enjoys traveling the country with his wife, who is a nurse. Together, they enjoy discovering local restaurants, staying active, exploring National Parks, and cheering on their favorite sports teams wherever life takes them. Having visited all 50 states and lived in 11 and counting, Stuart embodies a belief that the best opportunities come from embracing change and building community wherever you land.

Stuart is available to speak on career development, sports sales, networking strategies, and what it really takes to succeed in the sports industry. Reach out at www.StuartSokoloff.com.

Voices From the Industry

Throughout my career, I've been fortunate to learn from executives, Hall of Famers, scouts, trainers, and professionals across every corner of the sports world. When I told them I was writing this book, they didn't just offer encouragement – they shared the lessons they wish someone had told them when they were starting out. What follows are perspectives from people who've built careers at the highest levels of sports, from Olympians and General Managers to players and front office leaders, who understand what it actually takes to break in and stay in. Their words aren't just endorsements, they're the collective wisdom of an industry that rewards those who show up, work hard, and genuinely care about the craft.

"In sports and in business, individual success only happens when the team succeeds first. The people who last in this industry understand their role, do their job at a high level, and make the group better every day. Early in your career, stop chasing credit and start chasing contributions. Learn how organizations really work, support the people around you, and take pride in being dependable. When you prove you can help the team win, opportunities come faster and careers take care of themselves." **David Lane, CEO, Sports Illustrated Tickets**

"Stuart is someone I respect immensely for his professionalism, passion and integrity as a sports management professional. He is an incredible resource for anyone looking for pragmatic advice about not only how to kickstart a sports career, but also thrive long-term. Thanks to his first-hand experience building his career from scratch into one of constant success in so many different areas of the sports profession, Stuart is the perfect author for this book." **Nate Mulberg, Head Baseball Coach, Johns Hopkins University**

"Breaking into sports is often described as if there's a clear, straight path, but that wasn't my experience. When I was starting out, I took whatever opportunities I could find, whether it was volunteering at PGA golf events, attending sports conferences, to volunteering as a referee for intramural sports and trying to learn how the industry actually worked from being around the action. Like many students, I spent a lot of time searching for direction, facing rejection, and wondering how interest in sports could realistically turn into a career. I didn't follow a traditional path, and I didn't break in right away. Instead, I built experience wherever I could and focused on developing real, transferable skills outside of sports. That background ended up being the reason I was ready when an opportunity finally came. While my early exposure came through golf and other areas of the industry, the path eventually led me to professional soccer, something I never would have predicted at the beginning. That's why this book matters. It sets realistic expectations without being discouraging and doesn't pretend there are shortcuts. It shows students how to approach the process with patience, how to use early experiences, whether paid or unpaid, to build credibility, and how to stay open to opportunities that may look different from what they first imagined. It encourages a long-term mindset built around skill development, resilience, and adaptability. I'm proud to support a resource that puts students first and prepares them not just to get into sports, but to build careers that last." **Varun Desai, CFO of Blue Crow Sports Group**

"If you want to excel in sports, you need to be a solutions provider. That means being a student of the game, developing a strong business sense, paying attention to the details, and bringing an undeniable work ethic every day. But what really matters in the long run is building relationships that last and creating a personal brand people respect, one that shows leadership and creativity. This industry is like no other. It's truly a gift to work in sports, and you should enjoy it through all the memorable moments you create, one game at a time." **Kerri White, Sr. Vice President, Corporate Partnerships, South Carolina Stingrays**

"Everyone who has success in sports business can look to a handful of people in their careers who spent countless hours developing them, preparing them to take on more opportunities, and coaching them through the challenges (personally and professionally) of an early career in sports sales. We all owe it to the next generation of sports business leaders to make the industry better than we found it. Breaking Into Sports: The Real Guide to Landing Your Dream Job will give readers an in-depth guide on how to create success early in their career, to ultimately become the next great sports business leader." **Blake Pallansch, Sr. Vice President, Revenue & Strategy, QuickAyst**

"Breaking into the sports business starts with understanding that it's not about glamour, it's about value creation. Sports today is a mix of media, technology, business development (both buy and sales side), and relationships. Young professionals who stand out are the ones who are curious, coachable, and willing to do the work others avoid. I'd recommend starting early, saying yes before they feel ready, and building real experience through internships, side projects, event work, or content creation. Experience and reliability matter more than titles and recognition. Treating a role like it's your own business goes a long way. The most important attributes I look for are work ethic, communication skills, comfort with ambiguity, and intellectual curiosity. Whether you want to be in business development, content, operations, or partnerships, being able to learn quickly, communicate clearly, and build trust is critical. The sports industry rewards people who are humble, hungry, and dependable, especially when things get fast or messy. My advice is to be valuable before visible. If you consistently show effort, curiosity, and results, opportunities tend to follow." **Mike Levy, Sr. Vice President, Global Rights Acquisition, FloSports**

"The secret to success you will learn from Stuart is not a secret at all. It's all about showing up every day, being awesome, and providing real value to your team. I have had the privilege of working with Stuart for nearly a decade, and that's exactly what he does in real life and in this book." **Nate Fish, CEO, Israel Baseball Americas**

"The biggest piece of advice I give folks is to make your own path. No one is going to hand you anything in this business. If you know the place you're trying to get to in your career, you have to steer your own ship to get there. Create opportunities for yourself - no one else is going to. Be proactive." **Max Alpert, Vice President, Partnerships, SponsorUnited**

"The sports industry moves fast and demands flexibility with your time and responsibilities, but the rewards make it worth it. As a four-year collegiate athlete balancing school and full-time work, I never had the chance to take on sports-specific internships or volunteer roles. Looking back, that's my one regret. Now that I'm in a hiring position, I see how much those experiences matter. When a resume shows someone's already worked in sports, even unpaid, it immediately sets them apart. It proves they took initiative and, more importantly, that they understand what they're signing up for. Working in sports isn't a typical 9-to-5, and having that experience shows you're willing to put in the dedication it takes to succeed in this space." **Seth Kimberlin, Vice President, Marketing & Club Growth, Indy Eleven Professional Soccer**

"Breaking into the sports and live event industry can be exciting but is also extremely competitive and challenging. Remember that we work when everyone else plays. Dip your toes in all sides of the business because it's all the puzzle pieces that come together to make the experience memorable for guests. The best piece of advice I ever received was that 'it's not rocket science, but if you don't pay attention to the details, it will blow up in your face'. Stay organized, stay detail-oriented and always remember to see the event from the spectator's perspective." **Amber Musgrave, General Manager of Mullett Arena, Oak View Group**

"After 15 years playing professionally, I moved into broadcasting. One day, a group of college communication majors toured our studio. Our host shared her path, communications degree, internship, sideline reporting, then finally, network host. Then she pointed at me and joked, 'Or you can just play professionally first, it's easier!' At that moment, it hit me: breaking into pro sports when you haven't played is tough, and nobody hands you a roadmap. That's why this book matters. It shows you how to navigate the path, build relationships, and earn your place in the world of professional sports." **Ryan Lavarnway, Former Professional Baseball Player**

"Having a growth mindset has to be a big pillar going into professional sports. Understanding that we don't know what we don't know and choosing to treat every day as an opportunity to learn something new. Some of the most valuable lessons come from places you don't expect, so keeping an open mind is essential. Progress in this industry requires truth-telling as well as being willing to admit when you don't have the answers and having the humility and drive to go find it. That commitment to learning, honesty, and continuous growth is what ultimately creates real opportunity." **Alon Leichman, Professional Baseball Coach**

"Breaking into an industry like baseball can be very challenging. Anyone who's ever picked up a bat or ball dreams of being able to play or work for a professional organization. Baseball has been very good to my family and me. I have lots of mentors to thank for helping guide me in this game. I am grateful to help the next generation like many have done for me. As you navigate this journey in professional sports, an important pillar is to be a lifelong learner. Continuously pushing the envelope to learn new things and be curious is important to becoming the best version of yourself. The other pillar for me is resiliency. You're going to hear a lot of No's before you get a Yes. And once you get a Yes, the journey is just beginning. Be resilient, put your head down and be willing to do the work. It's usually not an easy path, but it will be a fulfilling one. Enjoy the journey and always be where your feet are!" **Tyger Pederson, Professional Baseball Coach**

"As both a professional athlete and someone looking to find their footing in the business world, I've found two best things you can do are to meet people with careers you admire and use their insights to build a marketable skill set. On the people front, you'd be surprised how many smart and accomplished people are willing to lend their time to give advice or be a sounding board. The key part is turning those connections into progress. Getting the 30-minute intro call does not mean these people will find you your dream job the next day. What comes after that is taking the insights you learned and using them to figure out what skills you can develop. The CEO of McDonald's recently said "...remember, nobody cares about your career as much as you do." (McDonald's CEO Chris Kempczinski) Surround yourself with kind people who are willing to hear you out, and then use their input to go into every future meeting with a more robust skillset." **Evan Kravetz, Professional Baseball Player**

"Be tenacious. Early in my journey, someone told me, "For every person in the sports industry, three people are there ready to take that job." I say that, not to scare current professionals, rather to give aspiring individuals the grace to accept breaking into the industry is tough. Have a "Yes!" attitude and be willing to do the dirty work to build your experience. It's a fun and competitive industry. Be resilient as you start your journey!" **Chris Jensen, Sports Business Executive**

"Breaking into sports isn't about having the perfect résumé. It's about demonstrating a relentless work ethic, a genuine willingness to learn, and a positive attitude. Working in sports means long hours, nights, and weekends, and as a hiring manager, I always looked for people who understood that commitment and embraced it rather than shied away from it. My advice to anyone trying to break in is simple...respect the brand, outwork expectations, build meaningful relationships, and stay humble. Longevity in this industry comes from consistency, curiosity, and treating people the right way." **Dave Sibelman, Director of Sales, One Times Square, Elevate**

"Breaking into sports isn't just about getting a job, it's about choosing the right first step. Be intentional about the roles you pursue and honest about the places you're willing to move. Take time to understand your strengths, whether that's relationship-building, strategy, operations, event management, or sales, and pursue opportunities that align with them. The industry will ask you to relocate, to stretch, to start where you can, but when your moves are aligned with both your skillset and your long-term vision, every position becomes a building block instead of just a paycheck." **Lindsay Stewart, Director, Membership Services, Arizona Cardinals**

"Breaking into sports isn't about waiting for someone to hand you a shot- it's about chasing it down with zero apologies for who you are. Stuart's book nails what I wish I'd heard earlier: be relentlessly genuine, because fake passion gets sniffed out fast. Some folks will see your drive and pour back into you; others won't- so what? Keep moving. Double down on polite persistence - follow up, stand out, use every tool (yeah, even AI for mock interviews) to sharpen your edge. When you land in the room, make it count: be concise, positive, unforgettable. The industry rewards the ones who show up as the trusted, no-brainer teammate every time. Surround yourself with people who match that energy, and watch doors keep opening. And when you finally get your shot? Grab it with both hands and prove the belief others have in you isn't misplaced. In every role as you climb, step out of your comfort zone, keep innovating, push the work forward, and constantly collaborate. That's how you turn a foot in the door into a real legacy." **Kyle Ingram, Sr. Director, Ticket Sales & Service, UFL**

"My advice for students is to remember that learning doesn't end with your diploma. When entering a career in sports, it's important to remember that you still have a lot to learn and years of growth ahead of you. Be open to new opportunities and remember the right job might be across the street or across the country but you won't know unless you apply." **Baylor Nicole Love, Assistant Director of Corporate Partnerships, Knoxville Smokies Baseball**

"Something I wish more people understood is that while working in Major League sports is a great goal, there are way more Minor League teams than Major League teams, and even more universities that all need the same roles. If you're only applying to the majors and it's not working, widen your scope. Look at Minor League teams, collegiate sports, and leagues outside the 'Big 5.' You'll find more opportunities. The same goes for geography. Keeping your options open location-wise creates more opportunities than fixating on one specific market. Breaking into this industry is already hard, don't make it harder on yourself by being too narrow. And remember, resumes get you interviews, but your attitude and how you relate your skills to the role get you the job. And don't discount game day roles if full-time positions or internships aren't panning out. A game day role still puts a professional sports organization on your resume and gives you access to network with leadership. That access can open doors you didn't even know existed." **JT McCreary, Sr. Director, Guest Services, Arizona Diamondbacks**

"Every opportunity I've had in this industry can be traced back to relationships built on trust, consistency, and mutual respect. Sports is a relationship business, and those connections only stay strong when we invest in each other. Giving back, through mentorship, guidance, and transparency, is how we ensure the next generation is better prepared." **Clay Cardenas, Associate Director, VaynerTalent, VaynerX**

"College athletics is built on relationships. Strong relationships and genuine kindness will consistently take you further in this field than even the strongest résumé. An athletic director friend of mine once said, "In our world, it's not who you know, it's who knows you." Today, more people than ever are trying to break into the sports industry. The key is to identify what sets you apart and lean into it with confidence. Be exceptional at what you do and authentic in who you are. Invest in meaningful relationships with everyone around you. When you do those things, opportunities don't just appear; they find you. And in time, your career path won't need to be forced; it will unfold exactly as it's meant to." **Jenny Hollabaugh, Director, Industry Relations and Events, LEARFIELD**

"Something I learned the value of very early on in my career is 'it's not who you know, it's who knows you.' One thing all the top sports executives have a powerful & eclectic network. From the start of your first internship and onwards throughout all points of your career, it's paramount to spend time networking & sharing best practices with those above, below, and alongside you. Don't be afraid to ask for help and always remember to pay it forward, you never know where that connection may lead you." **Adam Tuval, Commercial Development Director, Playfly Sports Europe**

"When a hiring manager reviews 200 applications and is trying to narrow that list to 7-10 first-round interviews, standing out matters. Find a way to do that. Send a thoughtful LinkedIn message to the hiring manager. FedEx a hard copy of your résumé and cover letter. And when you do, draw a meaningful connection and give them a clear sense of how you'll add value to their organization. I can speak for many colleagues across the industry who actively recruit: any application that arrives directly on our desk, assuming it's sharp and the candidate is qualified, immediately moves to the top of the pile. These extra steps take effort, but over time they pay off. Very few candidates are willing to take them." **Anthony Parilla, Vice President, Property Sales, Elevate**

"Stuart's dedication to his profession and helping others is admirable. One piece of advice I always give to those looking to break into the sports industry is that everyone's journey is different, and to keep their options open. As a student, myself included, we all have the dream of playing a significant role in the front office of one of our favorite major sports teams. While it may happen for some, at the end of the day, it is not very common. However, there is no reason to get discouraged! Many opportunities exist in sports, whether that be at the professional level, collegiate, youth, or through other non-profits. Partnerships, such as the one Little League has with Athletes Unlimited, make many things possible to be able to work on and have relationships with different sports properties from different angles. Pave your path!" **Kevin Feinberg, Director of Partnership Marketing, Little League International**

"An acronym I use in my day-to-day that I wish I had as a mindset when I was first looking to break into the sports industry is C.A.R.E. This acronym stands for Coachable, Accountable, Resilient, & Empathetic. Hiring Managers want individuals who want to be coached and seek feedback, who will PROACTIVELY hold themselves accountable, be able to be resilient and power through hard times, as well as showing empathy as you will connect with people from all walks of life. Showing this on the front end during an interview process can help separate yourself from the thousands of other applicants that want the same job you want. The acronym reads as CARE because it reflects one of the first things I was taught during my inside sales days from my leaders at the 76ers. "People don't care how much you know, until they know how much you care!" **Jake Goodman, Sr. Director, Ticket Sales & Service, Houston Dynamo FC, Houston Dash, Shell Energy Stadium**

"The advice I have for students trying to break into the sports/entertainment industry is to network your ass off! "Network" is an overused term, so what I mean is ask those who have the careers you'd love to have and ask about how they got there and what advice they'd give to a college student who aspires for the same thing. You can get a message, voicemail, email, or social DM in front of just about anyone you want to if you put your mind to it and exercise your resourcefulness. The more doors you knock on, the higher chance of someone opening." **Aaron Kelly, Director, Revenue & Operations, QuickAsyst**

"Focus on the intangibles and small things. So many sales executives stop trying after the sale is done, however, that's when the real work begins. Create relationships, remember birthdays and important milestones, make sure your facility is clean, LISTEN, and work hard. You can't control what your co-workers say or do, but you can control your work ethic, ability to be coached and willingness to learn and take risks." **Jenn Sylvester, Assistant Director, Corporate Partnerships, Fort Wayne TinCaps**

"I've had the chance to learn from some of the very best in professional baseball, they were kind enough to share their time and thoughts with me, so it's important to pay that forward onto the next group of folks who will keep our games moving forward. For an individual looking to break into the industry, one of the most important things to remember is that these entities are all businesses with accounting, finance, marketing, sales, HR, and administrative departments. Being a fan is awesome, but having hard skills that fit into these roles is really important. Don't just say "I want to work in baseball." Have an idea of how you can be an asset to a team." **Nick Bernabe, Assistant General Manager, Gwinnett Stripers**

"Always continue to watch how other networks or teams run their shows. I'm constantly thinking of new ideas to improve the Worcester Red Sox broadcast, and there's no better place to get ideas than watching different networks or going to live sports at other venues. I'll always be watching NESN, ESPN, or FOX's coverage of baseball games and say "Oh! I like how they did that graphic." or 'that camera shot was really cool.' And then think of ways to replicate it using your own brand. And it doesn't even have to be baseball or the sport you are working on. I've gotten ideas for videos and graphics based on what I saw at hockey games or while watching an NFL game on TV. Take the best ideas from everyone you watch and use it as a template to create your own brand to build around." **John Canavan, Director of WooSox Productions at Worcester Red Sox**

"One thing I always tell students is not to focus solely on professional sport organizations. Look at minor league teams, Olympic teams, collegiate programs, start there and grow from there. A lot of times professional organizations are looking for talent that already knows what a pro team requires. College studies don't necessarily provide that kind of application; it's more theory and a 'here's a start' kind of approach. My main talking point when college students reach out to me about breaking into sports is: start small and grow your skills from there. If they get lucky enough to accept an offer from a pro team right away, they're in the top percentage of talent, that's the exception, not the rule. My opinion on how colleges are marketing these degrees to students is that it's not doing them justice. A lot of times we get applications and the students think it's cut and dry coming into the workforce. They might understand the theory of the major, but the practical application isn't there, and that's what teams are looking for. It's great you can read a book, study, and pass a test, but unless you have real working knowledge, you're going to get overlooked. And that's hard for a college student to get without actual experience in the field." **Graham Howe, Director of IT Operations and Service, Indianapolis Colts**

"Breaking into sports isn't about loving the game more than the next person, it's about being useful faster. Every break I got early in my career came from being curious enough to learn how the business really worked, sharpening my capabilities beyond my job description, and earning trust from my colleagues. When opportunity presented itself, I wasn't guessing or hoping, I was ready because I'd been studying it, thinking about it, and had a plan if I was ever called upon." **Nick Cartan, Managing Director, Head of Media, Playfly Sports**

"Breaking into the sports industry is a lifestyle, not just a job. To succeed, you must move beyond being a fan and master the business fundamentals while embracing the grind of working nights, weekends, and holidays. Don't wait for opportunities to find you…chase them down with relentless effort and approach every experience with a learner's mindset. In the end, long-term success is built on authentic relationships and a disciplined focus on what you can control: your work ethic, your coachability, and your relentless commitment to improving every day." **Larry Sinclair, Director of Sales, Solheim Cup, LPGA**

"The amazing thing about working in the sports industry is that you can build genuine friendships without ever meeting in person. In a post-COVID world, creating and maintaining those connections has become even easier. I met Stuart through mutual friends in the industry, and we've connected countless times since. Whether he's inviting me to speak to his class, guiding me through career decisions, or those random moments when we're talking to colleagues who light up and say, "Oh, you know Stuart?" or "You know John?!", you quickly learn to hold onto these people. Those relationships matter. Stuart is a great friend, mentor, and resource. Anybody reading this book will be set up for success, thanks to Stuart. If you are looking to break into the sports industry, learn about roles you want, reach out to people in those positions on

LinkedIn and set up informational interviews. Nurture these relationships. Build upon them. You never know where they can lead to over time. The last three jobs I've had came from informational interviews, networking in the industry and connections built over time. The resume and applications came after because they already knew me, my body of work and my references in the industry spoke about me when I wasn't in the room. Good luck and enjoy the ride!" **John Michos, Premium Sales Manager, New York Mets**

"Being a fan of the team is good, but in sports sales it is your work ethic, your process, and the attitude you bring to the office every single day that truly make you stand out. The people who last are the ones obsessed with learning, who consistently outwork everyone around them, and who show up with a genuinely positive attitude day after day. The best advice I ever received was this: "Anyone can bring great energy for a day. Anyone can lock in for a week, or even grind for a month. But who is willing to do it, with the same standard, for years on end? Those are the people who make a name for themselves in this business." **Kyle Kaminsk, Manager, The Foundation, Cleveland Cavaliers**

"Stuart is somebody special who not just understands a past or present with sports but who also will influence, especially the future of our industry! He's a visionary a number of miles ahead, for all of Tomorrow's Thinking, you need to know today, as in right now. This book can influence lives, and change them in the form of launching careers (maybe yours) as a great read and educational tool! Both in-person and as well online, I will think of all the hundreds of university, college, plus high school youth who connect to be in my network, and to ask the personal advice which I am able to give them in terms of navigating sports, work, internships, and jobs. They want to know how they can get involved and noticed to be trained, developed, and then hired as they start out building a resume for years ahead, and dreams they do hope are realized. I'm quite thrilled to say to all of them here from this day forward, you have a reference which is like no other ever put out or authored in the past. For the next generation, and all the ones ahead, Stuart can be the catalyst for all those picking up and reading this book as a game changer in the wide world of sports!… He's a visionary capable of really expressing how to be able to make your dream or vision a professional reality as a great success story." **Shane McCoy, Scouting Analyst & Consultant, NHL**

"This business is built on people. Working for good people and networking with good people will forever have a lasting impact on a successful career in sports. I've been fortunate to know Stuart for more than 10 years and can say, without a shadow of a doubt, that he is the definition of what it means to work with and network with good people." **Justin Peterson, Sr. Manager, Ticket Sales, Anaheim Ducks**

"The sports industry is super small, and luckily for me, I was able to meet Stuart because of it. He has provided much insight because of his many years of experience. His journey is the ideal route any person wanting to get into the sports industry should follow. Working in the sports industry is a lot like playing sports. You have to have will and determination with a chip on your shoulder. If you want to make it to the big leagues, you have to give it your all every single day." **Chris Harpster, Sr. Group Sales Account Executive, New Orleans Pelicans**

"Breaking into the sports industry isn't about having a perfect resume, it's about persistence, relationships, and showing up with genuine passion. Network with intention, build real connections, and don't be afraid to ask questions or learn from every opportunity. For women in sports, don't be afraid to be bold, trust your voice, make your own decisions, and carve your own path. Doors don't always open right away, but consistency, confidence, and resilience will set you apart. The next generation will shape this industry, and those who invest in people will always find a place in it." **Autumn Bolton, Manager of Game Presentation, Buffalo Sabres**

"One thing I've learned working in sports is that no one starts with all the answers. Most of us begin to feel uncomfortable, unsure and learning as we go. That's why Breaking Into Sports feels so honest. It doesn't sugarcoat the industry or pretend there's a single right path; instead, it reflects the reality that careers are built through showing up consistently and staying humble. Titles come and go, but being dependable, kind and relationship-driven is what ultimately shapes a career you can be proud of." **Kelly Ross, Manager, Internal Communications, Pittsburgh Pirates**

"Not getting the job. Not making the sale. Not getting the promotion. That's okay. Learn from those experiences and keep going. Truly stepping out of your comfort zone and pushing yourself is going to feel awkward and even embarrassing at times, but that is where the real growth occurs." **Derek Anderson, Sr. Manager, Client Sales & Service, LA28 Olympic & Paralympic Games**

"Supporting the next generation of sports professionals matters because sometimes all it takes is one person willing to open a door or share honest advice. I know firsthand how intimidating it can feel to break into the sports industry without a clear roadmap. Though I didn't get here on my own. I learned by asking questions, networking, leaning on mentors, and saying yes to opportunities that helped me grow. Identify what area of sports you resonate with and connect with folks in those positions as soon as possible. Continue to seek feedback from every interview and don't be afraid to start at the ground level. Sports is a relationship-driven industry, and learning how to intentionally connect with people early on can set you up for long-term success!" **Emele Chaddock, Sales Manager, Seattle Kraken**

"Landing a job in sports happens on purpose. Be intentional about learning from people who are where you want to be, and stay connected with them. Seek out opportunities to gain experience through shadowing and internships, especially when they are outside of your comfort zone. If you don't get the role you applied for, it means you're one step closer to getting a "yes." Learn from it and let it fuel you. Ultimately, you will reach your goals not because you were lucky, but because you built genuine relationships, sought out learning, and consistently showed up on purpose." **Erica Slye, Manger, New Business Team, Arizona Diamondbacks**

"Being a fan doesn't replace strong sales fundamentals, but the best ticket sellers are bought into the fan lifestyle. They thrive in the energy of live events, being involved in their local community, and take pride in creating memorable experiences for others. When your passion is authentic, customers feel it, and that connection ultimately sells more tickets than any script ever could." **Marc Rogers, Ticket Sales Manager, New England Revolution**

"Learn how to frame where you are today as preparation for where you want to go. Whether you're in your first role or still chasing that initial opportunity, break your current responsibilities down and ask yourself how each one is building skills, habits, or perspective for the next level. Everything is transferable if you take the time to understand how it translates. When you connect the small, often unglamorous work to the bigger picture, it gives purpose to the grind and positions you to be ready when the opportunity comes. That mindset is what ultimately pays off." **Zeb Stock, Premium Sales Manager, Halo Sports & Entertainment**

"My advice for those looking to break into the industry is to be open to new and unique opportunities. A lot of people want to work for a team or a sport they are a fan of, and while that means you shouldn't chase your dreams, you need to be realistic. Many jobs at a Big Four sports organization see hundreds of applicants for one role and there are less teams available. Being able to work at a smaller organization may provide an easier opportunity to break in, but also provide a much more well-rounded experience that may open a variety of opportunities for future roles. Chase a mentor and a job that you will enjoy, not a logo you get to wear on your shirt. You never know what may happen, and the joy you can get from trying something new if you take the chance." **Ryan Ireland, Marketing Manager, Phoenix Suns**

"Early in my career, my first goal wasn't to figure out exactly what I wanted to do for the rest of my life; it was to discover what I didn't want to do. That felt far less daunting. By pursuing a variety of internships and opportunities, I was able to narrow in on the work that truly gave me energy. I found that purpose in producing the ultimate fan experience and helping make sports a place where everyone feels welcome, even those who may not love the game itself, is what truly brought me joy. Breaking into sports requires genuine passion for what you do, because the early years don't always come with the best pay or the easiest hours. But if you can show up every day energized, knowing you're creating moments people will remember forever, you may realize you've never truly worked a day in your life. I'd say that's the magic of sports." **Adele Huffman, Supervisor, Patriots Hall of Fame, New England Patriots**

"Start by understanding why you want to be involved in the sports industry and what aspects specifically about this industry interest you more than working in any other. That way you will stay motivated throughout the process as you grow your career. Then, don't be afraid to pivot. Whether it's changing cities to work for a new team, working for different leaders, or even departments within your team. That way you'll be more well-rounded and see opportunities through a different lens, better than everyone else around you." **Cooper Farrer, Sr. Premium Sales Manager, Orlando Magic**

"As a sales professional, you are an ambassador for your organization's brand, not only in the office, but in your daily interactions as well. The logo you represent is often the easiest icebreaker in the city, so use it to your advantage. If your name isn't yet associated with delivering high-level experiences at your arena, there are countless opportunities to build that reputation." **Bobby Mainor II, Manager of Inside Sales, Houston Rockets**

"Early in my career, I was obsessed with timelines and hitting certain milestones to prove I was successful. That mindset put me in a dangerous place where I was constantly comparing myself to my peers and defining my career based on what everyone else was doing, not my own journey. Here's what I learned: everyone has a different path. The more you focus on your own growth, cheer on your teammates and colleagues, and work on being the best version of yourself, the more opportunities will come your way. My advice for students breaking in? Be curious and ask questions, real questions that help you understand how things actually work. And don't be afraid to reach out to people for coffee or lunch to network. Just make sure you have a plan. Know what you want to learn from their career path, and offer to volunteer or shadow them to see how their department operates. People respect initiative, and that willingness to learn will set you apart." **Matt Menard, General Manager of Ticket Sales, Taymar Sales U**

"The best thing you can do when trying to break into sports is publish your ideas for people to see. Be open to feedback early on and continue to develop and adapt your ideas until something sticks. If nobody will publish you, create your own website. Find a way to get your ideas into the hands of decision makers." **Sam Goldberg, Head of Player Personnel, New York Red Bulls**

"My biggest piece of advice would be to stay the course. When you treat others well, keep your faith strong, and put the work in, good things will happen. Remember, all it takes is one opportunity to change the whole trajectory of your journey. So, you never know when that one call or that blessing will come. But if you throw the towel in too soon, you'll never know if that call would've come the next day. So, it's important to win from within mentally and to put yourself out there. Utilize social media as a resource to spotlight your work. Take pride in the work that you do, don't worry about the likes and impressions, consistency matters most. Network and establish authentic relationships with the mindset of "What can I do for you?" Ultimately, let your passion for what you do fuel your drive. Lastly, as you're climbing that ladder towards your goals, remember to take a moment to stop and embrace each chapter as part of your journey. Sometimes we are so focused on the end goal that we don't stop to truly appreciate the moments along the way. It's good to strive for more, but it's also okay to stay present, because those moments may not always happen twice. You got this!" **Derek Spallone, Social Media Manager, Wilson Sporting Goods Co.**

"The sports industry runs on people long before it runs on wins or revenue. My career has been shaped by perseverance, genuine relationship-building, and a belief that serving the community matters just as much as individual success. Opportunities didn't come from asking for favors, they came from earning trust over time. I faced rejection, uncertainty, and plenty of moments where quitting would've been easier, but perseverance and people carried me through. This industry is built on trust and community, not transactions. If you focus on helping others, investing in genuine relationships, and doing the work when no one is watching, doors open over time. And once you're in, you have a responsibility to pay it forward, because someone once did the same for you. If you want longevity in this business, invest in people, give more than you take, and never forget where you started. Helping the next generation isn't optional, it's how we as a whole take everything to the next level" **Branden Estrada, Corporate Hospitality Account Manager, Anaheim Ducks**

"Throughout my time at LA Galaxy and now Formula 1 Las Vegas Grand Prix, I am commonly asked by aspiring individuals "How can I work for [insert team name]?" When applying to a company in any industry, one should know as many details as they can about the role they're applying for and should be able to articulate to the hiring managers how they envision themselves being a valued employee. Sports are no different. No matter the role you are applying for, a sports team is just the product. I am a sales representative for F1 Vegas. I didn't apply to a F1 role. I applied to a sales role. During my interview with Galaxy and F1, I had to exemplify how my previous skillsets can apply to the role I was applying for, just like any other job. I barely knew anything about MLS or F1 before accepting their positions. I had not worked a typical sales role before the Galaxy, which was my first job in sports and sales. During my interview process with various sports teams, I found it very valuable to connect with other sales associates and leaders in the sports industry to learn more about the specific roles I was applying for. I shared my previous work experiences and asked for advice on which role would be a potential fit and how my previous skills would apply. I shared my resume drafts with hiring managers I was not interviewing with and asked what they would be looking for and how my resume could stand out more. I considered every potential advantage I could think of to get me in front of the right people and more prepared than other candidates. Ultimately, being a fan is great. Obviously, fans keep the business going, but you don't need to be a fan to succeed at your job. Narrow down the search to a specific role. Do your diligence. Thoroughly prepare for each interview. It will be noticed." **Derek Gaines, Premium Sales Manager, F1 Las Vegas Grand Prix**

"In 2010, when I was a junior in college, I read a book about breaking into the sports industry through ticket sales. That book played a key role in helping me land a job in Major League Baseball. Today, thanks to Stuart, current and future students have the same opportunity to learn how to break into sports" **Joshua Avart, Account Manager, Group Sales & Hospitality, Pittsburgh Pirates**

"As a former collegiate athlete, I've learned quickly that working in sports has similarities to the sports I grew up playing – I'm just putting on a different uniform every day. I've noticed that everyone here has an edge. Maybe it's your networking abilities, your hustle, your ambition, or your strategic thinking. Use your edge and leverage it. Your strengths get you in the door, but it is professionalism that keeps you in the room. Trust in the industry is earned through preparing well, putting in the effort on long days, and being a reliable teammate. From what I have seen, the people who approach working in sports with that mindset are the ones who build careers that last." **Annabelle Kubinski, Account Manager, Premium Service, Arizona Cardinals**

"Too often, particularly in the sales industry, I see professionals viewing clients as opportunities, or as a vehicle towards hitting their sales goals. On a first appointment with a brand new inside sales account executive, he remarked that he had been surprised about how well our conversation had flowed, and that we had genuine connection that led to a sale. My advice would be to stop seeing people as dollar signs or opportunities, but to see them as people. In the industry as a whole, nobody gets anywhere without help from others. Honest connection with others will naturally lend itself to career growth, as well as lifting up yourself and those around you." **Jonah Hirsch, Sr. Account Executive, Membership Services, Detroit Tigers**

"One of my favorite things working in the sports industry is working with younger professionals; helping establish their careers in sports. This book will be a tremendous help with providing guidance for younger professionals wanting to enter the sports industry. I started my career path while as a student at Central Michigan University, and early-on realized I wanted to pursue a sales career in sports. Which ultimately led me to the Arizona Diamondbacks. I'm excited to see the impact this book will have on the next Account Executives, Directors, and Vice Presidents of the sports industry's future." **Daniel Folkert, Account Executive, Arizona Diamondbacks**

452

"The sports industry may seem large, but it operates like a close-knit community. Everyone knows everyone, which makes relationships and connections essential. In the sports world, your network truly matters! The relationships you build can ultimately shape the opportunities you receive." **Jake Kling, Group Sales Account Executive, Carolina Panthers**

"Explore as many areas of the sports industry as you can. The more experience you gain, the more transferable skills you develop. Internships and volunteer opportunities aren't just about discovering what you want to do. They're just as valuable for learning what you don't see yourself doing in the future." **Jessica Beer, Sr. Manager, Membership & Inside Sales, Philadelphia Flyers**

"Be comfortable with being uncomfortable. Take risks and say yes to any opportunity you may have, because you never know what you may fall in love with. I find it important to do as much as you can, to gain experience in different departments and skills, because sometimes it is more important to figure out what you don't want to do versus what you do want to do." **Brandon Ferris, Premium Account Manager, Club Lexus, Denver Nuggets**

"When I was a college student at Springfield College, Stuart was an invaluable resource for his industry knowledge, connections, and recommendations to everyone who reached out. Through outreach, introductions to his contacts, and countless conversations, he provided a framework that encouraged students to step outside their comfort zones and grow as young professionals. Looking back now, as someone entering my third season working in professional sports and sales specifically, I realize that networking was the foundation of my sales career. The ability to connect with individuals for a purpose greater than your own motives, such as getting a job or internship, and to build genuine relationships is something that can be consistently replicated throughout a career, from start to finish." **Nick Ruffler, Sr. Business Development Specialist, Cleveland Cavaliers**

"Be willing to wear many hats and approach every task with humility, because no job is too small. Step beyond your defined role, stay curious, and keep learning. The sports industry is highly competitive and unlike any other. Be grateful for the opportunities, stay humble in your success, and always be willing to put in the work." **Sarah Himmelstein, Corporate Partnerships Analyst, Anaheim Ducks**

"Working in sports is a lot like playing a sport, no one is going to hand you anything or give you a starting position. You have to earn it. It really comes down to three components: you've got to want it, you've got to work for it, and you've got to win it. That mindset is essential. The sports industry is extremely competitive, as you can imagine. The people who rise to the top, the ones who land the internship, secure the job, earn the promotion, and work their way up, are those who refuse to settle. They stay hungry, driven, and committed to being the best. You have to find a way to stand out. If that means working longer hours, going the extra mile, or putting in more effort than others, then so be it. The question is: how badly do you want it, and how badly do you want to make a name for yourself? Remember, 'no' just means the next opportunity, and every mistake is a lesson. It's okay to be hard on yourself, but don't forget to give yourself grace along the way." **Cate Decker, Team Lead, Ticket Sales, Oklahoma City Thunder**

"If you're trying to break into pro sports, my advice is simple: seek out every opportunity you can to get experience, internships, game day help, whatever you can find. Then, once you're in the building, focus on making the full-time employees' lives easier. Show them you're there to help, not just to observe. If you provide real value and make their jobs smoother, people will remember you. And when they remember you, they'll use their network to help you find a job. That's how doors open in this industry." **Brian Betz, Soccer Medical Professional**

"Instead of saying, 'I don't know,' say, 'Let me find out." Then, do the work, research with intention, think critically, and above all, listen. Seek perspectives beyond your usual circle and be willing to learn from those who see the world differently. Not knowing isn't a weakness. It's an opportunity. It gives you the space to grow, to sharpen your judgment, and to increase your value. Curiosity and humility are signals of strength, not uncertainty. When you show a genuine eagerness to learn, people notice. Leaders trust you more, colleagues respect you more, and players respond to you differently. The habit of learning will set you apart" **Dan Clemens, Former Professional Baseball Player and Award-Winning Screenwriter**

"As Stuart has demonstrated throughout his career, successful sports business professionals don't just follow their passion - they channel it into creating measurable value for their organizations. The way players and fans engage with sports is evolving faster than ever, creating more entry points and opportunities to prove to organizations how you can not only come in and get the job done, but help them take an evolutionary mindset." **Aaron Gillette, Sports Marketing Director**

"For anyone that is fortunate to work in sports in any capacity, we have a responsibility and obligation to serve our athletes, fans, supporters, donors, and stakeholders on a daily basis. You have to be willing to adapt, change, refine, and adjust philosophies, thoughts, and processes to align and exceed the current day needs while also preparing and planning for the future. Sports at all levels are rapidly evolving and our industry needs individuals who are willing to lean into what makes us great while being open to the evolution of what will make us better." **Carter Hicks, General Manager, Baseball, University of North Carolina**

"Everyone is going to take their own path in sports and there definitely isn't a "right" one. Jobs and opportunities can come from the most unexpected of places. The breaks I've had in my career have most often come from my peers and friends; be good to those around you." **Savanna Collins, Sports Reporter**

"True advantage comes from discipline, humility, and hunger. Focus on what you can control, commit to the grind, embrace learning, and demand growth from yourself daily. Live up to this standard, and you'll operate on a level most never reach" **David Retan, Group Sales Executive, Detroit Pistons**

"Stuart's passion to help others is inspiring. He does a phenomenal job staying connected with his peers and embodying what it takes to be an elite sports professional. I am excited to see the impact this playbook makes! I challenge you to live by three principles: Work Hard, Be Kind, Stay Humble." **Hunter Arbogast, Account Executive, Global Business Development, F1 Miami Grand Prix**

"When breaking into the game, I believe Stuart learned as I did this valuable lesson. It's not what you know, and it's not who you know, the most important thing in navigating your way is 'Who Knows You!' Find a way to make yourself be remembered! Positively!" **Adam Gladstone, COO, Israel Baseball Americas**

"There are many ways to start a career in sports or to pivot from a non-sports career toward sports. I'm living proof of that! I got my Bachelor's Degree in Social Sciences and Master's Degree in Business Administration from Bar-Ilan University in Israel. No one from Bar Ilan University has ever worked at Major League Baseball before, much less baseball at all anywhere. The odds were stacked against me. Some online applications with school selection drop-down menus didn't even list my school, so I was left to indicate that I got my degrees from "Other." That only made my determination

stronger to pave a new path and achieve my goal of positively impacting the sport I love so much. Through genuine relationship-building, a consistent personal branding presence on LinkedIn, and an unwavering belief and persistence, I made it happen. Who says you can't, no matter where you're from, where you go to school, or what degree you study! My journey to working in sports, specifically baseball, was anything but a straight path. Many people took valuable time in their day to support me, share some advice and insight, pass along a job opening they saw, or put in a recommendation for me, even if they didn't know me so well. I have not forgotten all that kindness, and my current existence in the baseball world would not be fulfilling if I'm not trying to do as much paying forward as I realistically can to help and guide others pursuing a similar goal. Cherishing what I'm a part of and paying it forward is the best part of having gotten an opportunity to be a part of this special industry."
Zack Raab, Sr. Coordinator, MiLB Club Services, MLB

"One of the most important things in getting that first (or second) job is to not just get excited with the team you've always wanted to work for or a major league team that offers you a starting position. The key is to interview each just as much as they interview you. That first job is essential to your growth and finding the right fit, be it major league, minor league, independent sports, college or any other will matter more than the name of the team. How they grow and develop you and the investment they will make in you, just as you are making in them, can make or break a career. Find mentors along the way who will help keep you focused and grounded. Above all, never be solely enamored with titles. More important is what you can learn in the role." **Kathy Burrows, Chief Innovation and Energy Officer, Sold Out Seating**

"Breaking into sports can seem like a daunting task for those on the outside, looking in. I believe the traits that separate those who make it in, and those who don't, is firstly the ability to recognize an opportunity. Secondary to that, but just as important, is the discernment to take the appropriate action when it arises. Opportunities come in all shapes and sizes, and present different possibilities. Having a growth mindset, the willingness to fail, and the confidence to say yes or no will allow a prospect to better see where the opportunity can take them. Recognize the opportunity, assign the appropriate action, and gain the experience whether positive or negative. You'll look back at your career and be surprised where you end up if you learn to do these simple things at a high level" **Greg Woods II, Sr. Footwear Developer, Lifestyle, New Balance**

"I have known Stuart for many years, since one of his first internships in the Sports Industry. From the very beginning, he truly showed an uncommon drive to learn and network. He was never afraid to volunteer for a task, no matter how mundane, or stay late to get a job done. His passion for the sports industry, paired with a tireless work ethic, set him apart as an intern and now a veteran professional in this industry. I am confident that this book is a reflection of that journey filled with insight, honesty, and real-world value. Anyone looking to break into the sports industry will find inspiration and guidance within these pages." **Bridget McCabe, Help Desk Coordinator, Washington Commanders**

"Everything I've learned in sports has come from people who were willing to open doors, share the truth, and invest in those coming next. The future of this industry depends on our willingness to guide, mentor, and make space for the next generation to find their own path; and then go further than we ever did. No matter how individual the journey may feel, progress in sports is always collective, carried forward by the people who steady us, push us, and believe we don't have to run alone. Take that chance and reach out to someone you always admired, you never know where it will take you." **Curtis Diggins, Former Nike and TikTok Sports**

"The sports industry is truly a tight-knit community that thrives on innovation, creativity, and finding new ways to elevate the fan experience and improve processes; it is constantly evolving, and as a professional, there are so many things I wish I had known when I was graduating. Something I would tell anyone trying to break into this world is don't be afraid, send that email to an executive, go out and volunteer with different sports organizations, or intern across different areas of the industry to discover what you genuinely enjoy. Not every day is glamorous, but we are fortunate to work in a field that is built on connection, with fans, teams, and colleagues alike, so make an effort to meet anyone and everyone because once you're in, the opportunities are endless." **Nick Alo, Ticket Operations Coordinator, Savannah Bananas**

"It is never too early to start building your resume and relationships in the sports industry. Think of what your interests are and how you would build a career off of that. From there, research different organization directories to get an idea of what kind of jobs are out there that best align with you. Plan a career path from there, but be mindful that a career path isn't always linear. Research open positions including internships and part time roles to begin building your resume to put yourself in the best position to be in the industry upon graduation. Use that time to network develop relationships with industry professionals and be more than just someone applying for a job. You never know what a 'hello' can do." **Brad Herson, Sports Business Executive**

"The advice I would give to college students or recent graduates looking to go into sport is to decide what area of sport you want to work in. When you discover your why you want to work in sport, that needs to include if you want to work for the fans or the team. That will help keep you on track and motivated on why you put in the stressful moments!" **Addison Butler, Sports Business Executive**

"Stuart is one of the friendliest, most outgoing students we've ever had in our sport management department at Springfield College. When it comes to networking, Stuart flew before he ran, ran before he walked and walked before he crawled. In fact, he did an excellent job of modeling the importance of establishing personal relationships to many of his classmates while he was an undergraduate student. I'm not a bit surprised he was able to land a job so soon after graduation. I believe he was born for sales, but I also see big things for Stuart in the future because of his understanding of the importance of true, authentic relationships. He understands that sport organizations have to be more than ticket-takers and purveyors of entertainment. They have to be community partners. They are important entities in the lives of their fans. Stuart is already a driven professional in his early 20s, and I will be eagerly watching his career as he continues to mature and grow. I have no doubt he will accomplish great things." **Dr. John Borland, Former Springfield College Professor**

"After a career of about 45 years spent in college athletics and about 20 years teaching sports management, what I can tell you is that the sports industry contains so many opportunities, but finding that first job or the next one will not be easy for most people. While the industry continues to grow and change, the competition is real and growing too. I tell all the student-athletes I have worked with and the students I teach that you must be ready to do more than the people you are competing with for the jobs you want. Network more, build your skills, knowledge, and reputation. Because if you don't do that, someone else who wants that job will. And never be afraid to ask for assistance, especially from someone who has been in your shoes, someone who knows this world like Stuart." **Dr. Bob Dranoff, Professor, St. John's University, Former Director of Athletics and Division II Commissioner**

"Breaking in as a public address announcer is similar to landing any first job. I started with no direct background, used my public speaking and business experience, and created opportunities by networking and showing how my skills translated to the role. For those starting out, I recommend three things: first, develop your speaking skills through any public speaking opportunities, organizations like Toastmasters, or improv. Second, take every chance to call games at any level, paid or unpaid, to gain experience and improve your craft. Finally, and most importantly, brand yourself and network consistently so people remember you when opportunities arise. Focus on improving your skills, gaining experience, and promoting yourself, and you'll give yourself the best chance to succeed." **Craig Stevens, Public Address Announcer**

"Own your process and gamify your networking. Set a clear goal: connect with five new people each week. Commit to a daily minimum of 25 cold LinkedIn messages to people whose careers you admire. Do it for a week. That's 125 messages. How many responded? Did you hit your five connections? If not, throttle up your outreach. Patterns create pathways to success. Don't wait for opportunities to happen, go make them. In sports, roles change in an instant, a wide receiver turns into a defender after an interception. The more value you bring outside the scope of your role, the faster you grow and the more essential you become to your team. In this industry, promotions aren't given; they're earned by proving you can already do the work." **Alex Rothschild, Director of Brand Partnerships, SRS Partners**

"Being innately curious is a powerful way to showcase your intentions. Not just when you need something, but strategically networking to learn more. Having a genuine interest in someone's role, their career path, and the "why" behind what they're accomplishing. This, combined with asking questions that compel someone to share more on a human level, is what breaks through the noise and leads to true connection." **Max Simpson, Director of Partnerships, PHNX Sports & ALLCITY Network**

"My career in sports hasn't followed a straight line, and that's been one of my biggest strengths. I originally dreamed of building a career in journalism, but instead spent over 15 years working in professional sports abroad with several top basketball clubs and the National Team. After relocating to the U.S., I chose to re-enter the industry, and it wasn't easy. I took baby steps, learning, listening, and proving myself all over again. Even after all these years, I'm still passionate about sports, but I don't romanticize it. The work is routine-heavy, demanding, and sometimes tough. Titles matter less than effort, attitude, and consistency. For students: stay curious, be dependable, and don't be afraid of the long game, it's worth it." **Elena Kulagina, Program Operations Manager, Lucas Oil Stadium**

"Work hard to land an internship as your first level of experience. Once you do, ask a lot of questions of those who work for the team. Take lots of notes. Find out what they do and what makes them tick. Ask how you can do more every day. Show that you want to learn more and contribute in every way possible. Do everything you possibly can to stand out from your competition. Don't pigeonhole yourself into one department. If your internship allows it, ask to gain experience in different departments. You may find that you like another department more than the one you wanted to be in. If you have big goals (for example, to work towards becoming a General Manager), don't look to fast track to that goal. Take it slow. Learn as much as you can and get as much experience as you can. That will serve you well long-term. Working in sports has been described by many as a "lifestyle". It does involve a huge commitment of time however it is also very gratifying and enjoyable in many ways. I've never had a "boring" day in my 38 years in professional baseball." **Steve Gliner, CEO Home Run Professional Sports Consulting**

"Major sporting events succeed behind the scenes through clear communication, respect for every role, and calm leadership. My early years taught me that no task is too small, every credential checked, and statistic logged builds the foundation for leadership. In sports, longevity isn't about chasing the biggest event; it's about earning trust through preparation and professionalism. Your reputation is built long before the spotlight arrives." **Steven Torres, Sports Business Executive**

"If you want to work in sports, stop asking how to get the job and start asking how to create value. Be early, be curious, be useful, and be coachable. The industry is small, reputations travel fast, and the people who get opportunities are the ones others want around when things get hard." **Zach Lutz, Former Professional Baseball Player**

"If you want a career in sports, prepare yourself to be a five tool front office player. Learn every area of the organization, hone your sales, negotiating skills and build respected relationships alongside transferable skills that travel with you no matter the role. Be willing to support any project, at any level, and embrace the work ethic the industry demands. Titles change and teams change but versatility, trust, and service are what sustain a long, meaningful career in sports." **Katie Dannemiller, Sports Business Executive**

"Passion may get you in the door, but professionalism, coachability, and a genuine commitment to excellence are what keep you there. The young professionals who truly stand out are the ones who treat every role, every opportunity, and every relationship with intention and care, because in this business, every moment matters." **Becca Hogan, Sports Business Leader**

"I wish I had been able to read something like this when I was coming out of college. I had no idea what I wanted to do, and this would have helped me find my way into Sports Sales much faster. Success in this industry comes down to controlling what you can control; the rest will fall into place. Whether you are an intern, entry-level, or senior position, show up as the hardest worker in the room, stay coachable, and maintain a mamba-like mentality to your everyday life. Do this consistently, and you'll achieve the success you're striving for and then some. If you want to take this a step further, find someone who shares this mentality. When you hold each other accountable, you'll push one another to career heights you never thought possible." **Myers Dean, Enterprise Account Executive, Teak, Former Atlanta Hawks**

"The sports industry is deeply interconnected. Whether you work in sales, marketing, operations, player development, or any other role, everyone contributes towards a shared goal. That's why I strongly believe in developing a diverse skill set. I've been fortunate to work across many areas of the sports industry, and each experience prepared me for the next. I encourage sport management students to explore as many facets of the industry as possible early in their careers. At the very least, this approach builds a clear understanding of the many moving parts required to create a successful sports organization. There is no one better suited to pass these lessons on to the next generation of sports professionals than Stuart. A true Swiss-army knife, he understands what it takes to succeed at every level of the industry. Working in sports is tough, and hopefully this resource helps students navigate the challenges, gain clarity, and ultimately turn their passion into a career in the sports industry." **Ben Kropp, Player Development Coach, Gonzaga College High School, Former Oakland Athletics**

"As a recent college graduate trying to break into sports, Stuart's mentorship has been unmatched. His honesty, confidence, and selfless care for the people he works with are hard to find in the business world. I can't wait for his genuineness to leap off the pages of this book." **Natalie Teague, Intern, Miami Marlins**

"While I have always played and loved sports, I never imagined having a career in sport. In fact, after a career in the federal government and business, I found the adaptive and Paralympic sports movement through the birth of my first son when I was in my mid 30's. Twenty years later, I have had a variety of interesting roles in sport and frequently advise young leaders. A few quick tidbits: 1) Focus on your three Ps. When I coach individuals on career pathing, my recommendation is to find the intersection of your passion, purpose, and proficiency. If you are proficient at your work, you will be more successful than otherwise. If you are passionate about your work, it will help you get out of bed every morning to attack the day. And if you find purpose in your work, you will have the resilience to survive the tough times (i.e. bad reviews, failed projects, missed KPIs, demotions, etc). 2) Chase impact. Regardless of where you end up in sport, leagues, team, media, agency, or brands, search for ways to leverage your role, assets, and influence to do some good in the world. My belief is that too many of us are chasing careers, status, and income, but not always focused on doing good. Imagine that everyone at your place of work was chasing impact? There are many, many social problems, and we need as many good ideas and as many well-intentioned people as we can find to start to solve them. 3) Don't forget about non-profits. In fact, I suggest everyone, regardless of where they are in their career, find an organization or cause to align with. Then get involved, volunteer, and learn. This will give you expanded relationships, new skills, and a more nuanced understanding of the world. Don't just make random donations. Show up. Engage. And most importantly, pick one organization/cause and stick with it.

Nonprofits struggle to find supporters who will stay with them in the long run. We need consistency, and reliability." **Clayton Frech, Founder of Angel City Sports, Creator and Producer of ADAPTIVE**

"In sports sales, the high failure rate is the filter that separates the professionals from the fans. Most people quit because they are addicted to the result; the ones who make it are those who have learned to value the process over the outcome. To survive and thrive in this business, you have to be willing to be wrong, rejected, and redirected a thousand times until the process becomes your greatest competitive advantage." **Evan Flagg, Founder of Reach Capacity**

"There's no single 'right' way into sports. My path included nonprofit work, youth sports, and professional clubs; and each step mattered. Early in your career, focus less on where you work and more on what you're learning. Build a reputation for showing up, doing the work well, and caring about the mission. That consistency is what creates long-term opportunity." **Stefanie Caliri, Director of Partnerships, Soccer Parenting**

"Stuart has delivered invaluable information for the next generation of sports executives who seek to understand which path to follow and land a career in sports. The sports industry thrives when individuals are positioned to make contributions aligned with their strengths, and there is always space for someone who gets it. Bravo for putting this project together and giving back in a way that makes an impact for all who follow his guidance." **Bobby Bramhall, Sports Attorney and Law Professor**

"I graduated as a Division 1 athlete with a Media Arts degree and zero sports media experience. No sports management classes. One internship in the beauty industry. No connections beyond my coaches. I thought living in NYC with an athletic background would get me anywhere. It didn't. I applied. I got rejected. I was too scared to ask for help because I didn't realize that asking is everything. My career zigzagged. Stationery company, equipment manager, startups, nannying, freelancing, back to equipment management during COVID. I watched my peers get raises while I kept starting over from the bottom. But every skill I picked up was building my portfolio. I grinded. I networked with everyone. I didn't stop. Four years later, I landed my dream job: Social Media Coordinator at U.S. Soccer, managing 25 of 27 national teams. Here's what I learned: Don't stay in your lane. I built skills and relationships across every department. That's what made me valuable. No experience is wasted if you can translate it. Those 'random' jobs gave me skills I use every day. I learned to show how I could solve their problems. Pivot and pause aren't curses. Success isn't a lightning bolt. Its small wins strung together. The early chapters no one sees when you're working alone in the dark. Even the greatest athletes fail and still make it to the pros. Your setbacks don't disqualify you. They're part of the path. The sports industry can feel like a closed circle. It's not. Ask for help, say yes to uncomfortable opportunities, and trust that the zigzag is moving you forward." **Brittany Barbosa, Founder of Nobody Rides The Bench**

"My advice sits at the intersection of how I got into sports, why I was able to rise, and what I learned about relationships along the way. I have been self-sufficient since the age of 18, and yes, people looked out for me, but that help wasn't handed out for free. I earned it by treating people at every level with respect, working harder than expected, and becoming someone others could count on. The best networking happens when you give before you get, when you show up with good energy and add value without keeping score. Over time, that's what leads to your name being mentioned in rooms you're not in, and when someone does recommend you, they're putting their credibility on the line, so you honor that by showing up prepared, following through, and never squandering the opportunity." **Arielle Moyal, Founder, Moyal Enterprises**

"Breaking into sports isn't just about talent. It takes strategy, resilience, and the ability to create value where others don't see it yet. Stuart shares the kind of insider insight most people only learn through experience. My own unconventional path into this industry came from identifying a need and building something teams genuinely valued. This book reinforces what I've learned firsthand: strong careers are built by people willing to innovate, adapt, and step forward before they feel completely ready." **Stephanie Frusteri, Founder & CEO, Zone Performance**

"For someone starting out in sports, internships are incredibly important. They give you the chance to test out the career path and see if it's really for you. The hours are way longer than most people imagine, and the home schedule can be brutal. You need to know what you're getting into. But internships aren't always an option, so here's my other piece of advice: understand that sports careers are a series of stepping stones. If you want to work in marketing but the only open job is a seasonal role in inside sales, take it. Commit to it with your whole heart, learn everything you can about that department and the organization, and use that knowledge and those connections to take the next step. Having a complete view of how different departments work gives you insight and empathy, and that will make you a better colleague and a better leader down the road." **Ayron Sequeira, Founder, and then**

"Jobs in sports rarely exist in a vacuum. Like the teams our industry revolves around, an individual's impact is more profound when they understand how their own contributions help shape the bigger picture. The tactical skills you refine within your chosen discipline can help you break in and succeed in the day-to-day. But knowing how your role integrates across every business unit, and how it directly contributes to broader organizational goals, will position you as a well-rounded business pro with growth potential towards bigger roles." **Brad Friedman, Account Manager, Fresh Content Society**

"There's no single roadmap to success in sports. I started in minor league sports, which may not be the big stage, but it's one of the best training grounds in the industry, you gain hands-on experience across every part of an organization and learn how the business truly works. Just as important, you learn that every person you meet matters. Treat every relationship with respect, because the people around you today can become invaluable resources and partners down the road." **Brad Eisen, Philanthropy Officer, Former LA Galaxy and Los Angeles Clippers**

"If you truly want to work in sports, start now. This is what a professor told me when I was a sophomore in college and I took it to heart. She said don't wait until after graduation to figure it out, and get ahead of others before they get ahead of you. Say yes to opportunities, even the unpaid ones, because experience and relationships open doors. I started in ticket sales and kept showing up, doing good work, and staying in touch with people who believed in me. One opportunity led to another, and that's how I built a career in sports." **Matt Whewell, Director, Global Communications, HARMAN International**

"Who you know gets you into the office, and what you know keeps you there. Make sure you build connections during and after college, and don't forget to nurture those relationships because once you're at a company, prove your worth and show off your hard work. Make sure to build bridges, maintain bridges and don't burn bridges. The sports world is smaller than you know." **Aaron Eisman, Founder and CEO of Eisman Digital**

Recommended Readings

The books below have shaped how I think about sales, relationships, leadership, and building a career in sports. These aren't coffee table books, they're tools that will change how you approach your work if you actually read and apply them. Pick the ones that resonate with what you need right now and work through them intentionally.

Sports Industry Specific

Hustle Your Way to $ucce$$ in Sports Sales by Travis Apple - Written specifically for sports sales professionals, covering everything from mindset to tactics to building elite performance in the unique environment of sports business. Travis has lived it, and his playbook is directly applicable to ticket sales and revenue roles.

Shoe Dog by Phil Knight - Knight's memoir of building Nike from nothing into a global brand is one of the best business books ever written and deeply relevant to sports. You'll learn about persistence, relationships, risk-taking, and what it actually takes to build something great in the sports industry.

Fundamentals of Ticket Sales and Revenue Management by Dr. Nicholas Zoroya, Dr. Brandon Podgorski, Dr. Joshua Greer, and Dr. Alexander Atwood – Provides a comprehensive overview of how organizations price, sell, and optimize tickets to maximize revenue. The authors combine theory with real-world examples to explain demand forecasting, pricing strategies, and data-driven decision-making. This book is ideal for students and professionals seeking a practical foundation in ticket sales and revenue management.

So You Want to Work in Sports: Advice and Insights from Respected Sports Industry Leaders by K. P. Wee - A practical, student-friendly guide with interviews and real-world advice from professionals across many sports fields (marketing, broadcasting, management, analytics, etc.). Great for seeing the variety of roles in the industry and what the work is really like.

The Comprehensive Guide to Careers in Sports by Glenn Wong - A broader overview of career paths, required skills, salary expectations, and how professionals got started. It's especially helpful for planning and setting realistic expectations.

Careers in Sport, Fitness, and Exercise - This book focuses on careers related to kinesiology, sport science, fitness, and exercise, which is valuable if you're interested in roles like athletic training, coaching, or exercise science.

Working in Sport: A Practical Approach to Understanding Your Sport Journey by Rocco Porreca - Designed for students and early career pros, this gives a straightforward look at how to build a career in sport, including practical steps to stand out.

Sports Marketing: A Strategic Perspective by Matthew D. Shank & Mark R. Lyberger* - A widely used textbook in sports marketing education. It explores market research, consumer behavior, promotions, products, pricing, sponsorship, and digital strategy, essential for understanding how teams and events attract fans and partners.

Sports Marketing: A Practical Approach by Larry DeGaris - Focuses on real-world sports marketing actions that connect ticket sales, sponsorships, media, and fan experience into coherent campaigns.

Sport Promotion and Sales Management by Irwin, McCarthy & Sutton - Excellent if you want a focused look at selling tickets, corporate partnerships, and fan-focused sales strategies.

Moneyball: The Art of Winning an Unfair Game by Michael Lewis - A classic that popularized analytics in professional sports and scouting by showing how data was used to evaluate players and build teams more effectively. It's invaluable for understanding modern scouting and analytics roles.

Sports Event Management and Marketing Playbook by Supovitz & Goldwater - Offers practical guides to planning, producing, and marketing live sporting events, including how to think strategically about game presentation, fan experience, hospitality, and revenue streams.

The Agent: My 40-Year Career Making Deals and Changing the Game by Leigh Steinberg - A memoir by one of the most famous sports agents in the world, the real-life inspiration for Jerry Maguire. He shares his career in negotiation, representing top NFL players, and how he built influence in pro sports.

Olympic Turnaround: How the Olympic Games Stepped Back from the Brink by Michael Payne - Written by the former Director of Marketing for the International Olympic Committee, this book reveals behind-the-scenes decisions that transformed the Olympics into a global commercial powerhouse.

Fast Tracks and Dark Deals by Michael Payne - A newly published autobiography by the same IOC marketing legend, covering five decades of influence in global sport business, including sponsorship deals, media strategy, and how big sport became big business.

What You're Made For: Powerful Life Lessons from My Career in Sports by George Raveling - Written by a pioneer in sports marketing and coaching, this tells career and life lessons from decades in the sport world, blending athletic and business insights.

Business

What They Don't Teach You at Harvard Business School by Mark McCormack - Though not exclusively about sport, McCormack is considered a pioneer of sports marketing and this book is full of practical career lessons relevant to sport business.

Ice to the Eskimos by Jon Spoelstra - This business and sports marketing book is about how to sell products in saturated or highly competitive markets. Drawing on his experience in professional sports, Spoelstra shares practical strategies for creativity, differentiation, and finding new customers when it seems like everyone already has what you're selling.

Career Development and Professional Growth

Start with Why by Simon Sinek - Sinek's concept of the Golden Circle, starting with why you do what you do, not just what or how. This framework is transformative for understanding organizational purpose, building authentic brands, and connecting with fans and partners on a deeper level. In sports, where passion drives everything, understanding and communicating your "why" differentiates you from competitors.

The 7 Habits of Highly Effective People: Powerful Lessons in Personal Change by Stephen Covey - Covey's classic framework for personal effectiveness. The seven habits provide a comprehensive system for professional growth and interpersonal effectiveness, teaching you to focus on what you can control, prioritize what matters, and build relationships based on mutual benefit. This book is dense and requires real engagement, but the principles serve you throughout your entire career.

Never Eat Alone by Keith Ferrazzi - This book is about networking as generosity rather than transactional relationship-building.

Rich Dad Poor Dad by Robert Kiyosaki - A foundational personal finance book that contrasts two mindsets about money, work, and wealth-building, one rooted in traditional employment and security ("Poor Dad"), and the other focused on financial education, assets, and entrepreneurship ("Rich Dad"). Rather than technical investing advice, it reshapes how you think about money, risk, and long-term strategy.

Grit by Angela Duckworth - Duckworth explores why passion and perseverance matter more than talent alone in achieving long-term success. Drawing on research from education, sports, business, and the military, she shows that sustained effort over time is the real driver of excellence. *Grit* reframes success as a marathon rather than a sprint, emphasizing resilience, deliberate practice, and commitment to long-term goals. Especially relevant in competitive fields like sports and leadership, the book challenges the myth of "natural talent" and highlights how consistent effort compounds into elite performance.

The Happiness Advantage by Shawn Achor - Achor shows that happiness fuels success, not the other way around. Packed with practical strategies, the book teaches how optimism, positive habits, and resilience improve performance, relationships, and long-term career growth, essential for high-pressure fields like sales and sports.

So Good They Can't Ignore You by Cal Newport - Newport argues against "follow your passion" advice and makes the case for building rare and valuable skills.

The First 90 Days by Michael Watkins - This book is about successfully transitioning into new roles, which you'll do many times throughout your career.

Atomic Habits by James Clear - James Clear's book about building systems and habits rather than setting goals changed how I approach professional development.

Mindset by Carol Dweck - Carol Dweck's research on fixed versus growth mindsets is foundational psychology that applies to everything.

Sales

How to Win Friends & Influence People by Dale Carnegie - The timeless classic on building genuine relationships and influencing people through authentic interest rather than manipulation. Everything in this book about making people feel valued and important applies directly to sales, networking, and succeeding in sports business.

The Challenger Sale: Taking Control of the Customer Conversation by Matthew Dixon and Brent Adamson - Challenges the conventional wisdom that relationship-building alone drives sales success and introduces the "Challenger" approach, teaching customers something new, tailoring your pitch, and taking control of the conversation. Essential reading for anyone in partnerships or corporate sales where you're selling solutions, not just tickets.

How I Raised Myself from Failure to Success in Selling by Frank Bettger - One of the best books ever written on sales fundamentals, based on Bettger's transformation from a failed insurance salesman to an industry legend. His principles about enthusiasm, organization, and genuine service are as relevant today as when he wrote them decades ago.

The Greatest Salesman in the World by Og Mandino - A short, powerful parable about persistence, positivity, and the habits that separate average salespeople from great ones. Read it when you need motivation or when rejection is getting to you – it will reset your mindset.

The Sales Bible by Jeffrey Gitomer - Comprehensive, practical advice on every aspect of selling, from prospecting to closing to building long-term relationships. Gitomer's direct, no-BS style makes this an excellent reference you'll return to throughout your sales career.

The Little Red Book of Selling by Jeffrey Gitomer - Gitomer's condensed principles of sales greatness in a quick, digestible format. If you only read one Gitomer book, make it this one. It distills the essentials of what makes salespeople successful.

Virtual Selling by Jeb Blount - The definitive guide to selling in virtual environments, covering video calls, technology, and how to engage buyers remotely. Critical reading in an era where much of sales happens over Zoom rather than face-to-face.

Selling is an Away Game by Lance Tyson - Focuses on sales as understanding the customer's world rather than pushing your product, emphasizing preparation, research, and adapting your approach to what the buyer actually needs. Particularly relevant for corporate partnerships where you're solving business problems, not just selling sports entertainment.

Be Our Guest: Perfecting the Art of Customer Service by Disney Institute - Disney's legendary approach to customer service breaks down the systems, culture, and philosophy that make Disney parks exceptional. For anyone working in sports, where creating memorable fan experiences is central to the business, Disney's principles are directly transferable. You'll learn about attention to detail, empowering frontline employees, and creating magical moments that turn customers into lifelong fans.

Leadership and Managing People

The Energy Bus: 10 Rules to Fuel Your Life, Work, and Team with Positive Energy by Jon Gordon - Gordon's parable about positive energy, leadership, and team culture. The ten rules for creating a positive environment are directly applicable to sports organizations where culture and energy can make or break a season. Especially valuable when you're trying to maintain positivity during losing streaks, organizational changes, or challenging work environments.

Leadership and Self-Deception: Getting Out of the Box by The Arbinger Institute - A business fable about how we deceive ourselves about our own motivations and behaviors, particularly in how we view and treat others. The concept of being "in the box" – seeing others as objects rather than people – explains countless workplace conflicts and leadership failures. This book is challenging because it forces uncomfortable self-reflection, but understanding these principles transforms how you approach leadership and collaboration.

Leaders Eat Last by Simon Sinek - Sinek argues that great leadership is about creating environments of trust and psychological safety where people feel valued and protected. Drawing on biology, military examples, and business case studies, he shows how effective leaders put the needs of their teams first, fostering loyalty, collaboration, and long-term performance. In high-pressure, team-driven environments like sports and organizations, *Leaders Eat Last* demonstrates that when leaders prioritize people over short-term results, teams become more resilient, engaged, and successful.

The Five Dysfunctions of a Team by Patrick Lencioni - This is a business fable about a dysfunctional executive team learning to work together.

Radical Candor by Kim Scott - Scott's framework for giving feedback that's both caring and direct changed how I think about management.

Turn the Ship Around! by L. David Marquet - Marquet commanded a nuclear submarine and transformed it from worst to best in the fleet by changing the leadership model from leader-follower to leader-leader.

Dare to Lead by Brené Brown - Brown's research on vulnerability and courage applies directly to leadership.

Books That Changed How I Think About Life and Work

Living with a SEAL: 31 Days Training with the Toughest Man on the Planet by Jesse Itzler - Itzler, co-owner of the Atlanta Hawks, invites a Navy SEAL (David Goggins) to live with him for a month and overhaul his life. Entertaining, inspiring, and occasionally insane stories about intense physical training and mental toughness. Beneath the humor are serious lessons about pushing past self-imposed limits and discovering reserves of toughness you didn't know you had.

Man's Search for Meaning by Viktor Frankl - Frankl survived Nazi concentration camps and wrote about finding meaning in suffering.

The Obstacle Is the Way by Ryan Holiday - Modern interpretation of Stoic philosophy argues that obstacles aren't impediments to success, they're the path.

Essentialism by Greg McKeown - Makes the case for doing less, better.

Range by David Epstein - Epstein argues against early specialization and makes the case for broad experience.

Ego Is the Enemy by Ryan Holiday - Another Ryan Holiday book, this one about how ego sabotages success at every stage: aspiring, succeeding, and failing.

Communication and Influence

Made to Stick by Chip Heath and Dan Heath - The Heath brothers analyze why some ideas stick in people's minds while others don't.

Influence by Robert Cialdini - Cialdini's research on the psychology of persuasion is foundational.

Crucial Conversations by Kerry Patterson - This book teaches you how to have high-stakes conversations when emotions run high.

How to Actually Read and Apply These Books

Buying books doesn't make you smarter. Reading them does, but only if you're reading actively rather than passively consuming words. Here's how to get value from reading:

Take notes while you read. Underline key passages. Write in the margins. Keep a notebook where you capture insights, questions, and ideas. The physical act of writing helps you process and remember ideas. Discuss books with others. Start or join a book club. Talk about what you're reading with mentors, colleagues, and classmates. Articulating ideas out loud deepens your understanding and exposes gaps in your thinking. Apply what you learn immediately. When you read something useful, try implementing it within 48 hours. Don't just collect ideas, test them. This is how reading translates into growth.

Revisit important books. The books that truly matter deserve to be read multiple times at different life stages. You'll get different insights at 25 than you did at 20, and different insights again at 35. Don't just read and move on, return to the books that shaped you.

Build a reading practice, not a reading list. Don't chase quantity. Focus on reading regularly and reading well. One book per month, truly absorbed and applied, beats twelve books skimmed and forgotten. Consistency matters more than speed.

The Long Game: Becoming a Lifelong Learner

The books aren't the endpoint, they're the beginning of a learning practice that extends across your entire career. The executives I most admire are still reading voraciously in their 50s and 60s. They're curious about new ideas, new frameworks, and new ways of thinking. They haven't stopped learning just because they've "made it."

That's the approach you want to cultivate. Read widely. Read deeply. Read with purpose. Let books challenge your assumptions, expand your thinking, and give you frameworks for navigating your career. The investment you make in reading today will compound over decades. Your reading list will evolve as your career evolves. What matters at 22 isn't what matters at 32 or 42. Stay curious. Keep learning. And remember: the goal isn't to read every book on this list, it's to develop the habit of learning from books throughout your career.

Classic Sales Movies

Sales is one of the few departments in business that has its own film genre. There are little to no beloved classics about accounts payable or human resources, but sales has spawned dozens of iconic movies. Watching these isn't really about learning sales techniques, though you'll pick some up. It's more like watching Christmas classics during the holidays. You watch *A Christmas Story* or *Elf* not to learn about December 25th, but because they're part of the culture, because everyone references them, and because understanding the jokes and callbacks makes you part of the tradition. Same with sales movies. When someone in your office quotes Glengarry Glen Ross or references Jerry Maguire, you need to get it immediately or you're missing half the conversation.

Glengarry Glen Ross (1992) – The ultimate sales pressure cooker. Alec Baldwin's "Always Be Closing" speech is burned into the brain of every salesperson who's ever faced a quota. This film shows the dark side of commission-based sales, the desperation when numbers aren't there, and the cutthroat competition among colleagues. It's brutal and depressing, but it's also required viewing because every sales office references it. When someone says "coffee's for closers" or talks about leads, they're quoting this movie. Understanding these references means you're in the language of sales culture.

Jerry Maguire (1996) - A sports agent loses everything and has to rebuild from scratch with one client and one believer. This isn't just about the "show me the money" scene everyone knows. It's about integrity in a business that often rewards the opposite, about building genuine relationships with clients, and about what happens when you try to do things differently than everyone else. The film captures the humanity behind the deals and reminds you that relationships matter more than transactions. Plus, in sports business, this movie gets referenced constantly. You need to know it.

Moneyball (2011) - While not a traditional sales movie, it's about selling an idea nobody believes in. Billy Beane had to convince scouts, coaches, and ownership that his analytics-driven approach could work, despite overwhelming skepticism. He was selling a vision of baseball that contradicted everything the industry believed. In sports, you'll constantly face situations where you need to sell concepts, strategies, or changes that go against conventional wisdom. This film shows how data, persistence, and conviction can overcome institutional resistance.

Boiler Room (2000) - Shows the seductive appeal and moral compromises of high-pressure sales environments. Young salespeople get rich quick by selling questionable investments to people who can't afford to lose. It's a cautionary tale about what happens when revenue becomes the only thing that matters. Watch it to understand what not to become, and to recognize toxic sales cultures when you see them. The techniques shown are aggressive and often unethical, but understanding them helps you identify when you're being pushed toward practices that compromise your integrity.

The Wolf of Wall Street (2013) - Jordan Belfort's rise and fall in the stock brokerage world is excessive in every way, but it demonstrates raw sales skill and motivation techniques, even if applied to fraudulent ends. The "sell me this pen" scene is endlessly discussed in sales training. The movie shows how charisma, storytelling, and creating urgency can move products, and how sales success without ethics ultimately destroys everything. It's entertainment, not a blueprint, but the sales psychology on display is real.

The Big Short (2015) - This movie is about a handful of people who saw the 2008 financial crisis coming and bet against the market. What makes this a sales movie? They had to sell their vision to investors who thought they were insane. They faced constant rejection, ridicule, and pressure to give up. The film shows how difficult it is to sell something counterintuitive, even when you're right. In sports business, you'll often need to convince people to take risks on unconventional ideas, and this captures that struggle perfectly.

These movies are part of the sales department's DNA. You watch them not to become a better seller, but to understand the culture you're walking into, to get the jokes, and to share the common language that makes sales its own weird, wonderful subculture within the business world.

TED Talks That'll Help

Something most college students miss is that the people hiring in sports aren't just looking at your resume. They're sizing up how you think, how you communicate, and whether you understand what actually drives success in this industry. TED Talks are like a masterclass in all of that, compressed into 18 minutes. The best ones don't just teach you concepts like body language or growth mindset. They give you frameworks you can actually use when you're sitting across from a hiring manager, trying to explain why you're worth taking a chance on. They help you understand how elite organizations think about performance, innovation, and leadership. And honestly? When you can reference ideas from people like Carol Dweck or John Wooden in an interview, you sound like someone who's serious about learning, not just someone who wants courtside seats. The talks I've listed here aren't random motivational fluff. They're practical tools that'll help you nail interviews, build confidence when you feel underqualified, and think more strategically about your career path. Watch them like you'd study game film. Take notes. Actually apply the ideas. Because in an industry where everyone wants in, the difference between getting the job and getting passed over often comes down to how you present yourself and how deeply you understand what success really looks like.

For the Business of Sports

How to Outthink Your Competition by Rasmus Ankersen – With a Lesson from Sports by Rasmus Ankersen - Uses sports analytics and strategy to teach how organizations can stay ahead of competitors. Great for understanding how sports executives and strategists think about competitive advantage.

Are Athletes Really Getting Faster, Better, Stronger? by David Epstein. Examines how performance evolves over time. Excellent for understanding performance limits and strategic thinking about athlete and team development.

The Math Behind Basketball's Wildest Moves by Rajiv Maheswaran. Shows how data and analytics get applied to basketball. A model for understanding sports tech, analytics integration, and innovation driving competitive advantage.

The Difference Between Winning and Succeeding by John Wooden. Classic leadership and values talk from a legendary coach. Ideal for understanding team culture and sports leadership principles that transcend any specific role.

How Augmented Reality Will Change Sports and Build Empathy by Chris Kluwe. Explores tech innovation and fan engagement. Vital for business leaders thinking about experiential innovation and future technologies in sports.

This Tennis Icon Paved the Way for Women in Sports by Billie Jean King. Insightful on leadership, equality, and brand impact. Valuable for sports business professionals focused on social impact and brand strategy.

Sports Management: A Goldmine of Opportunities by Nilesh Kulkarni. Directly tied to sports management as a career and business. Beneficial for those considering or already building careers in sports business.

The Puzzle of Motivation by Dan Pink. Explores what actually motivates people in teams and workplaces. Essential for understanding how to lead, manage, and perform in organizational settings.

How Great Leaders Inspire Action by Simon Sinek. The famous "Start with Why" talk about leadership and organizational purpose. Helps you understand how great sports organizations build culture and inspire loyalty.

For Getting a Job Out of College

Your Body Language May Shape Who You Are by Amy Cuddy. The gold standard for confidence in interviews, networking, and leadership presence. Practical tools for controlling how you show up in high-pressure situations like job interviews and presentations.

How to Speak So That People Want to Listen by Julian Treasure. Clear, persuasive communication is everything in interviews, networking, and early career success. Practical tools you can apply immediately at career fairs and informational interviews.

The Power of Believing That You Can Improve by Carol Dweck. Growth mindset for when you're underqualified, which is basically everyone out of college. Essential for handling rejection, learning on the job, and building early career resilience.

Why You Will Fail to Have a Great Career by Larry Smith. Calls out the real reasons people don't go after opportunities. Blunt, funny, and uncomfortably accurate for seniors who feel stuck, scared, or behind.

Fake It Till You Make It? Why Confidence Is Key by Ivan Joseph. Confidence as a skill you can train, not a personality trait. Pairs perfectly with Amy Cuddy and is especially relevant for athletes and performers transitioning into business roles.

How to Find Work You Love by Scott Dinsmore. Building a career intentionally instead of randomly applying online. Encourages networking and skill building over the "perfect job" hunting approach that keeps most people stuck.

What Makes a Good Life? Lessons from the Longest Study on Happiness by Robert Waldinger. A career isn't just about money or title. Relationships matter long-term. Helps you avoid burnout and bad early career choices that look good on paper but wreck your life.

Grit: The Power of Passion and Perseverance by Angela Duckworth. Employers love grit more than raw talent. Very interview-friendly concept for framing your story when your resume isn't perfect.

How to Get Your Ideas Across by David JP Phillips. Practical and neuroscience-based approach to selling yourself, your ideas, and your value. Essential for case interviews, presentations, and networking conversations.

Never, Ever Give Up by Diana Nyad. Resilience and persistence that maps directly to leadership and navigating the challenges of breaking into competitive industries like sports.